NEW YORK CITY

CHRISTOPHER KOMPANEK

CONTENTS

MAPS

1	Statue of Liberty
2	Times Square
3	The High Line
4	Radio City Music Hall
5	New York Public Library Main Branch
6	*Atlas* at Rockefeller Center

DISCOVER
NEW YORK CITY

New York City goes by many names: the Big Apple, Gotham, and the City That Never Sleeps. For those who have yet to see it up close, the city exists in outsized, mythic proportions, inspiring big dreams and endless wonder. It's filled with art deco skyscrapers such as the Empire State and Chrysler Buildings, storied institutions like the New York Stock Exchange and Apollo Theater, and an endless and ever-changing array of restaurants, shops, and bars and clubs that stay open until 4am and beyond.

Noise abounds—the siren call of the city is usually an ambulance stuck in gridlock traffic. People walk and talk quickly and are prone to rapid replies that can sound curt to the untrained ear. Contrary to our reputation, though, New Yorkers aren't rude: We just always have someplace to be.

Perhaps above all, this is a city of the arts. Famous masterpieces hang at The Met and MoMA, while new masterpieces are waiting to be discovered in neighborhood galleries. The gleaming theaters of the Great White Way now more than ever represent the diversity and cutting edge of the nation, while hundreds of black-box spaces in nondescript buildings provide a place for innovative playwrights to hone their craft.

Every time you think you have this complex city pinned down, it shows you another side. Look beyond the famed icons; there's always something new to discover. You may find surprising pockets of natural solitude in Brooklyn's Prospect Park, or learn that the building you're standing before was the childhood home of Teddy Roosevelt or the final drinking spot of Dylan Thomas. The city's myriad stories spill out onto the streets and into the creative imaginations of the individuals who make it come alive. The real way to fit in here is to go your own way.

10 TOP
EXPERIENCES

1 **Hang Out on The High Line:** Locals and visitors alike take pleasure in this industrial railway turned green space (page 88).

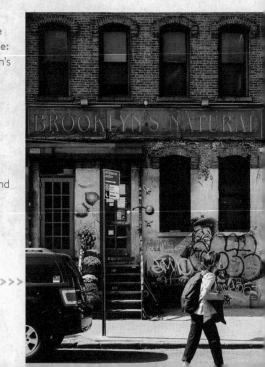

2 **Eat All the Food:** With the best bagels (page 13), authentic world cuisine (page 126), celebrity chefs (page 148), the country's largest open-air food market (page 173), and much, much more, New York is foodie heaven.

3 **Check Out the Brooklyn Scene:** Wander the borough's neighborhoods and discover a city unto itself, a hotbed for creative invention teeming with indie live music venues, brewpubs and bars, art spaces, shops, and restaurants galore (pages 62 and 68).

4 **Wander Amid World-Class Art:** Masterpieces born in ancient and modern times can be found at the **Whitney Museum of American Art** (page 90), the **Museum of Modern Art (MoMA)** (page 94), and **The Metropolitan Museum of Art** (page 105).

5 Experience America's Immigrant History: **Ellis Island** (page 76) was the first stop for many newcomers to this country; the **Tenement Museum** (page 86) tells their stories.

>>>

6 Seek Out Skyline Views: View the cityscape from famous vantage points like the **Empire State Building** and **Rockefeller Center,** as well as lesser-known perches like **Governors Island** (page 80).

<<<

7 Get Lost in Central Park: The trees, lakes, and meandering paths will make you forget the slabs of concrete that surround you (page 101).

>>>

8 **Go to the Theater:** Broadway musicals receive all the attention, but amazing theater can be found off the Great White Way and in almost every neighborhood in the city (page 234).

<<<

9 **Walk the Brooklyn Bridge:** Strolling from Manhattan to Brooklyn over this striking bridge is a classic city experience (pages 64 and 113).

>>>

10 **Admire the Statue of Liberty:** The enduring icon represents humanity's greatest ideals (page 77).

<<<

EXPLORE
NEW YORK CITY

THE BEST OF NEW YORK CITY

There will always be whole new worlds to explore in New York—even for longtime locals—but even in a short amount of time you can get a good taste of what makes it amazing. One of the city's greatest pleasures is its walkability, and these itineraries have been designed with this in mind. You won't be far from public transit options if you get tired; where particularly helpful, this information is included.

›DAY 1: UPPER WEST SIDE AND UPPER EAST SIDE

To the uninitiated, New York can be overwhelming in its vast density. To ease into your New York experience, begin your tour of the city in these quieter residential neighborhoods while checking a few big items off your list.

Start with breakfast on the Upper West Side at a classic Jewish deli, **Barney Greengrass,** where you can order everything from a bagel and cream cheese to decadent platters of smoked fish.

Once fortified, walk 15 minutes southeast to the **American Museum of Natural History.** Explore

American Museum of Natural History

A GUIDE TO THE CITY'S BEST BAGELS

Like New York pizza, New York bagels are hard to replicate. Most attribute this to the city's tap water, with its low concentration of calcium and magnesium said to make for a smooth taste while the pH level helps with fermentation of yeast. What this boils down to: Eat as many bagels as you can while here.

Russ & Daughters

RUSS & DAUGHTERS
The bagels at Russ & Daughters, available both at the store and café, make the best base on which to layer perfect slices of Gaspé Nova smoked salmon and other expertly cured meats (page 132).

MURRAY'S BAGELS
Murray's delivers solid bagels a bit on the firm side, making them perfect material for breakfast egg sandwiches or to hold heaping portions of deli meat (page 150).

ESS-A-BAGEL
Ess-A-Bagel creates the bagels by which all others are measured: giant, intensely flavored, and so airy that eating one is pure joy (page 155).

BARNEY GREENGRASS
Barney Greengrass is a premier uptown spot for bagels, whether holding together an epic egg sandwich or a healthy smear of cream cheese topped with sturgeon (page 162).

BERGEN BAGELS
Bergen makes some of the best bagels in Brooklyn and is within walking distance of BAM and the Barclays Center to boot. An everything bagel with vegetable cream cheese is a solid way to begin your day, or get a little adventurous with flavors like feta pesto (page 170).

its impressive collection of dinosaur fossils and mounted animals, and don't miss the space show at the **Hayden Planetarium.** For some real-life nature, pop into **Central Park,** which borders the museum. Wander through the leafy respite at your leisure, and revel in the greenery framed by skyscrapers.

When you've had your fill, exit on the Upper East Side, the opposite side of the park from which you started, at East 85th Street. Walk a block and then turn left onto Madison Avenue, where you'll find **Ristorante Morini.** Chef Michael White is known for his silky pastas, and the prix fixe lunch menu here is an especially good deal. For a tasty cheap-eats alternative, head a few blocks east and order a couple of hot dogs at **Papaya King.**

After lunch, head back east in the direction of Central Park and enter **The Metropolitan Museum of Art** at its main entrance on East 82nd Street and 5th Avenue, along a stretch known as **Museum Mile** for its many institutions. Spend the rest of the day wandering The Met's galleries, filled with art both ancient and modern, and make sure to visit its **Cantor Roof Garden,** an outdoor exhibition space that also offers great views of Central Park.

In the evening, head back to the Upper West Side's **Lincoln Center,** which showcases everything from theater to ballet to opera and film. It's a 30-minute walk southwest through the park from the museum.

Museum Mile

>DAY 2: TIMES SQUARE AND MIDTOWN

Today you'll tackle the cultural beast that is Midtown. Begin with a classic view of the city at either the **Empire State Building** or **Rockefeller Center**'s observatory deck, **Top of the Rock.** The former has slightly better views, but choose the latter if you want to squeeze in a studio tour of NBC and get a glimpse of sets from shows like *Saturday Night Live* and *The Tonight Show.*

MANHATTAN ORIENTATION

Most of the island of Manhattan is organized on a neat grid, making it easier to navigate than one might think. Avenues run the length of the island north-south from, roughly, 1st Avenue on the east side to 12th Avenue on the west side, with 5th Avenue being the dividing point between east and west sides. A few avenues are named; 3rd Avenue is followed by Lexington, Park, and Madison Avenues—then comes 5th Avenue. Uptown, avenues also change names (for instance, on the Upper West Side 9th and 10th Avenues become Columbus and Amsterdam Avenues, respectively, while in Harlem 6th and 7th Avenues become Malcolm X and Adam Clayton Jr. Boulevards, respectively). Streets run mostly east to west across the island's width, numbered north of Houston Street from 1st to 220th Streets. Anything south of 14th Street is loosely considered downtown, while anything north of 59th Street is considered uptown. Note that the grid gets twisty south of Houston Street. Even locals use Google Maps down here, but remember that getting lost is part of the fun.

Afterward, walk north from either attraction up **5th Avenue** to get a taste of the famous shopping street. You can continue up the avenue for more shopping or turn left onto 54th Street for the **Museum of Modern Art (MoMA),** whose permanent collection includes large-scale works by Pollock and Monet, among others. Also check out the museum's sculpture garden, which features fun rotating exhibits. After your visit, stop by the **MoMA Design Store** across the street to find some gifts or souvenirs.

For a decadent lunch, head southwest to nearby **Le Bernardin.** Chef Eric Ripert's French seafood

BEST PEOPLE-WATCHING

THE HIGH LINE
People of all nationalities flood The High Line daily for photos or just a stroll; grab a seat on a bench and watch the world pass by (page 88).

CHELSEA MARKET
Grab some ravioli or vegan sushi and watch the crowds of locals and tourists flood this foodie mecca (page 92).

UNION SQUARE
Take a seat on this public plaza's stairs or on a bench and observe this crossroads of east and west sides, uptown and downtown, where all boroughs converge at a major transit hub (page 92).

GREAT LAWN AT CENTRAL PARK
Softball games, picnics, and casual Frisbee tossing all occur regularly in the city's backyard (page 101).

WASHINGTON SQUARE PARK
The unofficial quad of New York University is rife with great people-watching, from competitive chess players in the southwest corner to impromptu street performances near the arch to the central fountain (page 267).

CHRISTOPHER STREET PIER
Impromptu hacky sack games, amateur break-dancers, and scantily clad sunbathers can all be found on expansive Pier 45 (page 268).

BROOKLYN HEIGHTS PROMENADE
This scenic elevated path is a popular place for locals to congregate, walk dogs, and let their children play together (page 275).

soon hit the heart of **Times Square.** It's home to the **TKTS booth,** where you can score same-day tickets to a range of Broadway performances. It opens at 2pm Tuesday and 3pm Monday and Wednesday-Sunday, so get in line early if you have your eye on something specific. If you're interested in seeing something more off the beaten path, **Playwrights Horizons** and **Signature Theatre Company** are also located in the Theater District and present top-notch productions of cutting-edge plays.

To kill time before your show and grab a break from the crush of crowds, you might take a 30-minute walk west to the quieter northern end of **The High Line,** accessible at 34th Street and 12th Avenue. A wide walkway is here, and there are excellent views over the Hudson River.

For a leisurely dinner before your show, try to get a seat somewhere no later than 6pm. Celebrity chef Daniel Boulud's **db Bistro Moderne** is right near Times Square, and a special pretheater prix fixe is available for a fair price.

>DAY 3: LOWER MANHATTAN AND DUMBO

Begin your day with a trip to the **Statue of Liberty** and **Ellis Island** via the Statue Cruises ferry that leaves from The Battery. Your ferry ticket includes general admission to both sights; you'll get up close to the iconic monument as well as visit the first U.S. landing spot for more than 12 million immigrants.

Once back in Manhattan, head to **The Dead Rabbit,** a short walk east of the ferry dock, for a stiff one and some delectable food to

restaurant is among the finest in the city. It's also one of the most expensive, but during lunchtime you can order a three-course meal in the lounge for about half the price of dinner.

After lunch, head south down 7th Avenue for four blocks. You'll

National September 11 Memorial

boot. Come night, this is one of the busiest bars in the city, so afternoons are best for soaking in its *Gangs of New York* vibe.

After you've refreshed yourself, walk northwest for about 15 minutes. Take some time to pause at the **National September 11 Memorial**'s cascading waterfalls, in the footprints of the Twin Towers. Continue northeast to **City Hall,** where you can admire the neoclassical building. On the east side of City Hall Park is Centre Street and the entrance to the **Brooklyn Bridge,** the starting point for a classic New York walk (page 64). The pedestrian walkway over the East River affords a unique angle on the city's skyline and the bridge's elegant construction. It takes about 30 minutes to cross, although you'll likely spend more time snapping photos and taking in the views.

Once on the Brooklyn side, head to **Juliana's** when you get hungry again for the city's best pizza, hop to some of **Dumbo's galleries,** and hang on the waterfront at **Brooklyn Bridge Park** or the **Brooklyn Heights Promenade.**

>> **Public Transit:** When you're ready to head back to Manhattan, you can take the A/C subway from High Street or the F subway from the York Street station.

WITH MORE TIME
> **DAY 4: LOWER EAST SIDE AND WILLIAMSBURG**
Few places tell the city's history better than the **Tenement Museum.** A morning tour here—check the website in advance, as the museum offers numerous types of tours at varying times, all guided—provides fascinating insight into how many New Yorkers lived around the turn of the century. Afterward, walk a few blocks north and choose between two epic Jewish American eateries, both off Houston Street: **Katz's Deli** for gut-busting

Katz's Deli

pastrami sandwiches and fresh bowls of pickles or **Russ & Daughter's Cafe** for latkes and silky smoked salmon and herring.

Next, get ready to explore the epicenter of New York's hipster culture. Just over the river from the Lower East Side, or LES, is Brooklyn's Williamsburg, sensibility-wise an extension of Manhattan's downtown artistic ethos.

>> **Public Transit:** Take the J or M train at the Essex Street subway station one stop to Marcy Avenue. Walk west on Broadway to Bedford Avenue.

Williamsburg Bridge

You could also just walk across the **Williamsburg Bridge**—it takes about 30 minutes from the Lower East Side at Clinton and Delancey Streets.

On the Brooklyn side, you'll exit the bridge right onto **Bedford Avenue,** Williamsburg's main thoroughfare. Enjoy the rest of the day exploring the neighborhood's numerous shops and businesses. You'll want to hit **Brooklyn Brewery,** a pioneer of the borough's craft beer scene. Book a tour in advance or just hang out in the tasting room to try some of its rare brews.

Stick around after dark as well, as Williamsburg offers some of the city's best **bars and restaurants.** End the night with a concert at **Baby's All Right** or a late movie at **Nitehawk Cinema.**

>> **Public Transit:** Take the J or the M subway from Marcy Avenue to return to the LES. The L subway—when it's back up and running again—can take you to Union Square and Chelsea from Bedford Avenue.

> **DAY 5: THE MEATPACKING DISTRICT AND CHELSEA**

Start your day with a hearty meal of southern comfort food at **Bubby's.** Next head one block west to the **Whitney Museum of American Art.** In addition to wandering its massive collection of 20th- and 21st-century art, make sure to check out its **terraces,** which hold sculptural and sound installations and offer great views over the Hudson River.

The Whitney conveniently sits at the southern base of **The High**

Line. Pop up and enjoy the curated green space with its art installations, artfully landscaped plants, and elevated views. Continue on, or, after a bit more than 0.5 mile (0.8 km), exit at 23rd Street, where Chelsea's famous galleries—including the **Gagosian** and **Pace Gallery**—are concentrated. Spend some time wandering the area. When you get hungry again, wander back south to **Chelsea Market,** where you can choose from a number of vendors for a delicious, casual meal.

>DAY 6: LOWER MANHATTAN AND GOVERNORS ISLAND

If you're here between May and October, today it's time to leave the city—well, not quite. **Governors Island** is 800 yards from Lower Manhattan and readily accessible by ferry. The terminal is in the heart of the Financial District, so it's possible to hit up a site or two before boarding. The **Federal Reserve Bank of New York** offers free tours (it books quickly—make reservations 30 days in advance) that end in a vault filled with gold. Several blocks southwest is the splendor of **Trinity Church,** where Alexander Hamilton is among the many buried in the adjacent cemetery. And just southeast is the **New York Stock Exchange;** the public can't enter the building, but outside you can admire the *Fearless Girl* statue— she moved here in 2018 after famously staring down *Charging Bull.*

When you're ready, walk 10 minutes south to the waterfront and hop on a ferry from the Battery Maritime Building. Once on Governors Island, you'll have great

Chelsea Market

views of the city skyline and acres of open land to wander on foot or by bike. **Food trucks** are plentiful, so grab something to eat while you're here. Lounge in a **hammock.** Walk the perimeter **promenade** or rent a **bike.** When you've had your fill, head back to Manhattan for a cocktail-driven dinner at **BlackTail**, northwest of the ferry dock.

If you're here outside the Governors Island season, consider spending a day in either Greenwich Village (page 42) or Harlem (page 58) instead. While both are light on major sights, they're ideal neighborhoods for atmospheric wandering.

> DAY 7: GRAMERCY, UNION SQUARE, AND THE EAST VILLAGE

Spend your final day traveling back in time to Old New York and doing some leisurely meandering. Begin the day at the **Theodore Roosevelt Birthplace National Historic Site** for a glimpse of what childhood was like for the 26th president of the United States. Just east down the block is the private **Gramercy Park.** Only residents can enter, but walking around the perimeter feels like stepping through a time portal, with its leafy streets and elegant 19th-century buildings.

A couple of blocks south is one of the oldest bars in the city, **Pete's Tavern.** Soak up the atmosphere over lunch and a pint.

Next head a couple of blocks west to **Union Square.** If it's a Monday, Wednesday, Friday, or Saturday, you'll get to check out the **Greenmarket,** a flood of fresh produce, meats, cheeses, and more from small farms in the tristate area. Some places give out samples and others sell irresistible small bites and drinks. The $1 cups of hot or cold cider (depending on the season) are a must. Even if you're not here during the market, the many seating options make this crossroads a great **people-watching** spot where you can simply sit back and take in the energy of the city.

While you're here, be sure to visit **The Strand,** just a couple of blocks south of Union Square, and get lost among the book-filled aisles. You can spend the rest of your day simply ambling the neighborhood, one of the great joys of the city. Head four blocks south and turn east on the 8th Street stretch known as **St. Mark's Place,** a nice entry point into the East Village (page 36), which offers numerous delicious options for dinner and drinks.

NEW YORK CITY WITH KIDS

New York can be overwhelming with kids. Waiting in endless lines tires everyone out, so break up attractions with time in the park. These two days combine a bit of both, with an emphasis on having a fun, active time.

›DAY 1: UPPER WEST SIDE AND UPPER EAST SIDE

Plan your first day around **Central Park.** Pack a picnic or pick up a bounty of food at **Barney Greengrass** on the Upper West Side. From there, it's just a couple of blocks east to the park. In addition to expansive fields to play in under the city skyline, Central Park contains a wealth of attractions. **Belvedere Castle** near the 81st Street entrance inspires fantastical adventures in kids of all ages. You can also wander south from here to **The Loeb Boathouse,** near 72nd Street, where you can rent a rowboat for four or take a gondola tour April-November.

Now it's time for a bit of culture. The **American Museum of Natural History,** bordering the park on its west side, is a famously kid-friendly museum. Without even paying admission, you can access its backyard, which becomes an impromptu water park in the summer. Inside, the special exhibitions often have an interactive component. Both kids and adults will enjoy the awesome **Hayden Planetarium** shows. If you have slightly older children, **The Metropolitan Museum of Art** on the park's east side is chock-full of wonders as

The Loeb Boathouse

biking in Central Park

HUDSON RIVER GREENWAY
Bike, run, or walk this 11-mile (17.7-km) path along Manhattan's west side. It offers excellent waterfront views and perches for resting (page 265).

CHELSEA PIERS
Don't be surprised if you feel like an American Gladiator at this active wonderland. Rock climbing, golfing, and ice-skating are just some of the fun options (page 269).

ROW A BOAT IN CENTRAL PARK
Rent a rowboat from The Loeb Boathouse and get a cardio workout at The Lake in Central Park (page 273).

BIKE THROUGH CENTRAL PARK
You can cover even more of this masterpiece of a park by renting a bike or hopping on a bike tour (page 273).

HIKE INWOOD HILL PARK
In upper Manhattan you'll find trails that traverse hilly terrain and the island's only forest (page 281).

well. The most popular for kids is the Temple of Dendur, an ancient Egyptian temple airlifted out of the Middle East and pristinely preserved. It's the closest thing to visiting the pyramids that you can get in the Western world.

End the day back near where you started with an early, hearty dinner at **Jacob's Pickles,** an upscale comfort food spot that caters to hipsters and high chairs alike in the early evening. Potent adult beverages abound as well as kid-friendly dishes like meat loaf and patty melts.

If you have time and energy to spare, head down to **Times Square** for the **New Victory Theater,** which stages smartly conceived children's theater with age-appropriate offerings (rated 6-plus, 10-plus, and so on) distilled to a kid-friendly hour.

>> **Public Transit:** From the restaurant, take the 1 train from 86th Street to the Times Square-42nd Street subway station.

>DAY 2: LOWER MANHATTAN AND GOVERNORS ISLAND

Let **Governors Island** be your first stop today if you're here in season (May-Oct.). Catch a ferry from the dock in Lower Manhattan just outside The Battery. Plenty of food carts can be found on the island, but feel free to bring your own picnic. On the island you'll find a huge kids-only (6 and up) playground, **play:groundNYC,** where getting dirty is encouraged. An expansive maze as well as a **zip line, mini golf,** and **rock climbing** are some of the island's other recreational options. Or you can just relax and take in some views—the **Statue of Liberty** is visible from many vantage points on the island.

If you're here outside the

One World Observatory

Governors Island season or seeking a more classic outing, spend your day instead getting up close to the Statue of Liberty, followed by an educational stop at **Ellis Island,** included in the same ticket. For a more intimate experience on the water, check out the sailboat tours from **Manhattan by Sail.**

Back at the ferry dock from either expedition, check out the **Castle Clinton National Monument,** a fort that protected the city from British invasion, in **The Battery.** From here walk north for about 10 minutes and pause at the **National September 11 Memorial.** Its waterfalls are breathtaking and provide a poignant experience that children can appreciate as well. Skip the museum—which is a bit heavy for kids—and continue north a block for **One World Observatory,** which offers panoramic views from on high and some high-tech experiences that might be particularly engaging for kids; for instance, you can rent an iPad for a more interactive experience in learning about the city's skyline.

Finally, head about two blocks west for dinner at **Parm,** an update on the red-sauce Italian American restaurant. Its kids' menu features classics like butter pasta and chicken tenders. For adults, the chicken parm is a must. Afterward, take the family for a stroll along the nearby waterfront and gaze at the glimmering skyline reflecting in the river.

PLANNING YOUR TRIP

WHEN TO GO

High season in New York includes the **summer** (June-Aug.) and the **end-of-year holiday season** (Nov.-Dec.). Summer is hot and uncomfortably humid. Temperatures around 85°F (29°C) are common but sometimes creep up into the mid-to-high 90°F range (35-37°C), with matching humidity percentages. On the upside, it can be easier to get coveted restaurant reservations in the summer because many New Yorkers with the means flee the heat to the Hamptons and Hudson Valley, and free cultural events abound, with free concerts and movie screenings all over town, as well as Shakespeare in the Park performances. Crowds and hotel prices surge during the winter holiday season in December as people pack into town for some of the city's bucket list events, including the Macy's Thanksgiving Day Parade, the Christmas tree lighting in Rockefeller Center, and New Year's Eve in Times Square.

To really experience the beauty of the city, though, come for a visit in **September, October,** or **early November,** typically the most pleasant months of the year weather-wise, when temperatures top out around 70°F (21°C), with lows around 50°F (10°C), allowing

Central Park in autumn

for long exploratory walks around the city. The end of summer and beginning of fall also signal the start of the year's cultural calendar, including the onset of theater season as award-winning companies return from summer hiatus and the commencement of major arts festivals such as the New York Film Festival and New Yorker Festival.

Hearty travelers looking for hotel discounts will find them outside the holidays during the winter **low season** (Jan.-Mar.). It may snow and temperatures might be freezing, but the cultural life of the city is in full swing and the crowds more manageable. Average highs and lows are 40°F (4°C) and 27°F (-2°C), respectively.

Spring (Apr.-May.) is variable, ranging from rainy and cold to pleasantly temperate, in the 60°F or 70°F spectrum (15-25°C), so come during this time if you're the gambling sort.

TRANSPORTATION

Travelers arriving by air to New York City typically fly into **John F. Kennedy International Airport** or **LaGuardia Airport,** both in Queens, or **Newark Liberty International Airport** in nearby New Jersey.

Driving isn't recommended in New York City. Besides the hassle of navigating the traffic and confusing one-way streets, parking is difficult to come by and expensive. And one of the great pleasures of New York City is that it's highly walkable and has an excellent transit system. **Subways** run frequently and are often the fastest way to get around during the day. **Buses** can take a long time but can be convenient

L TRAIN REPAIRS

Repairs to the L subway line—a primary transit artery between Manhattan and Brooklyn neighborhoods including **Williamsburg** and **Bushwick**—are underway, though the full scope of service disruptions and contingency measures is in flux. Years-long plans to address damage caused by 2012's Hurricane Sandy with a full shutdown were met with dread by New Yorkers and much discussed in the media, prompting an alternate proposal from Governor Andrew Cuomo to limit closure to nights and weekends (specifics are still uncertain at press time). Download the **Metropolitan Transportation Authority (MTA) Weekender App** (www.mta.info) to your smartphone for real-time updates on scheduled work and delays. The MTA plans to run additional **M, G, and 7 trains** during repairs; the M is probably your best alternate subway bet as it runs through Manhattan and into Williamsburg and Bushwick south of the L train. Williamsburg is also accessible from Manhattan via **NYC Ferry** (www.ferry.nyc).

for traveling between the east and west sides in Manhattan. Subways and buses run 24 hours a day. You can buy a **MetroCard** for $1 and add on any amount you like, which can be used on both subways and buses—it costs $2.75 for a single ride on either. Or you can buy a **7-Day Unlimited Pass** ($32), good

passengers traveling on the subway

DAILY REMINDERS

- **Monday:** Most theaters are dark on Monday nights.

- **Tuesday:** The National September 11 Memorial Museum offers free admission (5pm-8pm). The Whitney Museum of American Art is closed except in July and August.

- **Wednesday:** Broadway shows and some Off-Broadway productions have matinee shows. The Frick Collection offers pay-what-you-wish entry (2pm-6pm).

- **Thursday:** Galleries in Chelsea have show openings with free wine. Admission is pay-what-you wish at the New Museum (7pm-9pm) and free at the Brooklyn Museum (5pm-10pm).

- **Friday:** Many museums and other institutions host free admission or pay-what-you-wish hours today, including the Whitney Museum of American Art (7pm-9:30pm), Rubin Museum of Art (6pm-10pm), The Morgan Library & Museum (7pm-9pm), Museum of Modern Art (4pm-8pm), New-York Historical Society (6pm-8pm), and Brooklyn Botanic Garden (before noon). On the first Friday of the month, the Neue Galerie (6pm-9pm) and The Frick Collection (6pm-9pm, except Sept. and Jan.) offer free admission.

- **Saturday:** Admission is free to The Jewish Museum all day, and the Guggenheim Museum is pay-what-you-wish (5pm-7:45pm). The Brooklyn Museum is free on the first Saturday of every month (5pm-11pm) except in September. The Grand Army Plaza Greenmarket (8am-4pm) in Prospect Park takes place weekly. In season, Smorgasburg (Apr.-Oct.) takes place on Saturdays at Williamsburg's East River State Park.

- **Sunday:** Smorgasburg takes place in Prospect Park on Sundays April-October.

for both subway and local bus travel throughout the five boroughs.

A great way to get around and simultaneously sightsee is the **NYC Ferry,** a newly minted fleet of boats that shuttles riders between popular areas. It also costs $2.75.

RESERVATIONS

It's always a good idea to book your **accommodations** in advance but it's particularly essential for the holiday month of December, for which you should book ahead at least three months. At other times of year, a month ahead should suffice, and last-minute deals can also be found on the HotelTonight app (www.hoteltonight.com).

Tickets for popular **Broadway shows** like *Hamilton* and *Dear Evan Hansen* should be booked far in advance, as soon as a new block of tickets is released (announced on websites including www.playbill.com and www.theatermania.com), but for other shows a couple weeks prior is typically sufficient. But remember that the TKTS booths—selling same-day Broadway tickets at discounted prices—reward spontaneity.

Restaurants typically take

Hamilton on Broadway

reservations up to a month in advance, and the most popular fill up within minutes of releasing a new block of dates through their website or **OpenTable** (www.opentable. com), so stay vigilant if you have your eye on a specific place. Try logging on a few minutes before the release time and then refreshing the browser to increase your chances of nabbing a coveted table. Popular restaurants that don't take reservations often allow you to put your name on a list along with your cell number, so you can hit up a bar or otherwise explore a neighborhood while waiting.

Statue of Liberty and **Ellis Island** tickets should be purchased in advance to avoid ticket lines. About a month in advance typically suffices—unless you want to go up to Lady Liberty's crown, then at least six months in advance is advisable. Buying tickets to big museums like The Met, MoMA, and the Whitney in advance isn't necessary, but you can avoid long ticket lines if you do. This is also true of sights like the Empire State Building and the National September 11 Museum.

PASSES AND DISCOUNTS

If you plan on hitting some of the main sights, a **CityPASS** (www. citypass.com; $126 adults, $104 children) could save you money. It includes admission to six attractions, such as the Statue of Liberty and Ellis Island and The Metropolitan Museum of Art, over a period of nine days. For those wanting to pack more in, the **New York Pass** (www.newyorkpass.com; $127-425 adults, $94-285 children) offers almost a hundred attractions and tours to be gorged on in spans

WHAT'S NEW?

- **Bike Friendliness:** With 25 miles (40 km) of new protected bike lanes added in 2017 alone, according to the Department of Transportation, along with Citi Bike bicycle shares, which have been operating since 2013, New York is increasingly becoming a cyclist-friendly city.

- **Brewery Explosion:** There was a time when Brooklyn Brewery had little competition. Now amazing breweries abound across the boroughs, offering plenty of places for beer lovers to get their fix straight from the source.

- **Brooklyn Heights Promenade Closure:** Enjoy this scenic stretch while you can. The city won't determine a course of action until 2020 at the earliest, but repairs for the highway upon which the beloved promenade sits are in the works and could necessitate its closure for up to six years.

- **Going Green:** In recent years, the city's industrial and abandoned waterfronts have been turned into stunning green spaces—such as Hudson River Park and Brooklyn Bridge Park—with expansive lawns on which to stretch out and biking/walking paths for exercise with a view.

- **New Ferry Service:** Launched in 2017, the NYC Ferry offers low-cost routes and full bar service to popular neighborhoods like Williamsburg and Dumbo from Manhattan, making for more pleasant commutes or a fun excuse for an excursion.

ranging from 1 to 10 days, and frequent online sales can knock as much as $100 off the pass's price.

Many New York attractions offer discounts for seniors (65 and older) and students, and many museums offer free or pay-what-you-wish hours.

GUIDED TOURS

Shorewalkers (http://shorewalkers.org) and **Freewalkers** (http://freewalkers.org) each organize epic free walks around the city and surrounding areas. **Free Tours By Foot** (http://freetoursbyfoot.com/new-york-tours) also offers an extensive array of pay-what-you-wish walking tours.

New York Adventure Club (www.nyadventureclub.com) offers unique, small-group tours, such as one to Shakespearean actor Edwin Booth's private social club, The Players, in Gramercy Park.

CALENDAR OF EVENTS

JANUARY

Party with a million other people and watch the ball drop during **New Year's Eve in Times Square.**

FEBRUARY

Manhattan's Chinatown is awash in color during the **Lunar New Year Parade,** featuring fireworks, dancers, and floats. Similar celebrations take place in the city's Chinese communities in Flushing, Queens, and Sunset Park, Brooklyn.

MARCH

New York's **St. Patrick's Day Parade** down 5th Avenue draws about two million people and is purportedly the oldest and largest of its kind in the world. Also this month is **The Armory Show,** a major international showcase that brings together prestigious galleries from around the world.

JUNE

June is Pride Month, and the **NYC Pride March** is the celebratory culmination. Also this month is the

St. Patrick's Day Parade

city's largest parade, the **Puerto Rican Day Parade,** which brings close to three million spectators.

Free outdoor arts and entertainment abound during summer in the city, with many festivals kicking off in June, including **SummerStage** and **Shakespeare in the Park** in Central Park, the **BRIC Celebrate Brooklyn! Festival** in Prospect Park, and **Bryant Park Movie Nights.**

JULY

Celebrate the country's birthday on the waterfront and enjoy the **Macy's 4th of July Fireworks,** the largest fireworks show in the country. Alternatively, head out to Coney Island for **Nathan's Famous International Hot Dog Eating Contest** to watch the world's top competitive eaters vie for the Nathan's Mustard Belt.

AUGUST

The summer ends with the **U.S. Open** in Queens, one of tennis's biggest events, which starts in late August and continues into September.

SEPTEMBER

Fall kicks into gear with the prestigious **New York Film Festival** in late September, which runs into October and features premieres of anticipated films from around the globe.

OCTOBER

A couple of big festivals this month include the **New Yorker Festival,** organized by the namesake magazine and featuring talks, tours, and other events with heavy hitters of the arts and culture worlds. For food and drink, there's the **New York City Wine**

NYC Pride March

Rockefeller Center Christmas tree as seen from 5th Avenue before the tree lighting

& Food Festival, with extravagant dinners and parties. Also this month is the **Village Halloween Parade,** featuring tens of thousands of participants dressed in their finest costumes.

NOVEMBER

Runners hit the road every year on the first Sunday in November for the **New York City Marathon.** It crosses through all five boroughs, making it a highlight for athletes and spectators alike.

The **Macy's Thanksgiving Day Parade,** with its giant balloons, and the lighting of the massive **Christmas tree in Rockefeller Center** kick off the end-of-year holiday season and draw big crowds.

DECEMBER

While the Rockefeller Center tree-lighting ceremony happens in November, the tree remains lit all through December and into the new year. **Ice-skating** at The Rink at Rockefeller Center, as well as at the Winter Village in Bryant Park and Wollman Rink in Central Park, are in their prime season. The Rockettes perform their *Christmas Spectacular* at **Radio City Music Hall.** Macy's and other major department stores around the city deck out their **window displays** with elaborate decorations that not only show off their offerings but create theatrical tableaus that draw big crowds for their creativity and meticulous attention to detail.

NEIGHBORHOODS

Lower Manhattan

Map 1

Home to government institutions and gleaming office towers, Lower Manhattan is characterized by its workaday black-clad business bustle. It may feel the least distinctly New York of any neighborhood, but it's also the city's heart in many ways, and littered with **historical landmarks.** It's home to the **Financial District,** where you can walk **Wall Street** and access some of New York's most famous sights—including the **Statue of Liberty** and **Ellis Island**—and visit the

site of the **September 11** attacks that forever imprinted the city and country.

TOP SIGHTS
- Ellis Island (page 76)
- Statue of Liberty (page 77)
- Governors Island (page 78)

TOP NIGHTLIFE
- The Dead Rabbit (page 179)

TOP RECREATION
- Staten Island Ferry (page 265)
- Hudson River Greenway (page 265)

TOP HOTELS
- Conrad Hotel (page 310)

GETTING THERE AND AROUND
- Metro lines: 1/2/3, 4/5/6, A/C/E, J/Z, R/W
- Metro stations: Chambers Street, Fulton Street, Rector Street, Wall Street, Bowling Green, City Hall, Brooklyn Bridge, Park Place, Broad Street, World Trade Center, Whitehall Street, South Ferry
- Major bus routes: M1, M6, M9, M15, M20, M22

Soho and Tribeca   Map 2

Dominated by 19th- and 20th-century cast-iron buildings that serve as reminders of the neighborhoods' industrial past, the syllabically abbreviated Soho (South of Houston Street) and Tribeca (Triangle Below Canal) are now beacons for **high fashion,** the **arts, design,** and inventive **upscale restaurants.** Haute couture **boutiques** and **galleries** line the streets, and the spaces above them are now the extravagant lofts of celebrities such as Justin Timberlake, Jake Gyllenhaal, and Jennifer Lawrence. Meanwhile, on the edges of Soho and Tribeca, you'll find New York's historic **Little Italy** and **Chinatown.**

TOP RESTAURANTS
- Sarabeth's (page 123)
- Jungsik (page 128)

TOP NIGHTLIFE
- City Winery (page 181)

TOP ARTS AND CULTURE
- Mmuseumm (page 216)
- Soho Rep (page 218)
- Film Forum (page 219)

TOP SHOPS
- Jacques Torres Chocolate (page 289)
- Ingo Maurer (page 290)

GETTING THERE AND AROUND
- Metro lines: 1/2, 6, A/C/E, J/Z, N/Q/R/W
- Metro stations: Canal Street,
  Spring Street, Franklin Street,
  Prince Street, Houston Street
- Major bus routes: M20, M21, M55

East Village and Lower East Side

Map 3

The East Village's **free-spirited past**—this is where Basquiat hung out, the setting for Broadway musical *Rent*'s bohemians, and the former home to legendary punk club CBGB—reverberates in the neighborhood's vibrant creativity. Next door in the Lower East Side (LES), low-rise **tenement buildings** dot the skyline, housing a rich immigrant history. In both neighborhoods you'll also find influential **arts** and **live music** venues and some of the city's most exciting **bars** and **restaurants** (think revolutionary ramen and crème brûlée doughnuts).

TOP SIGHTS
- Tenement Museum (page 86)

TOP RESTAURANTS
- Katz's Deli (page 132)
- Ippudo (page 134)
- Dirt Candy (page 138)

TOP NIGHTLIFE
- Bowery Ballroom (page 183)
- Big Bar (page 186)

TOP SHOPS
- John Varvatos (page 290)
- The Strand (page 291)

GETTING THERE AND AROUND
- Metro lines: 4/5/6, B/D/F/M, L, J/Z, N/Q/R/W
- Metro stations: Astor Place, 1st Avenue, 2nd Avenue, 3rd Avenue, 8th Street, Delancey Street, Bowery, East Broadway, Essex Street, Grand Street, Union Square
- Major bus routes: M1, M8, M9, M14A, M14D, M15, M21, M22

EAST VILLAGE AND LOWER EAST SIDE WALK

TOTAL DISTANCE: 3 miles (5 km)
WALKING TIME: 1 hour

Times have changed in these formerly gritty neighborhoods, but you can still catch glimpses of their punk rock, bohemian, and im- migrant pasts. Head out for this walk in the late afternoon or early evening so you can stroll as night falls, a great time to explore the

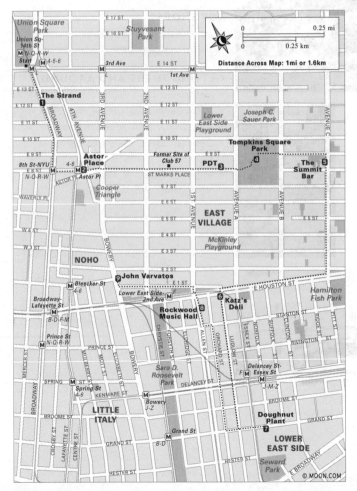

Astor Place subway station, completed in 1904

area with its many bars and eateries lining the streets and lighting the way.

1 Begin at **The Strand,** a mecca for book lovers and easily accessible from public transport stops at Union Square. Take your time perusing its storied, soaring shelves—you could spend a lifetime doing so, but when you're ready, head out the store's west exit onto Broadway.

2 Turn left to head south on Broadway. After four blocks, turn left onto East 8th Street and walk down the block to arrive at **Astor Place.** The centerpiece of this public space is Tony Rosenthal's steel sculpture *Alamo*. It's also known as The Cube and, yes, you can spin it. During the warmer months, you'll find café-style seating here if you'd like to stop for some people-watching.

3 From here, continue heading east down East 8th Street, which, after crossing 3rd Avenue, becomes St. Mark's Place, a famed East Village thoroughfare. Few streets in the city have changed more than St. Mark's Place over the past few decades. It used to be filled with used-record stores and vintage clothing shops and the bohemians and artists who frequented them; now you'll find a slew of fast-casual restaurants and the population skews more toward college students, young professionals, and tourists. The St. Mark's Place Hotel on the corner of 3rd Avenue used to rent by the hour. Cross 2nd Avenue; half a block down, look for number 57, now the Unitas mental health institute. It was formerly Club 57 (not to be confused with shuttered Midtown disco Studio 54), born out of a church basement and a hub for artistic

The Summit Bar

experimentation of all stripes from the late 1970s to early 1980s when artists including Keith Haring, Madonna, and Jean-Michel Basquiat hung out here while developing their voices. Continue on. The block between 1st Avenue and Avenue A remains the least corporate of the three-block stretch of street. Near the end of it you'll see Crif Dogs, tucked away a few steps below street level but easy to spot due to a large hot dog that hangs above the entrance emblazoned with the words "eat me." Go inside; the phone booth here is actually the entrance to celebrated cocktail bar **PDT.** Wait times are notoriously long, so pop in to put your name on the list for later before continuing your walk. Advance reservations can also be made.

4 Continue east on St. Marks Place to the end of the block at Avenue A, where you'll cross into the Alphabet City section of the East Village (so named for its alphabetical single-letter avenue names) and **Tompkins Square Park.** Walk through the small, pleasant green space, once infamous as a meeting place for drug dealers and users. But that gritty Alphabet City, where Jonathan Larson set his musical *Rent,* is—like most other hardscrabble vestiges of the city's past—long gentrified. Now you'll see people strolling their children and walking their dogs.

5 Exit the park at East 9th Street and Avenue B, and continue straight to head east one block to Avenue C, which used to be a no-man's-land rife with crime, but now houses condos, fine eateries, and some of the city's best cocktail bars. To sample the latter, pop half a block south into **The Summit Bar** for its terrific happy hour (5pm-8pm daily).

Katz's Deli

6 Turn right after exiting the bar to continue heading south down Avenue C about seven blocks until you hit East Houston Street, where you'll turn right and walk west. At the intersection with Ludlow Street is **Katz's Deli** on the corner. Around since 1888, the thing to get here continues to be the massive pastrami sandwich. Unless you're starving, it's a meal for two.

7 After stuffing yourself happy, turn right out of the exit to head south on Ludlow Street and into the Lower East Side. This is one of the neighborhood's main thoroughfares, with restaurants, bars, and clubs lining the storefronts of renovated tenements. After five blocks, turn left onto Grand Street. Walk two blocks, and to your right you'll find the original **Doughnut Plant,** a perfect place for dessert if you have stomach space to spare. For the widest selection, it's better to come earlier in the day, but as there isn't a bad doughnut here, evening is a fine time to snag one.

8 Backtrack from the direction you came, crossing Ludlow Street, and turn right on Orchard Street, another of the neighborhood's main streets. Continue four blocks north past many other trendy eateries, bars, and shops. Make a left onto Stanton Street and then a right onto Allen Street. You'll see **Rockwood Music Hall** to your right. The LES is a great spot for live music, and this venue has three stages to choose from, at least one typically without a cover—so it's a great spot to non-committally check out an up-and-coming band.

9 If you'd prefer to pay your respects to the neighborhood's legendary punk club, continue to the end of the block, cross East Houston Street, and turn left onto East 1st Street. Turn right onto Bowery after two blocks. Housed at the former site of CBGB, the **John Varvatos** store (open until 8pm Mon.-Sat. and 6pm Sun.) is the closest we have to a museum for the club that hosted up-and-comers bound for glory, including the Talking Heads and Patti Smith. While the iconic awning has been replaced with the designer's minimalist signage, he's preserved the walls, instruments, and other mementos from the club's heyday.

The Village and the Meatpacking District

Map 4

Greenwich Village is perhaps Manhattan's most romanticized neighborhood, a cornerstone of **1960s bohemianism** and the site of the **Stonewall** riots. Still host to **legendary nightlife venues,** it also has some of city's **best restaurants.** It serene western end, the **West Village,** is home to well-kept brownstones and quiet **tree-lined streets.** Next door the Meatpacking District, former home to slaughterhouses and biker bars, now trades in lavish **fashion stores** and **nightclubs.**

TOP SIGHTS

- The High Line (page 88)
- Whitney Museum of American Art (page 90)

TOP RESTAURANTS

- Minetta Tavern (page 140)

TOP NIGHTLIFE

- Village Vanguard (page 188)
- Le Bain (page 193)

TOP RECREATION

- Washington Square Park (page 267)

TOP SHOPS

- Madewell (page 293)

GETTING THERE AND AROUND

- Metro lines: 1/2/3, A/C/E, B/D/F/M, L
- Metro stations: West 4th Street, Christopher Street, 14th Street, Houston Street
- Major bus routes: M8, M11, M20

GREENWICH VILLAGE WALK

TOTAL DISTANCE: 2 miles (3.2 km)
WALKING TIME: 45 minutes

Greenwich Village is one of the loveliest areas in the city for a stroll, with numerous spots still resonant of its artsy, countercultural past. Quaint, leafy streets dominate the neighborhood, with 6th Avenue and 7th Avenue South being the two busiest thoroughfares. While most of the city is built on a grid, these lines bend in the Village, creating cozy enclaves easy to get lost in. Late afternoon, perhaps around 4pm, is a good time to take this walk, which will ideally coincide with sunset and an earlier dinner.

1 Begin in the tranquil **Jefferson Market Garden** (10am-5pm Tues.-Sun. Apr.-Oct.), named for the country's third president. When it opened in 1833, it was a lively trading site for fishmongers. Today it features a koi pond and benches popular with locals seeking quiet contemplation. The adjoining building is a former Victorian courthouse where Mae West was convicted on obscenity charges for her Broadway play *Sex*. The stunning original architecture has been preserved and the building now serves as an active branch of the New York Public Library.

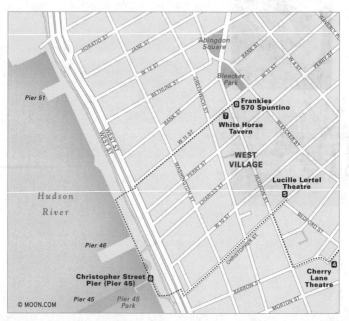

2 Exit the park on Greenwich Avenue, then make a right onto West 10th Street. Cross 6th Avenue, and continue east on 10th Street. Toward the end of the block, look for #14. This 1850s Greek Revival brownstone was purchased by Mark Twain at the turn of the 20th century and is rumored to have been his favorite residence, despite his living here for only a year. At the end of the block, turn right onto 5th Avenue and walk several blocks to **Washington Square Park.** You'll be greeted by the famous arch designed by Stanford White in the late 19th century. On a morbid note, White was murdered by his mistress's husband, who was subsequently tried at the Jefferson Market Courthouse. Walk through the arch to the fountain, where impromptu performances by street musicians often occur, making this a lively spot for people-watching.

3 Head to the southwest corner of the park to exit at West 4th Street. Continue a few blocks to its intersection with Jones Street. Picture a young Bob Dylan walking arm in arm with then-girlfriend Suze Rotolo—the cover photograph for *The Freewheelin' Bob Dylan.* It's still a fairly quiet street, making it easy to create your own replica. Continue down 4th Street for a couple more blocks and you'll reach Christopher Park and an important marker of 1960s history. Part of the **Stonewall National Monument,** the park's white statues commemorate the people who fought for LGBTQ rights. The monument also encompasses the namesake bar across the street where infamous police raids took place;

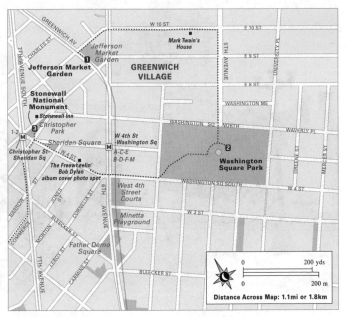

Stonewall Inn's two-for-one Big Gay Happy Hour (2pm-7:30pm Mon.-Fri.) makes it a nice stop if you're ready for a refreshment.

4 Exit onto Grove Street and head west, turning left to head south down 7th Avenue for several blocks. Make a right onto Commerce Street. About 1.5 blocks in, the street dead-ends at the **Cherry Lane Theatre.** Aside from its location on one of the more scenic streets in the Village, the theater has hosted premieres of works by Edward Albee and Samuel Beckett and continues to produce cutting-edge work by emerging and established playwrights alike. Head inside to see if its current offering catches your fancy; if the tickets are pricey, check the Theater Development Fund's half-price ticket booth website (www.tdf.org/nyc) for real-time offerings.

5 For more theater history, head west on Commerce and follow it to Barrow Street; then make a right on Hudson Street. Turn right on Christopher Street, walk a block, and look down. The Playwrights Walk of Fame, located in front of the **Lucille Lortel Theatre** and modeled after the Hollywood Walk of Fame, is one of the best monuments to the art form in the city. Among the playwrights alive and dead honored with a star are David Mamet, Sam Shepard, Tennessee Williams, Bertolt Brecht, and Arthur Miller.

Washington Square Park

Christopher Street Pier (Pier 45)

6 Next head the opposite way, walking west on Christopher Street for a few blocks. Cross West Street and head north for **Christopher Street Pier (Pier 45)**, one of the longest piers in the city. It offers striking views of the Hudson River along with One World Trade Center. If you've timed your visit for sunset, you can watch the light bounce off the gleaming Daniel Libeskind-designed tower.

7 Amble north along the water to West 11th Street, then head back east, crossing West Street again and walking three blocks to **White Horse Tavern.** This bar opened as a longshore workers' hangout in 1880. In the 1950s, it was frequented by Jack Kerouac and Dylan Thomas, who had his last drink—actually, it's said to have been 18 shots—before dying in his room at the Chelsea Hotel. The dizzying list of literary luminaries who've imbibed here goes on: Norman Mailer, Frank O'Hara, Anaïs Nin, Allen Ginsberg, Hunter S. Thompson. Have a drink in their honor.

8 Conclude your walk right across the street with dinner at **Frankies 570 Spuntino.** The Tuscan-style eatery uses locally sourced ingredients in shareable light bites like roasted beets with avocado and pastas like a tagliatelle with short ribs.

Chelsea and Union Square

Map 5

Chelsea is humming with activity. Home to the largest concentration of **art galleries** in the city and artisanal food hall **Chelsea Market,** the neighborhood is also known for its **LGBTQ nightlife.** To the east, Union Square is a major hub, encompassing park grounds, the city's largest **farmers market,** and a convergence of convenient subway lines. Nearby neighborhoods include **Gramercy,** defined by its tranquil private park, and nascent **NoMad** (North of Madison Square Park), also defined by its park.

TOP SIGHTS
- Chelsea Market (page 92)

TOP RESTAURANTS
- Eleven Madison Park (page 146)

TOP NIGHTLIFE
- Barracuda (page 194)
- Flatiron Lounge (page 195)

TOP ARTS AND CULTURE
- Gagosian (page 225)
- Petzel Gallery (page 225)
- Rubin Museum of Art (page 228)

TOP HOTELS
- Carlton Arms Hotel (page 317)

GETTING THERE AND AROUND
- Metro lines: 1/2/3, 4/5/6,
  A/C/E, F, L, N/Q/R/W
- Metro stations: 14th Street,
  23rd Street, 28th Street
- Major bus routes: M7, M11, M14, M23

CHELSEA WALK

TOTAL DISTANCE: 3 miles (4.8 km)
WALKING TIME: 1 hour

Take this art-focused walk in Chelsea late in the morning or early in the afternoon. Most galleries open at 10am and are closed on Sundays and Mondays.

1 Start your day at **Chelsea Market** to fuel up for your art-heavy walk. Here you'll find an array of food vendors to satisfy all appetites, and you can also peruse handmade offerings from Artists and Fleas, an Etsy-like flea market in the building where local artists show their wares.

2 Exit on the market's west side, at 10th Avenue, and notice The High Line above (convenient for a quick respite should you desire a break at any point). Turn right to head north about two blocks. Turn right onto West 18th Street, and on your right you'll see the **Petzel Gallery,** which showcases some of the best international artists.

3 Head back the way you came to 10th Avenue and walk north one block to 19th Street. The floor-to-ceiling glass walls of **STORY** will appear. This concept store operates more like a gallery, changing out its offerings, organized around themes, frequently. It's a fun stop for browsing or gift buying.

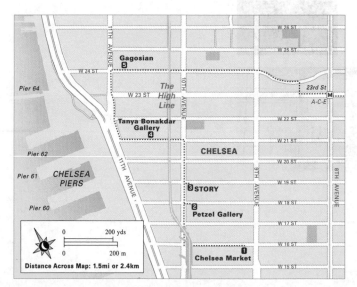

4 Exit the store and continue heading north on 10th Avenue for two blocks. Turn left on West 21st Street, and on the north side of the street you'll see the **Tanya Bonakdar Gallery.** This duplex gallery regularly exhibits major contemporary artists like Olafur Eliasson.

5 Across the street is one of Larry Gagosian's galleries, but his largest is a few blocks away. Turn right as you exit Tanya Bonakdar to head west on West 21st Street. At the end of the block, turn right onto 11th Avenue and walk three blocks. Turn right onto West 24th Street, and to your left will be the **Gagosian,** one of the most impressive gallery spaces in Chelsea.

6 Make a left as you exit the gallery on West 24th Street and head east. Past 9th Avenue, half a block down, you'll make a right and then a left onto West 23rd Street. Continue east on it, crossing 8th Avenue. The famed Chelsea Hotel of bohemian legend—artists from Leonard Cohen and Janis Joplin to Dylan Thomas and Arthur Miller kicked it around here—is in the middle of the block on the south side of the street. At the end of the block, turn right onto 7th Avenue and walk six blocks. Turn left onto West 17th Street and enter the **Rubin Museum of Art** to your right. This hidden gem has an impressive collection of Himalayan art that you could spend hours exploring. But you can also simply stop in at the café for a snack, as well as access the lower level—which usually has a few works on display—without paying admission.

7 Exit the museum and turn right, heading east down West 17th Street. At the end of the block, turn left and walk a block on 6th

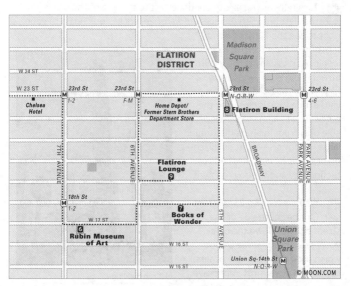

Chelsea Market

Avenue. Turn right onto West 18th Street, and about half a block down to your right you'll see **Books of Wonder,** a children's bookstore that even adults will love. The staff brings a sophisticated curatorial touch to children's literature with a series of author talks and a prized collection of first editions like the celebrated Eloise series. Artwork by Maurice Sendak, among others, is on display for purchase.

8 Turn right as you exit to continue east to the end of the block. Then turn left onto 5th Avenue and walk five blocks, looking up to your right to see the **Flatiron Building,** one of New York City's most iconic. At its skinny tip near 23rd Street is the Prow Artspace gallery. While the building houses private offices and is closed to the public, this unique space—viewable only from the outside through large windows—exhibits small, colorful shows with an emphasis on technology and the environment.

9 Walk west down 23rd Street. On the south side of the street halfway down the block, you'll see a giant Home Depot, which used to be Stern Brothers, one of the city's most impressive

Flatiron Building

Rubin Museum of Art

department stores in the 19th century when this neighborhood was a prime shopping district. You can still admire its Renaissance Revival architecture. Make a left at the end of the block on 6th Avenue and head four blocks to West 19th Street and make a left. Walk east about half a block on the north side of the street. Depending on how leisurely your stroll has been, you may be just in time for happy hour (4pm-6pm Mon.-Fri.) at the throwback-elegant **Flatiron Lounge,** where you can kick back with an artful cocktail to toast your day of exploration.

Midtown, Hell's Kitchen, and Times Square

Map 6

Midtown is where the city's iconography peaks, home to beloved beacons of the New York skyline, the **Empire State** and **Chrysler Buildings,** as well as sights like **Rockefeller Center** and **MoMA.** **Times Square** beckons with bright lights. Multistory department stores and international flagships line **5th Avenue.** Historic hotels and skyscrapers housing countless businesses tower over intense pedestrian traffic. Meanwhile, Hell's Kitchen offers a more residential and restaurant-filled respite from **Broadway's Theater District.**

TOP SIGHTS
- Museum of Modern Art (MoMA) (page 94)
- Empire State Building (page 95)
- Rockefeller Center (page 96)

TOP RESTAURANTS
- Ess-a-Bagel (page 155)
- Le Bernardin (page 157)

TOP NIGHTLIFE
- Rudy's (page 200)

TOP ARTS AND CULTURE
- Playwrights Horizons (page 231)
- Signature Theatre Company (page 231)

TOP SHOPS
- MoMA Design Store (page 299)

TOP HOTELS
- The Plaza (page 317)
- WestHouse Hotel (page 318)
- Algonquin Hotel (page 319)
- Yotel (page 320)

GETTING THERE AND AROUND
- Metro lines: 1/2/3, 4/5/6, 7, B/D/F/M, N/Q/R, S, A/C/E
- Metro stations: 34th Street, 42nd Street, 47-50th Streets-Rockefeller Center, 50th Street, Lexington Avenue, 5th Avenue, 7th Avenue
- Major bus routes: M1, M2, M3, M4, M5, M6, M7, M11, M12, M34, M42, M50, M57

Upper West Side and Upper East Side

Map 7

The **leafy streets** of the posh and predominantly residential Upper East and West Sides are lined with brownstones and wonderfully preserved prewar buildings. But these neighborhoods flanking **Central Park** are also home to top New York cultural institutions. **Museum Mile** on the Upper East Side comprises 20-odd blocks with some of the city's most revered museums, including **The Met** and the **Guggenheim,** while the Upper West Side has **Lincoln Center** and the **American Museum of Natural History.**

TOP SIGHTS
- Central Park (page 101)
- The Metropolitan Museum of Art (page 105)

TOP RESTAURANTS
- Gray's Papaya (page 164)

TOP ARTS AND CULTURE
- Lincoln Center (page 244)

TOP SHOPS
- Fivestory (page 300)
- Barneys New York (page 300)

TOP HOTELS
- The Surrey (page 321)

GETTING THERE AND AROUND
- Metro lines: 1/2/3, 4/5/6, A/C, B, Q
- Metro stations: 59th Street-Columbus Circle, 66th Street-Lincoln Center, 72nd Street, 81st Street, 86th Street, 96th Street, 103rd Street
- Major bus routes: M7, M11, M66, M72, M79, M86, M96

Harlem and Morningside Heights

Map 8

Manhattan's upper reaches are steeped in historical reminders, from the American Revolutionary War to the influential **Harlem Renaissance,** as well as home to grand **Gothic churches.** Today its neighborhoods are among the city's fastest growing, with an increasing number of businesses, including a new incarnation of a legendary bebop supper club. Harlem is rich in **black culture** past and present, while residential Morningside Heights is defined by **Columbia University.**

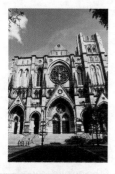

TOP SIGHTS
- Cathedral of St. John the Divine (page 109)

TOP RESTAURANTS
- Charles' Country Pan Fried
  Chicken (page 166)

TOP NIGHTLIFE
- Minton's Playhouse (page 203)

GETTING THERE AND AROUND
- Metro lines: 1/2/3, 4/5/6, A/C, B/D
- Metro stations: 110th Street, 116th Street,
  125th Street, 135th Street, 145th Street
- Major bus routes: M1, M2, M3, M4, M5,
  M7, M10, M60, M100, M101, M104

HARLEM WALK

TOTAL DISTANCE: 3 miles (4.8 km)
WALKING TIME: 1.25 hours

Crowds are considerably thinner in these northern parts of Manhattan, making the area nice for a wander anytime, especially on the weekends when much of Manhattan is mobbed. Sundays are livelier in Harlem, with a heavy church crowd, though the Cathedral of St. John the Divine closes earlier that day. To take best advantage of this itinerary, which aims to encompass some of the neighborhood's lively past and present, head out a bit later on a weeknd afternoon.

Note that gentrification in the neighborhood has given rise to frustration among some locals that is important to be aware

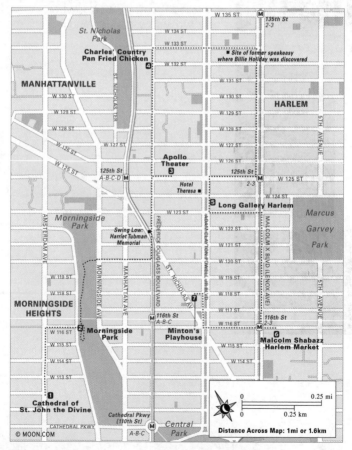

Cathedral of St. John the Divine

of—large groups of tourists are a particular target at which to voice these grievances. A gracious attitude and open mind goes a long way. Most people are friendly and welcoming when they see a genuine interest in learning about their culture and history. A good rule of thumb is to remember that this is a living community and not just a tourist attraction.

1 Start your walk at the architectural wonder that is the **Cathedral of St. John the Divine** (9am-5pm Mon.-Sat., 1pm-3pm Sun.), quite possibly the city's grandest church, with exhibits detailing its rich history. Its main entrance is at West 112th Street on Amsterdam Avenue.

2 Exiting the church, turn right and walk four blocks to West 116th Street, turning right again and heading a block down and into **Morningside Park,** one of the city's hilliest, offering expansive skyline views from its western ridge. Follow the park's winding staircase while taking in a bird's-eye view of its various playgrounds and the city skyline in the background. Walk north through the park and exit at West 120th Street and Morningside Avenue.

3 Continue down 120th Street for two blocks, turning left onto Frederick Douglass Boulevard. Head north, and near the West 122nd Street intersection, you'll see *Swing Low,* the Harriet Tubman Memorial statue commemorating the Underground Railroad heroine. Continue several blocks on Frederick Douglass Boulevard, and turn right onto West 125th Street, Harlem's most commercial stretch, where you'll see the marquee of the famous **Apollo Theater** mid-block. The iconic

Morningside Park

theater continues to be a cultural hub of the neighborhood; if you're here on a Wednesday, you might want to circle back later in the evening for its renowned Amateur Night (7:30pm), which has launched the careers of icons from Ella Fitzgerald to Jimi Hendrix. The theater also offers tours.

4 Backtrack to Frederick Douglass Boulevard and continue north to the corner of West 132nd Street, where you'll find **Charles' Country Pan Fried Chicken.** Don't be deceived by its low-key look; it serves the neighborhood's best fried chicken. Back on Frederick Douglass Boulevard, walk north a block and turn right onto West 133rd Street, which used to be known as Swing Street for its proliferation of clandestine watering holes during Prohibition; today the street is mostly home to renovated brownstones. About 1.5 blocks down the street, at number 148, you'll pass the site of the former 1st-floor speakeasy where Billie Holiday was discovered, now home to a dry jazz club called Bill's Place.

5 Continue walking down the street and turn right onto Lenox Avenue, also known as Malcolm X Boulevard, to begin looping back south and past numerous other notable eateries (take note for later) on this major commercial stretch. Walk eight blocks and turn right onto West 125th Street, then left on Adam Clayton Powell Jr. Boulevard. Look for the towering terra-cotta building to your right; this is the former Hotel Theresa, a historic landmark that's hosted such disparate leaders as Fidel Castro, John F. Kennedy, and Eleanor Roosevelt. On the next block south, check out the tiny **Long Gallery Harlem,** dedicated to showcasing contemporary works by artists of the African diaspora, to see if it's open. It keeps regular hours on the weekends when exhibitions are happening.

6 Turn left to leave the gallery and then left again at the end of the block to walk down West 123rd Street back to Lenox Avenue/Malcolm X Boulevard, continuing south on it for seven blocks. You'll walk through part of the Mount Morris Park Historic District, one of the only areas in Harlem protected by the Landmarks Preservation Commission. Ornate 19th- and 20th-century row houses line the blocks between 118th and 124th Streets. When you get to West 116th Street make a left and you'll find the **Malcolm Shabazz Harlem Market** on the south side of the street. Here you can browse and shop for African arts and crafts.

7 If the timing is right, end your day with drinks and jazz (and supper, if your stomach's ready for it) at **Minton's Playhouse,** which opens at 6pm. Walk back the way you came on 116th Street, continuing an extra block before turning right onto Adam Clayton Powell Jr. Boulevard. Walk two blocks, then turn left to find yourself at the birthplace of bebop.

Apollo Theater

Downtown Brooklyn, Dumbo, and Fort Greene Map 9

Brooklyn is a city unto itself. Dumbo (Down Under the Manhattan Bridge Overpass) and the largely residential **Brooklyn Heights** sit on the **waterfront,** which has been transformed from an industrial hub into a **green refuge** offering dramatic views of the Manhattan skyline and **Brooklyn Bridge.** Once a haven for artists seeking cheap lofts, Dumbo still has impressive **galleries,** while farther inland Downtown Brooklyn is home to the borough's government buildings and office complexes as well as, increasingly, **hip eateries and bars,**

also prevalent in Fort Greene, home to the **Brooklyn Academy of Music.**

TOP SIGHTS
- Brooklyn Bridge (page 113)

TOP RESTAURANTS
- Bella Gioia (page 169)
- Juliana's (page 170)

TOP ARTS AND CULTURE
- St. Ann's Warehouse (page 248)
- Brooklyn Academy of Music (BAM) (page 249)

TOP RECREATION
- Brooklyn Heights Promenade (page 275)

GETTING THERE AND AROUND
- Metro lines: 2/3, 4/5, A/C, B/D/F, G, N/Q/R
- Metro stations: Atlantic Avenue, Lafayette Avenue, Fulton Street, Nevins Street, Hoyt-Schermerhorn Street, DeKalb Avenue, Bergen Street, Clark Street, Hoyt Street, High Street-Brooklyn Bridge, York Street
- Major bus routes: B25, B26, B37, B38, B45, B52, B54, B61, B63
- Ferries: East River route to Dumbo or South Brooklyn route to Brooklyn Bridge Park Pier 6/Atlantic Avenue or Dumbo

BROOKLYN BRIDGE AND DUMBO WALK

TOTAL DISTANCE: 4 miles (6.4 km)
WALKING TIME: 1.25 hours

Walking the Brooklyn Bridge is a classic New York experience. Once you're in the borough, it's nice to spend the day wandering around its green waterfront spaces and galleries. Afternoon is a good time to take in what this walk has to offer. If you go on a Sunday in the warmer months, you'll also be able to catch the Brooklyn Flea.

1 Start on Centre Street on the southeastern perimeter of City Hall Park to access the **Brooklyn Bridge.** The bridge's entrance is conveniently located across from the Brooklyn Bridge City Hall Station servicing the 4, 5, and 6 subway lines. Unlike other bridges, there isn't a tricky staircase to find. Just follow the pedestrian path onto the bridge. Admire the exposed bridge cables and gorgeous views in all directions: Downtown Brooklyn ahead, Manhattan skyline behind, and the East River below. Crossing the 1.3-mile (2 km) bridge takes roughly half an hour.

2 While the pedestrian path continues on, you'll exit down a staircase to Cadman Plaza East/Washington Street in Dumbo. Head north to the corner of Prospect Street and walk one block west to Cadman Plaza

Brooklyn Bridge

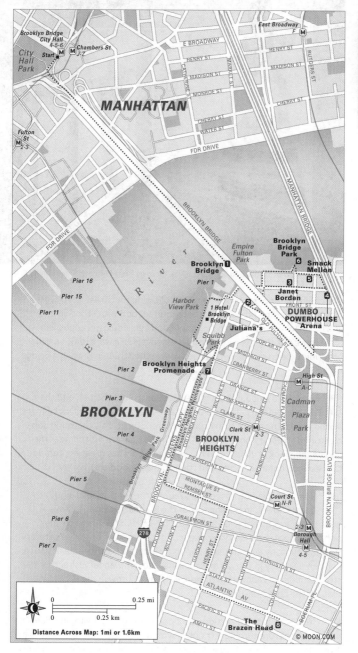

MANHATTAN

Brooklyn Bridge
City Hall
4-5-6

Ⓜ Start

City Hall Park

Ⓜ Chambers St
J-Z

E BROADWAY

East Broadway
F Ⓜ

HENRY ST

HENRY ST

MADISON ST

MADISON ST

RUTGERS ST

S CATHERINE ST

MONROE ST

CHERRY ST

Ⓜ Fulton St
2-3

CHERRY ST

WATER ST

FDR DRIVE

FDR DRIVE

BROOKLYN BRIDGE

MANHATTAN BRIDGE

East River

Pier 16

Pier 15

Pier 11

Empire Fulton Park

Brooklyn Bridge Park

Brooklyn ❶ **Bridge**

Pier 1

Harbor View Park

1 Hotel Brooklyn ■ Bridge

Juliana's

❷

Squibb Park

Brooklyn Heights Promenade ❼

Pier 2

Pier 3

BROOKLYN

Pier 4

Brooklyn Bridge Park Greenway

COLUMBIA HTS

Brooklyn Heights Promenade

❻ Smack Mellon

❸ ❺

Janet Borden

❹

FRONT ST

DUMBO POWERHOUSE Arena

OLD FULTON ST

POPLAR ST

MIDDAGH ST

CRANBERRY ST

ORANGE ST

PINEAPPLE ST

CLARK ST

BROOKLYN HEIGHTS

High St Ⓜ A-C

Cadman Plaza Park

CADMAN PLAZA WEST

Clark St Ⓜ 2-3

MONROE PL

Pier 5

Pier 6

Pier 7

QUEENS

Brooklyn Heights Promenade

WILLOW ST

PIERREPONT ST

MONTAGUE ST

REMSEN ST

JORALEMON ST

HENRY ST

GARDEN PL

SIDNEY PL

STATE ST

ATLANTIC AV

PACIFIC ST

AMITY ST

Court St Ⓜ N-R

LIVINGSTON ST

BROOKLYN BRIDGE BLVD

2-3 Ⓜ
Borough Hall
Ⓜ
4-5

CLINTON ST

COURT ST

The Brazen Head ❽

278

0   0.25 mi

0   0.25 km

Distance Across Map: 1mi or 1.6km

© MOON.COM

65

installation view of *Spread Wild: Pleasures of the Yucca* by Paula Wilson at Smack Mellon

West/Old Fulton Street. Make a right, following the street northwest. Just after passing Old Fulton Street's intersection with Front Street, you'll see **Juliana's** to your right, where you can indulge in coal-oven pizza by one of the city's local foodie legends. On a warm day, consider ordering a pie to go and eating it just down the street in Brooklyn Bridge Park.

3 Turn left to exit Juliana's, make a left onto Front Street, and then take another left after a block at the intersection onto Dock Street. At the end of the block, turn right on Water Street. This charming cobblestoned street is home to some of Dumbo's galleries. Stop near the end of the block at **Janet Borden,** which not only has great contemporary exhibits but a very cute and friendly black poodle.

4 Continue heading east down Water Street until it dead-ends at Adams Street, in the shadow of the Manhattan Bridge. Make a right on Adams Street and you'll find **POWERHOUSE Arena** to your right. This bookstore is a great place to get a sense of Brooklyn's literary talent, with many autographed copies by local authors for sale. If you're here on a Sunday in the warmer months, you can wander just across the street under the Manhattan Bridge archway to browse the Brooklyn Flea (10am-5pm Apr.-Oct.).

5 Head back in the direction you came from, going north on Adams Street before turning left onto Plymouth Street. **Smack Mellon** is a block down the street. Housed in an old warehouse, this gallery provides a dramatic exhibition space for artists, while its architecture captures

Broooklyn Bridge Park

both the neighborhood's gritty industrial past and chic present.

6 Continue west on Plymouth Street for one block and enter **Brooklyn Bridge Park** to your immediate right. Walk north toward the water, and you'll see Pebble Beach, one of the only points in the city where you can get right down to the water's edge. Continue west along the waterfront. Ramble around or follow pedestrian paths as the park curves south. You'll walk past a carousel. Human-made hills muffle the noise here and create an interesting topography to trek through.

7 You'll pass under the Brooklyn Bridge and come upon a ferry ticket purchase window near Pier 1. From here follow the Brooklyn Bridge Park Greenway as it curves left and south. You'll see the trendy woodwork of 1 Hotel Brooklyn Bridge on your left. As you pass the hotel, you'll access the Squibb Park Bridge to your left. The bridge brings you to Squibb Park. Exit at Middagh Street, turning right to walk about two blocks south on Columbia Heights to the entrance of the **Brooklyn Heights Promenade** at Orange Street. On the promenade, you'll gain a sublime perspective of the Manhattan skyline and Statue of Liberty. It's about a third of a mile long (just over half a km). Have a rest on one of the many benches and soak up the views. As you walk along the promenade, check out the brownstones that abut the elevated passageway.

8 Exit at Remsen Street and walk a couple of blocks east to Henry Street. Make a right to head south down to Atlantic Avenue. Make a left and **The Brazen Head** will be 2.5 blocks east on the south side of the street. End your day at this bar with ramshackle charm; there often is an interesting craft beer or cider or liquor event going on.

Williamsburg, Greenpoint, and Bushwick

Map 10

These formerly industrial working-class neighborhoods in Brooklyn are now the city's **hippest zone,** home to some of the best **craft beer bars, live music,** indie **arts venues,** and **world-class restaurants.** While Williamsburg is the polished center of hipsterdom, the Polish neighborhood of Greenpoint just north is its quieter cousin. Bushwick to the southeast has a **funkier edge,** with **working studios, bars,** and makeshift warehouse events. While ongoing work on the L train between Manhattan and the neighborhoods makes transit challenging, people will keep coming no matter what.

TOP SIGHTS
- Brooklyn Brewery (page 114)

TOP RESTAURANTS
- Brooklyn Cider House (page 175)

TOP NIGHTLIFE
- Beer Street (page 207)
- Noorman's Kil (page 211)

TOP ARTS AND CULTURE
- Nitehawk Cinema (page 252)

TOP SHOPS
- Beacon's Closet (page 304)
- Rough Trade (page 304)

TOP HOTELS
- Wythe Hotel (page 325)

GETTING THERE AND AROUND
- Metro lines: L (see page 24), G, J/Z, M
- Metro stations: Bedford Avenue, Lorimer Street, Graham Avenue, Grand Street, Montrose Avenue, Morgan Avenue, Jefferson Street, Greenpoint Avenue, Nassau Street, Central Avenue, Myrtle Avenue, Marcy Avenue, Hewes Street, Broadway, Metropolitan Avenue, DeKalb Avenue
- Major bus routes: B24, B32, B43, B48, B54, B59, B62
- Ferries: NYC Ferry East River route to Greenpoint, North Williamsburg, or South Williamsburg

WILLIAMSBURG AND GREENPOINT WALK

TOTAL DISTANCE: 2 miles (3.2 km)
WALKING TIME: 45 minutes

Welcome to the center of New York cool, where indie businesses thrive. Take a walk and get a taste of the hipster lifestyle. Williamsburg and Greenpoint are foodie destinations, so ideally you'll visit the neighborhoods during the warmer months on a Saturday so you can experience the wonder that is Smorgasburg, the country's biggest open-air food market, full of local vendors. Because the area is also a lively nightlife destination, it's a good idea to time this walk for late afternoon/early evening so you can experience a bit of both day and night.

1 A pleasant and convenient way to get to Brooklyn via Manhattan is by ferry service, which is frequent. From East 34th Street in Midtown or Wall Street/Pier 11 in Lower Manhattan, you can hop on the East River route and land here in Brooklyn 20-25 minutes later. From the North Williamsburg ferry landing, head east toward Kent Avenue. Turn left and walk a block to arrive at **East River State Park,** which on

East River State Park

Saturdays spring-fall hosts Smorgasburg (11am-6pm Apr.-Oct.), an out-door market featuring hundreds of local vendors to sate all foodie desires. Even when it's not Smorgasburg season, you'll catch great views of the Manhattan skyline from this waterfront park.

2 Exit the park at North 9th Street. About half a block down, you'll find **Rough Trade** to your right. Check out its schedule (it's also a live music venue) posted out front and then head inside to peruse rare vinyl albums.

3 Continue down the block, then turn left on Wythe Avenue. Walk two blocks, then turn right onto North 11th Street. You'll smell the hops and barley wafting through the air as you arrive at the renowned **Brooklyn Brewery.** Head inside and enjoy a pint in the taproom, where crowds jockey for seats at picnic tables and order food delivery from neighboring restaurants for sustenance.

4 From the brewery, continue down North 11th Street, then turn left onto Berry Street. In a block, you'll reach **McCarren Park,** which divides Williamsburg from Greenpoint and is the neighborhoods' main recreation spot. Meander through this oddly shaped park, a favorite for locals to walk their dogs and sunbathe.

5 Exit the park to the north at Nassau Avenue and Guernsey Street. About half a block down Guernsey Street is where you'll find **Beacon's Closet,** relocated from its original Williamsburg digs into this much larger Greenpoint space. This is one of the best places for vintage shopping at reasonable prices. Shirts by designers like Paul Smith are squeezed into stuffed circular racks, so careful examination is necessary to avoid missing gems.

6 Head back to Nassau Avenue the way you came and continue walking east down the street, one of Greenpoint's main commercial stretches. You may also catch glimpses down the tree-lined side streets of row houses, some elaborately renovated into sleek single-family residences and condos. After two blocks, turn right onto Manhattan Avenue for **Tørst,** an acclaimed beer bar from the founder of Denmark's Evil Twin Brewing. Beer is big in Brooklyn, so you may as well do as the locals do if you're so inclined and have another pint.

7 Go back to Nassau Avenue and toward McCarren Park. Cut again through the park via Bedford Avenue, or the pedestrian path that runs parallel inside the park. Exit the park at North 12th Street and continue down Bedford Avenue—this is Williamsburg's main thoroughfare, full of trendy eateries, shops, and bars. Peek into **Brooklyn Industries** on the corner of North 8th Street to check out clothes and accessories exporting the borough's cool.

8 If you're feeling peckish or weren't able to catch Smorgasburg, now is as good a time as any to stop for a slice at **Anna Maria Williamsburg,** just a block down Bedford on North 7th Street.

McCarren Park

Tørst

9 Walk another block southwest and turn right on North 6th Street, another of Williamsburg's bustling thoroughfares lined with restaurants and bars. Walk about 2.5 blocks down the street to arrive at the **Music Hall of Williamsburg.** Catching a live show is a great way to end a night in the neighborhood, so if time and serendipity align you might catch the latest indie act. Shows here tend to sell out for popular bands, so it's best to get tickets in advance if there's a particular performance that piques your interest.

SIGHTS

New York is a city of immigrants, and its most cherished sights reflect that. Over 12 million people entered the country through Ellis Island, greeted by

the Statue of Liberty. The Empire State Building, among many others, was built by their labor. The Tenement Museum today tells their stories.

Each neighborhood has its attractions. Lower Manhattan is home to Wall Street's New York Stock Exchange. The High Line runs from the Meatpacking District to Midtown, home to Rockefeller Center, Times Square, and Broadway theaters. The Upper East Side's Museum Mile boasts a stretch of renowned institutions flanking Central Park.

Besides such well-known stars, the city contains a plethora of other attractions, including island getaways, walkable bridges, and significant historical and cultural sites—from Founding Father Alexander Hamilton's house to the country's first LGBTQ national monument.

Empire State Building

As impressive as its sights are, New York is so much more than their sum. The best way to see the city is by walking the lively streets as much as possible, observing how each neighborhood blends into the next. Watch the skyscrapers of Midtown morph into the prewar apartment buildings and grand museums of the Upper East and Upper West Sides. Notice how Chelsea's neatly organized street grid dissolves into the crooked cobblestones of Greenwich Village. Cross the Brooklyn Bridge for a dramatic shift between boroughs. There's never a dull moment. And if you get tired, you're never far from a subway stop…

HIGHLIGHTS

✪ **BEST GLIMPSE OF THE IMMIGRANT JOURNEY:** Walk in the footsteps of millions of our immigrant ancestors at **Ellis Island** (page 76).

✪ **BEST MONUMENT TO OUR BETTER ANGELS:** The hopeful symbolism of the **Statue of Liberty** endures (page 77).

✪ **BEST ISLAND GETAWAY:** Wander the promenade, bike the trails, or just lounge in a red hammock on **Governors Island** (page 78).

✪ **BEST TIME MACHINE:** Experience what it was like to be an immigrant newly arrived in the Lower East Side at the **Tenement Museum** (page 86).

✪ **BEST URBAN REINVENTION:** Wander and lounge amid the greenery of **The High Line,** which has become a model for reclaiming industrial space (page 88).

✪ **BEST AMERICAN ART WITH A VIEW:** The **Whitney Museum of American Art** holds a world-class collection indoors and offers stellar views outdoors (page 90).

✪ **BEST INDOOR MARKET:** Get a sense of the city's breadth of foodie offerings at **Chelsea Market** (page 92).

✪ **MOST MODERN ART PER SQUARE FOOT:** The **Museum of Modern Art (MoMA)** has a world-class art collection and just keeps growing (page 94).

✪ **BEST SKYSCRAPER:** In a city filled with iconic buildings, the **Empire State Building** is the most iconic of all (page 95).

✪ **MOST NEW YORK ICONOGRAPHY IN A SINGLE COMPLEX:** Catch grand city views from Top of the Rock, tour NBC Studios, pose with *Atlas*, and, in winter, behold the giant Christmas tree and ice-skate at **Rockefeller Center** (page 96).

✪ **MOST FAMOUS CITY PARK:** Discover for yourself what makes **Central Park** the country's most visited urban green space (page 101).

✪ **GRANDEST MUSEUM:** The breadth of **The Metropolitan Museum of Art**'s collection will take your breath away (page 105).

✪ **MOST COLOSSAL CATHEDRAL:** The sheer scale of the **Cathedral of St. John the Divine** makes it a must-see (page 109).

✪ **BEST BRIDGE WALK:** Stroll the scenic **Brooklyn Bridge,** an active way to take in amazing views (page 113).

✪ **BEST BREWERY TO SEE WHERE IT ALL STARTED: Brooklyn Brewery** was here long before the borough was saturated with craft beer (page 114).

✪ **BEST LOCALS' PARK: Prospect Park** is the Central Park of Brooklyn and the borough's backyard (page 115).

Lower Manhattan

Map 1

✪ Ellis Island

Fun fact: Nearly half of all Americans are descended from immigrants who passed through Ellis Island. Now the Ellis Island National Museum of Immigration, the former immigration center offers visitors an impactful experience. Simply walking the halls here—where 12 million immigrants entered the country between 1892 and 1954—puts into focus the country's multicultural foundations.

The main building's 1st floor is where people checked their luggage before going through inspections. Today an exhibit examines how immigration and the slave trade shaped the landscape of the country from 1550 to 1890, providing industries in the city with free or cheap labor, while oral histories recount the individual struggles of immigrants as they resettled in a foreign country. Over 5,000 people were shuttled each day through the 2nd-floor registry room for medical examinations and legal reviews that would determine their eligibility to enter the country, and the cavernous grandeur of the floor has been restored to its appearance circa 1918-1924, with giant arched windows lining an expansive perimeter and featuring the original benches hopeful citizens sat upon as their future was determined. Listening to stories on the included audio tour about the grueling waits, while sitting in the same room, makes palpable the anticipation and anxiety.

Ellis Island

76

For a deeper peek, take a 90-minute hard-hat tour of the unrestored Ellis Island Hospital Complex. Now a ruin, this is where the arriving sick, or those who failed medical examinations, were held, and the tour offers an experience beyond the shiny museum sheen of the main building. Tours are pricey ($65.50 adults, $61 seniors) but include the ferry and regular museum admission. Seven tours a day are offered between 10:30am and 3:30pm in the summer, with reduced schedules in other seasons.

Access to both Ellis Island and the Statue of Liberty is available only via Statue Cruises. Ferries run roughly every 20 minutes 8:30am-7pm daily in the summer, weather permitting, with reduced operating hours off-season. Ferry tickets include general admission to both Ellis Island and the Statue of Liberty and should be purchased online in advance to avoid long lines, but you can also buy tickets at major hotels or the Castle Clinton ticketing window in The Battery.

MAP 1: Statue Cruises, The Battery opposite 17 State St., 877/523-9849, www.statuecruises.com; Ellis Island, 212/363-3200, www.nps.gov/elis; begins closing 30 minutes before final ferry departure; $18.50 adults, $14 seniors, $9 children 4-12, free for children under 4

TOP EXPERIENCE

✪ Statue of Liberty

New York has spawned many iconic images, but none so recognizable as the Statue of Liberty. Given as a gift of friendship from the French in 1886, she stands as both a symbol of democratic freedom and reminder to embrace our better nature.

Lady Liberty offered a hopeful first glimpse of the country as immigrants waited to be admitted at Ellis Island, and whether you see her from near or far today while you're in the city, she remains a welcoming sight. The word "liberty" was controversial—our democracy was still in its infancy and there were few other examples in the world—when the French political thinker and abolitionist Édouard de Laboulaye conceived of the 305-foot (93-m) sculpture that would be created by artist Frédéric-Auguste Bartholdi.

Different levels of access are possible. General admission brings you to Liberty Island, on which Lady Liberty is located. You can also go inside the statue and up to her pedestal—included in admission, though reservations are recommended. Crown access costs an extra $3, and reservations are required and should be made at least several months in advance. This is the highest accessible point and makes for a unique, if crowded, lookout point. It's 354 steps up (note there are no elevators), about 20 stories high, and a fairly narrow thoroughfare—this is not a spot for the claustrophobic.

Access to both Ellis Island and the Statue of Liberty is available only via Statue Cruises. Ferries run roughly every 20 minutes 8:30am-7pm daily in the summer, weather permitting, with reduced operating hours off-season. Ferry tickets include general admission to both Ellis Island and the Statue of Liberty and should be purchased online in advance to avoid long lines, but you can also buy tickets at major hotels or the Castle Clinton ticketing window in The Battery.

Statue of Liberty

MAP 1: Statue Cruises, The Battery opposite 17 State St., 877/523-9849, www.statuecruises.com; Liberty Island, 212/363-3200, www.nps.gov/stli; begins closing 30 minutes before final ferry departure; $18.50 adults, $14 seniors, $9 children 4-12, free for children under 4

NEARBY:

- Grab a hand-rolled bagel and choose from an array of cream cheeses and spreads at Leo's Bagels (page 123).

- Pair delicious drinks with a meal at The Dead Rabbit (page 179).
- Kick back in a Havana-inspired atmosphere with a cocktail at BlackTail (page 179).
- Relax under a tree or explore historical attractions at The Battery (page 264).
- Find the Financial District's famous *Charging Bull* statue at Bowling Green (page 264).
- Bike or walk along the water via the Hudson River Greenway (page 265).

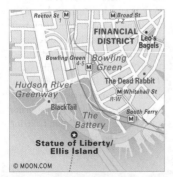

✪ Governors Island

First home to the Lenape people, who called it Pagganuck (Nut Island) for its abundance of oak, hickory, and chestnut trees, then a former military base, Governors Island has become a mini-getaway for locals and tourists alike. The island is small at 172 acres (70 ha), and you can walk around its perimeter via a 2.2-mile (3.5-km) promenade that offers striking skyline views of the city as well as the

Statue of Liberty, Brooklyn, and New Jersey. Dozens of red hammocks are in the aptly named Hammock Grove for lounging, while 7 miles (11.3 km) of bike trails trace through the expansive landscaped parkland. Blazing Saddles (www.blazingsaddles.com) offers free hour-long cruiser bike rentals Monday-Friday 10am-noon in season; outside these hours, cruisers are $15 for two hours or $25 for a full-day rental. Food trucks abound on the island, and alcohol is available. On summer Saturdays 11am-4pm The Downtown Boathouse offers free kayaks and instruction on a walk-up basis from Pier 101, near where the Manhattan ferry docks. Also on the island are free, site-specific art installations, a kids-only playground comprising 50,000 square feet (4,645 sq m) called play:groundNYC, and Adventures at Governors Island (www.adventuresgovisland.com;

typically 10am-6pm May-Oct.), a recreational complex with a maze ($8) and mini-golf course ($7) as well as zip line ($12) and rock-climbing ($6) options. Numerous events are held here, including the Jazz Age Lawn Party and countless others you can learn about on the island's website. It's a perfect nearby destination if you're looking to escape the weight of the summer heat or just for a respite from the bustle of the city.

In season, the island is accessible by ferry from Manhattan leaving from the Battery Maritime Building (10 South St., $3 round-trip), with 1-2 departures per hour daily starting at 10am; the final ferry leaves Manhattan at 4:15pm Monday-Thursday, with later departure times added Fridays May-September and Saturdays July-September (until 10pm and 11pm, respectively). You can also catch a ferry from Brooklyn Bridge Park (Pier 6,

Governors Island

BEST SKYLINE VIEWS

GOVERNORS ISLAND
Situated near the convergence of the Hudson and East Rivers just south of Manhattan, Governors Island affords a rare perspective on the surrounding topography, beholding the New York skyline as well as Brooklyn to the east and the Statue of Liberty and New Jersey to the west (page 78).

THE HIGH LINE
Elevated 30 feet (9 m) above Manhattan's far west side and snaking through the hip neighborhoods of the Meatpacking District and Chelsea, a walk along The High Line gives great views of both the Empire State and Chrysler Buildings, along with the Hudson River (page 88).

THE TERRACES AT WHITNEY MUSEUM OF AMERICAN ART
Take a break from art gazing on the Whitney's terraces—the museum has 13,000 square feet (1,208 sq m) of outdoor space—for expansive views of the Hudson River and city, including a bird's-eye glimpse of The High Line (page 90).

walking on the Brooklyn Bridge

EMPIRE STATE BUILDING
From the art deco grandeur of New York's most iconic building, the city skyline elegantly reveals itself, encompassing everything from Midtown skyscrapers and the Hudson River to New Jersey (page 95).

TOP OF THE ROCK
Atop Rockefeller Center you'll find vivid views of the city, inclusive of the Empire State Building (page 96).

THE MET'S CANTOR ROOF GARDEN
Dream about what it's like to have a 5th Avenue penthouse while taking in one of the most dramatic views of Central Park—and surrounding skyscrapers—available to the public (page 105).

ROOSEVELT ISLAND TRAMWAY
Gliding above the Queensboro Bridge mere feet above luxury condos, with the city spreading out beneath you, the tramway to Roosevelt Island provides a highly affordable alternative to a helicopter ride (page 108).

BROOKLYN BRIDGE
Don't forget to look up at the historic bridge itself as you take in panoramic views of Manhattan, Brooklyn, Queens, and beyond (page 113).

STATEN ISLAND FERRY
This free ferry passes right by the Statue of Liberty, and you'll get a good glimpse of Manhattan's downtown skyline to boot (page 265).

BROOKLYN HEIGHTS PROMENADE
From the promenade's elevated tree-lined perch, you'll see sweeping panoramas of Manhattan's skyline, as well as the Statue of Liberty and the Brooklyn Bridge, from the comfort of a shaded bench (page 275).

twice-hourly departures 11am-5:30pm Sat.-Sun., $3 round-trip).

MAP 1: http://govisland.com; May 1-Oct. 31; free

New York Stock Exchange

The New York Stock Exchange (NYSE) is the leading stock exchange in the world, trading 1.46 billion shares each day. While there are no longer public tours of the NYSE, you can get a good glimpse of the main entrance from the steps of Federal Hall. The iconic bell is rung at opening (just before 9:30am) and closing (just before 4pm) each weekday, and the people chosen for this honor have ranged from Hillary Clinton to *Sports Illustrated* swimsuit models to Snoop Dogg. Enterprising folks might be able to catch a glimpse of the comings and goings if they arrive around opening and closing. Also of note, the sculpture *Fearless Girl* was moved here in 2018. A powerful monument to female resilience and strength, sculptor Kristen Visbal created the 250-pound bronze statue, which previously stared down Arturo Di Modica's hulking *Charging Bull* in Bowling Green.

MAP 1: 11 Wall St., 212/896-2830, www. nyse.com

Federal Hall National Memorial

Federal Hall served as New York's city hall when it was built in 1700, and later as the first capitol building of the United States from the country's founding until 1791, when the government moved to Philadelphia. George Washington was inaugurated here as well. The current building—the original was demolished in 1812—was built in the style of Greece's Parthenon in 1842 as a customs house. Just standing in the large rotunda, with its imposing marble columns, evokes the colonial era. The building includes exhibits on its 1st floor detailing its role in the early days of the U.S. government. The Bible Washington was sworn in with is on display; it was also used for the inaugurations of Dwight D. Eisenhower and Jimmy Carter. Rotating exhibits, for example on individuals such as influential naturalist and conservationist John Muir, occupy other gallery spaces. Free, half-hour ranger-guided tours are available based on staff availability at 10am, 1pm, 2pm, and 3pm.

MAP 1: 26 Wall St., 212/825-6990, www. nps.gov/feha; 9am-5pm Mon.-Fri.; free

Trinity Church

This Gothic Revival Episcopal church is one of the most stunning in the city, recalling the grandeur of those in Europe. It holds 20 services a week—many streamed online—and offers tours weekdays at 2pm and after the 11:15am mass on Sundays. While the nave is an attraction unto itself for its intricate architectural construction and glowing stained glass windows, don't miss the smaller prayer room tucked away in the northwest corner of the building. It's an incredibly intimate space that encourages contemplation. But it's the church's graveyard that's drawing the largest crowds today: A giant tombstone marks the grave of Alexander Hamilton, who was buried here after his ill-fated duel with Aaron Burr. The church also hosts an array of concerts and lectures.

MAP 1: 75 Broadway, 212/602-0800, www. trinitywallstreet.org; 7am-6pm daily; free

Federal Reserve Bank of New York

The fortress-like Federal Reserve Bank of New York takes up a full block but hides in plain sight on a narrow street in the Financial District. Free public tours are offered twice daily on weekdays, and the entrance is through a door marked "employees only" that's guarded around the clock. After passing through security, you're escorted up to the bank's museum, a floor of exhibits detailing the founding of the Federal Reserve by Alexander Hamilton in 1791 and the branch's current role in holding gold for other countries. The 508,000 bars—equaling a combined weight of over six tons—are stored in an impenetrable vault 50 feet (15 m) below sea level and resting on the bedrock of Manhattan. Their current value is $240-260 billion. Walking into the vault is the highlight of the hour-long tour, which concludes with a tiny souvenir packet of shredded money gathered from the four million old bills the bank shreds each day. Reservations must be made online and fill up very quickly; for the best chance, check the website 30 days before your desired visit at 9am EST.

MAP 1: 33 Liberty St., 212/720-6130, www.newyorkfed.org; tours 1pm and 2pm Mon.-Fri.; free

South Street Seaport

As a rule, New Yorkers detest malls, and, though technically a historical district with roots in the 17th century, South Street Seaport feels somewhat like one, if a quaint incarnation. But though it used to house standard suburban chains along the lines of Abercrombie & Fitch, the area is now home to an upscale movie theater reminiscent of a private Hollywood screening room, restaurants by Michelin-starred celebrity chefs Jean-Georges Vongerichten and David Chang, and stores like Milan-based boutique 10 Corso Como. With its cobblestone streets, East River waterfront setting clustered around a series

of piers, and plenty of outdoor space and views of the Brooklyn Bridge and Statue of Liberty, the seaport has always had charm, and now it's becoming trendy to boot.

MAP 1: 19 Fulton St., www. southstreetseaport.com; 11am-9pm daily; free

St. Paul's Chapel

Built in 1766, this chapel is the oldest church in Manhattan and the only colonial-era one still in existence on the island. George Washington prayed here after his inauguration in 1789. More austere than its sister Trinity Church, the chapel's brick facade is particularly striking against the backdrop of the gleaming new World Trade Center. The interior likewise exudes 18th-century austerity. The chapel remained remarkably unscathed by 9/11 and served as a refuge for relief workers in the weeks following the attacks. A small exhibit details its use during this harrowing time.

MAP 1: 209 Broadway, 212/602-0800, www.trinitywallstreet.org; 10am-6pm daily; free

City Hall

Built over a decade (1802-1812) after New York lost its place as the nation's capital, this neoclassical building, flanked by City Hall Park, has a simple but elegant structure. You can sometimes see protests on the building's wide steps, and this is also where press conferences occur. City Hall consists of two wings connected by a grand circular staircase. The mayor's wing is off-limits but the city council room is a regular stop on public tours, which are free and last about an hour. Another highlight is the governor's room, which features a desk used by George Washington.

MAP 1: Broadway, Park Row, and Chambers St., 212/639-9675, www1.nyc.gov; tours 10am Thurs. (reservations required) and noon Wed. (first come, first served); free

City Hall Park

whether you choose a basic, standard, or deluxe tour, and give you access to the lobby, and in the case of the latter two tours, the lower level. Entering the building is like walking back in time.

MAP 1: 233 Broadway, 203/966-9663, http://woolworthtours.com; tours 2pm Sun.-Thurs., 1pm and 2pm Fri., 11:30am, 1pm, and 2pm Sat.; $20-45

Woolworth Building entrance

Woolworth Building

Designed by Cass Gilbert and completed in 1913, this neo-Gothic building was one of the world's first modern skyscrapers. It was also the most expensive, costing tycoon Frank Woolworth $13.5 million (roughly $350 million in today's dollars), which he paid in cash. Today, the building remains a gleaming example of American ingenuity and decadence. The vintage lobby is astounding: 1.5 million tiles make up the Romanesque ceiling, while marble and gold leaf detailing traces throughout the lobby. Also of note is that the building is fully electric—unheard of in its time—and produced all of its own electricity, with a generator in the basement until World War II. The only way to get inside is to take an architectural tour. Tours must be booked in advance and range 30-90 minutes, depending on

One World Observatory

The centerpiece of the World Trade Center site designed by Daniel Libeskind, One World Trade Center is an exquisite building featuring artfully angled lines and a spire that reaches to a symbolically significant 1,776 feet (541 m)—symbolizing the year in which the U.S. Declaration of Independence was signed. This also makes it the tallest building in the country. It sits just north of the 9/11 Memorial's twin reflecting pools marking the site of the felled twin towers. While most of this building's space is taken up by private offices leased to tenants such as Condé Nast, an observatory on the top floors (100-102) provides 360-degree views of the city via floor-to-ceiling windows that stretch around the building's perimeter, revealing New York's intricately plotted grid system, and opening out to views of the Hudson River, Queens, Long Island, and New Jersey. The experience is a bit gimmicky and, at points, unnecessarily high-tech—for example, the elevator that whisks you to the top features full-screen digital views of the city in place of actual windows, and you can rent an iPad ($15) to learn about the skyline—but the views are nice, and if you have kids with you this may be a fun way for them to engage. Buy tickets in advance online to avoid a long wait.

MAP 1: 285 Fulton St., 844/696-1776, http://oneworldobservatory.com; 9am-10pm daily; $34-67

National September 11 Memorial & Museum

Two giant reflecting pools with continuously cascading waterfalls occupy the footprint of the World Trade Center's twin towers, felled on September 11, 2001, when hijackers crashed planes into them in the largest terrorist attack in U.S. history. The names of the victims are engraved on walls that line the perimeter. To fully absorb the impact of the memorial, take time to pause for several minutes at each wall. When you get close enough, the sound of the water drowns out the city noise, and there's something solemn and ethereal about the moment when the wind covers you in a mist of water. The memorial is freely accessible to the public 24 hours daily.

The 9/11 Museum sits between the two memorial pools and explores the events and wreckage of that day in its main exhibit. The slurry wall, a subterranean concrete structure 3 feet (0.9 m) thick that surrounded the original

World Trade Center to prevent flooding from the Hudson River, remained intact after the buildings fell, and it's one of the first things you'll see as you descend an escalator to the museum's expansive single-floor space. Charred fire trucks and building remains are here; one of the eeriest pieces is a sign recovered from the Warner Bros. Studio store, previously located inside the mall of the original World Trade Center, that reads, "That's all Folk"; the "S" didn't survive. Excerpts of phone calls people made to loved ones from the hijacked planes as well as video and images of people who decided to jump from the towers rather than go down with them are tucked discreetly behind a corner in the main room.

Some notable exclusions are problematic; for example, a picture of a tank from Operation Iraqi Freedom with names of 9/11 victims scrawled on it appears absent a footnote detailing the lack of connection between 9/11 and Iraq.

Don't miss the small art gallery next to the main exhibit, which

National September 11 Memorial

captures modern artists' responses to the attacks.

Purchase your museum tickets online in advance to avoid long lines. Admission is free on Tuesdays after 5pm.

MAP 1: 180 Greenwich St., 212/312-8800, www.911memorial.org; 9am-8pm (last entry 6pm) Sun.-Thurs., 9am-9pm (last entry 7pm) Fri.-Sat.; $24 adults, $18 seniors, U.S. college students, and veterans, $15 children 7-17

Soho and Tribeca   Map 2

African Burial Ground National Monument

Set amid a cluster of government buildings just north of Chambers Street, this monument came about following the discovery of human remains during the digging of the Ted Weiss Federal Building's foundation in the early 1990s. An estimated 10,000-20,000 African Americans were buried here in the 17th and 18th centuries, when enslaved people helped build the city. It's the continent's oldest and largest excavated burial ground of African Americans, a dark reminder of the United States' brutal history of slavery and devaluation of African Americans. A gravesite as well as a memorial to others discarded in unmarked graves across the country, it was designated a national monument by President George W. Bush in 2006. An outdoor memorial and visitors center are here today, featuring a 20-minute movie and exhibits about the archaeological digs and history of slavery in the city.

MAP 2: 290 Broadway, 212/637-2019, http://www.nps.gov/afbg; 10am-4pm Tues.-Sat.; free

A PORTAL TO NEW YORK CITY'S PAST

Tribeca is filled with some of the city's best architecture, from the ornate flourishes of Italian Revival to the more utilitarian brick Federal style. One notable stretch is the two-block portion of **Staple Street** between Harrison and Duane Streets just west of Hudson Street. The cobblestone street once housed stables for horse-drawn ambulances and still conjures what New York looked like centuries ago. Because the street dead-ends, it receives little traffic, allowing you to imagine the city before cars as well as wander down the middle of the street to admire the well-preserved buildings dating back to the 1800s. Today, these are some of the most coveted residences in Tribeca. Look up to see the Instagram-popular skybridge that connects a townhouse on one side of the street to an apartment on the other; this unique property was listed in 2015 for a very modern $30 million.

East Village and Lower East Side

Map 3

✪ Tenement Museum

Before the Lower East Side housed bohemian artists and long before it became a trendy destination filled with top-notch restaurants, the area was a first home for many immigrants. They lived in tenement buildings, crowding multiple generations of a family into a small apartment. Most of these buildings have now been renovated into desirable residences, but the Tenement Museum has gone to great lengths to preserve 97 Orchard Street and give visitors a vivid glimpse into what life was like here in the 19th and 20th centuries.

Visits are available by guided tour only, typically lasting 1-2 hours. More than a dozen options are available, including various building tours focusing on a particular family's residence or merchant's business in the tenement, walking tours that illuminate the neighborhood's history, and interactive experiences during which actors portray building residents, telling stories of daily life and fielding visitor questions. On select Thursdays, Tastings at the Tenement combines a building visit with a meal culled from local, famous food purveyors that explores the influence of immigrants on the country's cuisine. Book the "Exploring 97 Orchard Street" tour to cover the most ground. It begins with a meet-and-greet orientation and then allows you to visit various floors in the building.

The Tenement Museum is at 97 Orchard Street but the visitors center is at 103 Orchard Street, at the corner of Delancey. Tours leave from the lobby gift shop and are often sold out, so it's a good idea to book in advance online or in person at the gift shop. The shop also carries a good selection of quirky and informative books on the city's history.

MAP 3: 103 Orchard St., 212/982-8420, http://www.tenement.org; visitors center 10am-6:30pm Fri.-Wed. and 10am-8:30pm Thurs., tour times vary; $25 adults, $20 seniors and students

Tenement Museum

THE AMERICAN DREAM OF THE LOWER EAST SIDE

While it's now considered one of the most desirable neighborhoods in the city, the Lower East Side was once a place of last resort. Beginning in the 19th century, a wide cross section of immigrants, including German, Jewish, Italian, Chinese, and, later, Dominican people, crowded into tenements here as a first stop after arriving via Ellis Island. These brick buildings were constructed with utility rather than design in mind. Fire escapes covered the front facade and provided a respite for residents from the heat during scorching summers pre-air-conditioning. The typical apartment clocked in at around 300 square feet (28 sq m) and often housed multiple generations of a family. By the 1860s, the population swelled to 240,000 people per square mile, causing the rampant spread of disease. A 1910 typhoid epidemic claimed the lives of many, including the first-born baby of Russ & Daughters founder and Polish immigrant Joel Russ. He began his legendary business just three years earlier, selling herring out of a barrel alongside many hopeful entrepreneurs, and established one of the most popular stores in the city. The founder of what would become Paramount Pictures, Adolph Zukor, from Hungary, grew up nearby. Many other New Yorkers' stories began on the Lower East Side, and while their ancestors would probably be pleased by their advancement they would most likely be equally perplexed by the high rent that one of those apartments now commands.

NEARBY:

- Order the classic pastrami sandwich at Katz's Deli (page 132).
- Get the bagel and smoked salmon at Russ & Daughters Cafe (page 132).
- Sate your sweet tooth with creative offerings from Doughnut Plant (page 138).
- Hang out in a classic neighborhood dive at The Library (page 187).
- Grab a cheap, cold beer at the warm Welcome to the Johnsons (page 187).
- Explore contemporary artworks at the edgy New Museum (page 220).
- Wander large-scale gallery exhibits at Perrotin (page 221).

Astor Place

Named for John Jacob Astor, who owned this stretch of land when it was mansions and bucolic gardens, Astor Place is a now a public open space most recognizable for Tony Rosenthal's sculpture *Alamo*, which sits prominently at its center. Installed in 1967 and known as The Cube, the steel box sits on a single point and can be spun around. Skater kids used to congregate here in droves, and now others pause here as well, following completion of a redesign in 2016 that made way for food trucks and outdoor café-style seating. It's a good spot for people-watching in warmer weather.

MAP 3: E. 8th St. between Lafayette St. and Cooper Sq., 212/777-2173, http://astorplace.nyc; 24 hours daily; free

The Village and the Meatpacking District

Map 4

✪ The High Line

Formerly an industrial train line, this elevated passageway is now a brilliantly realized and beloved park for both strolling and lounging. It snakes 1.45 miles (2.3 km) over the city from the edge of the Meatpacking District through Chelsea, to the latter's border with Midtown, affording visitors a unique vantage, including views of the Empire State and Chrysler Buildings as well as the Hudson River.

Benches are scattered throughout the park, and wooden lounge chairs can be found between 14th and 15th Streets. Don't miss the park's stadium-style seating near 17th Street, offering a perch to look out through glass windows onto 10th Avenue below. Wood-covered walkways flank clusters of perennials, shrubs, and even a large (for Manhattan) patch of grass near 23rd Street with space to sprawl out in nice weather. In warmer months, food vendors and crafts merchants set up shop in a covered section near a seasonal outpost of lauded wine bar **Terroir** (at 15th St.).

Stroll the whole thing in one leisurely go, or if you're in the bordering neighborhoods you can use it as a green break from whatever you're

The High Line

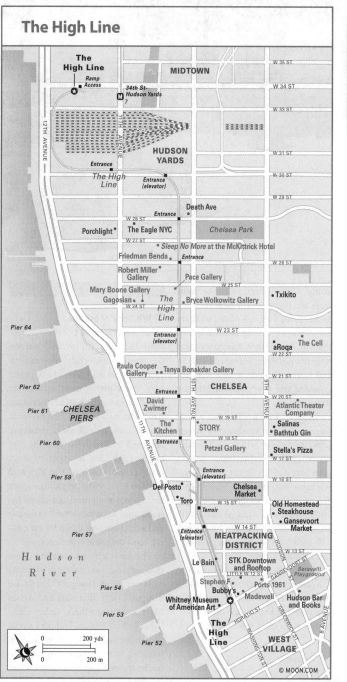

The High Line

The High Line

Ramp Access

34th St-Hudson Yards
7

MIDTOWN

W 35 ST

W 34 ST

W 33 ST

12TH AVENUE

11TH AVENUE

The High Line

Entrance

Entrance (elevator)

HUDSON YARDS

W 31 ST

W 30 ST

W 29 ST

Entrance

Death Ave

W 28 ST

Porchlight

The Eagle NYC

W 27 ST

Sleep No More at the McKittrick Hotel

Friedman Benda

Entrance

Chelsea Park

W 26 ST

Robert Miller Gallery

Pace Gallery

W 25 ST

Mary Boone Gallery

Gagosian

The High Line

Bryce Wolkowitz Gallery

Txikito

W 24 ST

Pier 64

Entrance (elevator)

W 23 ST

aRoqa

The Cell

W 22 ST

Paula Cooper Gallery

Tanya Bonakdar Gallery

W 21 ST

Pier 62

Pier 61

CHELSEA PIERS

10TH AVENUE

9TH AVENUE

CHELSEA

Entrance

David Zwirner

W 20 ST

Atlantic Theater Company

Pier 60

The Kitchen

STORY

W 19 ST

Salinas
Bathtub Gin

Entrance

Petzel Gallery

W 18 ST

Stella's Pizza

Pier 59

11TH AVENUE

W 17 ST

Entrance (elevator)

Chelsea Market

W 16 ST

Del Posto

Toro

Old Homestead Steakhouse

Terroir

W 15 ST

Gansevoort Market

Pier 57

Entrance (elevator)

W 14 ST

MEATPACKING DISTRICT

HUDSON ST

W 13 ST

Hudson River

Le Bain

STK Downtown and Rooftop

LITTLE W 12 ST

GANSEVOORT ST

Seravalli Playground

Pier 54

Stephen F.

Ports 1961

Bubby's

Madewell

Hudson Bar and Books

Whitney Museum of American Art

HORATIO ST

GREENWICH ST

WASHINGTON ST

8 AVENUE

Pier 53

The High Line

WEST VILLAGE

Pier 52

0   200 yds

0   200 m

© MOON.COM

Whitney Museum of American Art

doing. Crowds tend to choke pathways during most times of day; the best bets for a more isolated walk are early in the morning or during less-than-idyllic weather. A wide walkway near the northern entrance (34th St. and 12th Ave.) remains relatively uncrowded and overlooks the Hudson River.

The High Line has 11 access points: Gansevoort and Washington Streets (elevator access), 14th Street (elevator access), 16th Street (elevator access), 18th Street, 20th Street, 23rd Street (elevator access), 26th Street, 28th Street, 30th Street (elevator access), 30th Street and 11th Avenue, 34th Street and 12th Avenue (ramp access). The 14th-30th Street access points are just off 10th Avenue.

MAP 4: southern entrance Gansevoort St. and Washington St., 212/206-9922, www. thehighline.org; 7am-7pm Dec. 1-Mar. 31, 7am-10pm Apr. 1-May 31 and Oct. 1-Nov. 30, 7am-11pm June 1-Sept. 30; free

TOP EXPERIENCE

✪ Whitney Museum of American Art

Founded by sculptor and patron Gertrude Vanderbilt Whitney in 1930 with her collection of 600 paintings, the Whitney now houses over 21,000 works of 20th and 21st century American art. In 2015, the museum moved into a sleek glass structure designed by Renzo Piano at the foot of The High Line. Multiple terraces offer grand views of the city and Hudson River while providing a space for outdoor sculptural and sound installations. Take the elevator to the top and work your way down for the easiest, most complete experience.

The museum's permanent collection includes vast holdings of works by Jasper Johns, Georgia O'Keeffe, Ed Ruscha, Cindy Sherman, and Agnes Martin, among others. Other highlights include Edward Hopper's iconic 1961 painting *A Woman in the Sun*, featuring its subject standing naked in her bedroom—cigarette in hand and awash in melancholic contemplation—and Alexander Calder's epic moving sculpture *Calder's Circus, 1926-31,* which uses hundreds of finely crafted pieces to re-create the circuses the artist saw while living in Paris.

Daily tours (free with admission) provide insight into specific exhibitions, and admission is pay-what-you wish on Fridays 7pm-9:30pm.

The Whitney's signature **Biennial** exhibition is the longest-running survey of American art, and while it's a hit-or-miss affair, it remains an important event in the New York art world. With works that veer toward eye-catching aesthetics, it's accessible to general audiences and provides an introduction to new artists.

MAP 4: 99 Gansevoort St., 212/570-3600, www.whitney.org; 10:30am-6pm Wed.-Thurs. and Sun.-Mon., 10:30am-6pm Tues. July-Aug. only, 10:30am-9pm Fri.-Sat.; $25 adults, $18 seniors and students, free for children 18 and under

NEARBY:

- Take a scenic walk along **The High Line** (page 88).
- Find artisan-made food, clothes, and crafts at **Chelsea Market** (page 92).
- Fortify with a hearty brunch at **Bubby's** (page 139).

- Enjoy a classic NYC meal at the **Old Homestead Steakhouse** (page 149).
- Savor a cheap, yummy slice from **Stella's Pizza** (page 150).
- Eat or grab a drink at a smaller alternative to Chelsea Market, **Gansevoort Market** (page 152).
- Shop for women's fashions in a historic building at **Madewell** (page 293).

Stonewall National Monument

President Barack Obama inaugurated the Stonewall National Monument in 2016, the first national monument dedicated to preserving LGBTQ history. The monument comprises Christopher Park, the Stonewall Inn bar across the street, and some of the surrounding area. It commemorates the spot where lesbian, gay, bisexual, and transgender people ignited a movement in 1969 when the Stonewall Inn was raided by police and patrons and allies rioted in reaction to a long history of discrimination; the upheaval lasted six days and is considered the beginning of the gay rights movement that would eventually lead to marriage equality, along with greater recognition and human rights.

Situated at the bustling intersection of 7th Avenue South and Christopher Street, the monument exists in contrast as a place for remembrance and reflection. Christopher Park is shaped like a skinny triangle and includes a series of benches surrounding artist George Segal's sculptures of same-sex couples openly showing affection. Take a break in the park or cross the street to the Stonewall Inn and raise a toast to it.

MAP 4: W. 4th St. between Grove St. and Christopher St., 212/825-6992, www.nps.gov/ston; 9am-sunset daily; free

Chelsea and Union Square

Map 5

✪ Chelsea Market

Occupying a full block, this indoor upscale market focuses on artisanal foodie goods, from fresh-baked loaves at Amy's Bread to inventively vegan offerings at Beyond Sushi to one of the best lattes in the city at Ninth Street Espresso. Whether you're feeling like a Cambodian sandwich from Num Pang or the savory street delicacies of Berlin Currywurst, options abound. Non-edible offerings include Artists and Fleas, a smartly curated gathering of handmade crafts, clothes, and other one-of-a-kind items on the 10th Avenue side of the market, and a pop-up space near the 9th Avenue entrance that features sample sales from designers like Theory. These often last only a few days and draw large crowds for deeply discounted designer threads. The market is especially popular in winter.

MAP 5: 75 9th Ave., 212/652-2110, http://chelseamarket.com; 7am-9pm Mon.-Sat., 8am-8pm Sun.; free

Union Square

This urban park and plaza sits at a vibrant crossroads near the borders of the city's east and west sides and uptown and downtown, and it's also the site of a major subway hub connecting Manhattan to Brooklyn, Queens, and the Bronx. Often the site of protests, freestyle rap circles, and street performances, it makes for a wonderful

Chelsea Market

people-watching spot, whether from the stairs on the park's south side or the many benches strewn about the Greenmarket (www.grownnyc.org/greenmarket; 8am-6pm Mon., Wed., and Fri.-Sat.), the largest farmers market in the city. Featuring more than 100 local vendors, the market takes over the north and west sides of the park four times a week year-round.

MAP 5: Broadway/University Pl. to 4th Ave./Park Ave. S. and E.14th St. to E. 17th St., 212/460-1200, www.unionsquarenyc.org; 24 hours daily; free

Theodore Roosevelt Birthplace National Historic Site

The original maverick president was born here—or, more accurately, in a town house on this site that was torn down in 1916, three years before his death. This reconstructed brownstone, managed by the National Park Service, is a faithful replica and has been open since 1924. Five 1860 period rooms do an excellent job of transporting visitors to the earliest years of the 26th U.S. president and can be accessed only through ranger-led tours, which leave on the hour 10am-4pm, excluding noon, on open days. They last about 40 minutes and cannot be reserved in advance, so if you're keen it's best to come earlier in the day.

MAP 5: 28 E. 20th St., 212/260-1616, www.nps.gov/thrb; 9am-5pm Tues.-Sun.; free

Flatiron Building

Shaped like an isosceles triangle and located near the foot of Madison Square Park, the Flatiron is one of the area's most iconic buildings. Completed in 1902, its steel-frame construction was unusual at the time and people feared it might tip over. Other building quirks included water-powered elevators that have since been replaced. A ground-level space—essentially a window gallery display—at the triangular tip called the Prow Artspace (operated by Sprint, which occupies the adjacent retail space) houses art exhibitions often with a focus on the environment or technology.

MAP 5: 175 5th Ave.; not open to the public

Flatiron Building

Midtown, Hell's Kitchen, and Times Square

Map 6

✪ Museum of Modern Art (MoMA)

New York's Museum of Modern Art (MoMA) houses one of the most comprehensive collections of modern and contemporary art in the world on its six floors, home to famous pieces including Van Gogh's *The Starry Night,* Picasso's *Les Demoiselles d'Avignon,* Jackson Pollock's *One: Number 31, 1950,* and Monet's triptych *Water Lilies.* The latter two works are located on the museum's 5th floor, complete with contemplation seating and somehow remaining blissfully uncrowded even when the rest of the museum is at peak capacity. The museum is in the process of another expansion—entailing its closure June-October 2019—that will increase its gallery space from 135,000 square feet (12,542 sq m) to 175,000 square feet (16,258 sq m).

MoMA also regularly stages blockbuster temporary exhibits that push the boundaries of standard shows, such as recent retrospectives on Tim Burton, Björk, and Marina Abramović that incorporated, respectively, movie storyboards, elaborate costumes and immersive sonic experiences, and an original live performance art piece.

Also not to miss at the museum is the 1st-floor sculpture garden,

Museum of Modern Art (MoMA)

which hosts a rotating array of pieces in a sleekly manicured setting, including a pair of reflecting pools. MoMA also holds an extensive film archive, and its programming across three screens rivals that of the Film Forum or Film Society of Lincoln Center. The Contenders series, which shows a curated selection of the year's best films November-January, is extremely popular. Tickets to individual screenings often include Q&As with the writer, director, and/or the cast; they go on sale two weeks beforehand at 9:30am and sell out almost instantly.

Admission to the museum is free on Fridays 4pm-8pm.

MAP 6: 11 W. 53rd St., 212/708-9400, www.moma.org; 10:30am-5:30pm Sat.-Thurs., 10:30pm-8pm Fri.; $25 adults, $18 seniors, $14 students, free for children 16 and under

NEARBY:

- Explore iconic Rockefeller Center (page 96).
- Find the freshest seafood at star chef Eric Ripert's Le Bernardin (page 157).
- Eat a high-quality burger in a no-frills setting at Burger Joint (page 159).
- Play Holly Golightly and peruse

luxury jewelry at Tiffany & Co. (page 297).

- Wander the many floors of the original Saks Fifth Avenue (page 298).
- Commemorate your visit with a stylish souvenir from the MoMA Design Store (page 299).

✪ Empire State Building

Completed in 1931 and rising 1,454 feet (443 m), the Empire State Building lights up the New York skyline, marking special events and holidays with color configurations that can be seen across the city, from rainbow Pride displays to red, white, and blue on Independence Day (although lights are turned off at midnight during migration season to prevent birds from slamming into the building). Most of the art deco building houses office space and is closed to the public, except the two observatories, which stay open until 2am and have served as the backdrop for countless movie scenes, from *King Kong* to *An Affair to Remember* and *Sleepless in Seattle* to *Elf*. Evenings are the best time to go, to see the city as it lights up, so consider making this your last stop on an evening out. If you'd rather beat the crowds, there tends to be less traffic around the hours of 8am and 3pm.

The 86th-floor observatory is the highest open-air deck in the city and sometimes features a live jazz saxophonist (9pm-midnight Thurs.-Sun. Labor Day-Memorial Day, 10pm-1am Thurs.-Sun. Memorial Day-Labor Day). You can see a bit farther beyond the city limits from the indoor 102nd-floor deck but it's not as vivid an experience and probably not worth the extra $20 unless you're a vintage elevator buff—the ride up

from the main deck is in a manually operated Otis elevator.

It's wise to purchase tickets at least a day in advance to mitigate lines, though a wait of about 45 minutes is usually inevitable. Prices range from expensive to outrageous, but if you want the classic 360-degree skyline views, this is the place to go.

You also don't need to formally visit the Empire State Building to feel its comforting presence in the city. You can find great views of the building itself from many spots, but one of the best is north of The High Line on 10th Avenue between 38th and 39th Streets. Come after dark for maximum effect. **MAP 6:** 350 5th Ave., 212/736-3100, www.esbnyc.com; 8am-2am daily; $37-57 adults, $35-55 seniors and military, $31-51 children, free for military in uniform and toddlers, $65-85 express pass

❂ Rockefeller Center

Rockefeller Center may at first glance appear unremarkable. It consists of 19 buildings staggered around a plaza area, with chain stores like Michael Kors and Kate Spade lining the shop fronts of each building, and a lower-level concourse hosting a food court, albeit with high-quality offerings including outposts of Blue Ribbon Sushi and Jacques Torres Chocolate.

But it's also home to many icons of the city, most famously a giant Christmas tree during the winter that typically ranges in height from 70-100 feet (21-30 m), decked out in 50,000 lights that are first illuminated each year during **Christmas in Rockefeller Center** (late Nov.), a ceremony celebrated with live performances, including one by Radio City Music Hall's high-kicking Rockettes. An estimated 125 million people come to view the tree each year. Set below

ice-skating at The Rink at Rockefeller Center

the tree is **The Rink at Rockefeller Center** (8:30am-midnight Oct.-Apr.), popular for ice-skating with its great views of the tree and the center's art deco buildings.

The most prominent building in the group is home to **NBC Studios** (30 Rockefeller Plaza), where you can take a tour or attend one of its TV tapings. On the 5th Avenue side of the center, you may recognize the bronze statue *Atlas*, featured in many episodes of Tina Fey's *30 Rock*, which immortalized the studio.

A popular alternative to the Empire State Building is also here at **Top of the Rock** (8am-12:30am daily, $36 adults, $34 seniors, $30 children), an outdoor observation deck with 360-degree views. While its 70th-floor perch is at a considerably lower vantage, it offers striking views of the Empire State Building itself, as well as unobstructed views of Central Park. You can also take a one-hour **tour** ($25) of Rockefeller Center, offered every 30 minutes from 10am to 7:30pm, which can be combined with the Top of the Rock for a slightly better deal ($50). **MAP 6:** 45 Rockefeller Plaza, 212/588-8601, www.rockefellercenter.com; 7am-midnight daily; free

Radio City Music Hall

Radio City Music Hall is home to the *Christmas Spectacular* with the high-kicking Rockettes, New York's renowned precision dance company (Nov.-Jan., $56-599). You'll feel the venue's grandeur immediately upon entering. Constructed in 1932, it's adorned in beautifully preserved art deco elegance and has a uniquely illuminated dome that will be instantly recognizable to Tony Awards viewers. Outside the holiday season, live music acts as diverse as pop star Christina Aguilera and neo-soul singer Leon Bridges grace the stage. If you're coming for a concert, note that acoustics are less than desirable; avoid the extreme sides of the orchestra where sound becomes distorted and unbalanced. Prices vary wildly depending on the act. Radio City Music Hall tours ($28 adults, $24 seniors, students, and children 12 and under) are available daily 9:30am-5pm and last about an hour.

MAP 6: 1260 6th Ave., 212/247-4777, www.msg.com/radio-city-music-hall; box office 10am-6pm Mon.-Sat.; prices vary

St. Patrick's Cathedral

Sandwiched between office buildings and flagship stores in the most congested stretch of 5th Avenue, this neo-Gothic Roman Catholic cathedral stands in sharp contrast to its neighbors. Simply walking through the stunning main nave, with its ceilings that tower up to peaks 330 feet (101 m) high, is the attraction for many visitors here. Presidents and celebrities alike have sat in these pews and gazed up at the altar designed by Louis Comfort Tiffany. Marble panels depicting the stations of the cross won recognition at the 1893 World's Fair in Chicago. Public tours of the cathedral are offered some days ($5 suggested donation) at 10am depending on volunteer/staff availability, or you can download a self-guided audio tour app from iTunes or Google Play. MAP 6: 5th Ave. between 50th St. and 51st St., 212/753-2261, http://saintpatrickscathedral.org; 6:30am-8:45pm daily; free

St. Patrick's Cathedral

Times Square

Spanning 7th Avenue and Broadway between 42nd and 47th Streets, Times Square is aglow 24 hours a day thanks to a multitude of Jumbotron billboards that are displayed prominently on most buildings. Here's where you'll find One Times Square, a giant tower of screens where the famous Waterford crystal ball drops on New Year's Eve. Picture Vegas but sub out the gambling for shopping. Like that desert metropolis, Times Square once featured expansive wide-open spaces, as late as 1900. Back then it was known as Longacre Square. Soon enough the section of Broadway that runs through the Theater District earned the nickname the Great White Way for how its signage lit up surrounding side streets. At the heart of Times Square—at Broadway and 47th Street, in Father Duffy Square—is the

TKTS booth (Broadway and W. 47th St.; 3pm-8pm Mon. and Fri., 2pm-8pm Tues., 10am-2pm and 3pm-8pm Wed.-Thurs., 10am-2pm and 3pm-8pm Sat., 11am-7pm Sun.), where you can buy discount theater tickets. In warmer months the square is surrounded by pedestrian seating, from which you can marvel at the intense crowds. On the pedestrian island opposite Father Duffy Square, between 45th and 46th Streets, look down through a large section of metal grates and listen; you'll hear a persistent drone more precise and subtler than the blunt rumble of the subway. This is Max Neuhaus's *Times Square*, a sound installation maintained by the Dia Art Foundation since 1977.

MAP 6: Broadway and 7th Ave. between 42nd St. and 47th St., 212/768-1560, www.timessquarenyc.org; 24 hours daily; free

Times Square

New York Public Library Main Branch

There are few buildings in the city open to the public that contain as much high-society punch as the main branch of the New York Public Library. This beaux arts landmark stretches two city blocks and is covered in stately white marble—six times more than was used for the New York Stock Exchange and New York Chamber of Commerce combined. When it opened in 1911, it was the largest marble building in the country. To feel its grandeur, walk up the main stairs into the library from 41st Street, in between the two marble lions known as Patience and Fortitude—so popular they're the library system's mascots and featured in its logo. Other notable features of the library include its 1st-floor special exhibits—on topics ranging from Manhattan's map history to Timothy Leary's notes on acid trips—as well as the ongoing 2nd-floor exhibit detailing the branch's extensive research collection and history. But the star is the grand Rose Main Reading Room on the 3rd floor, with its high ceilings adorned with gold-and-copper-leaf-accented murals stretching almost the length of a football field. Live from the NYPL ($40) is a popular ticketed interview series hosted by the library in its elegant lower-level event space, featuring guests from *Bad Feminist* author Roxane Gay to former U.S. poet laureate Billy Collins.

MAP 6: 476 5th Ave., 917/275-6975, www.nypl.org/locations/schwarzman; 10am-6pm Mon. and Thurs.-Sat., 10am-8pm Tues.-Wed., 1pm-5pm Sun.; free

Grand Central Terminal

This beaux arts building dates back to the late 19th century, its entrance adorned with the world's largest Tiffany clock, encased in a massive sculpture of Greek gods by French artist Jules-Felix Coutan. Head inside to the main concourse to fully take in both the chaos and beauty of this expansive and pristinely preserved space. It features a striking dome ceiling, with constellations rendered in gold leaf and LED lights; it's fun to simply stop for a few moments to look

NBC's *Seinfeld* captured authentic cadences of New York life over the course of its nine seasons. Although filmed on a soundstage in Los Angeles, real New York venues were used for exterior shots. Fans can still find some echoes of *Seinfeld* across the city. With the exception of Tom's Restaurant, perhaps the show's biggest icon and located uptown, sites are in Midtown, so you might string together your own walking tour.

- Seinfeld cleverly conveyed diner culture in the city, often circling around Jerry, Elaine, George, and Kramer's go-to spot, the fictitious **Monk's Café**, which serves as the gang's kitchen-away-from-home and hub for numerous conversations about "nothing," dissecting small annoyances and slights over club sandwiches and big salads. Exterior shots were of Morningside Heights' **Tom's Restaurant** (2880 Broadway, 212/864-6137, www.tomsrestaurant.net; 6am-1:30am Sun.-Tues., 6am-midnight Wed., 24 hours Thurs.-Sat.), which makes a good spot for a cool photo op—incidentally, Suzanne Vega also paid it tribute in her song "Tom's Diner"—but the food itself is as mediocre as it is overpriced.

- Soup is definitely a meal at **The Original Soupman** (259 W. 55th St., 212/956-0900; 11am-8pm Mon.-Sat., 11am-7pm Sun.), on the edge of Times Square, where Elaine gets banned for not respecting the rules of the "Soup Nazi." In reality, it's not intimidating to order here, and the shop features a rotating selection of savory concoctions like lobster bisque and jambalaya (Newman's favorite).

- **Westway Diner** (614 9th Ave., 212/582-7661, www.westwaydiner.com; 6am-1am daily) in Hell's Kitchen is where Larry David and Jerry Seinfeld are rumored to have written the show's pilot. David lived nearby, across the hall from the real-life Kramer, who runs the **Kramer's Reality Tour** (http://www.kennykramer.com/RealityTourText.html) and frequented the spot. It's a solid place for a quick bite though not particularly notable.

- George gets scammed by a prostitute and misses a job interview at the **Hotel Edison** (228 W. 47th St., 800/637-7070, www.edisonhotelnyc.com). In reality, the art deco hotel is a bargain for the city and offers convenient accommodations in Times Square.

- The gang goes to see the opera *Pagliacci* and run into "Crazy" Joe Davola, who's dressed as the eponymous deranged clown, at the **Town Hall** (123 W. 43rd St., 212/997-1003, http://thetownhall.org). The concert venue, built in 1921, is a National Historic Landmark.

- What constitutes a meal is famously argued over (does soup count?) by Jerry and annoying aspiring comic Kenny Bania at **Mendy's** (www.mendysdeli.com). The Upper West Side location where the discussion explodes has since shuttered, but the Jewish deli has convenient locations in Midtown at **Grand Central** (lower-level dining concourse, 212/856-9399; 10:30am-9pm Mon.-Thurs., 10:30am-3pm Fri. winter and 10:30am-4pm summer, 11am-6pm Sun.) and **Rockefeller Center** (37 W. 48th St., 212/262-9600; 10am-7:30pm Mon.-Thurs., 10am-3pm Fri.). The pastrami, corned beef, and matzo ball soup are solid in a pinch.

up (away from the main human traffic arteries, of course—hundreds of thousands of commuters pass through here each day). Over a dozen vendors, including a bakery and mini farmers market run by famed fine-food purveyor Eli Zabar, make up the **Grand Central Market** on the main level, while a lower-level dining concourse includes Jacques Torres and Shake Shack outposts, as well as the famous Grand Central Oyster Bar, which has been sating the shellfish cravings of commuters since 1913. Self-guided audio tours of the building ($9 adults, $7 seniors, students, military, and children) are available at the GCT Tours windows in the main concourse.

MAP 6: 89 E. 42nd St., 212/340-2583, www.grandcentralterminal.com; 24 hours daily; free

Grand Central Terminal

Chrysler Building

This 77-story gleaming achievement of art deco architecture soars 1,046 feet (319 m) high and can be glimpsed from afar throughout the city. Its crown, with cascading semicircles that layer on top of each other until they reach a singular thin spire, is as iconic to New Yorkers as the more accessible and heavily trafficked Empire State Building. The public is free to walk through the lobby, once a showroom for Chrysler, and admire its walls of Moroccan marble. When the building opened in 1931 there was an observation deck on the 71st floor, but it closed to the public in 1945. Anyway, the best way to appreciate the building is from afar while walking through the city. You'll find a particularly good nighttime view just outside of Bryant Park on the southeast corner of 42nd Street and 6th Avenue.

MAP 6: 405 Lexington Ave., www.tishmanspeyer.com/properties/chrysler-center; lobby 8am-6pm Mon.-Fri.; free

United Nations Headquarters

In 1945, 51 countries banded together to form the United Nations with the goal of preventing World War III. Today there are 193 member states who meet each September. While the complex of buildings is under tight security, tours are given on weekdays when the UN isn't in session so the public can visit the General Assembly Hall and Security Council Room, among others. Tours last 45-60 minutes; visitors must pass through security, so arrive at least an hour beforehand. Check-in for tours is on 45th Street across from the General Assembly building. It's also a good spot to snap photos of the UN. Each member country has given the UN a gift, displayed in the halls; a popular attraction on the tour is the U.S. gift, a mosaic by Norman Rockwell titled *Golden Rule* and featuring a diverse array of people with the inscription, "Do Unto Others as You Would Have Them Do Unto You."

MAP 6: 405 E. 42nd St., 212/963-8687, http://visit.un.org; 9am-4:45pm Mon.-Fri.; $22 adults, $15 seniors and students, $13 children 5-12

Upper West Side and Upper East Side

Map 7

SIGHTS

UPPER WEST SIDE AND UPPER EAST SIDE

✪ CENTRAL PARK

The city's iconic park encompasses 843 acres (341 ha) in the center of Manhattan and runs from 59th to 110th Street and 5th to 8th Avenue, separating the Upper East and Upper West Sides. Midtown is directly south while Harlem abuts the northern border. Central Park sees 42 million visitors every year, making it the most visited urban park in the country. This can make for a crowded experience, particularly on warm weekend days, but it's still a respite from the concrete jungle, with many lush places in which to get lost. It's easy to spend a full day here, but you can also take in the park's peaceful beauty on breaks between museum visits—Museum Mile borders the park on its east side and the American Museum of Natural History abuts its west side.

Sights

Central Park is wonderful for a simple wander but has many notable sights. One of the most popular is Strawberry Fields (71st St. to 74th St.), accessed most easily from West 72nd Street—a convenient entry point that puts you within spitting distance of many notable spots, and is also across the street from the Dakota apartment building where John Lennon lived and was shot. A flower-covered mosaic memorial to the legendary singer-song-writer-activist welcomes visitors to a landscaped section often filled with fans singing songs. Just east along

The Lake is Bethesda Terrace (72nd St.), which has grand staircases, eye-catching arches, stately columns, and lake views. On the terrace is Bethesda Fountain, featuring the Angel of the Waters statue created by Emma Stebbins, which was the city's first public art commission awarded to a woman. Posing in front of the fountain is a popular photo op.

Heading north around the lake, you'll find The Ramble (73rd St. to 79th St.), which contains 36 acres (15 ha) of wooded paths and is a popular area for wandering or birding, with around 40 species year-round. Continuing north you'll come upon Belvedere Castle (79th St.), a tiny castle built in 1869, which has some of the best views in the park and also houses the Central Park weather station and a visitors center. The Delacorte Theater (80th St.), where The Public Theater's Shakespeare in the Park productions take place in the summer, is literally just across the pond. The Great Lawn (79th St. to 85th St.) to the north is the park's most sprawling space, a great gathering and thus people-watching spot. It also hosts popular events like free New York Philharmonic concerts in the summer. And yet farther north is the lake-sized Central Park Reservoir, now called the Jacqueline Kennedy Onassis Reservoir (85th St. to 96th St.) in honor of the late long-time resident of the Upper East Side's Carnegie Hill area. The reservoir holds billion gallons of water but is no longer

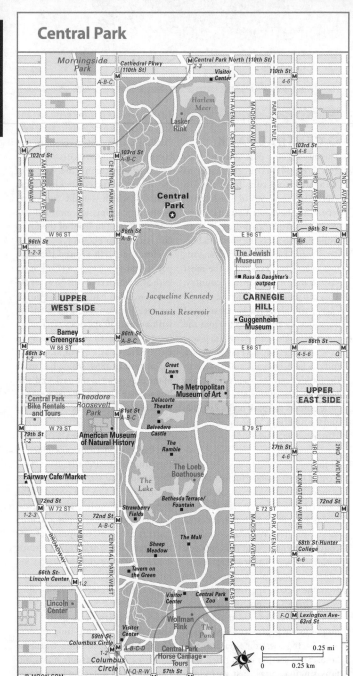

Central Park

Morningside Park

Cathedral Pkwy (110th St)

Ⓜ Central Park North (110th St) 2-3

Visitor Center

110th St 4-6

A-B-C

Harlem Meer

Lasker Rink

Ⓜ 1 103rd St

Ⓜ 103rd St A-B-C

Ⓜ 103rd St 4-6

BROADWAY

AMSTERDAM AVENUE

COLUMBUS AVENUE

CENTRAL PARK WEST

5TH AVENUE (CENTRAL PARK EAST)

MADISON AVENUE

PARK AVENUE

LEXINGTON AVENUE

3RD AVENUE

2ND AVENUE

Central Park ✪

W 96 ST

Ⓜ 86th St A-B-C

E 96 ST

Ⓜ 96th St 4-6

Q

Ⓜ 96th St 1-2-3

The Jewish Museum

■ Russ & Daughter's outpost

UPPER WEST SIDE

Jacqueline Kennedy Onassis Reservoir

CARNEGIE HILL

• **Guggenheim Museum**

• Barney Greengrass

Ⓜ 86th St A-B-C

W 86 ST

E 86 ST

Ⓜ 86th St 4-5-6

Q

Ⓜ 86th St 1-2

Great Lawn

Central Park Bike Rentals and Tours

Theodore Roosevelt Park

The Metropolitan Museum of Art ■

UPPER EAST SIDE

Delacorte Theater ■

Ⓜ 81st St A-B-C

W 79 ST

American Museum of Natural History

Belvedere Castle ■

E 79 ST

Ⓜ 79th St 1-2

The Ramble

Ⓜ 77th St 4-6

2ND AVENUE

3RD AVENUE

LEXINGTON AVENUE

The Loeb Boathouse

■ Fairway Cafe/Market

The Lake

Bethesda Terrace/ Fountain ■

Ⓜ 72nd St W 72 ST 1-2-3

Strawberry Fields ■

Ⓜ 72nd St A-B-C

E 72 ST

Ⓜ 72nd St Q

COLUMBUS AVENUE

CENTRAL PARK WEST

Sheep Meadow ■

■ The Mall

5TH AVE (CENTRAL PARK EAST)

MADISON AVENUE

PARK AVENUE

■ Tavern on the Green

Ⓜ 68th St-Hunter College 4-6

Ⓜ 66th St-Lincoln Center 1-2

BROADWAY

Visitor Center ■

■ Central Park Zoo

Lincoln Center

Ⓜ 59th St-Columbus Circle 1-2

Visitor Center ■

Wollman Rink

The Pond

F-Q Ⓜ Lexington Ave-63rd St

A-B-C-D

Central Park Horse Carriage Tours ■

Columbus Circle

N-Q-R-W

57th St

Ⓜ F

0   0.25 mi

0   0.25 km

© MOON.COM

Central Park

used for the city's water supply. The 1.58-mile (2.5-km) path around it is popular with joggers and has served as a backdrop for countless scenes in movies and television; you may recognize it as Charlotte's running route from *Sex and the City*.

From Bethesda Terrace, you can also head south in the park via **The Mall** (66th St. to 72nd St.), which features some of the largest and only remaining American elm trees in the country, shading a wide pedestrian path busy with street musicians, vendors, and a steady stream of visitors. Veer off west to find **Sheep Meadow** (66th St. to 69th St.), a popular place for sunbathing.

In the park's southeast corner is the small **Central Park Zoo** (E. 64th St. and 5th Ave., 212/439-6500, http://centralparkzoo.com; 10am-5pm Mon.-Fri., 10am-5:30pm Sat.-Sun. spring-fall, 10am-4:30pm daily fall-spring; $13.95 adults, $8.95 children 3-12, free for children 2 and under), which houses penguins, polar bears, and a rainforest that makes for a nice winter escape to the tropics.

Restaurants

West of Sheep Meadow is the iconic **Tavern on the Green** (W. 67th St. 212/877-8684, www.tavernonthegreen.com; 11am-4pm and 5pm-11pm Mon.-Fri., 9am-4pm and 5pm-11pm Sat.-Sun.; $$$). The restaurant dates back to the 1930s and received a modern revamp under new owners in 2014. It remains a draw for tourists looking to dine in the park, but prices are high and exceed culinary execution. To take in the ambience, you could also just grab a drink at the bar.

There's a lakeside restaurant in **The Loeb Boathouse** (212/517-2233; noon-3:45pm and 5:30pm-9pm Mon.-Fri., 9:30am-3:45pm and 6pm-9pm Sat.-Sun.; $$)—though note that views of the serene body of water are the main attraction at this beautifully situated tourist trap, with dishes like cedar plank salmon and petit filet mignon mere supporting players. As

SCORING TICKETS TO SHAKESPEARE IN THE PARK

Going to the theater in New York can be expensive. The Public Theater's founder, Joe Papp, envisioned the art form as one that should be accessible to all, and his creation, Shakespeare in the Park, brings some of the most famous actors of stage and screen to Central Park's charming open-air Delacorte Theater (80th St.) for two full productions each summer.

Some past highlights include Jesse Tyler Ferguson in Shakespeare's *The Comedy of Errors*, Meryl Streep in Bertolt Brecht's *Mother Courage and Her Children*, and Amy Adams in Stephen Sondheim's *Into the Woods*. Al Pacino, Denzel Washington, and many other stars have appeared in The Public Theater's (mostly Shakespearean) productions.

The downside to the free aspect is that tickets aren't easy to come by unless you're willing to camp out at the Delacorte Theater. Central Park opens at 6am for noon distribution on the day of the performance, and many people arrive even before then and wait outside the park. There's also a mobile lottery through the app for TodayTix (www. todaytix.com), which you can enter between midnight and noon on the day of performance. Winners are notified between noon and 2:15pm and must confirm within 45 minutes, then pick up tickets between 5pm and 7:30pm. Unclaimed tickets are released to the standby line around 7:30pm, and some claim that arriving in the afternoon and waiting in this line is the best way to score tickets. Performances begin at 8pm.

an alternative, try the next-door café (8am-5pm daily spring-fall, 8am-4:30pm daily winter), which offers cheap, serviceable deli fare that can be taken to go and eaten on a grassy knoll overlooking the lake, or sidle up to the restaurant's outside bar for a drink with lake views.

For higher-quality food, pick up a picnic from outside the park. Nearby takeout options include Fairway Market (page 160) and Barney Greengrass (page 162) on the Upper West Side and The Jewish Museum's Russ & Daughters outpost (page 243) on the Upper East Side.

Recreation
Along the eastern edge of The Lake you'll find The Loeb Boathouse (E. 72nd St. and Park Dr. N.) where you can rent a rowboat (page 273). Other popular activities in the park include biking (page 273) and horse carriage tours (page 274), and, in winter, ice skating (page 273).

Information and Services
Wherever you go, remember that Frederick Law Olmsted designed the paths in the park to meander so as to encourage people to get a little lost. If you need a little formal direction, there are directory signposts throughout, as well as four other visitors centers in addition to the one at Belvedere Castle (212/772-0288; 10am-5pm daily), inside the park and open 9am-7:30pm daily: Columbus Circle Information Kiosk (W. 59th St. at Central Park W.), Chess & Checkers House (64th St., 212/794-4064), Dairy Visitor Center (between 64th St. and 65th St., 212/794-6564), and Charles A. Dana Discovery Center (110th St. between 5th Ave. and Lenox Ave., 212/860-1374).

Restrooms are located throughout the park and open roughly dawn-dusk year-round for the most part, with a few exceptions such Bethesda Fountain and Sheep Meadow, which are open late March-early November only. MAP 7: 212/310-6600, www. centralparknyc.org; 6am-1am daily; free

UPPER EAST SIDE

✪ The Metropolitan Museum of Art

In a city teeming with world-class institutions, The Metropolitan Museum of Art is the grandest. Since its opening in 1880, it has expanded numerous times and now stretches a quarter mile (0.4 km), encompassing more than two million square feet (185,806 sq m). The museum's massive permanent collection spans 5,000 years of history, with galleries devoted to Greek and Roman, African, Asian, Egyptian, and modern and contemporary art, with two of the largest wings devoted to American art and European paintings. The latter famously includes works by the likes of Van Gogh, Vermeer, and Monet. Other highlights from the permanent collection include the Temple of Dendur (built in 15 BC in Egypt), Edgar Degas' *The Dance Class,* and Jackson Pollock's *Autumn Rhythm: Number 30.*

The Met also puts on special shows of art masters covering a wide range of eras across history—recent exhibits have included the early drawings of Michelangelo and a comprehensive retrospective of David Hockney—and it's also the preeminent space for lavish fashion shows, from the striking creations of Alexander McQueen to the bling-saturated pageantry of the Catholic Church.

A must, particularly in warmer months, is the Cantor Roof Garden, which not only offers great views of Central Park but serves as an outdoor exhibition space for temporary exhibits that can hold their own against the dramatic views. There's a bar up here as well so you can take it all in with a cocktail.

The Metropolitan Museum of Art

Admission is valid for three consecutive days and also includes entrance to The Met's superb collection of medieval art at The Met Cloisters, farther uptown, and The Met Breuer, which hosts a large part of the museum's modern art collection, including large-scale exhibits, in the Whitney Museum's former space just a handful of blocks south.

MAP 7: 1000 5th Ave., 800/662-3397, www.metmuseum.org; 10am-5:30pm Sun.-Thurs., 10am-9pm Fri.-Sat.; $25 adults, $17 seniors, $12 students, free for children under 12

NEARBY:

- Go for a ramble in Central Park (page 101).
- Enjoy an elegant Italian meal at Ristorante Morini (page 160).
- Order a burger and perhaps some pie at JG Melon (page 164).
- Eat one of New York's best hot dogs at Papaya King (page 165).
- Drink craft beer at rustic-chic Bondurants (page 202).
- Continue your art explorations at The Met Breuer (page 243).
- Browse for books in a cozy atmosphere at Albertine (page 300).

© MOON.COM

Guggenheim Museum

Some of the most cutting-edge contemporary and modern art shows have graced the halls of this art palace, famously designed by Frank Lloyd Wright in a spiral design spanning six floors. Its permanent collection includes works by Goya, Picasso, Degas, Gauguin, and Kandinsky, among many other art giants. While a small selection is always on display, the museum is also known for its daring temporary exhibits, for instance Matthew Barney's *The Cremaster Cycle*, an epic nine-hour art film with accompanying sculptures, drawings, and photos.

The museum's popular Works & Process series peers inside the creative process with artists, dancers, writers, composers, and directors, who preview upcoming work, and its Art After Dark events on select evenings feature DJs and a cash bar for a more social art experience. Museum admission is pay-what-you-wish 5pm-7:45pm Saturday, and it stays open later on Tuesdays in the summer (10am-9pm Tues. June-Sept.).

MAP 7: 1071 5th Ave., 212/423-3500, www.guggenheim.org; 10am-5:45pm Sun.-Wed. and Fri., 10am-7:45pm Sat.; $25 adults, $18 seniors and students, free for children under 12

Gracie Mansion

Built in 1799 as the country house of wealthy merchant Archibald Gracie, this mansion didn't become the official residence of the mayor until 1942. It was in the city's possession for many years prior and even served as a concession stand and restroom for Carl Schurz Park, in which it sits. Today this mini-White House, which has been called "the people's house," offers free hour-long tours of its 1st floor (advance reservations required through the website), including a grand drawing room and smaller social spaces where business of the city has been conducted for decades. The 2nd floor is off-limits; it's where the mayor and his family live. Plan to arrive a few minutes before your scheduled tour.

MAP 7: E. 88th St. and East End Ave., 212/676-3060, www1.nyc.gov; tours 10am, 11am, 5pm Mon.; free

Temple Emanu-El

This temple was home to the first Reform Judaism congregation in the city when it was founded in 1845 and is one of the largest temples in the world. Designed in the Romanesque revival style, it's also one of the most well-preserved houses of worship in the city, with a gold-flecked color palate evoking the paintings of Gustav Klimt. In addition to religious services, the temple hosts a range of talks by people such as retired general Colin Powell and ABC political correspondent George Stephanopoulos. It also has a museum, open and free to the public, that contains hundreds of objects dating back to the 14th century, along with rotating temporary exhibits.

MAP 7: 1 E. 65th St., 212/744-1400, www.emanuelnyc.org; museum 10am-4:30pm Sun.-Thurs.; free

Smallpox Hospital on Roosevelt Island

Roosevelt Island

Roosevelt Island is a skinny mass of land in the East River between Manhattan and Queens. Setting foot on it feels a bit like passing through a portal into an episode of *The Twilight Zone* or *Stranger Things*; formerly a drab residential enclave with little more than a diner and dry cleaners, and also a former site for hospitals and prisons, an air of unsettled business wafts through the streets.

But development is afoot, with shiny condos and rentals and the gleaming new campus of Cornell Tech (2 W. Loop Rd., 7am-9:30pm daily), set to be the Cal Tech of the East. It sits in the center of the island, next to the tram terminal, and features a café, outdoor tables, and a wild field with small hills on which to picnic or simply walk around and gaze at Manhattan's skyscrapers.

Less than a 10-minute walk south of the campus brings you to the ruins of the Smallpox Hospital, though you have to admire the Gothic Revival architecture from a distance because it's completely fenced off. The stately structure has been abandoned since the 1950s and is listed in the National Register of Historic Places.

Right next to the Smallpox Hospital at the southern tip of the island is Four Freedoms Park (9am-7pm Wed.-Mon., free), designed by Louis Kahn to honor President Franklin D. Roosevelt. More a memorial than a green space, it features a large bust of the late president who called New York State home. From here you can see Queens to the west, marked by a large Pepsi-Cola sign that stands where the soda company's bottling plant used to be, and the World Trade Center and Lower Manhattan skyline to the east. You also have the rare vantage of peering down the center of the East River to the Williamsburg Bridge.

Just 800 feet (244 m) across at its widest point and two miles (3.2 km) in length, Roosevelt Island is very walkable, though there is the free Red Bus that makes stops throughout the island.

Roosevelt Island is just one stop away from Manhattan by F train, but you can also take the more scenic Roosevelt Island Tramway (6am-2am Sun.-Thurs., 6am-3:30am Fri.-Sat.) for the same price as the subway. The aerial tram runs every 7-15 minutes from East 59th Street and 2nd Avenue in Manhattan and provides a rare bird's-eye view of the city's grid, allowing you to gaze the entire length of 1st Avenue as you glide above. At its peak height, you also gain expansive views of the East River and city skyline, including (at night) the illuminated semicircle formed by the lights of the Chrysler Building. It's also possible to hop on the NYC Ferry's Astoria route from Midtown or Lower Manhattan for the approximately 10- to 15-minute ride to the island.

MAP 7: Roosevelt Island Tramway E. 59th St. and 2nd Ave., 212/832-4540, https://rioc. ny.gov; free

UPPER WEST SIDE
American Museum of Natural History

The American Museum of Natural History holds an extensive collection of fossils and wild animal exhibits in its 45 halls spanning four floors and a lower level. With over half a million square feet, it's the largest natural history museum in the world. Plan on spending at least half a day here. Awe-inspiring features of the permanent collection include full sets of dinosaur fossils assembled to scale; dioramas presenting the natural habitats of animals including bears, moose, bison, and extinct species such as mammoths; and a massive blue whale model made of fiberglass and weighing 21,000 pounds (9,525 kg).

Temporary special exhibits delve into specific aspects of the natural world and tend to be particularly child friendly, with interactive elements that turn learning into a game. The Butterfly Conservatory, an annual seasonal exhibition (Oct.-May.), is a wonder for all ages with its more than 100 butterfly species fluttering amid the tropical plant-strewn space. But it's the Hayden Planetarium that really brings the wow factor. Its space show, *Dark Universe*—which plays every half hour—conveys the thrills of scientific exploration, taking viewers on an immersive journey through our solar system.

For an adults-only experience at the museum, the DJ party One Step Beyond takes place on select Friday nights in the Rose Center for Earth and Space and hosts big-name acts like Grammy-nominated Felix da Housecat as well as a beer and wine cash bar.

MAP 7: Central Park W. and 79th St., 212/769-5100, www.amnh.org; 10am-5:45pm daily; $33 adults, $27 seniors and students, $20 children 2-12

Harlem and Morningside Heights

Map 8

SIGHTS

HARLEM AND MORNINGSIDE HEIGHTS

✪ Cathedral of St. John the Divine

Perhaps the grandest of all New York cathedrals, St. John the Divine takes your breath away, with arches that appear to reach for the heavens. Construction began in 1892, though the cathedral is considered unfinished—it continues to be constructed, interrupted by World War II, fires, and depleted funds, among other things—but it's still the largest Episcopal cathedral in the world, occupying 11 acres (4 ha). Inside, light floods through giant stained glass windows. Exhibits around the perimeter of the cathedral's nave illustrate the progressive church's history of fighting for social justice and artistic expression. In the 1980s, it offered direct aid and counseling to people with AIDS, and these efforts are commemorated today with a memorial that includes the Book of Remembrance, listing all who have died from the disease, and Keith Haring's *The Life of Christ*, a triptych the artist carved into clay using a knife; it was his final work before succumbing to the disease. Also notable is the poet's corner, which includes engraved plaques with quotes by authors including Gertrude Stein and E. E. Cummings. On the Pulpit Green outside, you'll find a towering carved-stone Gothic spire. Admission is free for worshippers, but tourists pay an entrance fee.

MAP 8: 1047 Amsterdam Ave., 212/316-7540, www.stjohndivine.org; 9am-5pm Mon.-Sat., 1pm-3pm Sun.; $10 adults, $8 seniors and students

Columbia University

New York University has a sizable presence in the Village, but Columbia is the only college in Manhattan that has a true campus feel, spanning 114th-120th Streets between Broadway and Amsterdam Avenue. Its gates remain open during the day, making it a pleasant place to stroll or have a picnic lunch on the quad, which is a good spot for people-watching and accessible through the gate at 116th. The Miller Theatre (2960 Broadway, 212/854-7799) is open to the public and features a wide range of programming from string quartets to lectures by noted academics like Noam Chomsky. Free hour-long pop-up concerts are held on select weeknights at 6pm.

MAP 8: W. 116th St. and Broadway, 212/854-1754, www.columbia.edu; free

Cathedral of St. John the Divine

Riverside Church

Only slightly less grand in scale than St. John the Divine, Riverside Church is actually the tallest church in the country and was conceived in 1927 by John D. Rockefeller. Modeled after 13th-century Gothic cathedrals in Chartres, France, its first service was held in 1930 and it's located on one of the highest points in Manhattan, overlooking the Hudson River. Dr. Martin Luther King Jr. delivered his famous anti-Vietnam War sermon here, and Nelson Mandela later addressed the congregation from the same pulpit. Progressive peace activist Rev. Dr. William Sloan Coffin Jr. led the congregation 1977-1987, and today pastor Amy Butler preaches a powerful message of inclusion. The interdenominational church also has great acoustics, which has made it the site of many notable concerts by artists such as pop violinist Andrew Bird. The majestic nave encourages contemplation on a grand scale.

MAP 8: 490 Riverside Dr., 212/870-6700, www.trcnyc.org; 10:30am-6pm Tues. and Thurs.-Sat., 10:30am-7pm Wed., 9:30am-4pm Sun.; free

General Grant National Memorial

Sitting above the Hudson River near the northern edge of Riverside Park, Ulysses S. Grant's tomb is the closest thing New York has to the Lincoln Memorial and is nearly as grand. The monument is fitting for a man who was instrumental in the unification of the country after the Civil War, known equally for his tenacity as general and humanity as president. "Let Us Have Peace" is inscribed on the mausoleum, which is the largest in North America and holds the remains of both Grant and his wife, Julia. Approach from Riverside Drive near 122nd Street opposite Riverside Church for the best view of the monument, flanked by two rows of trees. The mausoleum's interior is open during alternating hours and features an original 35-star flag from when Grant served under Lincoln. A visitors center with restrooms is also here. Stroll around the perimeter of the tomb to find colorful mosaic benches, a public art project created in the 1970s and inspired by the work of Spanish artist-architect Antoni Gaudí.

MAP 8: W. 122nd and Riverside Dr., 212/666-1640, www.nps.gov/gegr; visitors center 9am-5pm Wed.-Sun., mausoleum 10am-11am, noon-1pm, 2pm-3pm, and 4pm-5pm Wed.-Sun.; free

Apollo Theater

Originally a "whites only" burlesque house upon opening in 1914, the Apollo Theater didn't last for long. It gained a new life in 1934, welcoming African Americans and gaining renown for its signature Amateur Night (7:30pm Wed.; $22-44). The showcase played a pivotal role in launching the careers of legends such as Ella Fitzgerald, James Brown, Jimi Hendrix, and Michael Jackson, and it remains a raucous event where performers are praised and booed with equal fervor (a pre-Fugees Lauryn Hill was famously booed off the stage). While the show has largely lost its power to catapult contestants to stardom, it still draws an enthusiastic crowd. Buy tickets at least a month in advance to get prime orchestra seats. The 1,500-seat venue also hosts a range of mainstream concerts and talks. Daily one-hour tours (11am, 1pm, and 3pm Mon.-Tues. and Thurs.-Fri., 11am Wed., 11am and 1pm Sat.-Sun.; $17-19)

THE HARLEM RENAISSANCE

A social and cultural movement, the Harlem Renaissance was born out of a search for black identity in the 1920s and 1930s. Segregationist Jim Crow laws ruled the South, and the racial division was still powerfully felt up north. The Great Migration between 1915 and 1970—during which approximately six million African Americans moved from the South to the North and West—brought droves of people fleeing lynching and a dearth of employment opportunities to New York, specifically Harlem, and the beginning of a free and vibrant community was formed. Among the neighborhood's most noted and influential residents was essayist and activist W. E. B. Du Bois, the first black man to receive a doctorate from Harvard and a proponent of African American artists across a wide range of mediums. Writers Langston Hughes and Zora Neale Hurston and musicians Duke Ellington and Billie Holiday were also associated with this creative explosion.

During this period, **Striver's Row** (aka St. Nicholas Historic District) became the first upper-middle-class neighborhood for black Americans in New York. The pristine cluster of neo-Italian and Georgian town houses in Harlem between Adam Clayton Powell Jr. and Frederick Douglass Boulevards on West 138th and 139th Streets evoke the era of horse-drawn carriages; look closely as you stroll and you can still see signs that say, "walk your horses." Its residents included Harry Pace, who founded Black Swan Records, the first black-owned music label; entertainer Bill "Bojangles" Robinson; and the country's first black congressman, Adam Clayton Powell Jr. If this was any other movement, there would be landmarks dotting the neighborhood, but the truth is that many of the places most important to the Harlem Renaissance were torn down before the revaluation of this rich cultural heritage began.

Another musician to come out of the Harlem Renaissance was Louis Armstrong. He first played in New York with Fletcher Henderson, an influential bandleader and arranger recognized for helping define the big band sound. Armstrong went on to headline at clubs like The Cotton Club, a gangster-owned, whites-only nightclub that served as one of the era's most high-profile stages for black performers. A new incarnation of **The Cotton Club** (656 W. 125th St., 212/663-7980, http://cottonclub-newyork.com) sits on the far west edge of Harlem but is frequented mainly by tourists. For a more authentic experience, head to Minton's Playhouse.

Armstrong met his fourth wife, Lucille Wilson, at the original Cotton Club when she worked as a dancer there. In 1943 the couple bought a house in Corona, Queens, and lived there for the rest of their lives. Now the **Louis Armstrong House Museum** (34-56 107th St., Queens, 718/478-8274, www.louisarmstronghouse.org; 10am-5pm Tues.-Fri., noon-5pm Sat.-Sun.; $12 adults, $8 seniors, students, and children, free for children under 5), it remains remarkably preserved and offers visitors an intimate glimpse into the day-to-day life of the legendary jazz crooner and trumpeter. During the guided 40-minute tour, you'll hear a recording Armstrong made in his living room—while you're standing in the same room. To get here, take the 7 subway to the 103rd Street-Corona Plaza station. Exit on the north side of Roosevelt Avenue and walk two blocks north on 103rd Street. Make a right on 37th Avenue and continue four blocks to 107th Street. Make a left and you'll find the house halfway down the block on the west side of the street.

detail the theater's significance as a cultural center for the city's black community. Groups of 20 or more can reserve in advance while others can join existing tours on the day of if space permits.

MAP 8: 253 W. 125th St., 212/531-5305, www.apollotheater.org; box office 10am-6pm Mon.-Fri., noon-5pm Sat.; performance prices vary

Langston Hughes House

Langston Hughes lived the last 20 years of his life in this 19th-century Italianate row house, now listed in the National Register of Historic Places. It's fitting that the building is now home to an arts collective (I, Too Arts Collective): Hughes mentored young writers and created a theater company in 1935, Harlem Suitcase

Theater, to produce new works. You can visit the parlor floor of the house to see Hughes's typewriter and piano some days of the week, but it's best to call ahead because there are some exceptions.

MAP 8: 20 E. 127th St., 929/344-1179; www.itooarts.com; Tues., Thurs., and Sat. noon-5pm.; $5 suggested donation

Abyssinian Baptist Church

A New York City Landmark, this historic church was founded in 1808 and has been in its current Collegiate Gothic-style home since 1923. It was the largest black church in the world when Adam Clayton Powell Jr.—who went on to become the first black U.S. congressman—was preacher. His tenure began in 1938 when he took the reins from his father and ended when he won his congressional seat in 1944. Worshippers are welcome, and tourists are allowed at the 11:30am service on Sunday. Abyssinian requests that visitors be mindful that these services are intended as worship and not gospel performance or entertainment. If you attend, expect to adhere to a dress code (no tank tops, flip-flops, shorts, or leggings) and remain once seated until the conclusion of the service, which typically lasts 2.5 hours.

MAP 8: 132 Odell Clark Pl., 212/862-7474, www.abyssinian.org; free

Hamilton Grange National Memorial

Even if you don't score tickets to *Hamilton,* you can visit Founding Father Alexander Hamilton's country retreat, the only house he ever owned, on its current site in Saint Nicholas Park (the house has been moved twice), on a part of the original estate. Enter through the basement, where you'll find a welcome center with historical exhibits and a gift shop. Admission to the house is free, but visitors need to sign up for a ranger-led tour offered on a first-come, first-served basis (10am, 11am, 2pm, and 4pm Wed.-Sun.), or go during designated self-guided tour hours (noon-1pm and 3pm-4pm Wed.-Sun). The handful of rooms on view are all on one level; the most impressive space is the drawing room, which features several chairs that belonged to Hamilton and his family and a Clementi piano his daughter played. Most of the other furniture, including his desk in the study, are replicas.

MAP 8: 414 W. 141st St., 646/548-2310, www.nps.gov/hagr; visitors center 9am-5pm Wed.-Sun.; free

Downtown Brooklyn, Dumbo, and Fort Greene Map 9

✪ Brooklyn Bridge

Several bridges connect the island of Manhattan to its surrounding boroughs and neighboring states, but the Brooklyn Bridge holds a place in the city's iconography that no others can match. Built over the course of 14 grueling years, it cost $14 million (approximately $400 million in today's dollars) and was the first to connect Brooklyn to Manhattan, spanning the East River and becoming a symbol of the city's innovative drive.

Today over 4,000 people trek across the bridge each day. As you make the crossing, notice the bridge's impressive cable span and how the towers' archways frame the city skyline; this is particularly pronounced at night.

The pedestrian thoroughfare is 1.3 miles (2 km) and takes roughly 25-30 minutes to walk. Add time for crowds and stops to take photos. Sunset is a popular time to go. Or, if you want to avoid the crowds, your best bet is to go before 8am. The bridge is also safe to walk across at night and remains trafficked by pedestrians until about 11pm.

From Manhattan, access the Brooklyn Bridge on Centre Street on the east side of City Hall Park, conveniently across from the Brooklyn Bridge City Hall subway station. Be sure to leave time after your walk for further exploration once you're on the Brooklyn side (page 64).

Alternatively, for a stunning view of the Brooklyn Bridge itself, as well as the city skyline, you could do as the locals do and walk over the neighboring

EXPLORING BROOKLYN'S BROWNSTONES

Few architectural styles are more quintessentially New York than the brownstone, named for the soft earthy sandstone or freestone of the building's facade. These spacious single- and multiple-family residences—typically three or four stories, plus a basement—were constructed in the mid-to-late 19th century. Before this, the material was used for stoops and door and window trim of Federal and Greek Revival row houses. Unlike those more distinctive styles, the brownstone has the ability to meld, and it often takes a close eye to tell where one ends and the next begins.

Brownstones can be found throughout New York, but some of the most well-preserved ones are in Brooklyn. **Brooklyn Heights** in particular has a high concentration of them. Stroll on the parallel "fruit streets" (Pineapple, Cranberry, Orange) between Columbia Heights and Henry Street—just east of Brooklyn Bridge Park's Pier 2—to glimpse some lovely examples set amid lush tree-lined streets.

To see a famous brownstone, head to 142 Columbia Heights near the corner of Pineapple Street. **Norman Mailer** wrote *The Executioner's Song* in the upper duplex, which he outfitted to look like a ship; if you look closely, you can glimpse a dramatic skylight. And while you're in the neighborhood, stop by 70 Willow Street, just off Pineapple Street, to see the Greek Revival mansion that **Truman Capote** lived in while writing *Breakfast at Tiffany's* and *In Cold Blood*.

Manhattan Bridge (note that trains roar across it quite frequently). Enter at Bowery and Canal Street on the Manhattan side and through Trinity Park on the Brooklyn side near the intersection of Jay and High Streets.

MAP 9: Manhattan entrance at Centre St., Brooklyn entrance at Cadman Plaza East or Boerum Pl. and Tillary St.; 24 hours daily; free

Williamsburg, Greenpoint, and Bushwick   Map 10

Brooklyn Brewery

✪ Brooklyn Brewery

Back in the 1980s, before Williamsburg was a destination and Brooklyn was synonymous with craft beer, this working brewery opened its doors. Brewmaster Garrett Oliver has literally written the book on beer (two, in fact) and won a James Beard Award. His most widely distributed beer—the one you get if you ask for a "Brooklyn" in any bar in the tristate area—is a fairly standard lager but others, like the aptly named Blast, are fully of punchy, hoppy flavor. The first-come, first-served taproom gets crowded on the weekends when locals pile in to try Oliver's one-off concoctions. Free tours are held on Saturdays and Sundays every half-hour 1pm-6pm. On weekdays, 45-minute small-batch tours (5:30pm, 6pm, and 6:30pm Mon.-Fri., $18) are available; they're limited to 20 people, include tastings of four beers, and must be booked in advance online.

MAP 10: 79 N. 11th St., 718/486-7422, http://brooklynbrewery.com; 5pm-11pm Mon.-Thurs., 5pm-midnight Fri., noon-midnight Sat., noon-8pm Sun.; free

Williamsburg Bridge

When it opened in 1903, the Williamsburg Bridge was the longest suspension bridge in the world at over 7,000 feet (2,134 m). Walking across is a fun way to get between the neighborhoods of Williamsburg and the Lower East Side. The bridge is just under 1.4 miles (2.3 km) long and takes about 30 minutes to walk across. While views are more caged in than on the Brooklyn Bridge, this also means smaller crowds, and you'll have views of the Lower Manhattan skyline as well as the Brooklyn Navy Yard. The bridge lets out next to Baby's All Right and Peter Luger's on the Brooklyn side and just a couple blocks from the Delancey F train subway stop on the Manhattan side.

MAP 10: pedestrian entrance Clinton St. and Delancey St. (Manhattan), Bedford Ave. between S. 5th St. and S. 6th St. (Brooklyn); 24 hours daily; free

✪ Prospect Park

Prospect Park is Brooklyn's Central Park. Likewise designed by Frederick Law Olmsted and Calvert Vaux, it's the borough's gathering spot and much more relaxed than its Manhattan counterpart despite offering plenty to do. Set in between the neighborhoods of Park Slope, Prospect Heights, Windsor Terrace, and Prospect Lefferts Gardens, you could easily spend a day exploring the park's 526 acres (213 ha). Grand Army Plaza is the park's primary northern entrance, and its Greenmarket (8am-4pm Sat.) is the city's second largest after Union Square. Just south of this entrance you'll hit Long Meadow, the longest stretch of unbroken greenery in any NYC park. Stretching almost a mile (about 1.6 km) across the length of Prospect Park, it's popular for lounging, reading, and Frisbee. Farther south near the park's center is the Ravine, the only forest in Brooklyn—it boasts nearly 150 woodland acres (61 ha)—and a perfect place to get lost for a little while amid modest waterfalls that drown out the street noise. At the park's southeastern corner is Prospect Park Lake, where you can rent a paddleboat or kayak. Off the lake's eastern shore is Breeze Hill, where massive outdoor food market Smorgasburg (www.smorgasburg.com; 11am-6pm Oct.-Apr.) takes place on Sundays in season.

If you get hungry, pop outside the park's borders to the neighborhoods of Park Slope to the west and Prospect

autumn in Prospect Park

Heights to the north. Both have numerous restaurants on their main thoroughfares, 5th and 7th Avenues and Vanderbilt and Washington Avenues, respectively.

A day in Prospect Park can also easily be combined with visits to the Brooklyn Museum or Brooklyn Botanic Garden, both of which border the park.

To get here, take the 2, 3, or 4 subway to the Grand Army Plaza station. Prospect Park's main entrance is just southeast across the large traffic circle that resembles Paris's Arc de Triomphe.

MAP 11: northern entrance Grand Army Plaza, southern entrance Machate Circle, Brooklyn, 718/965-8951, www. prospectpark.org; 5am-1am daily; free

Brooklyn Museum

On the northeastern perimeter of Prospect Park is the Brooklyn Museum, a world-class institution with a large permanent collection of art and artifacts from countries and cultures around the world, including Africa, Asia, Egypt, Europe, and the Americas. The five-story museum also has an impressive collection of feminist art exhibited in its Elizabeth A. Sackler Center, the centerpiece of which is Judy Chicago's *The Dinner Party*, a large triangular banquet with 39 place settings for important women throughout history, including Virginia Woolf, Susan B. Anthony, and Georgia O'Keeffe. The Brooklyn Museum also programs rotating special exhibits, such as the recent immersive *David Bowie is* show, which put visitors in the mind of the late, great musician by equipping each visitor with wireless headphones to listen to clips of music, interviews, and other recorded materials matched to particular displays.

Admission is free 5pm-10pm on Thursdays and 5pm-11pm on the first Saturday of every month except September. A discounted combination ticket ($25 adults, $16 seniors and students) for the Brooklyn Museum and Brooklyn Botanic Garden is also available.

To get here, take the 2 or 3 subway to the Eastern Parkway station, located right in front of the museum. A visit to the Brooklyn Museum makes for a nice day out when combined with trips to Prospect Park and the Brooklyn Botanic Garden.

MAP 11: 200 Eastern Pkwy., Brooklyn, 718/638-5000, www.brooklynmuseum.org; 11am-6pm Wed. and Fri.-Sun., 11am-10pm Thurs.; $16 adults, $10 seniors and students, free for ages 19 and under

Brooklyn Botanic Garden

On the eastern perimeter of Prospect Park and just south of the Brooklyn Museum is the Brooklyn Botanic Garden. While considerably smaller than the New York Botanical Garden at just 52 acres (21 ha), it's quite stunning. Its lush grounds include more than a thousand species of roses as well as a Native Flora Garden displaying myriad indigenous plant species such as cultivated pine barrens. The most popular time to visit the garden is during cherry blossom season in the Japanese Hill-and-Pond Garden. This typically takes place over a week between March and May and sets the garden aglow in pink. Entry is free on Fridays before noon and winter weekdays (Mon.-Fri. Dec.-Feb.). A discounted combination ticket ($25 adults, $16 seniors and students) for the Brooklyn Botanic Garden and Brooklyn Museum is also available.

To get here, take the 2 or 3 subway to the Eastern Parkway station. Walk one block east and make a right onto Mary Pinkett/Washington Avenue. A visit to the Brooklyn Botanic Garden combined with trips to Prospect Park and the Brooklyn Museum makes for a nice day out.

MAP 11: 990 Washington Ave., Brooklyn, 718/623-7200, www.bbg.org; 8am-6pm Tues.-Fri. and 10am-6pm Sat.-Sun. Mar.-June and Sept.-Oct., 8am-8:30pm Tues., 8am-6pm Wed.-Fri., and 10am-6pm Sat.-Sun. July-Aug., 8am-4:30pm Tues.-Fri. and 10am-4:30pm Sat.-Sun. Nov., 10am-4:30pm Tues.-Sun. Dec.-Feb.; $15 adults, $8 seniors and students, free for children under 12

Green-Wood Cemetery

Covering 478 acres (193 ha) in Brooklyn southwest of Prospect Park and encompassing hills and glacial ponds, Green-Wood Cemetery sometimes feels more like a natural refuge than the final resting place for some of the city's most distinguished residents, including Jean-Michel Basquiat, Leonard Bernstein, Boss Tweed, and Brooklyn Dodgers owner Charles Ebbets. Scores of Civil War generals are buried here as well, and the land itself was the site of the Battle of Long Island during the Revolutionary War. Founded in 1831, the cemetery actually predates the creation of public parks. Winding paths weave through the cemetery grounds, shaded by century-old trees. Maps are available at all four of the cemetery's entrances, including the main one on 5th Avenue, which features spectacularly intricate High Victorian arches. Other entrances are at 4th Avenue and 35th Street (8am-4pm daily), Fort Hamilton Parkway and Micieli Place (8am-4pm Sat.-Sun.), and Prospect Park West and 20th Street (8am-4pm Sat.-Sun).

If you get hungry while here, pop outside the cemetery on its northwest side and walk a little more than four blocks straight down 5th Avenue to Korzo (667 5th Ave., 718/499-1199, http://korzorestaurant.com; 11:30am-11:30pm Tues.-Fri., 11am-11:30pm Sat., 11am-10pm Sun.-Mon.; $), a Czech-inspired gastropub that makes one of the city's best and most original burgers. After being seared, the burger is wrapped in *lángos* (a Hungarian dough) and finished in a deep fryer so burger and bun become a singular orb of deliciousness, with the toppings tucked inside like a pita.

To get here, take the R subway to 25th Street. Walk one block southeast to 5th Avenue to arrive at the cemetery's main entrance.

MAP 11: 5th Ave. and 25th St., Brooklyn, 718/768-7300, www.green-wood.com; 8am-5pm daily Oct.-Mar., 7am-7pm daily April-Sept.; free

Coney Island

Home to an annual mermaid parade to kick off the summer and the famous July 4th hot dog-eating contest, Coney Island—not an actual island but rather a peninsular beach district—lets its freak flag fly high and proud. An atmospheric boardwalk stretches across this part of Brooklyn's south waterfront, and off of it you'll find a number of renowned amusements. Coney Island's 1927 roller coaster, the Cyclone, still runs regularly alongside newer rides at the revamped Luna Park (1000 Surf Ave.; hours vary seasonally; unlimited ride pass $31-42 under 48 inches, $43-69 over 48 inches, purchase online for the best prices), which took the place of the famous Astroland amusement park. It's free to enter the park, but you'll need to pay to hop on any rides, whether with an unlimited pass or a

Luna Park at Coney Island

pay-per-ride card—credits are $1 each, with the Cyclone priced at 10 credits, for example. The Coney Island Circus Sideshow (1208 Surf Ave.; $10 adults, $5 children under 12, Mar.-Sept.) features sword-swallowers, fire-breathers, and other performers stretching the limits of the human body. And of course, Nathan's Famous (1310 Surf Ave., 718/333-2202; 10am-11pm Mon.-Thurs., 10am-midnight Fri., 9am-midnight Sat., 9am-11pm Sun.; $), founded in 1916, is still here slinging hot dogs.

To get here, take the D, F, N, or Q subway to the Coney Island-Stillwell Avenue station. Follow Stillwell Avenue south to reach the action. MAP 11: Surf Ave. and Stillwell Ave., Brooklyn, 718/946-1350, www.coneyisland. com; boardwalk 6am-1am daily, lifeguard on duty 10am-6pm during beach season; free

The Met Cloisters

Situated in Fort Tryon Park in the northern reaches of Manhattan and overlooking the Hudson River, this medieval castle is the ideal setting for more than 2,000 pieces of art and architectural remnants of the Middle Ages from the 12th to the 15th centuries. The castle itself is much older than any building in the country, having been brought over from Western Europe and reassembled here. Part of The Metropolitan Museum of Art, the Cloisters gets its name from its four open-air galleries, which are particularly enjoyable for browsing in the warmer months and landscaped with plants authentic to the era. Indoor spaces are equally dramatic with massive panels of stained glass illuminating a Gothic cathedral and large-scale tapestries vividly depicting the hunt for the elusive mythical unicorn, among the many highlights. Plan to spend a couple of hours to take it all in at a leisurely pace.

Admission is valid for three consecutive days and also includes entrance to The Metropolitan Museum of Art and The Met Breuer.

To get here, take the A subway to

the 190th Street station. Exit the station via elevator and walk about half a mile (0.8 km) north through Fort Tryon Park on Margaret Corbin Drive.

MAP 11: 99 Margaret Corbin Dr., Manhattan, 212/923-3700, www. metmuseum.org/visit/met-cloisters; 10am-5:15pm daily Mar.-Oct., 10am-4:45pm daily Nov.-Feb.; $25 adults, $17 seniors, $12 students

New York Botanical Garden

Founded in 1891, the city's largest botanical garden has 250 sprawling and artfully manicured acres (101 ha) of greenery. A great way to begin a visit to this National Historic Landmark is by taking the free tram tour, which snakes through the most scenic parts of the garden and allows for hop-on, hop-off viewing. The rock, rose, and azalea gardens in particular are standouts for their artful landscaping. On the garden grounds is also a Victorian-style conservatory, strikingly framed by a reflecting pool with water lilies and lotuses and offering year-round tropical splendor. A popular annual exhibit is the Holiday Train Show (Nov.-Jan.) inside the conservatory, where model trains snake through half a mile (0.8 km) of tracks past intricately constructed replicas of more than 175 New York landmarks, including the Brooklyn Bridge and Ellis Island. The New York Botanical Garden also programs exhilarating temporary shows, including pairing Georgia O' Keeffe's obscure Hawaii paintings with the flowers that inspired them inside the conservatory and exhibiting pieces from glass artist Dale Chihuly across its grounds.

A casual café and a fine-dining restaurant are on-site but get quite crowded on busy days. Because the gardens feature picnic areas, a better idea may be to bring your own feast from Grand Central Terminal before boarding a Metro-North train, which stops across the street at the Botanical Garden Station. The ride from Grand Central takes less than 30 minutes.

MAP 11: 2900 Southern Blvd., Bronx, 718/817-8700, www.nybg.org; 10am-6pm Tues.-Sun.; $23-28 adults, $20-25 seniors and students, $10-12 children 2-12, free for children under 2

RESTAURANTS

It's harder to have a bad meal in New York City than most places. Darwinian levels of competition ensure that the meek almost inevitably fail (well, outside of major tourist zones such as Times Square—beware!). There are so many restaurants here you could try a different one each day without repeating yourself for decades.

Fiat Cafe

Sampling the city's variety of cuisines is one of the great joys of dining in New York. The city benefits massively from its multicultural roots, profoundly felt in the diversity of options on offer, from Italian, French, and Chinese to Basque, Ukrainian, Cambodian, and beyond.

Must-eat items while you're here include pizza, to start. Arguing over which is best is a local pastime. Jewish deli staples like bagels, pastrami, and lox should also be on the foodie's checklist. Many New Yorkers also love meat, from humble hot dogs to high-end steak. While hot dogs from the ubiquitous street-corner vendors are fine in a pinch, for prime versions of the street treat, hit the Papayas (Gray's Papaya and Papaya King). You'll find classic steak houses around the city. Conversely, vegetarians and vegans will also find plenty to please the palate. There's something for everyone here.

Add to all this star chefs and artisan food halls and markets to explore and you've got a busy schedule ahead of you. Remember while planning your itinerary: Eating is as much an activity here as sightseeing.

HIGHLIGHTS

✪ **BEST BRUNCH:** Sarabeth's famous brunch features epic sweet breakfasts and overstuffed omelets (page 123).

✪ **BEST UNIQUE FINE DINING:** Jungsik serves a seasonal set menu or signature tasting of inventive Korean cuisine (page 128).

✪ **BEST PASTRAMI:** No one masters the art of pastrami better than **Katz's Deli** (page 132).

✪ **BEST RAMEN:** You'll find many great places to get ramen in the city, but none can compete with **Ippudo**'s authenticity (page 134).

✪ **BEST VEGETARIAN:** You'll understand why **Dirt Candy** chef Amanda Cohen requests that you "leave the vegetables to the professionals" once you eat here (page 138).

✪ **BEST BURGER COOKED WITH THE PRECISION OF A FINE STEAK:** The dry-aged Black Label burger at **Minetta Tavern** has few peers (page 140).

✪ **BEST RESTAURANT TO BLOW YOUR BUDGET:** Considered among the world's best restaurants, **Eleven Madison Park** is also one of the most expensive—and worth it (page 146).

✪ **BEST BAGELS:** Massive, pillowy, and usually warm, the classic New York treat doesn't get any better than at **Ess-a-Bagel** (page 155).

✪ **FINEST SEAFOOD:** Le Bernardin serves some of the freshest seafood in the city, exactingly prepared by chef Eric Ripert (page 157).

✪ **BEST HOT DOG:** Hole-in-the-wall **Gray's Papaya** serves up an unbeatable New York street treat (page 164).

✪ **BEST FRIED CHICKEN IN HARLEM:** Find the neighborhood's best at the no-frills **Charles' Country Pan Fried Chicken** (page 166).

✪ **BEST RESTAURANT WHERE OLD AND NEW BROOKLYN MEET:** Sicilian comfort food gets an artisanal update at **Bella Gioia** (page 169).

✪ **BEST PIZZA:** Find coal-oven pizza at its finest at **Juliana's** (page 170).

✪ **BEST AUTHENTIC BASQUE DINING:** Catch your cider from the barrel tap and stuff yourself with plates of grilled chorizo and Spanish omelets at the **Brooklyn Cider House** (page 175).

PRICE KEY

$	Entrées less than $20
$ $	Entrées $20-35
$ $ $	Entrées more than $35

Lower Manhattan

Map 1

CONTEMPORARY AMERICAN

Atrio $$$

A fine-dining spot that's casual in dress and based in the Conrad Hotel, Atrio serves breakfast, lunch, and dinner. Appetizers like veal and pork meatballs, salt-and-pepper calamari, and excellent scallops make it a great stop for impromptu meals. Ingredients are locally sourced and prepared in a skillful but unfussy way. The wine list focuses on American offerings, with Sonoma chardonnays and cabs and a selection of pinot noirs from the Russian River and Willamette Valleys.

MAP 1: 102 North End Ave., 646/769-4250, http://www.conradnewyork.com; 6:30am-11am, 11:30am-3pm, and 5pm-10pm daily

Temple Court $$$

Celebrity chef Tom Colicchio's new restaurant in The Beekman hotel replaces his namesake Colicchio and Sons. The five-course tasting menu includes his take on classics, with offerings like veal Wellington and Maine lobster with chanterelle mushrooms. There's an à la carte menu as well, and an extensive cocktail list featuring drinks named after famous American architects like Pierre Charles L'Enfant, who designed the city plan for Washington DC. The restaurant's decor stands out with its stained glass panels, exposed ducts, and chandeliers exuding a rough-hewed elegance. All-day dining at the bar allows maximum flexibility.

MAP 1: 5 Beekman St., 212/658/1848, www.templecourtnyc.com; 6:30am-11pm daily

STEAK HOUSES

Delmonico's $$$

For a side of history with your perfectly cooked steak, Delmonico's has you covered. Opened in 1837, it's credited as being the first fine-dining restaurant in the country as well as the first restaurant to admit unaccompanied female diners. The many dishes that originated here include the namesake steak, eggs Benedict, and baked Alaska. While the wet-aged steaks are now the most popular, order the dry-aged rib eye or the porterhouse for two (it actually serves closer to four) for the most authentic experience. The Caesar salad is another must, served with a soft-boiled egg on top and a thinly sliced anchovy.

MAP 1: 56 Beaver St., 212/509-1144, www.delmonicosrestaurant.com; 11:30am-10pm Mon.-Fri., 5pm-10pm Sat.

ITALIAN

Parm $

Chef-owners Mario Carbone and Rich Torrisi have made their careers elevating Italian American cuisine and reveling in its simple and decadent pleasures. Parm is their take on a casual sandwich shop, where the stars are the namesake meatball, eggplant, and chicken heroes. The house turkey sandwich is an excellent option for those wanting slightly lighter fare. Checkered red-and-white tablecloths add to the nostalgic appeal at this spacious location at The Battery, steps from the Hudson River.

MAP 1: 250 Vesey St., 212/776-4927, www.parmnyc.com; 11:30am-10pm Sun.-Thurs., 11:30pm-11pm Fri.-Sat.

BAGELS
Leo's Bagels $

Leo's has developed a large local following for its hand-rolled bagels. They're served fresh out of the oven with an array of flavored cream cheeses (maple raisin walnut and jalapeno are among the choices), tofu spreads, and, of course, lox. You'll find more than a dozen smoked fish options to choose from, including salmon from Nova Scotia, Scotland, Ireland, and Norway. While choice is king here, seats are in short supply, so head over to The Battery to enjoy your feast if the weather allows.

MAP 1: 3 Hanover Sq., 212/785-4700, www.leosbagels.com; 6am-5pm Mon.-Fri., 7am-5pm Sat.-Sun.

DINERS
Pearl Diner $

This classic diner is one of the last of its kind. Its single-story structure with protruding neon sign looks like it was air-dropped from a desolate highway down which tumbleweeds roll. Sit on a stool at the counter for the full experience and keep your order simple: eggs, burgers, a Reuben. Besides the addition of panini, the menu hasn't changed much in the past half century. Beware of early closing hours, particularly on the weekends.

MAP 1: 212 Pearl St., 212/344-6620, www. pearldinerny.com; 7am-9pm Mon.-Fri., 8am-2:45pm Sat.-Sun.

Soho and Tribeca   Map 2

CONTEMPORARY AMERICAN
David Burke Kitchen $$$

David Burke's namesake restaurant in The James hotel is filled with guilty pleasures—like the extra-thick candied bacon with pepper-maple glaze, an ideal table share that you'll probably want to hog for yourself. An expansive and gorgeously landscaped 2nd-floor, open-air garden is the place to sit in warmer months; it's the most romantic spot in the city where you can also enjoy a plate of barbecue pork belly with pineapple-shrimp fried rice.

MAP 2: 23 Grand St., 212/201-9119, www. davidburkekitchennyc.com; 7am-10pm Sun.-Wed., 7am-11pm Thurs.-Sat.

✪ Sarabeth's $$

This New York institution is known for its brunch—particularly the lemon-ricotta pancakes. But there are also several different kinds of French toast and other pancakes, not to mention a plethora of fluffy egg dishes and cold-pressed juices. While Sarabeth's is most celebrated for brunch, it also offers a good range of options all day long. A roasted chicken salad is elevated with smoked almonds, and the chicken pot pie is the epitome of comfort food. The restaurant started on the Upper East Side and now has a handful of locations, but this Tribeca outpost is sleeker and offers more seating than uptown counterparts, making it a more strategic choice when trying to snag a table during prime brunch hours (typically around 11am-1pm Sat.-Sun.). For those on a budget, the restaurant also has a great happy hour (4:30pm-7:30pm daily) with $5 bites.

MAP 2: 339 Greenwich St., 212/966-0421, http://sarabethsrestaurants.com; 8am-10:30pm Mon.-Thurs., 8am-11pm Fri.-Sat., 8am-10pm Sun.

The Mercer Kitchen $$

Located in the basement of The Mercer Hotel, this is the place to go when you're craving fish-and-chips. In the hands of world-renowned chef Jean-Georges, the fish is perfectly cooked so each bite is light and fluffy. The space has a sexy club-like vibe, but the music is kept low. An heirloom tomato crostini is a simple yet decadent way to start a meal, and peach pie and carrot cake are must-have desserts.

MAP 2: 99 Prince St., 212/966-5454, www.themercerkitchen.com; 7am-midnight Mon.-Thurs., 7am-1am Fri.-Sat., 7am-11pm Sun.

Tribeca Grill $$

Exposed brick walls flank white-tablecloth booths in Robert De Niro's comfort food haven. Fried calamari, lamb meatballs, and lobster cavatelli are among the classic offerings. The cavernous wine list stretches 78 pages and includes prized bottles of grand cru going for over eight grand, but there are also bottles to be found for $40 and under. For a bargain, come for a weekday lunch, when two courses can be had for $28.

MAP 2: 375 Greenwich St., 212/941-3900, www.myriadrestaurantgroup.com; 11:30am-10pm Mon.-Thurs., 11:30pm-11pm Fri., 5:30pm-11pm Sat., 11am-10pm Sun.

ITALIAN
Altesi Downtown $$

This casual Tuscan restaurant serves some of the best meatballs in the city, accompanied with a dollop of ricotta. Equally memorable are the

Locanda Verde

pastas (particularly the braised duck agnolotti served in a truffle puree), sourced from a mill in Salento, and a selection of wood-fired pizzas (try the Bolognese with veal ragù). Another must is the freshly made and addictively salty focaccia bread. Service is warm but unfussy, making this a great place to refuel or end a long day of sightseeing.

MAP 2: 200 Spring St., 212/431-1212, www.altesinyc.com; noon-4pm and 6pm-11pm daily

Locanda Verde $$

Andrew Carmellini's Italian restaurant exudes rustic farmhouse warmth with its dimly lit elegance. Although there's no dress code, dining here feels like a special occasion. On the menu you'll find dishes like "My Grandmother's Ravioli" (filled with braised short ribs and pork belly) and a simple but insanely delicious sheep's milk ricotta waiting to be spread on grilled ciabatta. The extensive wine list is exclusively sourced from Italy and pricey, with no bottles under $50.

MAP 2: 377 Greenwich St., 212/925-3797, www.locandaverdenyc.com; 7am-11am, 11:30am-3pm, and 5:30pm-11pm Mon.-Thurs., 7am-11am, 11:30am-3pm, and 5:30pm-11:30pm Fri., 8am-3pm and 5:30pm-11:30pm Sat., 8am-3pm and 5:30pm-11pm Sun.

Osteria Morini $$

Chef Michael White's casual spot for Emilia-Romagna cuisine is decorated with rustic 18th-century antiques complemented by exposed brick walls and dark wood rafters. The menu includes an extensive array of cured meats along with more than a dozen handmade pastas, all cooked to al dente perfection. White is a master of creating delicate pastas and turning them into savory flavor bombs with ingredients like truffled ricotta and pork shoulder ragù. While it's a fairly pricey affair, all of the pastas are just $12 after 9pm on Sunday and Monday nights.

MAP 2: 218 Lafayette St., 212/965-8777, http://osteriamorini.com; 11:30am-11pm Mon.-Wed., 11:30am-midnight Thurs.-Sat., 11:30am-10pm Sun.

Fiat Cafe $

This affable, cash-only mainstay follows the European café model of understated elegance and great value. Savory pastas like ricotta ravioli in brown butter sauce, an array of freshly grilled panini, and other comfort dishes can be had for prices unheard of in the area. An American-style breakfast is also served daily until late afternoon, and offers a relaxed alternative to the typical brunch madness.

MAP 2: 203 Mott St., 212/969-1809, www.fiatcafenyc.com; 8am-11pm daily

Forlini's $

An old-school red-sauce joint in Little Italy, Forlini's is packed during lunch hours on weekdays when judges and defendants alike from the nearby courthouses pile in for generous servings of homemade pasta, like the spinach-and-ricotta-stuffed ravioli, and family-sized salads. The dining room, with its wall-to-wall carpeting and oil landscape paintings, feels frozen in time from its opening in 1943, and prices are equally nostalgic.

MAP 2: 93 Baxter St., 212/349-6779, www.forlinisnyc.com; noon-11pm Sun.-Thurs., noon-midnight Fri.-Sat.

PIZZA
Lombardi's Pizza $

Founded in 1905, this landmark coal-fired institution is arguably the

EATING YOUR WAY AROUND THE WORLD IN NYC

New York is the ultimate melting pot, and the city is home to many ethnic enclaves where old-world cultures reign and everyone benefits from amazing, authentic cuisines.

LITTLE ITALY

Italian immigrants began arriving in the city in the 1880s and formed a vibrant community here. Little Italy once occupied a significant stretch of downtown from Houston Street to Worth Street between Lafayette Street and Bowery. Now shrunken to the blocks surrounding Mulberry Street between Canal and Broome Streets (just north of Chinatown), between Soho and the Lower East Side, and flooded with busloads of tourists, it's hard to avoid crowds and mediocre food, but you can still find one of the city's best red-sauce joints here at **Forlini's** (page 125), just off Mulberry, which has been serving gargantuan plates of pasta and classic Italian American fare like chicken parm since 1943.

Alternate Adventure: To avoid the tourist crush, venture farther out to **Arthur Avenue** in the Bronx, the epicenter of New York's Italian American food culture today. Portions are large and attitudes more so at the restaurants that line this five-block stretch between East Fordham Road and Crescent Avenue. Excellent bakeries and markets also abound. For a hearty meal, check out **Emilia's** (2331 Arthur Ave., 718/367-5915; noon-9:30pm Sun.-Thurs., noon-10pm Fri., noon-10:30pm Sat.; $$), which serves heaping portions of homemade pastas daily, like lobster ravioli with baby shrimp and fettuccine with sautéed eggplant. For dessert, you'll find the freshest cannoli, filled to order, at **Madonia Bakery** (2348 Arthur Ave., 718/295-5573; 6am-7pm Mon.-Sat., 7am-6pm Sun.; $). The easiest way to get here is to take the Metro-North train to the Fordham stop and head a handful of blocks east on East Fordham Road (about an eight-minute walk), and then turn right onto Arthur Avenue.

CHINATOWN

During the 1870s, Chinese immigrants began settling in what would become New York's Chinatown, today bounded by Hester Street, Worth Street, East Broadway, Essex Street, and Lafayette Street, straddling Tribeca and the Lower East Side. The heart of the

country's first pizzeria. Pies are big but made with such ethereal delicacy that a couple of enthusiastic eaters could easily polish off a large. It's best to keep toppings to a minimum in order to taste the full effect of the San Marzano sauce. Long waits are common and reservations are taken during the week for large groups only, so it's best to go during off-hours—say, weekday afternoons around 3pm for a late lunch or very early dinner.

MAP 2: 32 Spring St., 212/941-7994, www. firstpizza.com; 11:30am-11pm Sun.-Thurs., 11:30am-midnight Fri.-Sat.

FRENCH
Balthazar $$$

It's tempting to order the classic steak frites at Balthazar, but the cheeseburger is just as good—and at half the price, a bargain for Keith McNally's famed bistro. Other menu highlights at this beloved mainstay include the often-imitated goat cheese and onion tart and the bouillabaisse, served only on Fridays. Service is warm, making it easy to linger in the cushy maroon leather booths that look out onto a wall of oversized mirrors. Those in a hurry or on a budget should stop next door at the **Balthazar Bakery** (212/965-1785, www.balthazarbakery.com;

neighborhood—the area around Mott, Doyers, and Pell Streets—has remained largely unchanged for many years, and it's an atmospheric place to wander amid busy stores bearing signage written in Chinese characters. As in its early days, many of the area's inhabitants are immigrants from the old country. A classic New York experience is eating dim sum in Chinatown, and a popular spot is **Nom Wah Tea Parlor** (page 133), which has excellent dumplings and friendly service to boot.

Alternate Adventure: While Chinatown is great, if you really want to feel like you're in another country, head to Main Street in downtown **Flushing,** Queens, now widely considered the place to go for Chinese food in New York. Take the 7 subway to its last stop, Flushing-Main Street, and you'll be immediately immersed in a world of bustling businesses, bubble tea shops, and cheap eats at almost every turn. For a finer-dining experience with authentic food, try **Guan Fu Sichuan** (3916 Prince St., 347/610-6999, http://guanfuny.com; noon-11pm daily; $$$), just a block from the subway. The restaurant received rave reviews from the *New York Times* and Michelin Guide, among others, for items like its intensely flavorful boiled fish with pickled vegetables and rare dishes like a fiery spicy cuttlefish salad.

CURRY HILL

A more recent development is this three-block cluster north of Gramercy Park around Lexington Avenue, between 26th and 28th Streets, which gets its name from the couple dozen Indian restaurants that began lining its blocks in the 1970s (its name is also a play on Murray Hill, the neighborhood just to its north). One of the best of these is the Punjabi restaurant **Dhaba** (page 151), which features a menu with over a hundred items, including a whole section for British curries.

Alternate Adventure: For Indian food farther off the beaten path, make your way to **Jackson Heights** in Queens. With 167 languages spoken, Jackson Heights is the most diverse neighborhood in the city, and this extends to its cuisine. There are particularly good Indian restaurants here, including the beloved **Jackson Diner** (3747 74th St., 718/672-1232, www.jacksondiner.com; 11am-10pm Sun.-Thurs., 11am-10:30pm Fri.-Sat.; $). Known for large portions of dishes like lamb korma, this casual eatery has drawn everyone from Hillary Clinton to Sylvester Stallone. A daily all-you-can-eat lunch buffet is only $12. The Roosevelt Avenue-Jackson Heights subway station (E, F, M, R, 7) lets you out on the area's main drag, Roosevelt Avenue, which stretches from approximately 74th-82nd Streets.

7:30am-7pm Mon.-Fri., 8am-7pm Sat.-Sun.) for amazing croissants.

MAP 2: 80 Spring St., 212/965-1414, www.balthazarny.com; 7:30am-midnight Mon.-Thurs., 7:30am-1am Fri., 8am-1am Sat., 8am-midnight Sun.

The Odeon $$

A Tribeca mainstay that once counted John Belushi and Jean-Michel Basquiat among its regulars, The Odeon serves comforting, well-executed dishes like moules-frites, local roasted chicken, and French onion soup. The trick is keep your order simple; *New York Times* critic Pete Wells singled out the spicy chicken dumplings with blue cheese as a particular misfire in his otherwise warm review.

The Odeon

127

MAP 2: 145 W. Broadway, 212/233-0507, www.theodeonrestaurant.com; 8am-11pm Mon.-Tues., 8am-midnight Wed.-Sat., 10am-11pm Sun.

Raoul's $$

Opened by a pair of brothers from Alsace in the 1970s, this holdover from Soho's bohemian days retains its cozy, retro vibe amid a hodgepodge of flea market-chic decor. Black-and-white-striped booths line the walls of the bistro, where staff serve up plates of escargot, veal sweetbreads with pork belly, and other savory dishes. Come during brunch and you can order the au poivre burger (also available in limited quantities at the bar daily), considered among the best in the city.

MAP 2: 180 Prince St., 212/966-3518, www.raouls.com; 5:30pm-midnight Mon.-Thurs., 5:30pm-1am Fri., 11:30am-3:30pm and 5:30pm-1am Sat., 11:30am-3:30pm and 5:30pm-midnight Sun.

KOREAN
✪ Jungsik $$$

What distinguishes New York from other great cities is how much of the world it encompasses within its cozy borders. This fine-dining contemporary Korean restaurant is a shining example. With only one other location in Seoul, Jungsik is the real deal. Named for its inventive chef-owner, Jungsik Yim, whose first name aptly translates to "formal dinner," this sleek Tribeca spot exudes elegance in its minimalist design and dishes that quietly wow. Choose from a seasonal set menu or the signature tasting. Both begin with five small bites served on mini pedestals, including a transcendent fried oyster covered in squid ink breadcrumbs and a foie gras mousse. The Tuna Kim Bap is

a decadent interpretation of a popular street-food dish (think sushi roll), while the branzino comes with a tiny jar of sesame oil that's meant to be nosed like a fine whiskey before it's drizzled on the delicately cooked fish.

MAP 2: 2 Harrison St., 212/219-0900, http://jungsik.com; 5:30pm-10:30pm Mon.-Thurs., 5pm-10:30pm Fri.-Sat., 5pm-9pm Sun.

SUSHI
Blue Ribbon Sushi $$$

The just-below-ground-level entrance of this mainstay sushi den beckons diners into a small waiting area. Reservations aren't accepted, so crowds tend to build up around the prime 8pm dining hour at this original location of the Bromberg Brothers' expansive restaurant group. A wide range of à la carte rolls and sushi are available, but put yourself in Toshi Ueki's nimble hands with the *omakase* (chef's choice), served on two epic boards full of sashimi, sushi, and rolls, with delicious bites like fluke fin in a mustard miso, bluefin belly, and horse mackerel.

MAP 2: 119 Sullivan St., 212/343-0404, www.blueribbonrestaurants.com; noon-2am daily

MEDITERRANEAN
Estela $$$

This hip spot occupies the former space of the famed Knitting Factory music club and counts former president Barack Obama among its diners. Chef Ignacio Mattos crafts sharable plates like cod with cherries and beef tartare with elderberries that disguise Mediterranean cuisine under a layer of invention. Reservations are hard to come by and it can get noisy, but exposed brick, stylish pendant lighting, and rich wood floors give a warm vibe. Try for around 5:30pm during the summer when the city's elite are out of town.

MAP 2: 43 E. Houston St., 212/219-7693, www.estelanyc.com; 5:30pm-11pm Mon.-Thurs., 11:30am-3pm and 5:30pm-11:30pm Fri.-Sat., 11:30am-3pm and 5:30pm-11pm Sun.

SEAFOOD
Aquagrill $$

Over two dozen types of oysters—which change daily—are just the beginning of the extensive offerings at this beloved seafood restaurant. You can order the sampler, which contains one of each, as well as choose from entrées ranging from a rich bouillabaisse to a truffle-crusted cod from Maine's Casco Bay to simple fish preparations. While the decor is a bit dated and bland, an elevated porch overlooking 6th Avenue provides a good perch for people-watching and is packed during the warmer months.

MAP 2: 210 Spring St., 212/274-0505, www.aquagrill.com; 11:30am-10pm Mon.-Thurs., 11:30am-11pm Fri., 11am-11pm Sat., 11am-10pm Sun.

Grand Banks $$

Operating during the warmer months on a historic wooden schooner at the end of a long pier in Tribeca, Grand Banks is an atmospheric mini-get-away right in the city. The sustainably sourced menu focuses on wild-caught seafood, and the scallops are a particular standout, served with a tomato and bacon compote. Fresh oysters are another must, particularly the Navy Points from Long Island's North Shore. Many people come just for the cocktails, which hew toward the sweeter side. The Fracas—made with a blend of mezcal and tequila, pineapple, lime, and nutmeg—is a perfect

Estela

Aquagrill

summer drink for people who don't usually like summer drinks. It gets crowded, so arrive when it opens at 3pm on Mondays and Tuesdays and before 3pm other days of the week—or be prepared to wait.

MAP 2: Pier 25 Hudson River Park, 212/660-6312, www.grandbanks.org; 3pm-midnight Mon.-Tues., noon-midnight Wed.-Fri., 11am-midnight Sat.-Sun. late Apr.-Oct.

Lure Fishbar $$

This subterranean restaurant looks like the inside of a chic yacht. Offerings on board include a wide range of crustaceans and mollusks, including scallops, shucked oysters, and lobster rolls. Numerous sushi options are also available, making this a nice spot to sate all seafood cravings in stylish digs. For a deal, come during happy hour (5pm-7pm Mon.-Fri.), featuring $2 oysters, $10 cocktails, and half-price basic sushi rolls.

MAP 2: 142 Mercer St., 212/431-7676, www.lurefishbar.com; 11:30am-11pm Tues.-Sat., 11:30am-10pm Sun.-Mon.

CONTEMPORARY AMERICAN

Narcissa $$

Narcissa takes its name from the matriarch dairy cow at the restaurant's dedicated organic farm in the Hudson Valley. A sleek dining room and private garden exude a fittingly elegant farmhouse vibe. Chef John Fraser has the ability to make root vegetables taste decadent—try the carrots Wellington or rotisserie-crisped beets—and there's also plenty here for dedicated carnivores. A Long Island duck breast with smoked rutabaga and a 24-ounce rib eye for two are just a couple of the meaty offerings.

MAP 3: 25 Cooper Sq., 212/228-3344, www.narcissarestaurant.com; 5:30pm-10pm Mon.-Thurs., 5:30pm-11pm Fri., 10am-3pm and 5:30pm-11pm Sat., 10am-3pm and 5:30pm-10pm Sun.

Clinton Street Baking Co. $

The crowds at this neighborhood comfort food favorite are most intense during brunch; the restaurant is known for serving some of the best pancakes in the city. But the pancakes are available all day—making this a more strategic stop when you're in the mood for breakfast-for-dinner. Another must on the menu is the chicken and waffles with honey-Tabasco sauce and homemade maple butter. On Monday and Tuesday nights, all bottles of wine are half price, and February is pancake month—one reason New York is pretty awesome in the winter. Every few days during the month, the eatery rolls out a new pancake flavor, like German chocolate with roasted pecans or blueberry crumb streusel.

MAP 3: 4 Clinton St., 646/602-6263, http://clintonstreetbaking.com; 8am-4pm and 5:30pm-11pm Mon.-Fri., 9am-4pm and 5:30pm-11pm Sat., 9am-5pm Sun.

PIZZA

Motorino $

Motorino's Neapolitan-style pizzas are only available by the whole pie, which are just slightly larger than a personal size; if you're hungry, order an entire pizza for yourself (the Brussels sprout with smoked pancetta is particularly great). The best time to go is during lunch on the weekdays; not only will you avoid the crowds, you can snag any pizza with a salad for $15.

MAP 3: 349 E. 12th St., 212/777-2644, www.motorinony.com; 11am-midnight Sun.-Thurs., 11am-1am Fri.-Sat.

Nicoletta $

There were certainly skeptics when renowned chef-restauranteur Michael White announced his plan to bring Midwestern pizza to New York, but most have been won over by these thick-crust pies. Sampling the pizza is also a great way to try White's cuisine at a fraction of the price of his other restaurants. While hardly deep-dish, the hearty pizzas are denser than any in the city; two or more people can split one and be stuffed. If you have room, the porcini arancini, brick-oven-baked meatballs, and rotating selection of pastas are all quite good. There's been discussion of Nicolleta moving to a delivery-only model and then transitioning to a new sit-down location in 2019.

MAP 3: 160 2nd Ave., 212/432-1600, http://nicolettapizza.com; 4pm-11pm Mon.-Thurs., noon-midnight Fri.-Sat., noon-11pm Sun.

JEWISH DELIS

✪ Katz's Deli $$

Even if Meg Ryan had never faked an orgasm here in an iconic scene in *When Harry Met Sally. . .*, Katz's Deli would be the stuff of foodie legend. The fluorescent-lit dining hall features walls covered with autographed photos of the scores of celebrities who have dined here. The pastrami sandwich, piled high on fresh rye bread, is one of the best things you can possibly eat. Don't load it down with toppings; the flavor is dynamic enough to stand on its own or with just a little mustard. It takes up to a month to cure the pastrami. Each order comes with a heaping bucket of pickles that can take the place of fries. Other solid dishes include knishes, latkes, and hot dogs. Service is cafeteria-style and can be brusque. Your order is written on a ticket that's handed out upon entry, and you pay at the end; don't lose your ticket, as doing so will incur a stiff $50 penalty.

MAP 3: 205 E. Houston St., 212/254-2246, www.katzsdelicatessen.com; 8am-10:45pm Mon.-Wed., 8am-2:45pm Thurs., 8am Fri.-10:45pm Sun. (24 hours Sat.)

Russ & Daughters Cafe $$

Legendary Jewish appetizing store Russ & Daughters (179 E. Houston St., 212/475-4880; 8am-6pm Mon.-Wed. and Fri.-Sun., 8am-7pm Thurs.) is known for its impossibly fresh lox and herring that's as smooth as sashimi. The Houston Street storefront has passed through four generations of ownership since it opened in 1914. To celebrate 100 years in business, current owners Niki Russ Federman and Josh Russ Tupper opened this café, rife with old-world elegance, a few blocks south. Sit at one of the plush booths and order platters of Gaspé Nova and pastrami-crusted salmon to share with a group; the bagels here make the perfect base. The pastrami-crusted salmon is also available on a pretzel roll with muenster cheese and dubbed "Pastrami Russ." In colder weather, soups are a must and it's hard to do better than the smoked whitefish chowder, a slightly spicy flavor bomb of comfort. Russ & Daughters also makes all its own breads, and the challah bread pudding is the perfect way to cap off a meal here.

MAP 3: 127 Orchard St., 212/475-4880, www.russanddaughters.com; 9am-10pm Mon.-Fri., 8am-10pm Sat.-Sun.

CHINESE

Mission Chinese $$

As its name implies, chef Danny Bowien's Mission Chinese began in San Francisco's Mission District, and the bold and whimsical flavors of his inventive Sichuan cuisine have garnered him a well-deserved cult following on both coasts. The restaurant's youthful vibe and music make it a great spot to gather with small groups of friends. The star dish is a mouth-on-fire mapo tofu made with aged beef that will redefine your definition of spicy. It pairs well with the salt cod fried rice.

MAP 3: 171 E. Broadway, 917/376-5660, www.missionchinesefood.com; 5:30pm-11pm Mon.-Fri., 11am-4pm and 5:30pm-11pm Sat.-Sun.

Baohaus $

Celebrity chef Eddie Huang—whose memoir was adapted into the sitcom

Fresh Off the Boat—makes some of the best pork buns in the city, certainly the best for a take-out spot that's not much wider than a hallway. The classic is the Chairman Bao with Berkshire pork belly, but equally good is the Birdhaus Bao with fried chicken that's been brined for 24 hours. Orders are churned out quickly to a backdrop of hip-hop.

MAP 3: 238 E. 14th St., 646/669-8889, www.baohausnyc.com; 11:30am-11:30pm Sun.-Thurs., 11:30am-3:30am Fri.-Sat.

Nom Wah Tea Parlor $

Chinatown's Nom Wah Tea Parlor has been operating in various incarnations since 1920. Originally a bakery known for its mooncakes (round pastries with a sweet red bean filling), it's now a go-to spot for dim sum. The made-to-order dumplings are succulent and can be ordered all day long. The atmosphere is fluorescent-lit and no-frills, but unlike at some other places in the neighborhood, service is warm. It has another chicer location, Nom Wah Nolita (10 Kenmare St., 606/478-8242; 11:30am-10pm Sun.-Thurs., 11:30am-11pm Fri.-Sat.), a handful of blocks north.

MAP 3: 13 Doyers St., 212/962-6047, http://nomwah.com; 10:30am-10pm Sun.-Wed., Thurs.-Sat. 10:30am-11pm

Nom Wah Tea Parlor

Vanessa's Dumpling House $

You'll usually find a line of college students at this Beijing-style dumpling house—your first indication the food here is delicious and ridiculously cheap. You can have a feast here for a few dollars. The pork and chive dumplings are best fried but any of the dumplings will satisfy. The green bubble tea is good as well, though the sesame pancake sandwiches leave something to be desired. Because of its proximity to the Bowery Ballroom, this is a good spot to stop for a quick dinner before a concert.

MAP 3: 118 Eldridge St., 212/625-8008, http://vanessas.com; 7:30pm-10:30pm Mon.-Sat., 7:30pm-10pm Sun.

JAPANESE
Momofuku Ko $$$

All of David Chang's Momofuku restaurants are worth a visit, but this spot featuring a tasting menu ($255, including service) is the crown jewel of his empire. The 13-course extravaganza blends Asian and American sensibilities with dishes like *uni* (sea urchin) with chickpea puree. The main dining room offers table seating for parties of 4-6, but sitting at the dimly lit 12-seat counter offers the best experience; you'll get to watch each of the courses being carefully constructed in the open kitchen. It's such an engaging experience one wouldn't feel awkward dining alone here. Seating in the main dining room is by reservation only (www.opentable.com)—make sure to book online exactly 30 days prior to your desired date.

An abbreviated tasting of five or six courses culled from the larger tasting menu is available at the bar for less than half the price, but you'll miss out on the kitchen theatrics, and the amount of food is closer to a large

Momofuku Ko

snack than a decadent meal. A few dishes like dry-aged strip loin and bass belly are available à la carte. Bar seating is on a walk-in basis. Arrive when the restaurant opens for the best chance at nabbing a seat.

MAP 3: 8 Extra Pl., 212/203-8095, http://ko.momofuku.com; 5:30pm-midnight Tues.-Thurs., 12:30pm-3:30pm and 5:30pm-midnight Fri.-Sat., 12:30pm-3:30pm Sun.

✪ Ippudo $

The city is now home to a lot of high-end ramen spots; many are good but none come close to the perfection of Ippudo. Chef-owner Shigemi Kawahara built up numerous locations in his native Japan before opening here. His broth is more complex, noodles utterly slurpable, and the pork belly falls apart in your mouth. Hence the long lines at all locations (two outposts are in Midtown), almost always lasting several hours. This East Village location is his original New York

venue and offers the benefit of many nearby bars at which to while away the time after you've put your name and number on the waiting list. Otherwise go after 10pm to minimize the wait.

MAP 3: 65 4th Ave., 212/388-0088, www.ippudony.com; 11am-3:30pm and 5pm-11:30pm Mon.-Thurs., 11am-3:30pm and 5pm-12:30am Fri., 11am-11:30pm Sat., 11am-10:30pm Sun.

Momofuku Noodle Bar $

Opened in 2004, Momofuku Noodle Bar was David Chang's first restaurant—and thus a food empire was born. In the early years, it was possible to walk into the no-reservations eatery and sidle up to a stool surrounding the open kitchen without a wait to enjoy a transcendent bowl of ramen. Those days are long gone, so the best plan of action is to head there a couple of hours before you're hungry, put your name and cell number on the list, and wait in one of the East Village's many watering holes.

MAP 3: 171 1st Ave., 212/777-7773; noon-4:30pm and 5:30pm-11pm Mon.-Thurs., noon-4:30pm and 5:30pm-1am Fri., noon-4pm and 5:30pm-1am Sat., noon-4pm and 5:30pm-11pm Sun.

BRITISH
The Fat Radish $$

The Fat Radish gleefully dispels negative conceptions of British cuisine. With a locavore sensibility that informs its seasonally changing menu, this rustic-chic spot is about simple flavors turned decadent. Radishes served with oil and herbs whet the palate for dishes like a monkfish curry, roasted mushrooms in juniper butter, or a whole charred eggplant cooked in lemon. Save room for the house-made doughnuts.

MAP 3: 17 Orchard St., 212/300-4053, www.thefatradishnyc.com; 5:30pm-midnight Mon.-Fri., 11am-3:30pm and 5:30pm-midnight Sat., 11am-3:30pm and 5:30pm-10pm Sun.

AUSTRIAN
Edi and the Wolf $$

While the name of this cozy Austrian eatery sounds like it was inspired by a fairytale, it's actually a mashup of the executive chefs' names: Eduard "Edi" Frauneder and Wolfgang "the Wolf" Ban. A dinner here might start with seared octopus in chimichurri sauce followed by heritage pig Wiener schnitzel and an apple strudel with lemon yogurt. Brunch is worthwhile as well; come for the duck egg sandwich. Reclaimed barnwood lines the ceiling, and antiques like Victorian military boots are repurposed as vases. A rope from an old church has been

Ippudo

MORE MOMOFUKU!

It's hard to miss David Chang's presence in the New York food scene given his celebrated brand, **Momofuku** (http://momofuku.com). From gourmet renditions of fast-food-style fried chicken sandwiches to elaborate tasting menus, he offers meals to fit nearly every craving and budget.

Chang's opening salvo was **Momofuku Noodle Bar** (page 134), arguably introducing gourmet ramen (that is, beyond the instant variety) to the American mainstream. Next was the nearby **Ssäm Bar** (207 2nd Ave., 212/254-3500; 11:30am-3pm and 5:30pm-11:30pm Mon.-Thurs., 11:30am-3pm and 5pm-12:30am Fri.-Sat., 11:30am-3pm and 5:30pm-11:30pm Sun.; $$), which helped contain some of the Noodle Bar's overflow while widening the scope of Chang's culinary ambitions, expanding upon popular large-format fried chicken

Momofuku Noodle Bar

meals from the Noodle Bar to include a whole rotisserie duck and a Flintstonian 50-day dry-aged rib eye steak feeding up to six people. These meals must be booked in advance online and are intended for groups of 3-10. Each feast has its own person minimum/limit, so check the website to find the one that best fits your group.

At **Momofuku Ko** (page 133), Chang explores the world of tasting menus, eliminating the formality that usually accompanies such experiences. While the food is certainly dressed up, you don't have to be, and servers are just as happy to recommend a craft beer as a pricey bottle of wine to accompany your meal.

Chang's entry into Italian food came by way of **Momofuku Nishi** (232 8th Ave., 646/518-1919; noon-3pm and 5:30pm-11pm daily; $$), which takes reservations online through OpenTable—and they're not hard to get (yet).

More casual options include **Momofuku Fuku** (two locations in Lower Manhattan; $), which churns out crave-worthy spicy chicken sandwiches along with wings, fingers, and salads. Wash it down with a strawberry lemonade slushie or booze it up with some sake. It also has outposts at Madison Square Garden and Citi Field, open during games and events. **Momofuku Milk Bar** (various NYC locations; $), the brainchild of pastry chef Christina Tosi, a former Momofuku employee who founded Milk Bar with seed funding from Chang, has multiple locations across Manhattan and Brooklyn. These holes-in-the-wall are the most readily accessible of the company's venues, offering artful and intensely sweet concoctions like the butter-laden Crack Pie, which is as addictive as it sounds.

Momofuku Bang Bar (10 Columbus Circle, 3rd fl., http://bangbar.xyz; 8am-sold out Mon.-Sat.; $, cashless) is Chang's latest addition, opened in 2018. The takeout spot serves Korean flatbread wraps akin to gyros with tasty fillings like spit-fired mortadella, Zabar's smoked salmon, or spicy pork. Come early as it tends to sell out by early afternoon.

twisted and affixed with lights to create a chandelier.

MAP 3: 102 Ave. C, 212/598-1040, www.ediandthewolf.com; 5pm-10pm Mon.-Wed., 5pm-11pm Thurs.-Fri., 11:30am-11pm Sat., 11:30am-10pm Sun.

GERMAN
Zum Schneider $$

Plenty of German beer gardens can be found in Manhattan, but this spot feels the most authentic, with its well-worn wood walls and long tables that have weathered intense bouts of drinking. Liter steins combined with fresh potato salads, giant warm pretzels, and well-seasoned sausages makes it easy to imagine you're on the other side of the Atlantic.

MAP 3: 107 Ave. C, 212/598-1098, http://nyc.zumschneider.com; 5pm-2am Mon.-Thurs., 4pm-4am Fri., 1pm-4am Sat., 1pm-midnight Sun.

UKRAINIAN
Veselka $

Since 1954, this East Village mainstay has been serving heaping plates of Ukrainian comfort food like beef Stroganoff. The handmade pierogi are also on point, made daily in a variety of flavors including sweet potato and short rib. You also can't go wrong with the potato pancakes or all-day breakfast. Enjoy the latter after a long night of barhopping; the diner is open 24 hours a day

MAP 3: 144 2nd Ave., 212/228-9682, www.veselka.com; 24 hours daily

Veselka

MEXICAN
The Black Ant $$

The Black Ant is seductively styled, a restaurant with the trappings of an inviting lounge. Its sleek environs will lull you outside your comfort zone to try insect-dusted dishes. A good starting point is the yucca-manchego grasshopper croquettes with avocado; the little creatures sit crispy atop each fried orb and go down with a pleasing crunch. Excellent non-bug options, like rabbit enchiladas, abound as well. A sophisticated cocktail menu offers plenty of choices. Try the namesake negroni made with a chili-infused Campari, or the poblano old-fashioned made with 23-year-old Ron Zacapa rum.

MAP 3: 60 2nd Ave., 212/598-0300, www.theblackantnyc.com; 4pm-midnight Mon.-Wed., 4pm-1am Thurs.-Fri., 11:30am-1am Sat., 11:30am-midnight Sun.

La Palapa $$

This cantina on St. Mark's Place is known for its Mexico City-style tacos and quesadillas. You can pick from eight fillings, including a deeply satisfying chargrilled steak and spicy homemade chorizo. One is enough for a light meal, or you can share several for a feast. On Sundays, pitchers of sangria (both red and white) are just $10; they're on the watered-down side but have smooth, balanced flavors that go down easy. An atmospheric dining room encourages lingering.

MAP 3: 77 St. Mark's Pl., 212/777-2537, http://lapalapa.com; noon-midnight Mon.-Fri., 11am-midnight Sat.-Sun.

SEAFOOD
Zadie's Oyster Room $

There may be only one way to properly shuck an oyster, but there are many ways to eat them. Marco Canora, whose Tuscan restaurant Hearth draws big crowds down the block, explores the versatility of this popular mollusk in a rustic and intimate space that's lesser known but holds its own. The oysters are, of course, impeccably fresh and a delight to eat on their own; one variety is offered each night for $1.50 each. For heartier fare try the oysters Kilpatrick, baked with prosciutto, brown butter, and cured egg yolk. Pan-roasted oysters with squash are equally warming and pair well with a selection of craft beers, ciders, and wines by the glass. The delectable mollusks are also served pickled and smoked.

MAP 3: 413 E. 12th St., 646/602-1300, www.zadiesoysterroom.com; 5pm-11pm Mon.-Sat.

VEGETARIAN
✪ Dirt Candy $$$

Vegetables are rarely described as guilty pleasures, but Dirt Candy strives to change this. Its tasting-menu-only dinner, served in the restaurant's expansive, elegant space, includes dishes like jalapeno hush puppies with maple butter and a Korean fried broccoli that chef Amanda Cohen describes as crack. Many dishes induce giddy highs, like the portobello mousse with sautéed Asian pears, cherries, and truffle toast; it's basically foie gras for

Dirt Candy

vegetarians. À la carte dining is available during brunch and at the bar on a walk-in basis. Otherwise, reservations are highly recommended.

MAP 3: 86 Allen St., 212/228-7732, www. dirtcandynyc; 5:30pm-11pm Tues.-Fri., 11am-3pm and 5:30pm-11pm Sat., 11am-3pm Sun.

Superiority Burger $

Burger devotees often look at veggie burgers with sad bewilderment, but Superiority Burger might change that. This fast-food vegetarian spot churns out a seriously tasty burger with muenster cheese that mimics the consistency of its meaty rivals. You won't be fooled into thinking it's beef, but you'll find a worthy new flavor that satisfies a similar craving.

MAP 3: 430 E. 9th St., 212/256-1192, www. superiorityburger.com; 11:30am-10pm Wed.-Mon.

HOT DOGS
Crif Dogs $

This tiny hole-in-the-wall has a devoted following for its endless reimaginations of the simple hot dog. For extra-decadent deliciousness, get one wrapped in bacon. Or order the aptly named Good Morning, which adds melted cheese and a fried egg. Pineapple, cream cheese, and avocado are among the topping options. Lines are longest after 8pm on weekends, since these caloric bombs satisfy post-drinking cravings, but the hot dogs hold up with sober stomachs as well.

MAP 3: 113 St. Marks Pl., 212/614-2728, www.crifdogs.com; noon-2am Sun.-Thurs., noon-4am Fri.-Sat.

SWEETS
Doughnut Plant $

Mark Israel began toying with his grandfather's doughnut recipe in 1994 and opened up shop in a tenement building soon after. For the last two decades he's been leading the pack of doughnut innovation in the city, creating the world's first crème brûlée doughnuts. Other creations include tres leches, carrot cake, and peanut butter and blackberry jam-filled concoctions. These are intensely satisfying fried sugar bombs, though if you need help justifying the indulgence it might be good to know ingredients are seasonally sourced and there's no trans fat or artificial flavoring. Doughnut Planet has a handful of locations around the city now, but this is the original. Come in the morning to avoid sellouts of favorites.

MAP 3: 379 Grand St., 212/505-3700, ext.379, http://doughnutplant.com; 6:30pm-8pm Sun.-Thurs., 6:30am-9pm Fri.-Sat.

The Village and the Meatpacking District   Map 4

CONTEMPORARY AMERICAN

Blue Hill $$$

Local farming advocate and chef Dan Barber—who served on President Obama's fitness, sports, and nutrition council—uses his restaurants as a platform for his beliefs as well as an outlet for his creativity; it's not uncommon to see Brussels sprouts fashioned as a mini tree. To get the full experience, you need to venture up to his farm in Tarrytown just north of the city, but for those unable to make the trip, this provides a good taste of Barber's talents.

MAP 4: 75 Washington Pl., 212/539-1776, www.bluehillfarm.com; 5pm-11pm Mon.-Sat., 5pm-10pm Sun.

Bubby's $$

Curated rustic charm abounds at this locally sourced Southern comfort food brasserie. Wooden fans and exposed air ducts run across the ceiling above groups of neighborhood regulars and tourists alike devouring homemade toaster pastries, biscuits, grits, and other simple savory fare. Prices are high for this kind of casual fare, but so is the quality. The original location is in Tribeca but this second location is conveniently located next to the southern entrance of The High Line.

MAP 4: 73 Gansevoort St., 212/206-6200, www.bubbys.com; 8am-10pm Sun.-Thurs., 8am-11pm Fri.-Sat.

Dante NYC $$

Once a hangout for scrappy intellectual bohemians along with celebrities like Al Pacino, Jerry Seinfeld, and Whoopi Goldberg, this café has been reborn as an upscale small-plates boîte. You can munch late into the night on plates of octopus, beef tartare, and burrata, and wash them down with concoctions from the excellent negroni menu, which are specially priced at $10 from 3pm to 6pm.

MAP 4: 79-81 MacDougal St., 212/982-5275, www.dante-nyc.com; 10am-1am Sun.-Wed., 10am-2am Thurs.-Sat.

Minetta Tavern

STEAK HOUSES
✪ Minetta Tavern $$$

Now a part of Balthazar owner Keith McNally's restaurant group, this old-school restaurant with red banquettes and white tablecloths dates to the Prohibition era, when it was frequented by Ernest Hemingway and E. E. Cummings. Today the main draw is its Black Label burger, which is arguably the city's best. Made with dry-aged beef and featuring the same rib eye that's on the menu at triple the price, the delicious dish is a bargain.

MAP 4: 113 MacDougal St., 212/475-3850, www.minettatavernny.com; 5:30pm-midnight Mon.-Tues., noon-3pm and 5:30-midnight Wed., noon-3pm and 5:30pm-1am Thurs.-Fri., 11am-3pm and 5:30pm-1am Sat., 11am-3pm and 5:30pm-midnight Sun.

ITALIAN
Via Carota $$$

It can get noisy in this large, rustic "gastroteca." Via Carota doesn't take reservations and is usually crowded, but its throngs of devoted fans hardly notice. Inventive crostini are a good place to start, and pastas like wild boar ragù are traditionally made with subtle, well-rounded flavors. The menu as a whole avoids ostentatious flourishes, and there's special attention given to vegetables, like fennel bulbs with orange zest.

MAP 4: 51 Grove St., 212/255-1962, www.viacarota.com; 11am-midnight Sun.-Wed., 11am-1am Thurs.-Sat.

Frankies 570 Spuntino $$

Spuntino means "informal meal," but here refers more to the friendly service and warm vibe: Frankies takes its food very seriously. The menu changes seasonally and features an array of homemade pastas cooked in sauces like porcini ragù and browned sage butter. The wine list is on the pricey side compared to the food but features a well-curated selection of Italian varietals.

MAP 4: 570 Hudson St., 212/924-0818, http://frankies570.com; 11am-11pm Sun.-Thurs., 11am-midnight Fri.-Sat.

PIZZA

Arturo's $

Red walls and live jazz enhance the old-time New York feel at this coal-oven pizzeria. With generously sized pies, it's easy to walk away full, and the line never gets as intense as at Lombardi's. Just be warned: Like most sit-down pizza spots, Arturo's only serves whole pies, which two people would struggle to finish.

MAP 4: 106 W. Houston St., 212/677-3820, www.arturoscoaloven.com; 4pm-1am Mon.-Fri., 2pm-midnight Sat.-Sun.

Bleecker Street Pizza $

This classic slice joint is perfect for grab-and-go eating just about any time of day. Its footprint is just a tiny sliver on a busy corner of 7th Avenue South, but it serves a serious volume of pizza, ensuring you'll get a fresh slice with a perfect cheese-to-sauce ratio. Order "not too hot" to be able to devour immediately.

MAP 4: 69 7th Ave. S., 212/924-4466, www.bleeckerstreetpizza.com; 11am-2am Sun.-Wed., 11am-3am Thurs., 11am-5am Fri.-Sat.

Joe's Pizza $

Joe's has been popping up on best-of lists for decades for good reason: It consistently delivers a classic New York-style slice that seamlessly blends sauce and cheese into a single irresistible flavor. Despite its popularity, you won't have to endure the lines common at some of the city's other famed spots, especially on weekdays.

MAP 4: 7 Carmine St., 347/312-4955, www.joespizzanyc.com; 10am-4am Sun.-Thurs., 10am-5am Fri.-Sat.

John's of Bleecker Street $

A whole-pie-only establishment, John's is one of New York's seminal pizzerias and has been around since 1929. Sit at one of the beat-up wooden benches and order a plain or pepperoni pizza to experience the full coal-fired brick-oven taste. Beginner's tip: Keep it simple. Too many toppings overwhelm the flavor of these more classically authentic pies. Fountain soda is available by the pitcher, and prices average out to just slightly higher than a regular slice joint. Note that John's is cash only.

MAP 4: 278 Bleecker St., 212/243-1680, www.johnsbrickovenpizza.com; 11:30am-11:30pm Mon.-Thurs., 11:30am-12:30am Fri.-Sat., noon-11:30pm Sun.

OTTO $

Celebrity chef Joe Bastianich's pizzeria (cofounder Mario Batali is in the process of divesting from the restaurant) delivers hole-in-the-wall pricing with fine-dining ambience. Push past the brass revolving door to reveal a marble-covered bar where quartinos of wine and shareable plates can be consumed with gusto. Grab a table to sample the pastas and, of course, the finely crafted Neapolitan pizzas. It often gets quite noisy in here, but that's just because everyone's having such a great time.

MAP 4: 1 5th Ave., 212/995-9559, http://ny.ottopizzeria.com; 11:30am-midnight daily

Two Boots $

Opened by a pair of indie filmmakers who love Cajun food, Two Boots is the place to go for a spicy, inventive casual slice. Its concoctions are named for pop-culture characters like *Reservoir Dogs'* Mr. Pink (Creole chicken), *The Big Lebowski*'s Dude (Cajun bacon cheeseburger pie), and Andy Kaufman's Tony Clifton (mushrooms, onions, and red pepper pesto). Sit in a red-leather booth to soak in the quirky, retro atmosphere. MAP 4: 201 W. 11th St., 212/633-9096, www.twoboots.com; 11am-midnight Sun.-Wed., 11am-1am Thurs., 11am-2am Fri.-Sat.

FRENCH
Boucherie $$$
An expansive bistro ideal for walk-ins looking for hearty French fare with upscale flair, Boucherie makes a mean aged steak, in a variety of cuts, along with creamy homemade pastas and a tasty escargot with some of the plumpest snails around. Service can be a little absentminded, but the old-school vibe with exposed rafters provides a pleasant atmosphere for lingering with a finely crafted cocktail, like the restaurant's twist on a sidecar made with absinthe.
MAP 4: 99 7th Ave. S., 212/837-1616, http://boucherie.nyc; 11am-1am Sun.-Thurs., 11am-2am Fri.-Sat.

Buvette $$
A cute all-day café, Buvette serves authentic French fare (it has an outpost in Paris) to a steady stream of devoted locals. Antiques and flea market finds fill the tiny space, creating a welcoming atmosphere. The café doesn't take reservations, so it's best to visit during off-hours. Come after 11pm for its take on buttery croques.
MAP 4: 42 Grove St., 646/756-4145, www.ilovebuvette.com; 7am-2am Mon.-Fri., 8am-2am Sat.-Sun.

Dominique Bistro $$
This cozy, casually elegant bistro on a quiet leafy corner is a slice of the Marais in New York. Homemade linguine with peekytoe crab is great as an entrée, or you can split it—along with an order of mussels—with a friend. You also can't go wrong with the bistro burger topped with caramelized onions and aged gruyère. Ample, comfy barstools make it a good option for solo diners.
MAP 4: 14 Christopher St., 646/756-4145, http://dominiquebistro.nyc; 8am-midnight Sun.-Thurs., 8am-1am Fri.-Sat.

CHINESE
RedFarm $$
RedFarm serves Greenmarket-sourced Chinese fare. Among its many draws are an extensive array of soup dumplings made with decadent ingredients like black truffle as well as egg rolls made with Katz's pastrami. Exposed wood beams give the restaurant an inviting ambience. Atmosphere can also be had in the basement bar, Decoy, which feels less like a watering hole and more like an extension of the elegant upstairs dining room. The bar has its own menu, and Peking duck, served whole, is the thing to get here. It's offered à la carte subject to availability, but make a reservation for the prix fixe (from $79.95 pp) built around the dish for a sure thing.
MAP 4: 529 Hudson St., 212/792-9700, www.redfarmnyc.com; 5pm-11:45pm Mon.-Fri., 11am-2:30pm and 5pm-11:45pm Sat., 11am-2:30pm and 5pm-11pm Sun.

JAPANESE
Bar Moga $$
Although technically a bar, this corner spot on the border of the Village and Soho feels like your go-to neighborhood joint with its row of cozy tables and inventive but comforting plates of food. Its Japanese interpretations of American classics are well executed, from cocktails made with the earthy spirit *shochu* to novelty entrées like the

RedFarm

hamburger steak and vegetable ramen topped with parmesan cheese.
MAP 4: 128 W. Houston St., 929/399-5853, www.barmoga.com; 5pm-1am Sun.-Thurs., 5pm-2am Fri.-Sat.

SUSHI
Sushi Nakazawa $$$
You might recognize Daisuke Nakazawa, the namesake chef at this elegant cozy spot, as the apprentice in the documentary *Jiro Dreams of Sushi*. Opt to sit at the bar and he will personally serve you each course of the *omakase*, a tasting menu and your only option. Prices are steep and reservations are hard to come by, but a lucky few are rewarded with a transcendent experience of culinary mastery. Your best chances for scoring a reservation are in the dining room around 10pm; check OpenTable (www.opentable.com) for availability.
MAP 4: 23 Commerce St., 212/924-2212, www.sushinakazawa.com; 5pm-10:15pm daily

BRITISH
A Salt and Battery $
This tiny storefront hawks the most authentic fish-and-chips this side of the Atlantic. Choose between sole, haddock, cod, and whiting in a four- or eight-ounce portion. Chips are extra but easy to split with a friend. Save room for a deep-fried Mars bar, which hits just the right combination of fat and sugar. Head west a few blocks to the Hudson River for a scenic view with your meal.
MAP 4: 112 Greenwich Ave., 212/691-2713, www.asaltandbattery.com; 11:30am-10:30pm Mon.-Sat., 11:30am-10pm Sun.

MIDDLE EASTERN
Moustache $
For Middle Eastern comfort food, head to Moustache. Inspired by Lebanese bakeries, the cash-only eatery serves "pitzas"—pita bread baked in an oven and served with toppings ranging from tomato and fresh mozzarella to seafood and lamb. You can

also order traditional fare like hummus, baba ghanoush, and falafel to eat at the copper-topped tables, or nearby in Washington Square Park.

MAP 4: 90 Bedford St., 212/229-2220, www.moustachepitza.com; noon-midnight daily

SEAFOOD
Mermaid Oyster Bar $$

You could drop a considerable amount for dinner at this casually chic seafood spot—or come for its daily happy hour (starting at 5pm daily but all night on Mondays). Oysters are $1.25 and some of the freshest in town; at that price, you could make a meal out of them. Wash them down with a $5 craft beer or shell out a couple more bucks for a glass of wine or specialty cocktail.

MAP 4: 79 MacDougal St., 212/260-0100, www.themermaidnyc.com; 5pm-10pm Mon., 5pm-10:30pm Tues.-Sat., 4pm-10pm Sun.

Pearl Oyster Bar $$

Named for chef-owner Rebecca Charles's opera-singing grandmother, Pearl Oyster Bar was the first to bring a proper lobster roll (overstuffed and served with shoestring fries) to Manhattan. Other menu musts are the fried oysters and New England clam chowder with smoked bacon. The seaside-chic decor is likely to transport you to coastal Maine, where Charles spent her summers growing up. While the restaurant doesn't take reservations, if you arrive when it opens you shouldn't have to wait too long.

MAP 4: 18 Cornelia St., 212/691-8211, www.pearloysterbar.com; noon-2:30pm and 6pm-11pm Mon.-Sat.

BARBECUE
Pig Bleecker $$

This inventive restaurant proves that massive servings of meat don't have to be boring, and barbecue doesn't have to be casual. Some of the many highlights include pecan-candied bacon, barbecue chicken lollipops, and brisket ravioli. An impressive cocktail list and sleek decor add to the decadent experience.

MAP 4: 155 Bleecker St., 646/756-5115, www.pigbleeckernyc.com; noon-2:30pm and 5:30pm-11pm Mon.-Fri., 11am-3pm and 5:30pm-11pm Sat., 11:30am-3pm and 5:30pm-10pm Sun.

Mighty Quinn's Barbeque

Mighty Quinn's Barbeque $

Southern transplants complain there's no worthy barbecue above the Mason-Dixon Line, but Mighty Quinn's makes a solid case with ridiculously tender pulled pork slathered in a delicious sauce that doesn't overwhelm the flavor of the meat. While this fast-casual spot has numerous locations, this is the most stylish, with exposed brick walls, as well as the only one that accepts reservations.

MAP 4: 75 Greenwich Ave., 646/524-7889, www.mightyquinnsbbq.com; 11:30am-10:30pm Sun.-Thurs., 11:30am-11pm Fri.-Sat.

COFFEE SHOPS AND CAFÉS

Caffe Reggio $

With tiny bistro seats and Renaissance paintings, Caffe Reggio was already quirkily dated when Bob Dylan played here in the 60s, and not much has changed since—except the café no longer features live music. But this trapped-in-time quality is what makes the café such an appealing spot: It still conjures some of the heady atmosphere of those bygone days. Grab a cappuccino and sit with a book for the full experience, just like Jack Kerouac and his fellow beat generation writers did while licking their hangover wounds in the Village.

MAP 4: 119 MacDougal St., 212/475-9557, www.caffereggio.com; 9am-3am Sun.-Thurs., 9am-4:30am Fri.-Sat.

Caffe Vivaldi $

Long a spot for New York creatives famous and not, Caffe Vivaldi has even appeared in a few Woody Allen movies, including *Bullets Over Broadway*. This classic cash-only Village coffee shop, opened by a Pakistani impresario with old-world European flair, perfectly encapsulates the diversity that is the lifeblood of the city. Most nights the café features live music acts ranging from jazz to classical to folk.

MAP 4: 32 Jones St., 212/691-7538, http://caffevivaldi.com; 6pm-11:30pm Sun.-Thurs., 5pm-midnight Fri., 6pm-midnight Sat.

SWEETS

Magnolia Bakery $

Made famous by the *Sex and the City* ladies and responsible for kicking off the artisanal cupcake craze in the country, the original location of this popular bakery is unsurprisingly flooded with long lines. A wide range of specialty cupcakes, including chocolate truffle, and seasonal specials—like "back-to-school" cupcakes in the fall topped with edible apples and books—are the highlights of the extensive offerings. While the hype is earned—the delectable treats feature fluffy cake and often a buttercream frosting—if it's just the sugar fix you're after, head to one of the Magnolia's other, less scene-y outposts (including Rockefeller Center, Grand Central Terminal, and the Upper West Side).

MAP 4: 401 Bleecker St., 212/462-2572, www.magnoliabakery.com; 9:30am-11pm Mon.-Thurs., 9:30am-midnight Fri.-Sat.

Mah-Ze-Dahr $

Backed by celebrity chef Tom Colicchio, this bakery offers a sleek atmosphere in which to enjoy a pastry. Popular items like the brioche doughnut sell out early in the day, but founder and head chef Umber Ahmad always has some delicious confection on hand, like a slice of lemon cheesecake with chocolate crust or an unusually complex chocolate chip cookie made with two different kinds of flour.

MAP 4: 28 Greenwich Ave., 212/498-9810, http://mahzedahrbakery.com; 7am-6pm Mon.-Fri., 8am-5pm Sat.-Sun.

Chelsea and Union Square

Map 5

CONTEMPORARY AMERICAN

✪ Eleven Madison Park $$$

Widely considered one of the best restaurants in the world, Eleven Madison Park has few peers. It nabbed the number one spot on the World's 50 Best Restaurants list in 2017. Swiss-born chef-owner Daniel Humm bought it from his former boss, Danny Meyer, in 2011 and has since been gleefully expanding the definition of contemporary American cuisine, from dry-aged veal to smoked-sturgeon cheesecake. The restaurant's art deco environs feature soaring ceilings that are suitably dramatic to accompany the menu offerings, which consist of a constantly changing 8-10-course meal for $335 per person, service included. A 5-course option is available in the bar/lounge for $175 and offers a similar experience. Both are very popular and require reservations. For your best bet, book on the first of the month at 9am when the restaurant releases tables for the following month.

MAP 5: 11 Madison Ave., 212/889-0905, www.elevenmadisonpark.com; 5:30pm-10pm Mon.-Wed., 5:30pm-10:30pm Thurs., noon-1pm and 5:30pm-10:30pm Fri.-Sun.

Gramercy Tavern $$$

Tom Colicchio has long since departed this pioneering seasonal

Eleven Madison Park

fine-dining spot, but it remains one of the best places to have an unfussy yet world-class meal, now in the hands of Michael Anthony; both chefs have won James Beard Awards for the restaurant. The back room serves a set menu for dinner but the tavern is à la carte at all times. The all-domestic draft beer list features a superb rotating array from breweries like Hill Farmstead, Other Half, and Evil Twin. Pair them with a plate of Wagyu meatloaf for a decadent wallop of comfort.
MAP 5: 42 E. 20th St., 212/477-0777, www.gramercytavern.com; 11:30am-11pm Sun.-Thurs., 11:30am-midnight Fri.-Sat.

Park Avenue $$$

There's always been a theatrical aspect in the best of fine dining, but Park Avenue takes this tradition further by fully transforming the restaurant for each season. While this might sound gimmicky, the results are a pure aesthetic thrill. Rich orange hues dominate in autumn, with an expected dish like pumpkin ravioli flipped on its head by the addition of pickled cranberries. Performance artist Marina Abramović turned dessert into an event here one winter in a collaboration on a baked Alaska—it was served with a pair of earphones through which her recorded voice purred instructions on how to eat it.
MAP 5: 360 Park Ave. S., 212/951-7111, http://parkavenyc.com; 11:30am-10pm Mon.-Thurs., 11:30pm-11pm Fri., 11am-11pm Sat., 11am-9pm Sun.

Craft $$

Tom Colicchio's signature restaurant is the most complete expression of his understated approach to fine dining: Choose ingredients well and cook them with just enough flair and seasoning to make them shine—perhaps fitting for a man whose favorite appliance at home is the Crock-Pot. Lunch is a particularly good deal at $29 for two courses or $36 for three. Some items you might find on the menu include beef tartare with smoked eggs, a pork belly BLT, and butternut squash gnocchi.
MAP 5: 43 E. 19th St., 212/780-0880, www.craftrestaurant.com; noon-2:30pm and 5:30pm-10pm Mon.-Thurs., noon-2:30pm and 5:30pm-11pm Fri., 5:30pm-11pm Sat., 5:30pm-9:30pm Sun.

Union Square Cafe $$

Danny Meyer's first restaurant has been around since 1985 and is considered one of the pioneers of contemporary American cuisine. Dry-aged steak for two, homemade pastas, and burrata are a few of the draws. It moved into more spacious digs in 2016 following a rent hike and reopened to much fanfare, managing to retain its literati regulars, cherrywood floors, and even salvaged wood from the bar at its former location a few blocks away. If prices seem a bit high, it's because service is included.
MAP 5: 101 E. 19th St., 212/243-4020, www.unionsquarecafe.com; 11:45am-10pm Mon.-Fri., 11am-10pm Sat.-Sun.

Upland $$

Upland exudes casual chic in spades, its decor designed to put you instantly at ease—think oversized leather booths below towering shelves of illuminated wine bottles. Named for the California town where he first developed his love for cooking, chef Justin Smillie offers options perfect for days when you can't decide if you're feeling adventurous or craving comfort, with choices ranging from crispy duck wings with *yuzu kosho* (a Japanese seasoning incorporating chili, citrus, and

NEW YORK'S CELEBRITY CHEFS

New York is ground zero for celebrity chefs. Here's who they are and how to get to know their work.

- **Lidia Bastianich** lives in the Queens suburb of Douglaston, the setting for her early PBS cooking shows. Her restaurants range from formal **Del Posto** (page 149) to the more casual **Becco** (page 154), which features the best all-you-can-eat pasta deal in the city.

- **Daniel Boulud** has such prominence in the city that he's been rendered in a mosaic—wearing a blazer and holding a bag of groceries—by artist-friend Vik Muniz in the 2nd Avenue subway station at 72nd Street. But to get to his namesake flagship restaurant, **Daniel** (page 161), or **Bar Boulud** (page 162), you're better off taking the Q or F train to 63rd Street on the Upper East Side. Or, if you're looking for a pre-Broadway show dinner, try his **db Bistro Moderne** (page 155).

- **David Chang** worked in restaurants by celebrated chefs Tom Colicchio and Daniel Boulud before growing weary of the fine-dining scene and making his mark with a casual ramen counter spot in the East Village, **Momofuku Noodle Bar** (page 134), which has spawned an empire. **Momofuku Ko** (page 133), also in the East Village, is one of the finest spots in the city to dine, but jeans and T-shirts are still welcome. From gourmet renditions of fast-food-style fried chicken sandwiches to elaborate tasting menus, he offers meals to fit nearly every craving and budget (page 136).

- **Amanda Cohen** has transformed how New Yorkers think of vegetables, churning out craveable, meticulously constructed dishes at her LES herbivore den **Dirt Candy** (page 138).

- **Tom Colicchio** of *Top Chef* fame launched his career—together with fellow celebrity chef Danny Meyer—with Gramercy Tavern, where they pioneered locally driven menus. **Craft** (page 147), just a block away, is his signature restaurant and a good place to start to discover his culinary talents. His latest is **Temple Court** (page 122), which serves both an à la carte and a tasting menu.

- **Wylie Dufresne** once headed one of New York City's most innovative restaurants, WD-50, but since its closing now spends his time crafting mind-blowing doughnuts at his namesake coffee shop in Williamsburg, **Du's Donuts and Coffee** (page 176).

- **Danny Meyer** has had an impact that's hard to overstate. His restaurants have won 28 James Beard Awards, and he's mastered just about every level of American cuisine, from fast food to fine dining. Sample his empire's delights by stopping by his original **Shake Shack** (page 152), classic first restaurant **Union Square Cafe** (page 147)—one of the pioneers of contemporary American cuisine along with his other flagship, **Gramercy Tavern** (page 146)—or cocktail bar **Porchlight** (page 196).

- **Eric Ripert** is known for his frequent appearances on late friend Anthony Bourdain's shows and for hosting his own PBS show, *Avec Eric*. But he also has the talent to back up the fame, as evidenced by the meticulous perfection that is **Le Bernardin** (page 157), his stellar seafood restaurant.

- **Marcus Samuelsson** went from being the executive chef of Midtown's Aquavit, which has received two Michelin stars, to opening **Red Rooster** (page 165), his stylish den of soul food in Harlem near where he lives in a brownstone.

Upland

salt) to sausage and kale pizza. A decent selection of wines by the glass is culled from a range of vineyards, from the pinot-heavy Willamette Valley in Oregon to the Loire Valley in France. The restaurant also offers a quartet of draft beers by the likes of Evil Twin and Catskill Brewery.

MAP 5: 345 Park Ave. S., 212/686-1006, www.uplandnyc.com; 11:30am-3pm and 5pm-11pm Mon.-Sat., 10am-3pm and 5pm-10pm Sun.

STEAK HOUSES
Old Homestead Steakhouse $$$

This dark, wood-filled relic has been sating carnivores since 1868. A giant cow hangs out front to clear up any confusion about what's on the menu. Like most steak houses, the thing to get is evident but, for those on a budget, the Old Homestead offers a filet mignon burger served with truffle fries and a Caesar salad for just $19.

MAP 5: 56 9th Ave., 212/242-9040, www.theoldhomesteadsteakhouse.com; noon-10:45pm Mon.-Thurs., noon-11:45pm Fri., 1pm-11:45pm Sat., 1pm-9:45pm Sun.

ITALIAN
Del Posto $$$

New York elegance from the roaring '20s is conjured up in grand fashion at Joe and Lidia Bastianich's signature restaurant (former partner Mario Batali is in the process of divesting from the establishment). A high-ceilinged dining room features a piano player and feels luxuriously spacious for a New York restaurant. There are no misfires to avoid here, but the homemade pastas are a must and the truffled dressing on the herbs-and-lettuces salad is addictive. No matter when you come, plan on staying at least three hours to soak in the whole experience. Note that lunch is markedly cheaper than dinner and provides a similar experience.

MAP 5: 85 10th Ave., 212/497-8090, http://delposto.com; 11:30am-2pm and 5:30pm-11pm Mon.-Fri., 4:30pm-11pm Sat., 4:30pm-10pm Sun.

Eataly $$

What if someone invented a shopping mall dedicated to all facets of Italian cuisine, from cooking supply vendors to sit-down dining experiences? Founded by Oscar Farinetti along with partners Joe and Lidia Bastianich and Mario Batali (who's in the process of divesting from the enterprise), Eataly is it, and it may be a dream or a nightmare (steer clear if you don't enjoy particularly frenzied atmospheres) come true. It's billed as the largest food hall in the world—that is, behind Farinetti's food theme park in Bologna, which measures a million square feet (92,903 sq m). A wide range of Italian food experiences are available; you can eat fresh homemade pasta at Il Pastaio di Eataly or feast on a bountiful selection of small plates like crispy artichokes and Wagyu beef skewers at a rustic rooftop greenhouse. Also on the rooftop is a craft beer haven known as Birreria. Dogfish Head, which has an established relationship with brewers in Italy, creates unique citrusy pale ales exclusively for the place. The tap list also includes other Dogfish Head beers along with top-notch local beers from Other Half and Grimm Artisanal Ales.

MAP 5: 200 5th Ave., 212/229-2560, www. eataly.com; 9am-11pm daily

PIZZA
Stella's Pizza $

Many proper pizzerias (save for Joe's) close by midnight, forcing you to satisfy nocturnal cravings at the subpar $1 pizza joints that abound throughout the city. Stella's is a standout for serving cheap, classic slices with a good cheese-to-dough ratio. Note that prices are slightly higher than the standard $2.75 in the wee hours of the morning.

MAP 5: 110 9th Ave. #1, 212/462-4444; 10:30am-10:30pm Mon., 10:30am-1am Tues.-Wed., 10:30am-3am Thurs.-Fri., 11:30am-4am Sat., noon-1am Sun.

BAGELS
Murray's Bagels $

Murray's hand-rolled bagels are baked fresh daily and on the crispy side, excellent with a schmear of cream cheese or as a base for a cold-cut sandwich. Round bistro tables are available in a small seating area here, but the nearby High Line's lawn on 23rd Street makes for more ideal picnic grounds.

MAP 5: 242 8th Ave., 646/638-1335, http:// murraysbagelschelsea.com; 6:30am-7pm Mon.-Fri., 6:30am-6:30pm Sat.-Sun.

INDIAN
Junoon $$$

Junoon has the distinction of being the only Michelin-starred Indian restaurant in the city, taking classic dishes and elevating them for the white-clothed dining room. Serious spice fiends will want to try the ghost chili pepper-coated chicken thigh, while others will be wowed by offerings including a tandoori octopus with black garlic aioli and farm-raised lamb chops with charred pineapple. A bar area offers a more casual atmosphere for spontaneous or solo dining as well as a killer cocktail list, including a series of *Game of Thrones*-themed concoctions; the best is the Jon Snow, which features 10-year-old Ardbeg scotch with a heavy dose of intoxicating spice smoke.

MAP 5: 27 W. 24th St., 212/490-2100, http://junoonnyc.com; noon-3pm and 5:30pm-10:30pm Sun.-Thurs., noon-3pm and 5:30pm-11:30pm Fri.-Sat.

aRoqa $$

Combining the sleek appeal of a lounge with the full-service menu of a restaurant, aRoqa is a great place to linger with friends or a date. Most dishes, such as the Katafi Mushrooms (wild mushroom croquettes), Parsi Chimbori (beer-battered crab), and Vindaloo Momos (pork dumplings with bacon crumble) make for satisfying shares and go well with a range of cocktails. Seasons of Luck, made with chamomile-infused bourbon, comes with a mini playing card affixed to the

aRoqa

glass—if yours happens to be a joker, your drink is free.

MAP 5: 206 9th Ave., 646/678-5471, www.aroqanyc.com; 5pm-11pm Mon.-Wed., 5pm-1am Thurs.-Sat., 11am-3pm and 5pm-11pm Sun.

Dhaba $$

A dizzying menu selection stretches into triple digits at this Punjabi eatery in an area known as Curry Hill. An all-you-can-eat buffet is available for lunch, and à la carte items let you choose between dishes like smoky minced lamb kebabs and creamy *palak paneer* (spinach and cheese curry), or from about a dozen British curries. While the restaurant takes its name from truck stop eateries in India, the digs here are decidedly sleeker, with dim exposed light bulbs hanging over polished dark-wood tables and lime-green leather banquettes.

MAP 5: 108 Lexington Ave., 212/679-1284 www.dhabanyc.com; noon-midnight Mon.-Thurs., noon-1am Fri.-Sat., noon-10:30pm Sun.

MEDITERRANEAN

Salinas $$

This hidden gem features a magical glass-enclosed garden that elevates its Mediterranean cuisine year-round. Musts include the daily selection of croquettes, pan-seared octopus with salsa verde, and sea bream. Chef Luis Bollo hails from San Sebastián, Spain, which has the enviable distinction of having one of the highest concentrations of Michelin-starred restaurants per capita. Bollo's food draws on the region's tradition of rich yet simple flavors.

MAP 5: 136 9th Ave., 212/776-1990, http://salinasnyc.com; 6pm-10pm Mon.-Thurs., 6pm-11pm Fri.-Sat., 5pm-10pm Sun.

TAPAS AND PINXTOS

Toro $$

Housed in a cavernous industrial-chic space with Spanish hams hanging from the rafters, this Barcelona-inspired tapas joint—a second iteration of chefs Ken Oringer and Jamie Bissonnette's restaurant (the first is in Boston)—serves inventive dishes like a sea urchin and lobster chowder, and croquettes with pig's head. Come for the food happy hour (5pm-6pm daily and 9pm-10pm Mon.-Wed. and 10pm-11pm Thurs.-Fri.) for tasty discounted bites like blood sausage pigs in a blanket for $2 each.

MAP 5: 85 10th Ave., 212/691-2360, www.toro-nyc.com; 5:30pm-10pm Sun.-Wed., 5:30pm-11pm Thurs.-Sat.

Toro

Txikito $$

Soak in the wood-covered atmosphere at this cozy spot that feels like it belongs on a cobblestone street in Bilbao. Munch on *pintxos* (the Basque version of tapas) like deviled crab, homemade chorizo hash, and a mini porcini mushroom grilled cheese, the latter of which goes great with a glass of rioja. Or order a cider and watch as it's poured Basque-style: The waiter lifts his arm comically high to create a dramatic cascade into your waiting glass. This is a great stop after a show at the Atlantic Theater Company or The Joyce Theater, when the crowds will be thinner.

MAP 5: 240 9th Ave., 212/242-4730, www.txikitonyc.com; 5:30pm-11pm Mon.-Thurs., 5:30pm-11:30pm Fri.-Sat., 5:30pm-10:30pm Sun.

MEXICAN
Cosme $$$

Chef-owner Enrique Olvera's first restaurant outside of Mexico has many devotees who rave about his exquisitely plated dishes made from local ingredients that blow up conventional notions of the cuisine. Jicama scallops, uni tostadas with bone marrow salsa, and honeynut squash tamales are among the offerings. President Barack Obama dined here shortly before leaving the White House. Scoring a prime-time reservation can be difficult on OpenTable; you'll have a better chance calling the restaurant directly or settling for a 5:30pm Monday slot.

MAP 5: 35 E. 21st St., 212/913-9659, www.cosmenyc.com; noon-2:30pm and 5:30pm-11pm Mon.-Thurs., noon-2:30pm and 5:30pm-midnight Fri., 11:30am-2:30pm and 5:30pm-midnight Sat., 11:30am-2:30pm and 5:30pm-11pm Sun.

BARBECUE
Blue Smoke $

Blue Smoke serves authentic Southern-smoked comfort food like briskets, ribs, and pork shoulders, along with skillet mac and cheese and "lighter" options like a brisket salad with Alabama white sauce. Exposed brick walls and large skylights give the ground-floor dining space a warm vibe. Or if you want to pair your food with music, you can head to its basement club, the Jazz Standard, which offers spacious seating, including some comfy booths; nearly the entire Blue Smoke menu can be ordered here. The Mingus Big Band, which plays the music of legendary bebop bassist Charles Mingus, holds court every Monday night (sets at 7:30pm and 9:30pm, cover $30 per set) and delivers a massive brassy wallop that goes nicely with fried chicken and biscuits.

MAP 5: 116 E. 27th St., 212/477-7733, www.bluesmoke.com; 11:30am-10pm Sun.-Thurs., 11:30am-11pm Fri.-Sat.

FOOD HALL
Gansevoort Market $

Gansevoort Market is like a little sister to nearby Chelsea Market, offering an easy way to sample an array of artisan-crafted dishes across a wide range of world cuisines. The food hall's decor hews towards minimalist industrial and has ample seating. Vendors rotate often, but sample offerings include everything from Peruvian ceviche to fried chicken-stuffed waffle cones to coal-oven pizzas to macarons with Americanized fillings like birthday cake and s'mores.

MAP 5: 353 W. 14th St., 646/678-3231, www.gansmarket.com; 8am-9pm daily

BURGERS
Shake Shack $

Danny Meyer may have an array of fine-dining restaurants in his portfolio, but a hundred years from now he might be most remembered for elevating the fast-food burger. There are now numerous Shake Shack locations across the country and world, but it all started here, at this freestanding venue that looks like an urban interpretation of an old-fashioned ice cream shop. Meyer captures the addictive rush of the best fast food and serves it up with quality meat from butcher Pat Lafrieda, who supplies the

NEW YORK'S ARTISANAL FOOD HALLS

New York's artisan-driven food halls upgrade the variety and convenience of a typical mall food court with chicer settings and food offerings of restaurant quality. Chelsea Market was a pioneer of this type of venue when it opened in 1997, and now these spaces abound and make for meals both fast and memorable. They're typically housed in giant open spaces with communal seating, and you can easily wander around and try dishes from a few places during a visit.

- **Chelsea Market:** New York's original food hall is also its most popular, with vendors cooking up cuisines from around the globe. It's also conveniently located near the Whitney Museum and The High Line (page 92).

- **Gansevoort Market:** Just a couple of blocks away from big sister Chelsea Market, this intimate market on the border of Chelsea and the Meatpacking District features a rotating array of vendors with a focus on local ingredients and comfort food. A fully stocked bar is in back (page 152).

- **DeKalb Market Hall:** Housed in the basement of a mall in rapidly developing Downtown Brooklyn, this spacious food hall is a one-stop shop for New York deliciousness that peaks with an outpost of the famous Katz's Deli. It's also convenient to BAM, Theatre for a New Audience, and the Alamo Drafthouse (page 171).

city's best restaurants. The main draw is the beef burgers, of course, which are a perfect balance of flavor and texture, but there are also hot dogs and chicken sandwiches. If you're feeling decadent, the shakes are pretty awesome, too. It's conveniently located in Madison Square Park, offering plenty of benches for al fresco eating.

MAP 5: Madison Ave. and E. 23rd St., 212/889-6600, www.shakeshack.com; 7:30am-11pm Mon.-Fri., 8:30am-11pm Sat.-Sun.

SWEETS
The Donut Pub $

Most of the city's prized doughnut shops close early in the evening, leaving nocturnal cravings unsated. While more a diner than a pub, this sweet mecca has been delivering freshly baked fried orbs in a dizzying variety of flavors since 1964. Simple staples like a chocolate glazed or honey dip are the best bets, especially if you roll in during the wee hours of the morning when production slows.

MAP 5: 203 W. 14th St., 212/929-0126, www.donutpub.com; 24 hours daily

Midtown, Hell's Kitchen, and Times Square
Map 6

CONTEMPORARY AMERICAN

Friedmans $$

Located on a lonely stretch of 10th Avenue, Friedmans feels like a country farmhouse. Knotty wood abounds and the locally sourced menu is just as comforting. It's named after the economist Milton Friedman, in reference to his "There's no such thing as a free lunch" quote—which is borne out in the menu's prices. You get what you pay for, though, with high-quality ingredients and a range of gluten-free options. Highlights include a grain bowl with Japanese vegetables, a falafel burger, and a BLT with avocado that's satisfyingly smoky.

MAP 6: 450 10th Ave., 212/268-1100, www.friedmansrestaurant.com; 7:30am-10pm Mon.-Fri., 8:30am-4pm and 5pm-10pm Saturday, 8:30am-4pm and 5pm-9pm Sun.

ITALIAN

Becco $

Unlimited pasta ($19.95 lunch, $24.95 dinner) is the thing to get at this cavernous and popular pretheater spot by celebrity chef Lidia Bastianich and her son Joe. Waiters continuously serve three pastas, prepared daily, from giant pans. Served with an antipasto assortment or Caesar salad, this is a great bargain for a massive amount of intensely satisfying food. Bottles of wine are a reasonable $29.

MAP 6: 355 W. 46th St., 212/397-7597, http://becco-nyc.com; noon-3pm and 5pm-10pm Mon., noon-3pm and 4:30pm-11pm Tues., 11:30am-3pm and 4pm-11pm Wed., noon-3pm and 4:30pm-11pm Thurs., noon-3pm and 4:30pm-midnight Fri., 11:30am-3pm and 4pm-midnight Sat., noon-10pm Sun.

Il Melograno $

This tiny, out-of-the-way spot consistently turns out impeccably fresh pastas in a cozy space that easily gets crowded. Chef Alberto Tartari sticks to the traditionally smaller Italian portion sizes, so ordering a salad along with a pasta is a good bet. The wine list is culled largely from Tartari's home country, perhaps with an Argentinian malbec and Willamette Valley pinot noir thrown in.

MAP 6: 501 W. 51st St., 212/757-9290, www.ilmelogranonyc.com/ilmelograno.html; 4pm-9:45pm Sun.-Thurs., 4pm-11pm Fri.-Sat.

Manganaro's Heroboy $

This no-frills dining hall serves generous portions of classic Italian American fare with an equally classic dose of surly service. The chicken parmesan is particularly satisfying, with a generous dollop of sauce added for extra ooze. The eatery closes spectacularly early and doesn't seem to care if a delivery order falls through the cracks, so it's best to dine in. A sandwich makes for a meal and then some, and comes with a small bag of homemade chips (don't be afraid to ask if it slips the counter person's mind).

MAP 6: 494 9th Ave., 212/947-7325, http://heroboy.com; 11am-6:30pm Mon.-Fri., 11am-4pm Sat.

PIZZA
Don Antonio $

Don Antonio's Neapolitan pizza stands out for its deep-fried dough, whose aroma tantalizingly wafts through the air and lends each personal-sized orb an intense smokiness. White truffles are among the decadent toppings available. Unlike most other places, you can't customize the pies here, but it's a small price to pay for the deliciousness. Seating is at densely packed tables.

MAP 6: 309 W. 50th St., 646/719-1043, www.donantoniopizza.com; 11:30am-3:30pm and 4:30pm-11pm Mon.-Thurs., 11:30am-11:30pm Fri.-Sat., 11:30am-10:30pm Sun.

FRENCH
Gabriel Kreuther $$$

White tablecloths mixed with exposed wooden columns and abstract art pieces create a slightly more relaxed sense of refinement at this French-inspired restaurant. Dining here is by prix fixe only, with a three-course menu for the pretheater crowd and a four-course menu for everyone else.

A cassoulet made with Pennsylvania squab and brown butter and sage pork tenderloin are among the offerings. A smaller but still extensive menu is available à la carte at the bar.

MAP 6: 41 W. 42nd St., 212/257-5826, www.gknyc.com; noon-2pm and 5:30pm-10pm Mon.-Fri., 5:30pm-10:30pm Sat.

db Bistro Moderne $$

Most pretheater menus are a tired selection of standards like roast chicken, but Daniel Boulud's relatively casual bistro offers authentic French dishes like *pâté en croute* (think foie gras pastry) and a namesake burger that's a celebration of all things decadent, piled mightily high and incorporating goose liver, black truffles, and short rib. It paved the way for the high-end restaurant burger now ubiquitous in the city. A pretheater prix fixe ($55) as well as full à la carte menu are available for dinner, and breakfast and lunch are also served. During happy hour (3pm-6pm daily, and also after 9pm or 10pm depending on the day), beer and wine can be had for just $5 at the bar along with bites like truffled arancini.

MAP 6: 55 W. 44th St., 212/391-2400, www.dbbistro.com; 7am-10am and 11:15am-10pm Mon., 7am-10am and 11:15am-11pm Tues.-Thurs., 7am-10am and 11:15am-11:30pm Fri., 8am-11:30pm Sat., 8am-10pm Sun.

BAGELS
✪ Ess-a-Bagel $

Few things are more quintessentially New York than bagels and long lines, and you'll find both at Ess-a-Bagel. Queues stretch out the door even on brutally cold days, but for good reason: These bagels are hands-down the best in the city, bigger than those of

Gabriel Kreuther

WHERE TO EAT BEFORE (OR AFTER) YOUR BROADWAY SHOW

5 Napkin Burger

Pretheater dining is understandably popular around Broadway, and most restaurants in the surrounding area cater to the crowds with special preshow menus; many of these don't actually end up saving you much money though, so look closely. More than in most areas of the city, you'll need to stay alert for mediocre food here.

Daniel Boulud's **db Bistro Moderne,** a more casual take on his flagship Daniel on the Upper East Side, courts theatergoers with a special prix fixe menu of authentic French fare for a fair price. Or you could just order its famous burger. At popular places like Broadway hangout **Joe Allen** and unlimited-pasta mecca **Becco**—a bright spot amid a string of largely mediocre tourists traps on a block between 8th and 9th Avenues known as **Restaurant Row**—it's a good idea to make reservations at least a few days beforehand. Restaurants west of 8th Avenue, in Hell's Kitchen, can usually handle walk-ins; try raucously cozy Mediterranean spot **Mémé.** On 9th Avenue between 36th and 56th Streets, you'll find numerous Thai restaurants that make for fast and affordable dining. One of the most authentic of these is **Pure Thai Cookhouse,** but many offer decent curries, fried rice, and Thai iced teas.

Most shows start at 8pm, so plan on sitting down at 6pm at the latest for a leisurely meal. This of course means that everyone else will also be trying to dine in the area during this time frame. Many venues will ask if you're seeing a show upon taking your order, but if they don't feel free to mention it and your order will be expedited. It's worth noting that an increasing number of shows are adopting a 7pm curtain on weeknights, and if this is the case you might be more inclined to consider eating a late lunch and then dining after your show rather than deal with pre-curtain throngs. This will also allow for elated postshow conversations without the stress of tracking time. Places like **5 Napkin Burger** and **Kiabacca Bar** offer late-night specials. Regardless of where you eat, **Schmackary's** makes an ideal dessert stop, with cookie flavors like maple bacon, red velvet, and a classic chocolate chip with sea salt that's usually warm and gooey.

competitors, and with a tender chewiness that also somehow has the airiness associated with a great croissant. They're so good you could eat them plain—an express counter at the back of the store is set up for such ordering purposes—but there are almost two dozen tempting homemade cream cheeses to try. Classics like lox and vegetable are hard to beat. This location is more convenient to numerous attractions, but to avoid the crowds, you could also try the other shop on 1st Avenue and East 19th Street.

MAP 6: 831 3rd Ave., 212/980-1010, www. ess-a-bagel.com; 6am-9pm Mon.-Fri., 6am-5pm Sat.-Sun.

THAI
Pure Thai Cookhouse $

There are so many Thai restaurants on 9th Avenue between 36th and 56th Streets that if you blindfolded a friend and had them aimlessly wander into a storefront on any given block, they would most likely be able to find their way to plate of pad thai. But Pure Thai Cookhouse has a singular feel. Fashioned in the style of the tiny shops in Thailand where plates of food are scarfed down on stools, this is an ideal pretheater spot thanks to its fast turnover and delicious food. All the noodles are handmade from a recipe from the family of owners David and Vanida Bank.

MAP 6: 766 9th Ave. #2, 212/581-0999, www.purethaicookhouse.com; noon-10:30pm Mon.-Thurs., noon-11:30pm Fri.-Sat., noon-10pm Sun.

KOREAN
Baekjeong $$

Koreatown, the stretch of 32nd Street between 6th Avenue and Broadway, is a tiny respite from the blandness of the area around Penn Station. Baekjeong in particular draws local foodies for its high-quality ingredients, especially its brisket and short ribs. As at the many other Korean barbecue joints lining the street, you can cook your own meat here at a table grill or order dishes prepared in the kitchen. An array of *banchan* (side dishes), including kimchi, is served with your order. Small private rooms are available for groups, and the $45 party set menu provides a feast of food.

Map 6: 1 E. 32nd St., 212/966-9839, http://baekjeongnyc.com; 11:30am-1am Sun.-Thurs., 11:30am-5am Fri.-Sat.

CAMBODIAN
Num Pang Kitchen $

This restaurant's name means "sandwich" in Cambodian, and that's precisely what's on offer here. Highlights include pulled pork with spiced honey as well as one with spicy organic tofu. All sandwiches come with pickled vegetables and chili mayo on a semolina or quinoa baguette, and some are also offered in grain bowl versions. Num Pang has multiple locations throughout the city, sized as grab-and-go spots, but in warmer weather this outpost offers nearby Bryant Park as an ideal picnic spot.

MAP 6: 133 W. 38th St., 917/409-1134, www.numpangkitchen.com; 11am-9pm Mon.-Fri., noon-6pm Sat.-Sun.

MEDITERRANEAN
Mémé $$

Named after the owners' French-Moroccan grandmother, this dimly lit and often boisterously loud bistro makes a mean hummus and a fall-apart-tender organic salmon served with truffle risotto. The wine list features bottles from Greece as well as Spain and France, and the atmosphere has an easygoing Mediterranean elegance, with brightly colored walls and a wood ceiling.

MAP 6: 607 10th Ave., 917/262-0827, http://memeonhudson.com; 11:30am-11pm Mon.-Fri., 10am-11pm Sat.-Sun.

SEAFOOD
✪ Le Bernardin $$$

Considered one of the best restaurants in the city if not the world, Le Bernardin has received not only a coveted three Michelin stars but just about every other accolade, including more James Beard Awards than any other restaurant in the city and a four-star rating from the *New York Times* maintained through five reviews since its opening in 1986. Eric Ripert's fine-dining palace combines the decadent precision of French cuisine—he grew up in the south of France—with the freshest seafood available. The elegant space has sleek leather chairs and white-clothed tables spaced generously apart. Stools are brought out for ladies' purses, just one sign of the impeccable service. Each bite here, whether it's of the prized Dover sole, barely cooked scallop, or seared octopus in a red wine-mole sauce, is an ecstatic joy. This bucket list experience is priced accordingly: The standard four-course dinner prix fixe is $160 in the dining room, while a more affordable $57 three-course lunch is served in a lounge section; $5 of each lunch course goes to the charity City Harvest.

To nab a coveted reservation, check online or call on the first day of the month for the following month (i.e. Nov. 1 for Dec. seatings), or come by the lounge, which is always first come, first served.

MAP 6: 155 W. 51st St., 212/554-1515, www.le-bernardin.com; noon-2:30pm and 5:15pm-10:30pm Mon.-Thurs., noon-2:30pm and 5:15pm-11pm Fri., 5:15pm-11pm Sat.

Grand Central Oyster Bar $$

Open since 1913, this oyster bar has long been a favorite of both locals and tourists alike. Located in the center of Grand Central's lower-level dining concourse, seating in the cavernous space—featuring a Catalan vault ceiling made of terra-cotta tiles—is at large counters with leather stools, where commuters can often be found inhaling half shells before hopping on a train. The unparalleled oyster selection spans several pages and includes details about size, flavor characteristics, and origin. The freshest oysters are typically from Long Island. During happy hour (4:30pm-7pm Mon.-Wed. and 1pm-5pm Sat.) Blue Point oysters are a dollar and change and martinis $9, which is a spectacular bargain for this pricey institution.

MAP 6: 89 E. 42nd St., 212/490-6650, http://www.oysterbarny.com; 11:30am-9:30pm Mon.-Sat.

CLASSIC AMERICAN
Joe Allen $$

The exposed brick walls of this long-time theater hangout are lined with show posters spanning the decades of its existence. Open since 1965, when it served hamburgers for 75 cents, the restaurant continues to exude throwback comfort with menu items like meatloaf with mashed potatoes and gravy. The lobster roll is a solid choice as well. A few good craft brews are usually on draft and the wine list includes sancerre by the glass. Joe Allen's helpful website features a list of current Broadway show running times to help patrons make an accurate post-show reservation.

MAP 6: 326 W. 46th St., 212/581-6464, www.joeallenrestaurant.com; noon-11pm Mon.-Tues., 11:30am-11:30pm Wed., noon-11:30pm Thurs., noon-11:45pm Fri., 11:30am-midnight Sat., 11:30am-11pm Sun.

Shorty's $

The owners of this meat-lovers' mecca, which doubles as a sports bar, have their big, pillowy rolls shipped in from Philadelphia daily to create authentic cheesesteaks with Cheez Whiz, American, or provolone (and fried onions upon request) that melt in your mouth. Yuengling-battered onion rings are a nice accompaniment, and there's always a generous selection of craft beers on tap to wash it all down. Avoid prime football game times unless you want to get swept up in Eagles mania.

MAP 6: 576 9th Ave., 212/967-3055, www. shortysnyc.com; 11am-1am Sun.-Wed., 11am-2am Thurs.-Sat.

BURGERS
Burger Joint $

Hotels are usually not where bargain meals can be found; Parker New York in Midtown is the exception. Tucked inside its business traveler-sleek halls is the Burger Joint, which is exactly that: a crowded, no-frills spot with a simple menu scrawled on pieces of cardboard. The five-ounce Black Angus beef patties are ground daily, a fact that stood out more when it first opened in 2002, two years before Shake Shack. But burgers are still a bargain for the neighborhood at under $9. Come late in the afternoon to avoid the lunch crowd, or be prepared to wait.

MAP 6: 119 W. 56th St., 212/708-7414, www.burgerjointny.com; 11am-11:30pm Sun.-Thurs., 11am-midnight Fri.-Sat.

5 Napkin Burger $

This eatery's name suggests just how messy these delicious 10-ounce burgers—enough to feed two—will be. Choose from truffle, bacon cheddar, and ahi tuna options, among others. At brunch you'll find a bacon-and-egg cheeseburger. The atmosphere here is that of a warm bistro. The budget conscious will want to take note of the happy hour, every night after 10pm at the bar, when you can order oversized sliders for just $3 and cocktails like a Buffalo Trace whiskey sour for $7.

MAP 6: 630 9th Ave., 212/757-2277, http://5napkinburger.com; 11:30am-midnight Mon.-Fri., 11am-midnight Sat.-Sun.

SWEETS
Schmackary's $

Cookies are an art at this hole-in-the-wall around the corner from 5 Napkin Burger and just down the block from the shining marquees of Broadway theaters. Lines stretch out the door at all times but move quickly. Over 75 flavors rotate, including red velvet, cookies and cream, and M&M-speckled options, but the classic with semisweet chocolate chips and sea salt is among the best. The constant demand ensures new plates of cookies are frequently coming out of the kitchen, keeping offerings wonderfully fresh.

MAP 6: 362 W. 45th St., 646/801-9866, http://schmackarys.com; 8am-11pm Sun.-Tues., 8am-midnight Wed.-Sat.

CONTEMPORARY AMERICAN

Per Se $$$

Celebrated chef Thomas Keller's New York spin on his iconic French Laundry restaurant is an ode to lavish meals and is still considered by many a pinnacle dining experience in the city (despite a scathing review by the *New York Times* in 2016). At a service-inclusive price of $340 per person, excluding drinks, it's beyond most budgets, but those with the means to splash out will enjoy a nine-course tasting menu—created anew daily, one each for carnivores and vegetarians—in a plush dining room overlooking Central Park.

MAP 7: 10 Columbus Circle, 4th Fl., 212/823-9335, www.thomaskeller.com/perseny; 5:30pm-9:30pm Mon.-Thurs., 11:30am-3pm and 5:30pm-9:30pm Fri.-Sun.

Fairway Cafe $$

Occupying a space on the 2nd floor of the beloved Fairway Market (6am-1am daily), this casual café serves up organic omelets, buckwheat crepes, oven-roasted Cornish hens, and other unfussy artisanal dishes.

MAP 7: 2121 Broadway, 2nd Fl., 212/595-1888, www.fairwaymarket.com; 8am-9:30pm Sun.-Thurs., 8am-10pm Fri.-Sat.

Maison Pickle $$

The owners of wildly popular eatery Jacob's Pickles, just around the corner, bring their penchant for heaping plates of comfort food into a more upscale bistro atmosphere. The centerpiece of the menu is a quartet of overstuffed French dip sandwiches: three versions featuring beef, including a Reuben, and a leg of lamb with mint chimichurri. Also on the menu are duck fat-fried potato chips drizzled with fondue, several steaks, an extensive cocktail list, and a "cellared" beer list of craft bottles that have been aged for several years.

MAP 7: 2315 Broadway, 212/496-9100, www.maisonpickle.com; 11am-11pm Mon.-Thurs., 11am-midnight Fri., 9am-noon Sat., 9am-11pm Sun.

ITALIAN

Ristorante Morini $$$

Catering to museum-goers and socialites alike, Michael White's elegant Italian restaurant, located just a block from Museum Mile, has a fairly good lunch deal where diners can order tasty and hearty dishes like an overstuffed kale salad with candied almonds, a generously portioned pasta (low-gluten options available), and a scoop of gelato for $32. It's the perfect food to power up on before diving into that next museum. Happy hour runs 2:30pm-6:30pm Monday-Saturday and all day Sunday and features steep discounts on glasses of Italian wine and cocktails.

MAP 7: 1167 Madison Ave., 212/249-0444, http://ristorantemorini.com; noon-10pm Mon.-Fri., 11:30am-10pm Sat., 11:30am-9:30pm Sun.

Gennaro $$

Ask Upper West Siders what their favorite mainstay Italian restaurant is, and the answer will often be Gennaro. While the trattoria doesn't take credit cards or reservations, it's gained a loyal following for its relatively gentle pricing and family-friendly atmosphere. On the menu is classic fare like tortellini stuffed with spinach and ricotta, and the wine list—also reasonably priced—includes offerings from Tuscany. Waits can be long during peak dinner hours after 6pm, so put you name in and then head for a stroll in Riverside or Central Park.

MAP 7: 665 Amsterdam Ave., 212/665-5348, www.gennaronyc.com; 5pm-10:30pm Sun.-Thurs., 5pm-11pm Fri.-Sat.

FRENCH
Daniel $$$

Daniel Boulud's flagship restaurant has been a neighborhood favorite for fine dining since it opened in 1993; it's also among the best in the city. His cooking style is refined but not fussy, and he has a knack for capturing the essence of ingredients and then seamlessly blending them together—as in a foie gras flambéed with mezcal. Dinner is available as a three-, four-, or seven-course meal. The main dining room's coffered ceiling and neoclassical columns evoke the grand culinary palaces of Paris, while the bar and lounge area has a more modern vibe.

MAP 7: 60 E. 65th St., 212/288-0033, www.danielnyc.com; 5pm-11pm Mon.-Sat.

Vaucluse $$$

Chef Michael White made his name with authentic Italian cuisine, particularly exquisite handmade pastas. Here he ventures into French fine dining with equal aplomb. The foie gras with rhubarb jam makes a robust starter, and the precisely prepared branzino an excellent entrée. A few

Ristorante Morini

pastas are available as well, and one is included in the six-course tasting menu. White is a fan of negronis, and the house version is balanced yet potent. An extensive wine list includes a large selection by the glass from the Rhone, Loire, and Burgundy regions, among others.

MAP 7: 100 E. 63rd St., 646/869-2300, http://vauclusenyc.com; noon-10pm Mon.-Thurs., noon-10:30pm Fri., 5:30pm-10:30pm Sat., 11:30am-9pm Sun.

Bar Boulud $$

Located directly across the street from Lincoln Center, it's hard to find a better pre- or postshow dining spot than Bar Boulud. While there's ample sidewalk seating, opt for a booth inside to enjoy the tranquil minimalist decor under an artfully curved ceiling. The menu features an extensive array of charcuterie that pairs well with the comprehensive wine list culled from the Burgundy and Rhone regions. Standout dishes include a tender truffled pork sausage and specialty dishes like rabbit. Bistro mainstays like escargot in almond-herb butter are intensely satisfying as well.

MAP 7: 1900 Broadway, 212/595-0303, www.barboulud.com/nyc; 11:30am-11pm Mon.-Thurs., 11:30am-midnight Fri., 11am-midnight Sat., 11am-10pm Sun.

JEWISH DELIS
Barney Greengrass $$

Opened in 1908, and in its current location since 1929, this classic Jewish deli and appetizing store features a retro sign outside proclaiming it the sturgeon king—which is more than mere boasting. Locals rave about the buttery smoked fish as well as the smoked salmon, and the bagels here are some of the finest you'll find. Breakfast on the weekends is particularly crowded and cash is the only payment accepted by the gruff waitstaff, but the no-frills ambience is part of the charm. Seating is at small Formica tables by the counter or in a small dining room curiously lined with wallpaper from New Orleans' French Quarter, despite no NOLA specialties on the menu.

MAP 7: 541 Amsterdam Ave., 212/724-4707, www.barneygreengrass.com; 8am-6pm Tues.-Sun.

2nd Floor Bar and Essen $$

Dimly lit, with small tables that encourage intimate conversation, Bar and Essen lets you combine a delicious deli meal with cocktails in a speakeasy-style space. Located on the 2nd floor of the 2nd Avenue Deli, one of the city's old-school Jewish delis, you'll find comfort staples transformed into elegant small plates like pastrami deviled eggs and pastrami-stuffed potato latkes, though purists can just order a plate of the prized meat and eat it with rye bread and mustard in classic style. The potent cocktail list is divided into two categories (Shaken & Sours and Stirred & Spirited), and drinks range from refreshing and citrus-forward to heavier concoctions like the Unforgiven, made with bourbon, apple brandy, and a syrah reduction.

MAP 7: 1442 1st Ave. (entrance at E. 75th St. between 1st Ave. and York Ave.), 212/737-1700, www.2ndavedeli.com/2nd-floor; 5pm-midnight Sun.-Thurs., 5pm-2am Fri.-Sat.

Zabar's Café $

Zabar's gourmet specialty shop is the go-to place for locals to buy lox, bagels, and other appetizing items to host lavish brunches. This café, located right next door, is a great place to grab a quick coffee, lunch, or savory sweet treat like a chocolate croissant, and a welcome alternative to the nearby American Museum of Natural History's sad cafeteria-style options.

MAP 7: 2245 Broadway, 212/787-2000, www.zabars.com; 8am-7:30pm Mon.-Fri., 8am-8pm Sat., 9am-6pm Sun.

THAI
Thai Market $

Thai restaurants can sometimes feel ubiquitous and homogenous in their offerings, so it's refreshing to find a standout like Thai Market. While pad thai is on the menu, so are scores of more adventurous dishes, like the Pia Dook Pad Ped, a spicy fried catfish with bird's-eye chili. Prices are reasonable and portions large. Waits are common during prime dinner hours (around 6pm-9pm); try lunchtime instead, when a two-course meal goes for around $10.

MAP 7: 960 Amsterdam Ave., 212/280-4575, http://thaimarketny.net; noon-10pm Sun.-Thurs., noon-10:30pm Fri.-Sat.

MEXICAN
Rosa Mexicano $$

There aren't a lot of great dinner options near Lincoln Center that aren't wildly expensive, and none are as close as Rosa Mexicano, a small chain that started in New York. The dining room is large, making for relatively easy seating and dramatic presentations of tableside guacamole. Plates of tacos and enchiladas are tasty and filling. The restaurant also features an extensive array of agave-based cocktails, a nice way to relax before taking in an epic opera.

MAP 7: 61 Columbus Ave., 212/977-7700, http://rosamexicano.com; 11:30am-11:30pm Tues.-Sat., 11:30am-10:30pm Sun.-Mon.

Taqueria y Fonda $

Taqueria y Fonda is as authentic as Mexican food comes on the northern edge of the Upper West Side. The no-frills hole-in-the-wall offers over-stuffed tortas, tamales, and a range of tacos at prices that draw large crowds from nearby Columbia University. Because your money goes to the food and not the atmosphere, order your picks to go and have an impromptu picnic in Central Park.

MAP 7: 968 Amsterdam Ave., 347/619-0383, http://taqueriayfondany.com; 11am-11:45pm daily

SOUTHERN
Jacob's Pickles $$

Jacob's Pickles is a joyful celebration of excess. From the heaping chicken biscuit sandwiches that are more efficiently eaten with a knife and fork to the warm cookie pie sized for four people, portions are uncharacteristically large for New York. The casual restaurant evokes Southern hospitality that's just a touch refined. It doesn't take reservations and is usually packed to the gills. Potent cocktails served in mason jars ease the sting of the sometimes very slow service while deep-fried Oreos are a decadently fitting end to a wondrously exorbitant

Jacob's Pickles

meal. As its name suggests, numerous house-cured pickles are also on the menu—and can, unsurprisingly, be enjoyed fried.

MAP 7: 509 Amsterdam Ave., 212/470-5566, http://jacobs.picklehospitality.com; 10am-2am Mon.-Wed., 10am-4am Thurs.-Fri., 9am-4am Sat., 9am-2am Sun.

VEGETARIAN
Candle Cafe $$

Candle Cafe has long been a refuge for vegetarians and vegans craving proper restaurant food. Colorfully plated dishes are served in a warm and casual atmosphere. The food's freshness, flavor, and quality—with offerings like seitan steaks, avocado tartare, and risotto with kale pine nut pesto—have won the eatery a loyal following over the past three decades, and this original spot is now supplemented by two other locations. Cocktails incorporate small-batch ingredients, and there's a local beer list as well.

MAP 7: 1307 3rd Ave., 212/472-0970, www.candlecafe.com; 11:30am-10pm Mon.-Fri., 11am-10pm Sat., 9am-9:30pm Sun.

CLASSIC AMERICAN
JG Melon $

The Upper East Side is filled with overpriced society hangouts, but this isn't one of them. The pub atmosphere here is as authentic as they come; the space dates back to the 1920s when it was a tavern during Prohibition. Burgers here are seriously good. Crowds form even late on weekday nights, but the line tends to move quickly, aided by efficient service and a limited menu. For dessert, opt for the pecan pie, which is served warm and with whipped cream. Single diners can usually find a stool at the bar and plenty of raucous company.

MAP 7: 1291 3rd Ave., 212/744-0585, http://jgmelon-nyc.com; 11:30am-3am Mon.-Wed., 11:30am-4am Thurs.-Sat., 11:30am-1am Sun.

Viand Cafe $

Located in the Hotel Beacon, prices are a bit high here, but the quality is a notch above typical diner fare. Soups and sandwiches are good bets, along with burgers. Viand also roasts its own turkeys. It's conveniently located next to the Beacon Theatre and so it can get crowded before a big show; plan accordingly or come by afterward for a late meal.

MAP 7: 2130 Broadway, 212/877-2888, www.viandnyc.com; 7am-midnight daily

HOT DOGS
✪ Gray's Papaya $

There are many great hot dogs to be had in New York City, but Gray's Papaya is the best. The long, thin franks are cooked so the casing is perfectly crisp, and they're served on toasted buns. Try one plain first to experience the simple mastery of this hole-in-the-wall favorite, but sauerkraut and other toppings are also available. The battered storefront evokes the neighborhood's less polished past and remains a favorite midday stop, as well as a great place to grab a quick bite before a show at the Beacon Theatre. But thankfully, you can get a hot dog at this cash-only spot whenever the craving hits since it's open 24 hours a day. Wash it down with a papaya drink—the fruit's enzymes aid digestion. The Recession Special is only $6.95 and includes two hot dogs and a medium drink. A second location is near Times Square.

MAP 7: 2090 Broadway, 212/799-0243, http://grayspapaya.nyc; 24 hours daily

Papaya King $

The product of a Greek immigrant's persistent dream, Papaya King was the city's first great hot dog stand and juice bar. The juice actually came first, and hot dogs were added in 1939. The all-beef hot dogs on toasted buns offer just the right amount of bounce for each bite—similar to Gray's Papaya, which started as a franchise and branched off to become a bitter rival in the 1970s. Prices are a little higher at Papaya King, but the papaya drinks are a little better. There's also a wide range of specialty dogs, including one with pastrami. It's cash only, and also has an outpost in Brooklyn near BAM.

MAP 7: 179 E. 86th St., 212/369-0648, www.papayaking.com; 8am-midnight Sun.-Thurs., 8am-1am Fri.-Sat.

SWEETS

Levain Bakery $

Opened in the 1990s by two friends fleeing jobs in banking and fashion, this neighborhood bakery has become a go-to spot for New Yorkers craving the tastiest (and largest) cookies in the city. They clock in at a whopping six ounces and are thick with gooey insides. Chocolate chip walnut is the bakery's classic but other tempting flavors include dark chocolate peanut butter chip and oatmeal raisin. In addition to cookies, Levain also make sticky buns, scones, muffins, and a variety of breads. This location is larger and keeps longer hours than the original store (167 W. 74th St., 212/874-6080; 8am-7pm Mon.-Sat., 9am-7pm Sun.), located just a couple of blocks north.

MAP 7: 351 Amsterdam Ave., 212/874-6080, www.levainbakery.com; 7am-8:30pm daily

Harlem and Morningside Heights   Map 8

SOUL FOOD

Amy Ruth's $$

Waffles are the thing to get at this beloved local favorite. A multitude of variations on the soul food staple occupy a large section of the menu, with over a dozen options—but the classic chicken and waffles option is named after Rev. Al Sharpton and available either fried or smothered. Other waffle-pairing options include fried shrimp, catfish, and pork chops. You can also order chicken and two sides—dubbed the "President Barack Obama"—or try the "Al Roker," boneless short ribs.

MAP 8: 113 W. 116th St., 212/280-8779, http://amyruths.com; 11am-11pm Mon., 8:30am-11:30pm Tues., 8:30am-11pm Wed.-Thurs., 8:30am-5:30pm Fri., 7:30am-5:30pm Sat., 7:30am-11pm Sun.

Red Rooster $$

Named for a speakeasy frequented by James Baldwin and Nat King Cole, Red Rooster serves up a wide range of comfort food, from neighborhood staples like chicken and waffles to Louisiana crab cakes and shrimp and grits. Celebrity chef Marcus Samuelsson, born in Ethiopia but raised in Sweden, made a name for himself as the executive chef of fine-dining Midtown spot Aquavit before opening this spot. He melds precision with a casual bistro experience and adds an extensive and inventive cocktail list that includes ingredients like chocolate bitters and bacon. Sidle up to the bar weekdays 4pm-7pm and grab a bourbon negroni for $10.

MAP 8: 310 Lenox Ave., 212/792-9001, www.redroosterharlem.com; 11:30am-10:30pm Mon.-Tues. and Thurs., 11:30am-2:30pm and 9pm-10:30pm Wed., 11:30am-11:30pm Fri., 10am-11:30pm Sat., 10am-10pm Sun.

Red Rooster

Sylvia's $$

Bill Clinton frequently visited this soul food icon when he had an office in Harlem post-presidency; many others have as well since its founding in 1962. At this point, the restaurant feels more like a crowded tourist attraction than a destination restaurant, and the food is on the disappointing side of adequate. Fried chicken is the safest bet while more elaborate dishes like a bone-in short rib should be avoided. The massive space seats over 400 in several dining rooms that hew traditional, with banquet chairs and white tablecloths. Still, Sylvia's is embedded in the neighborhood's history: When the namesake proprietor died in 2012, a block nearby was renamed in her honor, underscoring her enduring legacy in Harlem.

MAP 8: 328 Malcolm X Blvd., 212/996-0660, http://sylviasrestaurant.com; 8am-10:30pm Mon.-Sat., 11am-8pm Sun.

✪ Charles' Country Pan Fried Chicken $

Charles Gabriel is the true soul food king. His pan-fried chicken is the perfect blend of crispy and juicy and also attains the optimal level of saltiness. Collard greens are traditionally prepared, oozing their bacon aroma, and his mac and cheese makes an ideal starchy accompaniment. A full meal can be had for around $10. On weekday afternoons, *The People's Court* is likely to be playing on a TV in the corner of this unassuming hole-in-the-wall.

MAP 8: 2461 Frederick Douglas Blvd., 212/281-1800; 11am-midnight Mon.-Sat., 12:30pm-midnight Sun.

BARBECUE
Dinosaur Bar-B-Que $

This was the first NYC location of a popular upstate chain that serves heaping portions of barbecue ribs, pulled pork, and other smoked fare in a cavernous space, with wooden rafters lending the feel of a biker bar—but one where no one has ever gotten into a fight. Blues bands play live sets starting at 10:30pm on Fridays and Saturdays with no cover, and over 25 beers are on tap and available by the half pint, pint, and pitcher. While there are plenty of gluten-free options, vegetarians will be stuck with a salad or fried green tomatoes.

MAP 8: 700 W. 125th St., 212/694-1777, www.dinosaurbarbque.com; 11:30am-11pm Mon.-Thurs., 11:30am-midnight Fri.-Sat., noon-10pm Sun.

STEAK HOUSES
The Cecil Steakhouse $$

It's not uncommon to witness multiple birthday celebrations or waiters breaking out into funky song-and-dance numbers at this joyously upbeat meat haven. Prime cuts of filet mignon and sweet potato au gratin will likely be accompanied by a singer holding court in the front bar or a roaming tap dancer in a bright sport coat weaving through the spacious restaurant—perhaps unsurprising, as the proprietors also own the jazz club next door, Minton's.

MAP 8: 210 W. 118th St., 212/866-1262, www.thececilharlem.com; 5pm-midnight Tues.-Fri., noon-3pm and 5pm-midnight Sat.-Sun.

The Cecil Steakhouse

PIZZA
Patsy's Pizzeria $

Patsy's Pizzerias can be found around the city, but this is the original. It opened in 1933 to serve a growing Italian immigrant population in East Harlem and later became a favorite of singers Frank Sinatra, Dean Martin, and Tony Bennett, along with all-star Yankees Joe DiMaggio, Phil Rizzuto, and Yogi Berra. The exposed brick walls and white tablecloths have changed little since those days, and neither have the red sauce-based coal-oven pizzas, parms, and pastas. A casual counter next door serves slices, a find for pizza of this pedigree.

MAP 8: 2287 1st Ave., 212/534-9783, www.thepatsyspizza.com; 11am-midnight Mon.-Sat., 11am-11pm Sun.

DELIS
Blue Sky Deli (Hajji's) $

It doesn't look like much from the outside, but the Blue Sky Deli—known as Hajji's by regulars—is an integral part of Harlem. It created the "chop cheese" sandwich, a cheap-eats gem that's somewhere between a cheeseburger and an NYC spin on the Philly cheesesteak. Hajji's also inspired a documentary short and a high-end knockoff from celeb chef April Bloomfield, but in its purest (and cheapest) form, the "chop cheese" is a marvel of bodega hangover food. It's also one of the most filling under-$5 meals in the city.

MAP 8: 2135 1st Ave., 646/682-7488; 24 hours daily

MEXICAN
Sexy Taco/Dirty Cash $

During this eatery's boisterous happy hour (3pm-8pm Mon.-Fri., 5pm-7pm Sat.-Sun.), solidly mixed margaritas can be had for just $5, a good way to wash down an array of generously stuffed tacos—the best of which might be the fried codfish—or massive pressed burritos, a solid choice for the ravenous. It's also conveniently located near the 2/3 express train.

MAP 8: 161 Malcolm X Blvd., 212/280-4700, www.sexytacodirtycash.com; 11:30am-midnight Mon.-Thurs., 11:30am-2am Fri., 11am-2am Sat., 11am-11pm Sun.

SWEETS

Hungarian Pastry Shop $

Devoted locals rave about the pastries at this homespun coffee shop. It's reminiscent of the kinds of places that used to line Broadway and Amsterdam Avenue before Starbucks swooped in. Sweets including baklava and cherry strudel can be had for a few dollars—cash only, please—and eaten at the small, well-worn wooden tables. The shop makes an ideal sugar-rush stop after a visit to Cathedral of St. John the Divine or a Central Park stroll.

MAP 8: 1030 Amsterdam Ave., 212/866-4230; 7:30am-11pm Mon.-Fri., 8:30am-11pm Sat., 8:30pm-10pm Sun.

Downtown Brooklyn, Dumbo, and Fort Greene Map 9

CONTEMPORARY AMERICAN

Colonie $$

Sit at the chef's counter for the full experience at Colonie, a locally sourced gem where the menu changes daily and savory aromas waft through the air as you sip a cocktail or craft cider. The menu is divided into four main sections: small, large, pasta, and vegetable. Carnivores can order the short rib cavatelli or generously sized pork chop, while vegetarians will find satisfaction with items like a filling bowl of carrots with smoked ricotta. All can enjoy a deep-fried mushroom or decadent sticky date cake.

MAP 9: 127 Atlantic Ave., 718/855-7500, www.colonienyc.com; 6pm-10:30pm Mon.-Thurs., 6pm-11:30pm Fri., 11am-3pm and 5pm-11:30pm Sat., 11am-3pm and 5pm-10:30pm

The Vanderbilt $$

This gastropub has a more relaxed vibe than famed chef Saul Bolton's eponymous, Michelin-starred restaurant, but likewise turns out high-quality food, including artisanal sausages (also available at the Barclays Center and in grocery stores as Brooklyn Bangers), Brussels sprouts with sriracha, duck wings, and a curry chicken pot pie. A well-curated selection of microbrews on tap and a whiskey list that's as reasonable as it is comprehensive make it easy to linger.

MAP 9: 570 Vanderbilt Ave., 718/623/0570, http://thevanderbiltnyc.com; 5pm-11pm Mon. and Wed.-Fri., 10am-midnight Sat., 10am-10pm Sun.

Hudson Jane

Bella Gioia

Hudson Jane $

A passerby would be forgiven for mistaking Hudson Jane for a simple coffee shop. While you can definitely get your caffeine fix here, there's so much more on offer. Transcendently delicious egg sandwiches made with raw milk cheddar and perfectly crispy hash browns are just the beginning. Try the vegan BLT with mushroom transformed into bacon. It's hard to order badly here, but the tater tots are a must, proving that a great chef can make anything interesting.

MAP 9: 360 Myrtle Ave., 347/987-3881, www.hudsonjane.com; 7am-4pm and 5pm-10pm Mon. and Wed., 7am-4pm and 5pm-11pm Thurs.-Fri., 8am-4pm and 5pm-11pm Sat., 8am-4pm and 5pm-10pm Sun.

ITALIAN
✪ Bella Gioia $$

New Brooklyn innovation meets oversized Old Brooklyn portions at this rustically chic restaurant, a Sicilian comfort food den with a festive atmosphere. The deep-fried burrata and giant arancini with four dipping sauces make for epically tasty apps while a large cut of short rib that falls apart into sweet potato puree is easily sharable as a main course. The wine list is sourced solely from Sicily and reasonably priced while a mezcal negroni is one of many solid cocktails on offer. Chef Nico Daniele trained in Parma, Italy, before working as a pastry chef in Sicily, so it's good to leave room for dessert, specifically the warm chocolate brownie served in a bowl with corn gelato and topped with candied popcorn and caramel sauce. Bella Gioia is also conveniently located just a short walk from BAM and the Barclays Center.

MAP 9: 209 4th Ave., 347/223-4176, www.bellagioianyc.com; 5:30pm-10pm Tues.-Thurs., 5:30pm-11pm Fri., 5pm-11pm Sat., 2pm-9pm Sun.

PIZZA

✪ Juliana's $

This coal-fired gem sits in the shadow of the Brooklyn Bridge—steps from the impeccably landscaped waterfront—in the original storefront of Grimaldi's Pizzeria. Pizza god Patsy Grimaldi sold his namesake pizza chain, which now makes up a mini empire, over a decade ago to retire. He opened Juliana's shortly afterward, proving retirement ain't for everyone. The thin-crust pies (no slices) with just-sweet-enough sauce are possibly the best in the city. The pizza joint's proximity to St. Ann's Warehouse makes it an ideal pre- or postshow stop for simple delights like a pepperoni pizza and craft beer. There's also an extensive wine list that includes a barbera from Piedmont and a chardonnay from Chablis. Lines can stretch out the door after 5pm and on weekends but often move quickly.

MAP 9: 19 Old Fulton St., 718/596-6700, www.julianaspizza.com; 11:30am-3:15pm and 4pm-10pm daily

JEWISH DELIS

Junior's Restaurant and Bakery $$

Somewhere between a diner and a Jewish deli, Junior's serves gargantuan platters of NYC-style comfort food to an eager crowd. This original location has been around since 1950 and for many decades was a shining beacon in a food desert. It's success has spawned additional locations, including two in Times Square that replicate the retro decor with varying degrees of accuracy—but head to this one for the authentic experience. Oddball sandwiches like "something different" are a marvel of excess; why not serve a brisket sandwich using a pair of potato pancakes? Be sure to save room for the restaurant's dense and delicious cheesecake, which they ship across the country.

MAP 9: 386 Flatbush Ave Ext., 718/852-5257, www.juniorscheesecake. com; 6:30am-midnight Sun.-Thurs., 6:30am-1am Fri.-Sat.

BAGELS

Bergen Bagels $

Long lines form at this neighborhood favorite but move quickly thanks to the no-nonsense staff. Bagels here are delicious, especially topped with one of Bergen's inventive cream cheese flavors, like feta pesto. Egg sandwiches here are also solid. Take your bagel to either Fort Greene Park or Prospect Park; there's very limited seating here.

MAP 9: 473 Bergen St., 718/789-7600, www.bergenbagels.com; 6am-10pm daily

CHINESE

Yaso Tangbao $

There are several locations of this fast-food spot, but this outpost in Downtown Brooklyn makes for a great quick stop before a show at BAM or the Alamo Drafthouse. The extensive menu offers authentic Shanghai street food like spicy pork soup dumplings and pan-fried *baos* (buns). You order via touch screen and dishes are often whipped up within minutes. Keep

Yaso Tangbao

an ear out for your order number or someone might inadvertently snag it.

MAP 9: 148 Lawrence St., 929/337-7599, www.yasotangbao.com; 8am-10pm Sun.-Thurs., 11am-10pm Fri.-Sat.

FOOD HALL
DeKalb Market Hall $

DeKalb Market Hall is a subterranean food court with 40 vendors showcasing some of the city's best offerings. An outpost of Katz's Deli is here and serves the same pastrami sandwiches (at the same prices) that made its Lower East Side cafeteria-style restaurant so famous. Arepa Lady, formerly a Queens food cart, offers its outstanding namesake Columbian cornmeal cakes, a perfect blend of sweet and savory. While many toppings are available, it's hard to go wrong with just cheese. There was a time when sweet-tooth foodies had to trek to Brooklyn's Red Hook neighborhood for Steve's Authentic Key Lime Pie, but now it can be had in individual servings here.

Each vendor offers hearty options that can stand alone, but one of the joys to be had at the DeKalb, which could go toe to toe with Chelsea for best market hall, is mixing and matching the options. Come with a few people and create a decadent four-course meal with impossibly fresh pierogi from Pierogi Boys and inventive ice cream scoops from Ample Hills Creamery. Try riding through your food coma with a movie upstairs—DeKalb Market Hall is located in the basement of the same building as the Alamo Drafthouse.

Map 9: 445 Albee Sq. W., 929/359-6555, http://dekalbmarkethall.com; 7am-10pm daily

SWEETS
Four & Twenty Blackbirds Pie Counter and Bar $

For those who've ever sat at a bar and thought the experience could be improved upon with a piece of pie, this outpost of the popular Brooklyn-based mini-chain is the place to go. Owned by a pair of sister pie-makers, it uses locally sourced fruit to craft some of the most satisfying pies in the city. It's hard to go wrong but the salted caramel apple and chocolate chess are outstanding. Flavors sell out fast, so arrive before noon for the best selection. Snag a spot at the 10-seat counter and pair your slice with a local craft beer, wine, or cider.

MAP 9: 634 Dean St., 347/350-5110, www. birdsblack.com; 8am-9pm Mon.-Wed., 8am-11pm Thurs.-Fri., 9am-11pm Sat., 9am-9pm Sun.

Williamsburg, Greenpoint, and Bushwick
Map 10

CONTEMPORARY AMERICAN
Fat Goose $$

It's easy to feel like a regular when you sidle up to the cozy bar at this casually elegant, French-inspired American spot. Friendly servers and comfort plates like duck in huckleberry jus with braised kale make Fat Goose feel like a home away from home. During brunch, it serves a bourbon cider. The location a couple of blocks from the Music Hall of Williamsburg and National Sawdust makes it convenient for a pre- or postshow stop. Happy hour runs Tuesday-Friday 6pm-8pm.

MAP 10: 125 Wythe St., 718/963-2200, http://fatgoosewilliamsburg.com; 6pm-10pm Tues.-Thurs., 6pm-11pm Fri., 11am-4pm and 6pm-11pm Sat., 11am-4pm and 6pm-10pm Sun.

STEAK HOUSES
Peter Luger Steak House $$$

Famed Peter Luger's has been serving dry-aged porterhouses since 1887 when the neighborhood was predominantly German—and it's still the thing to get. The only real decision to make is how big: steak for two, three, or four? A burger served only at lunch has its fans, but it only provides a taste of the rich dry-aged beef that has made this place a city institution.

MAP 10: 178 Broadway, 718/387-7400, http://peterluger.com; 11:45am-9:45pm Mon.-Thurs., 11:45pm-10:45pm Fri.-Sat., 12:45pm-9:45pm Sun.

St. Anselm $$$

If Peter Luger had a kid, his rebellious child might be St. Anselm, where gargantuan cuts of meat share a menu with sweet tea-brined chicken, wine-braised octopus, and salads with burrata and butternut squash. It's actually the brainchild of local restaurateur Joe Carroll, whose mini-empire includes barbecue joint Fette Sau and craft beer pioneer Spuyten Duyvil. Unsurprisingly the drink selection here beats most steak houses, with local wines from Long Island and a craft cider available on draft.

MAP 10: 355 Metropolitan Ave., 718/384-5054, www.stanselm.net; 5pm-11pm Mon.-Thurs., 5pm-midnight Fri., 11am-3pm and 5pm-midnight Sat., 11am-3pm and 5pm-11pm Sun.

ITALIAN
Faro $$$

Michelin-anointed fine dining has been slow to come to Bushwick—though many locals don't seem to mind, preferring the plethora of places serving tasty dishes in a less exacting manner—but the neighborhood earned its first star with chef-owner Kevin Adey's Faro, for dishes like octopus with fermented pepper, creamy foie gras with milk jam, pig's head with cured egg yolk, and above all, homemade pastas that make nothing else in the world matter. High ceilings and exposed ducts give off a warehouse-chic vibe and the service is meticulously attentive.

SMORGASBURG

As its name implies, **Smorgasburg** (www. smorgasburg.com)—a spinoff of the Brooklyn Flea—offers a massive buffet of delectable offerings, from 100 rotating local vendors dishing out everything from Himalayan street food to whole grilled lobsters on a bed of garlic noodles, along with beer, wine, and cocktails. Smorgasburg, which launched in 2011, is now the country's largest open-air food market. April-October from 11am to 6pm, the outdoor foodie market draws large and lively crowds of tourists and locals alike to **East River State Park** (N. 7th St. and Kent Ave.) in Williamsburg on Saturdays and Breeze Hill in **Prospect Park** (East Dr. at Lincoln Rd.) on Sundays. An NYC Ferry conveniently stops at East River State Park and is just a 20-minute ride from Manhattan's East 34th Street dock. The Bedford Avenue station is the closest subway stop when

Smorgasburg

the L train is running, but otherwise the closest option is the Marcy Avenue station, serviced by the J and M lines. The closest subway stop to Smorgasburg in Breeze Hill is the Prospect Park station, which services the B, Q, and S subway lines. In 2018, Smorgasburg also became a year-round event, with an indoor winter market held November-March, along with Friday night markets November-December.

MAP 10: 436 Jefferson St., 718/381-8201, http://farobk.com; 6pm-11pm Mon.-Sat., 5pm-10pm Sun.

Faro

Antica Pesa $$

Riffing on the Roman cuisine of their ancestors—the restaurant's original location is in the Roman neighborhood of Trastevere—this family-run Italian bistro serves homemade pasta in a sleek, dimly lit setting. The menu, which changes seasonally, includes staples like lasagna Bolognese and an all-Italian wine list. There's also a decent cocktail menu with four different negronis.

MAP 10: 115 Berry St., 347/763-2635, www.anticapesa.com; 6pm-10pm Sun.-Thurs., 6pm-11pm Fri.-Sat.

Bamonte's $$

It doesn't get more old-school than Bamonte's, opened and family run since 1900. With tuxedo-clad waiters and white tablecloths, this mainstay red-sauce relic is a window into the neighborhood's immigrant past. There are regulars who have been coming for the past half century and staff members who've worked here just as long.

Classics like spaghetti and meatballs are served in heaping portions alongside glasses of cheap table wine, making a meal here one of the better deals in the neighborhood.

MAP 10: 32 Withers St., 718/384-8831; noon-10pm Mon. and Wed.-Thurs., noon-11pm Fri.-Sat., 1pm-10pm Sun.

PIZZA
Roberta's $$

Roberta's is the last remaining of the original pioneering restaurants in Bushwick. When it opened in 2007 it was the sole beacon of foodie goodness in a sea of warehouses. Its pizzas are now sold at Whole Foods, but the quality and alluring ingredients, like Calabrian chili, have remained intact. With so many other great options in the neighborhood now, though, a two-hour wait might seem less desirable.

MAP 10: 261 Moore St., 718/417-1118, www.robertaspizza.com; 11am-midnight Mon.-Fri., 10am-midnight Sat.-Sun.

Anna Maria Williamsburg $

Open until 2am, Anna Maria makes a great stop before heading back to your hotel after an evening out. Generously cut slices with slightly sweet sauce are served rapid-fire after midnight on the weekends when a line can snake out the door. Like most slice joints, it tends to overheat orders, so ask for "not too hot" to avoid a scalded tongue.

MAP 10: 179 Bedford Ave., 718/599-4550, www.annamariabrooklyn.com; 11am-2am daily

Paulie Gee's $

Rustic charm abounds at this local favorite. Wood-fired pizzas come with a dizzying variety of toppings, and 20 of the specialty pies are vegan, made with ingredients like cashew ricotta, kale pesto, and pumpkin puree. Each

is sized as a large personal pizza that's easily sharable with a salad. The warehouse-meets-farmhouse decor makes lingering over a craft beer or one of the vegan desserts easy. Reservations aren't accepted, and crowds can form on weekend evenings. A couple of blocks away is the more casual **Paulie Gee's Slice Shop** (110 Franklin St., no phone; noon-4pm and 6pm-11pm Mon.-Thurs., noon-4pm and 6pm-1am Fri., noon-1am Sat., noon-11pm Sun.).

MAP 10: 60 Greenpoint Ave., 347/987-3743, http://pauliegee.com; 6pm-11pm Mon.-Fri., 5pm-11pm Sat., 5pm-10pm Sun.

JAPANESE
Momo Sushi Shack $$

Most seating is communal at Momo, so be prepared to get to know your neighbors as you gorge on handmade *gyoza* (Japanese dumplings) and sushi bombs (orb-like dollops of rice topped with, for instance, barbecued eel or salmon belly). Inventive flourishes are a key draw, including several vegan options, but traditional rolls are available as well, as are noodle, fish, and meat dishes. Crowds form in the evenings and on weekends, so weekday lunch is the best time to come if you want more elbow room.

MAP 10: 43 Bogart St., 718/418-6666, www.momosushishack.com; noon-4:30pm and 5:30pm-11pm Sun.-Thurs., noon-4:30pm and 5:30pm-midnight Sat.-Sun.

Shalom Japan $$

Chefs and owners Aaron Israel and Sawako Okochi blend their Jewish and Japanese backgrounds, respectively, to create an utterly original menu that features dishes like matzo ball ramen with foie gras dumplings or *okonomi-yaki* (a savory Japanese pancake) with pastrami and a fried egg. Beverages include the Japanese spirit *shochu*, along with an extensive craft beer list and cocktails like the Meshugatini, made with gin, vodka, and pickle brine.

MAP 10: 310 S. 4th St., 718/388-4012, http://shalomjapannyc.com; 5:30pm-10pm Tues.-Wed., 5:30pm-11pm Thurs.-Fri., 11am-3pm and 5:30pm-11pm Sat.-Sun.

INDONESIAN
Selamat Pagi $

Top-notch Balinese-inspired cuisine made from local and organic ingredients is served in an intimate and colorful yet casual environment at this Indonesian restaurant that takes food very seriously. Its dishes don't shy away from spices in offerings such as a grass-fed beef curry or prawn vermicelli soup. Spring rolls with shiitake mushrooms make an ideal starter and can be made vegetarian or vegan, as can several other options on the menu. A well-curated selection of wines and craft beer is available along with soju-based cocktails, like a hard limeade, to wash it all down.

MAP 10: 152 Driggs Ave., 718/701-4333, www.selamatpagibrooklyn.com; 5:30pm-11pm Mon.-Fri., 11am-4pm and 5:30pm-11pm Sat.-Sun.

BASQUE
✪ Brooklyn Cider House $$

Brooklyn Cider House imports the joyous experience of Basque country dining to a smartly renovated warehouse on the industrial edge of Bushwick. You can order à la carte from the front bar or head to the back dining area where a feast awaits: four courses served family style, including a Flintstonian bone-in rib eye steak. Between courses, diners take trips to giant barrels and "catch" pours of cider with wide-rimmed glasses; this involves placing your glass by the barrel's spigot and lowering it until full, when the next person can jump in with his or her glass. It's a fun drinking game that tests your coordination skills. These craft concoctions are deceptively smooth, clocking in at almost 7 percent ABV, and generously doled out. Reservations are recommended on weekends.

MAP 10: 1100 Flushing Ave., 347/295-0308, www.brooklynciderhouse.com; 5pm-midnight Tues.-Thurs., 5pm-1am Fri., 11am-1am Sat., 11am-midnight Sun.

Brooklyn Cider House

MEXICAN
Mesa Coyoacan $$

Named for the borough in Mexico City where chef Ivan Garcia grew up, Mesa Coyoacan separates itself from a growing pack of upscale Mexican restaurants by delivering a craft approach to street food, such as tacos, at reasonable prices. Plates like enchiladas de mole, made from Garcia's secret family recipe, cost more. Mezcal margaritas and an extensive tequila selection invite you to linger at the bar, one of the long communal tables, or in the shaded sidewalk seating.

MAP 10: 372 Graham Ave., 718/782-8171, www.mesacoyoacan.com; 5pm-midnight Mon.-Tues., noon-midnight Wed.-Thurs., noon-1am Fri., 11am-1am Sat., 11am-midnight Sun.

Tortilleria Mexicana Los Hermanos $

This working tortilla factory is one of the few businesses to make the transition from old Bushwick to new. It remains popular with recent neighborhood transplants and nightlife revelers simply because the food here is cheap and good. Tortillas are made fresh daily and form the base for the variety of tacos, tostadas, and quesadillas on offer. Write you order on an index card and hand it to a counter worker. Grab a Mexican soda from the fridge or crack open a BYO-beer while you wait. The no-frills atmosphere—loading dock brutalist—adds to the experience.

MAP 10: 271 Starr St., 718/456-3422; 9am-11:30pm Mon.-Sat., noon-11:30pm Sun.

BARBECUE
Arrogant Swine $

Dressed as an industrial beer garden but with the soul of a North Carolina barbecue pit, this is an ideal place to while away a few hours under the sun in the ample concrete backyard. Sides like a sweet potato waffle with bourbon maple syrup decadently complement whole-hog pulled pork and chicken wings glazed with a Vietnamese caramel sauce. Over a dozen craft drafts include rarities like San Diego brewery AleSmith's Horny Devil, clocking in at a potent 10 percent ABV.

MAP 10: 173 Morgan Ave., 347/328-5595, http://arrogantswine.com; noon-2am Tues.-Thurs., noon-4am Fri.-Sat., noon-midnight Sun.

Fette Sau $

With bare-bones industrial decor and meat by the pound, served on metal trays, Fette Sau is a carnivore's haven. Drawing inspiration both from central Texas pits and New York delis, the restaurant features staples like pulled pork and brisket alongside beef tongue pastrami and veal hearts, all hormone- and antibiotic-free. Almost a dozen craft beers are available by the gallon, though the cost is virtually the same as ordering by the pint. Crowds during prime weekend evening hours after 6pm can be intense but McCarren Park, just a short stroll north, makes a good spot for an impromptu picnic if you decide to order out instead.

MAP 10: 354 Metropolitan Ave., 718/963-3404, www.fettesaubbq.com; 5pm-11pm Mon., noon-11pm Sun. and Tues.-Thurs., noon-midnight Sat.-Sun.

SWEETS
Du's Donuts and Coffee $

Wylie Dufresne's molecular gastronomy den WD-50, which closed in 2014, was one of the most influential restaurants in the world. The acclaimed chef is now devoting his second act to doughnuts. Housed in the posh William Vale hotel, Dufresne's tiny shop churns out a rotating array of delectable cake donuts from chocolate caramel brownie to pomegranate tahini. The latter pairs well with Du's scrambled egg grilled cheese for a decadent breakfast.

MAP 10: 107 N. 12th St., 718/215-8770, www.dusdonuts.com; 8am-5pm Mon.-Fri., 9am-5pm Sat.-Sun.

NIGHTLIFE

In a city that prides itself on never sleeping—most bars don't close until 4am, dance clubs stay open even later, and subways run 24 hours a day—options for nocturnal amusements are as endless as they are varied. People are always out and about and the city is always buzzing somewhere. Iconic jazz clubs and intimate rock venues regularly host world-renowned musicians, cocktails wow with each sip, and craft brews increasingly—especially in Brooklyn—abound. The only thing lacking is the time to take it all in.

BlackTail cocktail

You'll find trendy lounges in Soho and Tribeca, while dance clubs are largely concentrated in the Meatpacking District between 14th and Gansevoort Streets. Williamsburg, along with the East Village and Lower East Side, are teeming with many of the city's hippest bars and live music venues.

Greenwich Village, particularly in the vicinity of MacDougal and Bleecker Streets, has a high density of college hangouts—unsurprising, given New York University's presence in the area—but the neighborhood also has some great cocktail bars and historic jazz and rock clubs like the Village Vanguard, Smalls, and The Bitter End. The Village is also home to legendary LGBTQ spaces, including the Stonewall Inn. Chelsea is also known for its LGBTQ nightlife, particularly its gay bars.

HIGHLIGHTS

✪ **BEST COCKTAIL BAR:** Find a dizzying array of trendy cocktails in an old-school atmosphere at **The Dead Rabbit** (page 179).

✪ **BEST MUSIC-AND-MEAL PAIRING:** Enjoy live music with great food and wine at cozy **City Winery** (page 181).

✪ **BEST LIVE MUSIC VENUE:** See a show at the **Bowery Ballroom** to experience what many consider the city's best acoustics (page 183).

✪ **BEST BAR TO MAKE NEW YORK FEEL LIKE A SMALL TOWN:** **Big Bar** is a neighborhood mainstay exuding cozy conviviality (page 186).

✪ **BEST JAZZ CLUB:** The **Village Vanguard** has hosted countless musical legends over the years (page 188)

✪ **BEST SCENE-Y NIGHTCLUB:** **Le Bain** is the place to see and be seen—especially in the pool (page 193).

✪ **BEST PLACE TO SEE A TOP-NOTCH DRAG SHOW:** **Barracuda** has long been a go-to spot for flirty conversation and high camp (page 194).

✪ **BEST *MAD MEN*-STYLE LOUNGE:** Bygone style is in abundance at **Flatiron Lounge,** Julie Reiner's classic cocktail bar (page 195).

✪ **BEST DIVE BAR:** **Rudy's** is dirt-cheap and provides a glimpse of a pre-gentrification neighborhood (page 200).

✪ **MOST STORIED SUPPER CLUB IN HARLEM:** **Minton's Playhouse,** the birthplace of bebop, still features a solid lineup of musicians and good food and cocktails to boot (page 203).

✪ **BEST CRAFT BEER IN BROOKLYN:** Tiny **Beer Street** packs a punch with its selection of rare brews (page 207).

✪ **BEST PLACE FOR WHISKEY *AND* A GRILLED CHEESE:** Grown-up and childhood pleasures meet at **Noorman's Kil** (page 211).

Village Vanguard

COCKTAIL LOUNGES

✪ The Dead Rabbit

Owners Sean Muldoon and Jack McGarry take the best parts of a saloon from the Wild West—a rustic atmosphere, exposed wooden beams—and meld them with top-notch cocktails. The 1st-floor taproom has a more raucous vibe, while the tables in the 2nd-floor parlor encourage more refined conversation. The baby lamb chops are fall-off-the-bone tender and the lobster deviled eggs are as decadent as they sound, making this a worthy dining destination as well, but the dizzying array of cocktails are the main draw. Displayed as a graphic novel, the menu of creative concoctions like Holy Smoke (scotch, green *matcha* tea, curry leaf) and Shadow Boxer (aged gin, carrot, paprika) make it evident why The Dead Rabbit was dubbed number one on *The World's 50 Best Bars* list in 2016. An expansion recently doubled the space, cutting down on wait times for this popular bar.

MAP 1: 30 Water St., 646/422.7906, www.deadrabbitnyc.com; 11am-4am daily

BlackTail

The latest venture by The Dead Rabbit's owners, this large and elegant space on top of Pier A evokes the bars in Havana that well-heeled New Yorkers would flock to during Prohibition, with leafy oversized plants, dark wood paneling, and plush seating. The drink list is divided into five categories: highballs, punches, sours, old-fashioneds, and cocktails. Tasty novelties include the Rattlesnake (Islay scotch, fennel, Earl Grey tea, egg whites) and Arawak (Campari, coffee, rum, absinthe). As an added nicety, customers are served a small amuse cocktail to whet the palate, and a full food menu is available.

MAP 1: 22 Battery Pl., Pier A 2nd floor, 212/785-0153, http://blacktailnyc.com; 5pm-2am daily

Cedar Local

This dimly lit bar just a stone's throw from Wall Street caters to the after-work crowd with an array of creative cocktails cheekily divided into two categories: New Money and Old Money. The former features the bold Splash of Rose (rye, maple syrup, pinot noir) while the latter features more traditional libations like a whiskey sour. Bar bites include a wide range of charcuterie, Murray's cheeses, and savory dishes like smoked pork belly sliders.

MAP 1: 25 Cedar St., 212/344-3467, www.cedarlocal.com; 3:30pm-midnight Mon., 3:30pm-2am Tues.-Wed., 2pm-2am Thurs.-Fri., 5pm-2am Sat.

The Wooly Public

Tucked inside the historic Woolworth Building, but with its own entrance on Barclay Street, this modern cocktail bar and restaurant exudes the warmth of a library, with bookshelves lining the back wall. Paintings of wooly mammoths hang over tables where diners quaff finely crafted tiki concoctions like the Woolynesia (gin, aperol, chili, ginger, pureed stone fruit) and a sublime summery take on the Manhattan dubbed the Lower Manhattan Project (scotch, vermouth, mezcal, elderflower). The food is quite good as well, especially the tater tots with shredded Peking duck and queso

WHERE SPIRITS AND HISTORY MEET

The Dead Rabbit

Owners Sean Muldoon and Jack McGarry like to bring history to life at their bars, with modern updates.

The Dead Rabbit is named after an Irish street gang that ruled the neighborhood when it was known as the rough-and-tumble Five Points in the mid-19th century, an era captured in Martin Scorsese's *Gangs of New York.* "Dead" is slang for "very" and "rabbit" is the American pronunciation of the Celtic word "ráibéad," which means "man to be feared." The building in which the bar is based dates back to 1828, and the dozens of cocktails are designed to evoke the culture of that era—for instance, classic communal punches served in tea cups—though, as McGarry explains, "All of our cocktail recipes have been tweaked to suit contemporary palates." The bar itself exudes more of an upper-class refinement, though the lively 1st-floor Irish pub-style taproom feels like a spot where gang members might pop in for an invigorating shot of whiskey.

After the success of The Dead Rabbit, McGarry and Muldoon were looking to tell a different story: that of American bar culture in Havana during Prohibition. At **BlackTail,** brass plaques commemorate the famous and infamous who frequented Cuba for liquid vacations, like Ernest Hemingway and Al Capone. "In particular, we are championing the highball, the unsung high priest of tall drinks," McGarry notes. Eight are on the menu, and it's best to think of these as sessionable cocktails: easy to quaff and then repeat. Some, like a rum and cola, may sound classically familiar, but the BlackTail version is flavored with amaro and fig. With hundreds of photos at the bar documenting Cuban life, it's easy to drink here and feel like an expat on the island.

and the fried cod sandwich stuffed with coleslaw.

MAP 1: 9 Barclay St., 212/571-2930, www.thewoolypublic.com; 11:30am-midnight Mon.-Wed., 11:30am-1am Thurs.-Fri., 6pm-1am Sat.

PUBS

Woodrow's

Situated near City Hall, the National September 11 Memorial & Museum, One World Observatory, and the Woolworth Building, Woodrow's makes for a great mid-sightseeing refueling break, with solid pub grub including a sweet $10 burger and beer special that's a true bargain in the area. It's a popular after-work spot for the Wall Street crowd and can get packed from about 5pm-8pm on weekdays, but otherwise it's easy to nab a table or seat at the long wooden bar and sip pints of local craft beer from the Bronx Brewery, among others. If you're here on the first Monday of the month, you can catch trivia hosted by *Jeopardy!* winner Austin Rogers, whose 12-day winning streak in 2017 made him one of the most successful contestants in the show's history.

MAP 1: 43 Murray St., 212/676-0300, www. woodrowsnyc.com; 11am-1am Sun.-Wed., 11am-2am Thurs.-Sat.

Soho and Tribeca · Map 2

LIVE MUSIC
ROCK
✪ City Winery

Owner and music impresario Michael Dorf created City Winery because he wanted a place where you could sit down with a great glass of wine while watching a rock show. City Winery's offerings are made from West Coast grapes that ferment in large barrels on-site, and are served on tap by the glass. The Sohovignon Blanc is fresh (wink for the pun on the Soho location), with a clean finish, and the Pinot Noir Spring Street has a subtle complexity. A full kitchen is here as well, and serves up funky cheese flatbreads and an addictively sweet duck breast. Folk legend Billy Bragg, veteran guitarist Alejandro Escovedo, and buzzy up-and-comers Wye Oak are just a few of the musicians who have graced the winery's stage. Singer-songwriter-novelist Wesley Stace hosts his monthly indie rock/ literature variety show "Cabinet of

City Winery

Wonders" here, with guests from bands like Sonic Youth and the Mountain Goats and authors including Tom Perrotta and Sarah Vowell. The venue also hosts wine dinners and pairings with music. Scott Ian of Anthrax led a particularly memorable Led Zeppelin cover band that coupled nicely with an array of robust reds.

MAP 2: 155 Varick St., 212/608-0555, www.citywinery.com; 11:30am-11pm Sun.-Fri., 5pm-11pm Sat.; prices vary

COCKTAIL LOUNGES
The Bennett

This Tribeca cocktail bar seamlessly blends comfort and class. The majority of seating is at gold-colored high tops that line a wall opposite the bar. With drinks that incorporate spiced maple or celery bitters, the concoctions are anything but ordinary. Order a burger on Mondays and cocktails made with Bulleit Bourbon are just $10.

MAP 2: 134 W. Broadway, 212/902-9671, www.thebennettbar.com; 5pm-1am Mon.-Wed., 5pm-2am Thurs., 4pm-2am Fri., 11am-2am Sat., 11am-11pm Sun.

Pegu Club

Pegu Club has quite the pedigree: Owner Audrey Saunders did time at the famously fancy Bemelmans Bar in The Carlyle hotel, and her original slate of bartenders went on to start their own prized cocktail bars, including Death & Co., PDT, The Happiest Hour, and Attaboy. The bar's name, derived from an early 20th-century cocktail, is an inside nod to the bartending community, and fans gush that you can't go wrong with any drink on the menu; this could be because Saunders is known to have dozens of versions of each made before settling on the perfect recipe.

MAP 2: 77 W. Houston St., 2nd fl., 212/473-7348, www.peguclub.com; 5pm-2am Sun.-Wed., 5pm-4am Thurs.-Sat.

The Ship

The subtle nautical theme at this subterranean cocktail bar goes well with the unassuming crew who makes the half-dozen cocktails that change seasonally. The Ship's all-seated policy ensures a relaxed vibe to enjoy plates of dishes like Korean barbecue sliders and slow-cooked octopus, but it also might mean a wait on weekend evenings. It's best as a small-group hangout: booths hold six people or fewer.

MAP 2: 158 Lafayette St., 212/219-8496, www.theshipnyc.com; 5pm-1am Mon.-Thurs., 6pm-3am Fri.-Sat.

PUBS
Ear Inn

Located down the street from what was George Washington's Richmond Hill estate, one of New York City's oldest bars—dating back to 1817—sits in a Federal-style town house that once belonged to African American Revolutionary War hero James Brown, who made a fortune in the tobacco trade. The knick-knack-filled bar feels like a portal to a bygone era, with its ship's wheel mounted on the ceiling. Enjoy the quirky atmosphere with a pint of Guinness at the bar.

MAP 2: 326 Spring St., 212/226-9060, www.earinn.com; 11:30am-4am daily

Fanelli Cafe

While this saloon dates back to the 19th century and much of the old wooden decor has been preserved, it is far from a relic. Dogfish Head beer is served on tap and the burgers are deservedly reputed. Charred, smoky, and unfussy, the bison burger is particularly filling and deeply satisfying. Fanelli's also happen to make one of the better veggie burgers around, served with an addictive pesto sauce.

MAP 2: 94 Prince St., 212/226-9412; 10am-2am daily

East Village and Lower East Side — Map 3

LIVE MUSIC

ROCK

✪ Bowery Ballroom

Considered by many to have the best acoustics in the city, the Bowery Ballroom consistently draws an impressive array of up-and-coming buzz bands and legends alike. Vampire Weekend, Patti Smith, and Stephen Malkmus are just a few of the acts who have graced the stage. You'll head down a staircase upon entering and emerge in a bar-lounge area, a great place to enjoy a drink while waiting for the band to start. A staircase behind the semicircular bar leads up to the back of the venue while one to the right of the entrance, next to the women's bathroom, puts you right by the stage. Arrive when the doors open if you want to nab a spot right in front. Most shows are standing room and the venue only holds 575 people, so you'll never be too far from the stage.

MAP 3: 6 Delancey St., 212/260-4700, www.mercuryeastpresents.com/boweryballroom; door time varies by show; prices vary

Mercury Lounge

Think of this club as a mini-Bowery Ballroom. There are few standing room clubs that are as intimate, but be warned: It can get deafeningly loud in here depending on the act (keep earplugs on hand). Some of the many highlights have included Cloud Nothings, singer-songwriter Kyle Craft, and one of Moby's side projects. Prices are usually low (typically $10), making it a cool place to take a chance on a band. PBR on tap helps keep your bar bill low, but several craft brews are also on offer and there's a full bar.

MAP 3: 217 E. Houston St., 212/260-4700, www.mercuryeastpresents.com/mercurylounge; door time varies by show; from $10

Pianos

The name and faded sign in front of this popular Lower East Side music club are remnants of the piano shop that used to occupy this space. The lineup of up-and-coming indie acts draws crowds of adventurous young music lovers. For $10 or less, you can usually see five bands a night in the showroom, while the upstairs lounge features free DJ sets most nights. During happy hour (2pm-8pm), beer and wine is just $4.

MAP 3: 158 Ludlow St., 212/505-3733, http://pianosnyc.com; 2pm-4am daily; cover $8-10

Rockwood Music Hall

Rockwood Music Hall's front room, where there's typically no cover, feels like a 2.0 version of the legendary

WHERE ALL THE BANDS YOU READ ABOUT IN *PITCHFORK* PLAY

If you want to hear that hip new band that just got a coveted 9.2 in online music magazine *Pitchfork,* head to the Lower East Side or Williamsburg, both of them treasure troves of live music venues. Shows can sell out fast, so check schedules well in advance.

LOWER EAST SIDE

- Cream of the crop is the **Bowery Ballroom** (page 183), which regularly books acts that grace *Pitchfork*'s Best New Music list and other music blogs. You'll also see bands that have yet to reach the radar of music journalists; Vampire Weekend played here when their core fan base was primarily students from their alma mater, Columbia University.

- **Mercury Lounge** (page 183) keeps prices low and is a cozier version of the Bowery Ballroom—on less-crowded nights, it has the intimacy of a friend's living room.

- It's hard to ask for a more elegantly intimate experience than a café table at the front-room space of **Rockwood Music Hall** (page 183), which often has no cover.

WILLIAMSBURG

- **Baby's All Right** (page 207) serves Korean food in its front room and hosts promising acts—like singer-songwriter Phoebe Bridgers—in its tiny backroom.

- Formerly based in Manhattan, the **Knitting Factory** (page 207) features a steady array of up-and-coming acts.

- **Music Hall of Williamsburg** (page 207), similar to the Bowery Ballroom, books buzzy indie acts.

- In back of a record store, **Rough Trade** (page 304) has hosted shows by indie acts like Father John Misty and Amanda Palmer.

---

shuttered Living Room, with small candlelit tables arranged around an equally intimate stage. This singer-songwriter café is a great spot to check out new talent while enjoying a good glass of wine. Talking is shunned and focus is on the songs. In addition to the front room, there's a stage next door with a larger standing room area and some tables, and a third smaller space in the basement. With multiple bands on three stages, there's always someone playing their heart out here.

MAP 3: 196 Allen St., 212/477-4155, www.rockwoodmusichall.com; 5:30pm-1:30am Mon.-Thurs., 5:30pm-2:30am Fri., 2:30pm-3am Sat., 2:30pm-1:30am Sun.; Stage 1 usually no cover, with one-drink minimum per set standing, two-drink minimum per set seated, Stages 2 and 3 typically $10-15 per set

COCKTAIL LOUNGES
Angel's Share

This stylish speakeasy is hidden behind an unmarked door on the 2nd floor of unassuming Japanese restaurant Village Yokocho, around the corner from bustling St. Marks Place. The bar's name describes the portion of whiskey that evaporates during the aging process—so it's not surprising Angel's Share makes some of the most complex whiskey cocktails around; the one with foraged mushrooms and Virgil Kaine bourbon is a particular standout. But this is the kind of place where it's best to find your way to the perfect drink by having a conversation with the bartender. Groups over four aren't allowed in the intimate space; the bar is better suited for dates or chiller hangouts than a raucous night out. Reservations are a must.

MAP 3: 8 Stuyvesant St., 212/777-5415; 6pm-1:30am Sun.-Wed., 6pm-2:30am Thurs.-Sat.

Death & Co

Awarded the World's Best Cocktail Menu honor in 2010 by the venerable Tales of the Cocktail—the Oscars of the cocktail world—this bar remains a major influencer. Its extensive offerings are divided into four categories: In the Raw, Water of Life, Transformation, and Luxury. The last of those consists of pricey concoctions that clock in at almost double the standard $16 and features top-shelf spirits like Mic Drop bourbon and 12-year-old cask-strength Redbreast Irish whiskey.

MAP 3: 433 E. 6th St., 212/388-0882, www.deathandcompany.com; 6pm-2am Sun.-Thurs., 6pm-3am Fri.-Sat.

Holiday Cocktail Lounge

Around since 1835, this dive turned upscale lounge has been a favorite over the years for storied locals like W. H. Auden and Leon Trotsky. Madonna and the Ramones have also knocked back a few here. These days the bar serves up strong but masterfully mixed cocktails, has craft beers on draft, and offers an extensive food menu. The Cubano doughnut—the classic Cuban sandwich with a doughnut in place of bread—is a must; there's no better way to soak up all the alcohol you'll want to drink here.

MAP 3: 75 St. Mark's Pl., 212/777-9637, www.holidaycocktaillounge.nyc; 4pm-4am Mon.-Fri., noon-4am Sat.-Sun.

PDT

This low-ceilinged den of ramshackle elegance would feel like a secret (its initials stand for Please Don't Tell) if not for the mob of people that usually surrounds it. Make a reservation in advance by phone so you can bypass the crowds and enjoy its celebrated cocktails, like the Benton's old-fashioned; this inventive take on the classic drink is made with maple syrup and Four Roses Bourbon infused with bacon. It pairs nicely with one of the bacon-wrapped hot dogs from Crif Dogs—the bar is located through a "phone booth" inside the eatery.

MAP 3: 113 St. Mark's Pl., 212/614-0386, www.pdtnyc.com; 6pm-2am Sun.-Thurs., 6pm-3am Fri.-Sat.

Pouring Ribbons

Pouring Ribbons

Most renowned cocktail bars in the city are small and require a wait without reservations. Pouring Ribbons is the exception. A 2nd-floor space accommodates groups and often has open tables (unlike other neighborhood bars like Death & Co). The menu is a delight to behold, with drinks displayed on a chart measuring how they rank on a scale of potency (refreshing to spiritous) and complexity (comforting to adventurous). Drinks typically follow a theme; a milk-based drink named after British artist Damien Hirst—who often explores death in his work—came with a skull emblazoned in the foam.

MAP 3: 225 Ave. B, 917/656-6788, www. pouringribbons.com; 6pm-2am daily

The Summit Bar

Exposed brick walls and an inviting L-shaped bar make lingering easy at this cocktail bar-gastropub hybrid. Drinks here are already more afford-able than at competitors, but happy hour (5pm-8pm daily) offers a par-ticularly sweet deal, when a range of cocktails, from a classic old-fashioned to the more adventurous Ground to Glass (a blend of tequila, red bell pep-per puree, house-made orange bit-ters, and smoked salt), and dishes like pulled pork sliders can be had for just $7 each.

MAP 3: 133 Ave. C, 347/465-7911, www. thesummitbar.net; 5pm-2am Sun.-Thurs., 5pm-3am Fri.-Sat.

The Summit Bar

CRAFT BEER
Burp Castle

Don't be surprised if the bartender hushes you at this contemplative Belgian beer den. Come alone or for quiet conversation with a friend to sample the dozen taps. From your throne, er, barstool, you can enjoy tart lambics, bold tripels, and the oc-casional locally brewed craft, like a crème brûlée porter from Southern Tier. An Oriental rug and giant nauti-cal-themed wall mural give the place a cozy, quirky vibe.

MAP 3: 41 E. 7th St., 212/982-4576, www.burpcastlenyc.com; 5pm-midnight Mon.-Fri., 4pm-2am Sat.-Sun.

Eastwood

This gem on the eastern edge of the Lower East Side makes a great stop after seeing a show at nearby Abrons Arts Center. It has a warm and woodsy vibe, a laid-back crowd, and eight taps featuring a well-chosen array of mostly local offerings from the likes of LIC Beer Project, Finback, and Industrial Arts breweries. Service can be inattentive, so it's best to go when you're feeling leisurely. The bar also has some inventive food options, like an Israeli Scotch egg (it's wrapped in falafel before it's fried).

MAP 3: 200 Clinton St., 212/233-0124; noon-2am Mon.-Fri., 10am-2am Sat.-Sun.

BARS AND PUBS
✪ Big Bar

This ironically named watering hole is one of the smallest in the city. But what Big Bar lacks in square footage it makes up for in heart: With just a handful of stools, a few booths, and a jukebox, it has a charming big-city-interpretation-of-small-town vibe that emanates throughout the small, red-lit space. It feels a bit like an extension of your living room, if you had a steady stream of affable strangers stopping by.

MAP 3: 75 E. 7th St., 212/777-6969; 5pm-2am Sun.-Thurs., 5pm-4am Fri.-Sat.

The Library

Old and cult movies play on a projected screen in the back of this neighborhood hangout. Drawing a friendly punk-ish crowd and offering daily beer and shot specials at cut-rate prices, The Library used to be just one of many of a kind but now stands out as a reminder of a bygone bar scene. The tattooed bartenders are affable and quick on the draw, making this a good place to settle in and lose count of how many you've had.

MAP 3: 7 Ave. A, 212/375-1352; noon-4am daily

McSorley's Old Ale House

Serving since 1854, this saloon is the oldest continuously operated drinking establishment in the city. What other place could count both President Lincoln and John Lennon as patrons? E. E. Cummings captured his experience here in the poem "Sitting in McSorley's." The floors are sawdust-covered, and hints of the bar's vast history can be found in framed photos adorning the walls and memorabilia, including a pair of handcuffs supposedly worn by Houdini. One welcome change is that women are now allowed—that only happened in 1970. Ordering is a simple affair: The only choices are light and dark ale, served in smallish mugs, and best enjoyed in large quantities. Today, drinking here remains a festive experience with plenty of glasses clanging in spontaneous toasts.

MAP 3: 15 E. 7th St., 212/473-9148, http://mcsorleysoldalehouse.nyc; noon-12:30am daily

Welcome to the Johnsons

Wood paneling, a pool table, and retro video games that double as tables give this dive bar the feel of a 1970s basement. Prices are dirt cheap, and the vibe is warm, encouraging rambling stays that end with a stumble to a cab or the F train around the corner. The crowd is college-aged but not exclusively so.

MAP 3: 123 Rivington St., 212/420-9911; 3pm-4am Mon.-Fri., 1pm-4am Sat.-Sun.

LGBTQ
Club Cumming

Housed in the former space of shuttered gay bar Eastern Bloc, Club Cumming is a joyous and all-inclusive affair for people of all gender identities and persuasions. Its co-owner is the incomparably talented actor-singer Alan Cumming, who drops in regularly to perform cabaret sets along with a bevy of friends, including his piano player Lance Horne, who holds court Mondays after 9pm. Celebrity sightings are common and many wind up on stage; Paul McCartney stopped by once to accompany Cumming for a few songs. The sleek, narrow club oozes a playful sex-charged vibe with black ceilings, chandeliers, and a red-lit glow throughout. Burlesque shows and scantily clad go-go dancers are also regular fixtures.

MAP 3: 505 E. 6th St, 917/265-8006, www.nowherebarnyc.com; 7pm-3am Sun.-Thurs., 7pm-4am Fri.-Sat.; usually no cover, select shows $10-15

Nowhere

Nowhere exudes dive bar warmth with exposed brick, low ceilings, a pool table, a perpetual red hue, and a mirror ball that sets the intimate space aglow. While prices are reasonable, they get even better with $3 drink specials for events like the long-running Beers, Beards, and Bears; Ginger Appreciation Night; and go-go-boy-filled Macho Mondays.

MAP 3: 322 E. 14th St., 212/477-4744, www.nowherebarnyc.com; 3pm-4am daily; no cover except for Macho Mon. ($5-10)

The Village and the Meatpacking District   Map 4

LIVE MUSIC
JAZZ
✪ Village Vanguard

Jazz legends like Miles Davis and John Coltrane recorded some of their most iconic albums in this wedge-shaped basement club. Seating is tight and views are often obstructed, but the warm acoustics are unparalleled. Cover charges have remained low compared to the city's other major clubs and the lineup remains top-notch, with regular appearances by Fred Hersch, the Bad Plus, and Joe Lovano, among others. The club's namesake brassy orchestra holds court on Mondays.

MAP 4: 178 7th Ave. S., 212/255-4037, www.villagevanguard.com; sets 8:30pm and 10:30pm daily; $35 per set

The Blue Note

The grand piano-shaped entrance awning at this classic club is as gleefully from a bygone era as the neon sign above the bar near the entrance. Sitting at the bar is the cheapest option, though you'll be quite far from the action. Arrive when doors open to snag prime table seats for acts like Béla Fleck and the Flecktones, Chick Corea, and Maceo Parker. While there's an extensive food menu, you're better off having dinner at one of the restaurants nearby.

MAP 4: 131 W. 3rd St., 212/475-8592, www.bluenote.net; 8pm-10pm nightly; cover $30-45

Smalls

Smalls may feel like your parents' basement, but don't let the casual vibe fool you: This jazz club regularly books some of the most talented up-and-coming musicians. Although it's no longer BYOB, there's no drink minimum and on weeknights your ticket is good all night as well as at Smalls's sister club, Mezzrow, down the block, making this an ideal long evening out with friends. On weekends, admission is for a single set, though you might be allowed to stay for additional sets based on how crowded it is that night. Just remember: It's good etiquette not to talk while the musicians are playing.

MAP 4: 183 W. 10th St., 646/476-4346, www.smallslive.com; 7pm-3:30am Mon.-Fri., 4pm-3:30am Sat.-Sun.; cover $20

Zinc Bar

This tucked-away jazz club has a funky-chic vibe and a diverse lineup of emerging bands. From Afro-Cuban to bossa nova, the music is highly syncopated and often joyful,

From Frank Sinatra to Lou Reed to Sarah Jessica Parker to Tina Fey, New York has always had its share of stars. The list goes on and on, and with so many celebrities living in such a condensed space, it's not uncommon to run into them at a restaurant, on the street, in a movie theater, or even a grocery store. The etiquette here is be cool. Don't pull your camera out as you would to snap a photo of a landmark or a polar bear at the zoo. Smile and move on. Some celebrities have made public their willingness to engage in genuine conversations with fans, but this shouldn't be assumed. If you find yourself saying, "I don't mean to disturb you, but … (insert random compliment)," chances are you did.

and it continues into the wee hours of the morning. Crowds come in waves throughout the evening, and on weekends it's not uncommon for a line to form outside.

MAP 4: 82 W. 3rd St., 212/477-9462, www.zincbar.com; 6pm-2:30am Sun.-Thurs., 6pm-3am Fri.-Sat.; cover $10-20

BLUES
Terra Blues

This mainstay 2nd-floor club is the place to go when you want to consume a lot of blues. Unlike many clubs of this caliber, the cover charge is good for the entire evening (though there is a strict two-drink minimum per set) and the musicians, many of whom are regulars, have a knack for insanely spirited jams. An extensive whiskey menu includes a dizzying array of small-batch bourbons.

MAP 4: 149 Bleecker St., 212/777-7776, www.terrablues.com; 7pm-2am Sun.-Thurs., 7pm-3am Fri.-Sat.; cover $10-20

ROCK
The Bitter End

Founded in 1961, The Bitter End has the distinction of being the city's oldest rock club. Bob Dylan, Lady Gaga, Stevie Wonder, Randy Newman, and Neil Diamond have all performed here—though don't come expecting to spot stars. The club has an open-mic kind of vibe, providing a space for emerging musicians to showcase their talents.

MAP 4: 147 Bleecker St., 212/673-7030, www.bitterend.com; 7pm-4am Mon., 7pm-1am Tues.-Thurs., 7pm-4am Fri.-Sat., 7pm-1am Sun.; free-$15

Le Poisson Rouge

Formerly the site of the famed Village Gate music club, Le Poisson Rouge is a sleek venue appealing to a wide range of musical tastes. The late, great Lou Reed had the distinction of playing both, the former with the Velvet Underground and the latter with experimental classical composer John Zorn. Though the venue holds 700 people, you never feel like you're far from the stage. Earplugs are available at the bar.

MAP 4: 158 Bleecker St., 212/505-3474, www.lpr.com; 5pm-close daily depending on shows; prices vary

COCKTAIL LOUNGES
Bar Sardine

Aptly named, this cozy gastropub has mostly bar seating, with just a few tables. Craft beers, inventively named cocktails (the bar's Moscow mule is called Ferris Mule-er), artisanal ciders, and several wines by the glass provide plenty of options for imbibing. And the all-day food menu is a step above typical bar fare, including items like a burger with barbecue mayo or scallop crudo. Flooded with light during the day, it makes a nice destination for an afternoon drink.

MAP 4: 183 W. 10th St., 646/360-3705, www.barsardinenyc.com; noon-midnight Sun.-Wed., noon-2am Thurs.-Sat.

Employees Only

The bar's name references the fact that the owners of this stunning libations and culinary mecca previously worked in the service industry. What makes Employees Only such a special place is its ability to fuse simplicity and refinement. Fresh oysters are a great way to start, and the bone marrow poppers are a must—but there aren't any misfires on the menu. That goes for the cocktails as well, which are as creative as they are nuanced. A green awning and a neon "psychic" sign out front let you know you're in the right place.

MAP 4: 510 Hudson St., 212/242-3021, www.employeesonlynyc.com; 6pm-4am daily

Employees Only

The Happiest Hour

This tropical-themed cocktail lounge is an explosion of warmth and color. Sidle up to the horseshoe-shaped bar for quaffable inventions like Fall from the Tree, a comforting blend of fresh apple juice, cinnamon, lemon, and aromatic bitters. For most cocktails, you can pick your spike of choice from several spirits. When hunger strikes, order the Happiest Burger, a fine-dining execution of a fast-food classic. The kitchen stays open until 2am for those nocturnal cravings.

MAP 4: 121 W. 10th St., 212/243-2827, www.happiesthournyc.com; 5pm-late Mon.-Fri., 2pm-late Sat.-Sun.

Hudson Bar and Books

At this cigar club, which feels like a private establishment, you can smoke while you sip a cocktail. Emphasis is placed on conversation, and as the name implies, the place is filled with antique books. Regular promotions include a free cigar for women on Mondays, and everyone gets specially priced whiskeys on Tuesdays. There's a two-drink minimum during prime hours and a $5 surcharge if you choose not to purchase tobacco. Cocktail offerings include cigar-friendly classics like Manhattans and Sazeracs.

MAP 4: 636 Hudson St., 212/229-2642, www.barandbooks.cz/hudson; 5pm-3am Mon., 5pm-4am Tues.-Thurs., 3pm-4am Fri., 1pm-4am Sat., 1pm-3am Sun.

Little Branch

With just a plain black door to identify it and a long staircase to climb down, this top-notch cocktail bar feels more like a speakeasy than others that aim for the effect. The only password you'll need, though, is good manners. A creation of the late Sasha Petraske, whose bars helped revive cocktail culture, you can expect finely crafted concoctions here. Just tell the bartenders what kind of drinks you prefer, and they'll whip you up something special.

When Bob Dylan moved to New York in 1961, he lived in an apartment at 161 West 4th Street. At the time, it was dirt-cheap housing for struggling bohemians; today the six-unit walk-up, built in 1910, is among the city's most valuable real estate. The iconic album cover of *The Freewheelin' Bob Dylan* was photographed across the street at the corner of Jones and West 4th. A few blocks away, heading southeast on West 4th, right on 6th Avenue, and left on Minetta Lane, you'll find **Cafe Wha?** (115 MacDougal St.), where the famed troubadour played his first show. Today, the venue host bands seven days a week, though most are cover bands and locals tend to stay away.

Another way to soak up the vibe of the man who wrote "Masters of War" and "Don't Think Twice, It's All Right" is with a drink on the same block. Linger in **Caffe Reggio** (119 MacDougal St.) with a cappuccino. The café claims to have been the first to serve the espresso drink in America, and Dylan played here after being fired from Cafe Wha? Or hit up the **Up & Up** (116 MacDougal St.), a subterranean cocktail bar with a friendly vibe and storied history as the former site of the Gaslight Cafe, where Dylan recorded *Live at the Gaslight 1962* featuring "A Hard Rain's a-Gonna Fall," among other soon-to-be-classics.

Around the corner, heading south on MacDougal and turning left onto Bleecker, is **Le Poisson Rouge** (158 Bleecker St.), housed in the former site of another Dylan stomping ground, the Village Gate. The original marquee still hangs on the building's eastern corner, but the club's digs are decidedly swankier than its predecessor. Top-notch, eclectic bookings draw a local music geek crowd and provide an opportunity to expand your sonic palate. For a more no-frills atmosphere, cross the street to **The Bitter End** (147 Bleecker St.), which has the distinction of being the oldest rock club in the city. It's been decades since Dylan has taken the stage here, but each night includes a lineup of unknown bands who might capture your heart.

MAP 4: 22 7th Ave. S., 212/929-4360, www.facebook.com/Little-Branch-41435210381; 7pm-3am Mon.-Sat., 7pm-2am Sun.

Up & Up

Formerly the site of the famed Gaslight Cafe, where Bob Dylan recorded *Live at the Gaslight 1962*, this dimly lit and unassuming cocktail bar is hidden in a subterranean space below a busy stretch of MacDougal Street. Lines can be long to get in because it has a strict no-standing policy—but this also ensures a chill vibe. Service is friendly and the bartenders are happy to make recommendations. Head bartender Chaim Dauermann has a knack for subverting cocktail expectations.

MAP 4: 116 MacDougal St., 212/260-3000, www.upandupnyc.com; 5pm-2am Sun.-Wed., 5pm-3am Thurs.-Sat.

CRAFT BEER
Blind Tiger

One of the first serious craft beer bars in the city when it opened in 1995, the tiny Blind Tiger is often packed. Come in the afternoon for a more chill environment to sample from the extensive and frequently rotating drafts on tap. Look out for Brooklyn brewer Other Half, which makes aggressively hoppy beers. Brewery tap takeovers regularly provide an opportunity to sample one-off rarities.

MAP 4: 281 Bleecker St., 212/462-4682, www.blindtigeralehouse.com; 11:30am-4am daily

Upright Brew House

Located on a quiet block of Hudson Street, this craft beer bar feels like a restaurant. Very little room for standing crowds ensures a relaxed atmosphere. Homemade pretzels and sliders are the food must-haves and

pair well with the impressive beer list, which leans toward inventive sours. It's common on busy nights for kegs to be swapped out mid-meal, so best not get too attached to a particular brew.
MAP 4: 547 Hudson St., 212/810-9944, www.uprightbrewhouse.com; noon-midnight Mon.-Thurs., noon-2am Fri., 11am-2am Sat., 11am-midnight Sun.

PUBS
White Horse Tavern
It's best to keep your order simple at this cash-only spot, as the grub is pretty standard and the beer fairly bland (try a burger and Guinness). But you're here for the atmosphere: After a few drinks you might start to feel the presence of the literary giants who once sat on these barstools. Around since 1880, this old-school pub was particularly popular with writers during the 1950s and 1960s including, most famously, Dylan Thomas, who had his last drinks (18 to be precise) here. Norman Mailer, Allen Ginsberg, and Bob Dylan were also regulars.
MAP 4: 567 Hudson St., 212/989-3956, www.whitehorsetavern1880.com; 11am-2am Sun.-Thurs., 11am-4am Fri.-Sat.

LGBTQ
Cubbyhole
Colorfully decorated and suggestively named, Cubbyhole is a lesbian bar with an inclusive vibe (gay and straight welcome) and serves free popcorn to boot. Look up to see the multitude of lanterns strewn from the ceiling. Frequent specials, including Margarita Tuesdays and Whiskey Wednesdays, make for cheap fuel at this particularly festive bar.
MAP 4: 281 W. 12th St., 212/243-9041, www.cubbyhole.com; 4pm-4am Mon.-Fri., 2pm-4am Sat.-Sun.

Julius'
This wood-paneled spot is the city's oldest gay bar. It opened as a grocery store in 1840, became a bar in 1864, and started attracting a gay crowd by the 1960s. Regulars love the $6 burgers and frequent drink specials along with Julius's monthly Mattachine Night, a dance party started by John Cameron Mitchell and PJ DeBoy to honor trailblazing queers, held the third Thursday of each month; the popular event is named after the first gay rights organization.
MAP 4: 159 W. 10th St., 877/746-0528, www.juliusbarny.com; 11am-4am Mon.-Sat., noon-3am Sun.

Marie's Crisis
A legendary cash-only piano bar popular not only with the LGBTQ crowd but the musical theater community at large, Marie's Crisis often features intimate shows by Broadway stars and composers. Lea DeLaria and Alan Cumming are both known to unwind here, and Cristin Milioti once popped by to belt out "Own My Own." It gets crowded so it's best to arrive early, at the start of happy hour (4pm-9pm Mon.-Thurs.), or make a reservation.
MAP 4: 59 Grove St., 212/243-9323, http://mariescrisis.us; 4pm-3am Mon.-Thurs., 4pm-4am Fri.-Sat., 4pm-midnight Sun.; no cover

Stonewall Inn
As the site of the riots that bear its name, this iconic gay bar is now part of the Stonewall National Monument, and it remains a popular gathering place for the LGBTQ community. Its Big Gay Happy Hour offers two-for-one drinks during the week 2pm-7:30pm, and a regular lineup of entertainment includes drag bingo on Mondays and drag cabaret shows on Sundays.

Stonewall Inn

MAP 4: 53 Christopher St., 212/488-2705, http://thestonewallinnnyc.com; 2pm-4am daily

CLUBS
✪ Le Bain
Located on top of The Standard hotel, this all-black tiled nightclub, complete with hot tub, attracts world-famous DJs who spin late into the night. The roof deck overlooks The High Line and is popular for day drinking, while the inside is an EDM disco. During the summer there's a plunge pool on the dance floor for wet thrills. The crowd is young and stylish. This is one of the toughest doors to get past in the city. Things that help: being kind and wearing Prada and a smile.

MAP 4: 444 W. 13th St., 212/645-7600, www.standardculture.com/lebain; 4pm-midnight Mon., 4pm-4am Tues.-Thurs., 2pm-4am Fri.-Sat., 2pm-3am Sun.; cover varies

STK Downtown and Rooftop
When you feel like a steak and some clubbing, this chic restaurant/ lounge hybrid has you covered with premium cuts of meat and DJs spinning thumping beats. It also has a retractable roof for year-round enjoyment, but STK is a pricey affair. If you don't care about being here for the scene, come for happy hour (6pm-8pm Mon.-Fri.) for $10 cocktails and sliders.

MAP 4: 26 Little W. 12th St., 4th fl., 646/624-2444, http://togrp.com/venue/stk-downtown; 5:30pm-11pm Mon.-Tues., 5:30pm-midnight Wed.-Thurs., 5:30pm-12:30am Fri.-Sat., noon-5pm and 6pm-10pm Sun., no cover

COMEDY
Comedy Cellar
This is a comic's comedy club. It's not uncommon for regular shows to include name comedians like Colin Quinn and Judy Gold. Jerry Seinfeld, Chris Rock, and Amy Schumer have been known to drop in unannounced. The club has a friendly, laid-back atmosphere, so if you make a lot of noise, it will be noticed and dealt with swiftly; to this end, parties of more than eight people aren't allowed.

MAP 4: 117 MacDougal St., 212/254-3480, www.comedycellar.com; shows from 7pm daily; $14-24

Chelsea and Union Square

Map 5

LIVE MUSIC
ROCK
Irving Plaza

Now owned by Live Nation, Irving Plaza is one of the oldest rock clubs still kicking in the city. Its distinctive red marquee announces its presence on the otherwise quiet street of Irving Place. Like most clubs, it has a standing room-only main floor and a small balcony, but with a 1,200-person capacity it's one of the largest venues of its kind. Acts range from buzzy up-and-coming teenage singer Grace VanderWaal to 1980s noise rockers like the Jesus Lizard. Legends like the Ramones and Talking Heads have also graced the stage.

MAP 5: 17 Irving Pl., 212/777-6817, http://venue.irvingplaza.com; door time varies by show; prices vary

LGBTQ
✪ Barracuda

Barracuda's low-key lounge atmosphere makes it a swell spot to have drinks with friends or to meet new ones. This venerable gay bar frequently hosts live events at a small stage in back, like Miss Peppermint's Drag Show, a long-running variety show of comedy and kitsch. You'll find a welcoming vibe here on the friendly side of cruisy. Comfy couches encourage lingering in the dimly lit and cozy space.

MAP 5: 275 W. 22nd St., 212/645-8613; 4pm-4am daily

The Eagle NYC

Opened in 1970 and billed as a leather-and-Levi's jeans bar, this was one of the first gay watering holes to open after the Stonewall riots. From Foot Fetish Mondays to Jockstrap Wednesdays, it's filled with risqué theme nights for a multitude of tastes—but leather reigns. Each year, the bar dubs a new man Mr. Eagle to act as its Mr. Universe-like ambassador, whose duties include hosting benefits and workshops for the leather community. Sundays are for football and $3 domestic drafts.

MAP 5: 554 W. 28th St., 646/473-1866, http://eagle-ny.com; 10pm-4am Mon.-Sat., 5pm-4am Sun.

Gym Sportsbar

For dudes who like dudes who are into sports, Gym has you covered with a dizzying array of screens as well as a pool table. A generous two-for-one happy hour (4pm-9pm Mon.-Fri.) makes it easy to down a few while watching a game. The bar has a range of specials after 9pm as well, like $6 frozen margaritas on Tuesdays—and

Gym Sportsbar

even on weekends you'll find drink promotions here.

MAP 5: 167 8th Ave. #A, 212/337-2439, www.gymsportsbar.com; 4pm-2am Mon.-Thurs., 4pm-4am Fri., 1pm-4am Sat., 1pm-2am Sun.

REBAR

Part club and part bar, this sleek venue is the 2.0 iteration of gay nightlife, with polished wood barstools and Edison light bulbs hanging from the ceiling. Don't expect bright colors here except a Pride flag or two. With shirtless bartenders and scantily clad theme nights, REBAR is charged with sexual energy. The space doesn't have TVs in an effort to foster human interaction, and a rewards program encourages repeat visits.

MAP 5: 225 W. 19th St., 646/863-2914, http://rebarchelsea.com; 4pm-2am Mon.-Wed., 4pm-4am Thurs.-Sat., 2pm-2am Sun.

COCKTAIL LOUNGES
✪ Flatiron Lounge

From its blue-lit mahogany bar to the faint sounds of big band jazz on the speakers, Flatiron Lounge evokes a bygone period of elegance and stiff drinks. It doesn't take much imagination to picture *Mad Men*'s Don Draper, suave and brooding, sitting a stool over, although he might be surprised by Julie Reiner's fresh-squeezed juice concoctions, like the playful gin-based Toes First, featuring blackberries, grapefruit, and maple syrup. He might be more at home with another of her classics, made with bourbon, Tabasco, and peach; it's aptly named the Devil Went Down to Georgia. This is the rare serious cocktail den that also has a happy hour (4pm-6pm Mon.-Fri.), when select cocktails are just $10.

Bathtub Gin

MAP 5: 37 W. 19th St., 212/727-7741, http://flatironlounge.com; 4pm-2am Mon.-Wed., 4pm-3am Thurs., 4pm-4am Fri., 5pm-4am Sat.

Bathtub Gin

Hidden behind the back wall of Stone Street Coffee, the location of this dimly lit bar is only given away by the massive line that forms outside nightly. Arrive before 6pm to minimize the wait. As its name implies, you'd do just fine ordering a gin cocktail, but offerings are diverse. From concoctions made with fine whiskeys like Bruichladdich to punches and alcohol-infused pots of tea meant to be shared with a group, the menu satisfies a range of tastes.

MAP 5: 132 9th Ave., 646/559-1671, http://bathtubginnyc.com; 5pm-2am Mon.-Wed., 5pm-4am Thurs.-Fri., 11:30am-3:30pm and 5pm-4am Sat., 11:30am-3:30pm and 5pm-2am Sun.

Porchlight

Porchlight

Danny Meyer's cocktail bar on the far reaches of the west side is city slicker Southern charm at its best. Exposed wood beams, along with wooden tables, chairs, and some walls, give the space a warm log cabin vibe. Arranged into four categories based on drink strength and level of inventiveness, the bar's menu features two dozen offerings that change somewhat regularly. A few standouts have included a gin cocktail with Other Half IPA, a creole negroni with absinthe, and a Manhattan with porter beer syrup and brandy. If you find yourself in the city for New Year's, Porchlight throws a hell of a party, with a different theme each year. Past themes have included an immersive transplantation to the Big Easy and summer camp complete with roasted marshmallows and helpful counselors.

MAP 5: 271 11th Ave., 212/981-6188, http://porchlightbar.com; noon-midnight Mon.-Wed., noon-2am Thurs.-Sat.

Raines Law Room

Raines Law Room's name slyly refers to an arcane 1896 liquor tax law that was written to curtail the drinking habits of locals. Ring the bell to enter and a hostess shows you to your seat among the well-upholstered antique couches. Booths in the back add an extra level of privacy to the already secretive spot. Cocktails are potent, and spice lovers will be particularly satisfied—several offerings pack serious heat. Reservations can be made online for Sunday-Tuesday and groups are limited to six or less. Otherwise, plan to arrive a couple of hours early to put your name on the list.

MAP 5: 48 W. 17th St., no phone, www.raineslawroom.com; 5pm-2am Mon.-Thurs., 5pm-3am Fri.-Sat., 7pm-1am Sun.

CRAFT BEER
Cooper's Craft & Kitchen

Located right next door to The Joyce and down the block from the Atlantic Theater Company, Cooper's makes an ideal spot for a pre- or postshow beer. Its extensive draft list includes some of the city's best breweries like KCBC, Other Half, and Grimm, and unlike other craft beer spots in the neighborhood, the atmosphere is sleek, with a wood-paneled ceiling, dim lighting, and, most importantly, no TVs. Cooper's also makes great bar food like fish-and-chips with minted peas and a burger with cornichon remoulade. There's a food special each night, including $1 fish tacos on Mondays. Another location in the East Village has similar fare.

MAP 5: 169 8th Ave., 646/661-7711, http://coopersnyc.com; 11am-2am Sun.-Wed., 11am-3am Thurs.-Sat.

Death Ave

Part brewery and part restaurant, Death Ave offers a rotating selection of its own beers, including several cask ales, along with popular crafts from breweries like Founders and Stone. The rustic space feels like a stylized saloon, and there's an expansive back patio that makes it a sweet spot for day drinking when the weather is nice. The Greek-influenced menu is pricier than it is tasty, but Death Ave's location near the 30th Street and 11th Avenue entrance to The High Line makes it a convenient stop.

MAP 5: 315 10th Ave., 212/695-8080, www.deathave.com; noon-10pm Mon.-Thurs., noon-11pm Fri., 11am-11pm Sat., 11am-10pm Sun.

BARS AND PUBS
Old Town Bar

Open since 1892, Old Town Bar retains much of its original decor, from the tin ceilings to the mahogany and marble bar. The watering hole also boasts that it has the oldest functional dumbwaiters in the city. Historic relics extend to the urinals, made by high-end manufacturer Hinsdale and installed in 1910. The bar has long been favored by the literary crowd, and book covers from U.S. poet laureate Billy Collins and the late, provocative journalist Christopher Hitchens hang proudly among many others.

MAP 5: 45 E. 18th St., 212/529-6732, www.oldtownbar.com; 11:30am-1am Mon.-Fri., noon-1am Sat., 1pm-midnight Sun.

Pete's Tavern

Pete's Tavern glows with hospitality. Decked out in string lights long after the holidays—they cover the ceiling above the bar—you'll feel surrounded by a halo while downing a pint of Guinness. Little has changed (besides the prices) since the first beers were poured here in 1864; the rosewood bar still features intricate moldings across its base, as does the tin ceiling. Pete's also serves above-average pub grub and offers food specials Monday-Wednesday, along with a $5 beer and wine happy hour (4pm-7pm Mon.-Fri.). Occasional plates of complimentary hors d'oeuvres are passed out during happy hour.

MAP 5: 129 E. 18th St., 212/473-7676, www.petestavern.com; 11am-2:30pm Sun.-Wed., 11am-3am Thurs., 11am-4am Fri.-Sat.

Midtown, Hell's Kitchen, and Times Square   Map 6

LIVE MUSIC

JAZZ
Birdland

The original Birdland opened in 1949 just west of the 52nd Street jazz scene that boomed in the 1930s and 1940s following the repeal of Prohibition. More than a dozen clubs used to line the street, hosting acts like Billie Holliday, Miles Davis, and Charlie Parker, nicknamed "Bird," who head-lined often and played sets that some-times lasted until dawn. The club's current incarnation on 44th Street opened in 1996 with much more reg-ulated sets, but stellar acts continue with established performers like Joe Lovano and Catherine Russell as well as promising new acts like Chilean saxophonist Melissa Aldana, who up-dates the airy seductiveness of bossa nova for a millennial crowd.

MAP 6: 315 W. 44th St., 212/581-3080, www.birdlandjazz.com; 5pm-1am Mon.-Sat., 5pm-midnight Sun.; $30-50 per set

The Iridium

Tucked underground, just beneath the chaos of Times Square, The Iridium is one of the city's premier clubs, with programming that often stretches be-yond the traditional boundaries of jazz to include rock and blues acts. Les Paul held court here every Monday for de-cades and his presence still looms large. Recent shows have included a solo concert by Benmont Tench, best known as the keyboardist and a founding member of Tom Petty and the Heartbreakers. While the venue doesn't have the magical old-world ambience of the Village Vanguard or the views of Dizzy's Club, it offers a comfortable setting for acts that usu-ally play rowdier spaces.

MAP 6: 1650 Broadway, 212/582-2121, http://theiridium.com; 7pm-midnight daily; $15-45 per set

COCKTAIL LOUNGES

The Campbell

If you're walking through The Morgan Library and start wondering what it would be like to drink a negroni amid ornately appointed turn-of-the-century elegance, head over to the nearby Campbell for an approxi-mation. Its namesake was a financier who turned this space—located atop Grand Central Terminal—into an of-fice and reception hall in 1923. Hand-painted ceilings and a large leaded glass window are among the lounge's unique features. Reservations are a must to enjoy this luxurious spot in leisurely fashion. Walk-ins usually end up saddled with a long wait time or find themselves standing near the bar, hardly ideal for enjoying well-made drinks like the Penicillin, made with a peaty 10-year-old Ardbeg single malt scotch.

MAP 6: 15 Vanderbilt Ave., 212/297-1781, www.thecampbellnyc.com; noon-2am daily

Middle Branch

The eastern reaches of Midtown aren't known for fine cocktail bars, so Middle Branch stands out. Housed in a former antique store, this two-story space has a cozy vibe. It's part of the family of bars created by the late Sasha Petraske, credited with revitalizing craft cocktail culture in the city. The bar proves that rum can have a proper place in an old-fashioned and a pisco sour doesn't require tinkering. The Sazerac is served in an absinthe-rinsed glass while the bartender's choice lets drinkers put themselves in capable and inventive hands.

MAP 6: 154 E. 33rd St., 212/213-1350; 5pm-2am daily

The Pool Lounge

Perched above the swanky digs of what used to be the Four Seasons Restaurant, once a staple of New York power dining and now The Pool restaurant, The Pool Lounge is both a living testament to a bygone era of formality (the titular pool, a signature feature of the Four Seasons, has been preserved) and a lively revamp of the cocktail tradition. Barman Thomas

Waugh has created a line of drinks that adhere to classic flavors but add a dose of whimsy. Drinks are named for a dominant ingredient; one of the most satisfying is the Jalapeño, served in a martini glass with the whole chili pepper artfully dangling atop. The drink exercises restraint, with the spice barely peeking through the potency of reposado tequila and quinine-laced Cocchi Americano.

MAP 6: 99 E. 52nd St., 212/375-9001, http://thepoolnewyork.com; 5pm-11pm Tues.-Fri., 5pm-midnight Sat. and Mon.

CRAFT BEER
Beer Culture

Beer Culture has an abundance of charm, with its exposed brick walls, Edison light bulbs, and well-curated drafts featuring many microbrews in addition to well-established crafts. A large bottle selection has lower to-go pricing. The bar is smaller than nearby

The Campbell

Kiabacca Bar and prices are a bit higher, but it's a sweet place to linger over a postshow beer if you can score a seat at the often-packed bar.

MAP 6: 328 W. 45th St., 646/590-2139, www.beerculture.nyc; 11:30am-2am Mon.-Sat., 11:30am-midnight Sun.

The Ginger Man

You won't find a better craft beer bar in the vicinity of the Empire State Building than The Ginger Man. With 70 taps, it has one of the most extensive selections in the city, but note that the high-ceilinged space can become deafeningly loud when the post-work crowd comes piling in around 5pm.

MAP 6: 11 E. 36th St., 212/532-3740, www.gingerman-ny.com; 11:30am-2am Mon.-Thurs., 11:30am-4am Fri., 12:30pm-4am Sat., 12:30pm-2am Sun.

Kiabacca Bar

Craft beer, artisanal pizzas loaded with toppings, and wine on tap are the defining features of this neighborhood hangout. While the bar has a couple of screens to broadcast games, the wooden warmth of the space is more conducive to conversation than cheering. Prices are good for the selection and quality: a rotating selection of drafts from breweries like Finback, Long Trail, and Other Half dominate. Wine pours are exceedingly generous. Weekends boast all-day specials like $5 pints.

MAP 6: 639 10th Ave., 212/649-4675, http://kiabacca.com; 3pm-4am Mon.-Thurs., noon-4am Fri.-Sun.

BARS AND PUBS
✪ Rudy's

Little more than duct tape holds together the worn red booths at this granddaddy of dive bars. Rumored to have been a speakeasy in 1919, with regulars like Al Capone, before obtaining a liquor license in 1933 when Prohibition ended, Rudy's is a relic of Hell's Kitchen's rougher past and a find in corporate Midtown. Its original wood door has been retained, and looks as weathered as some of the longtime patrons. Arrive early to nab a booth because it gets crowded. On weekends it can be challenging to even get to the bar; come on weekdays or in the afternoon to avoid the most robust crowds. Rudy's serves a steady crowd of manual laborers and students alike who are drawn in by the impossibly cheap prices; there's no need for a happy hour when you can grab a beer and a shot for $5 anytime. Pitchers, the preferred serving size here, start at $8 for the house brew. Hot dogs are free. Become friends with bartender Neil and he might just offer you a cookie from nearby dessert haven Schmackary's.

MAP 6: 627 9th Ave., 646/707-0890, www.rudysbarnyc.com; 8am-4am Mon.-Sat., noon-4am Sun.

Jimmy's Corner

It's an understatement to say that Times Square is a lousy place to get a drink. All those humble-looking pubs come with steep prices. So finding Jimmy's Corner here is a delight. Decorated with the boxing memorabilia of owner and former professional trainer James Glenn, the narrow dive bar feels like a time capsule of 1970s New York airdropped into Times Square: It opened in 1971 and little has changed since then, from the well-worn tables in the back—the best spot to soak up the warm, no-frills atmosphere—to the photo of Jimmy with Muhammad Ali hanging on the wall opposite the long bar. A sign above the bar reads "let's not discuss politics

Upright Citizens Brigade

here." It's best to stick to the rules and simple mixed drinks, which are made with mid-shelf spirits like Maker's Mark and served strong. A Captain Lawrence IPA is on tap for hopheads at the throwback price of $4.50.

MAP 6: 140 W. 44th St., 212/221-9510; 11:30am-4am Mon.-Fri., noon-4am Sat., 3pm-4am Sun.

COMEDY
Upright Citizens Brigade

Amy Poehler, Matt Besser, Ian Roberts, and Matt Walsh started Upright Citizens Brigade (UCB) in 1996 to bring "Chicago-style" long-form improv to New York. Think of it as a play without a script. That show lives on every Sunday night as "Asssscat 3000," and Poehler and the gang have been known to stop by on occasion. UCB offers so much more, though, with multiple shows each night of the week. Gravid Water (8pm last Mon. monthly) features Broadway and Off-Broadway actors performing scenes from notable plays with improvisers making their part up as they go along, while Dirty Laundry (11pm Mon.) is a free show of up-and-coming alternative stand-up comedians. Make reservations in advance.

MAP 6: 555 W. 42nd St., 212/366-9176, http://hellskitchen.ucbtheatre.com; box office 6pm-11:30pm Sun.-Thurs., 6pm-1am Fri.-Sat.; free-$12

Upper West Side and Upper East Side

Map 7

LIVE MUSIC
JAZZ
Dizzy's Club Coca-Cola

Most jazz clubs in the city are located in basements or similarly dark spaces, but Dizzy's is perched high above the Time Warner Center and has commanding views of Central Park. Located inside Jazz at Lincoln Center, this club is the venue's most intimate stage and hosts a range of top-notch artists, from trumpeter Nicholas Payton and his joyously rhythmic brand of fusion to saxophonist Allen Lowe, with his Dixieland interpretation of John Coltrane's *A Love Supreme*. A full menu, including a bayou risotto, is served before and during shows and features an above-average single malt scotch selection, including Oban, Cragganmore, and Talisker.

MAP 7: 10 Columbus Circle, 212/258-9595, www.jazz.org/dizzys; 6pm-1am Tues.-Sat.; $5-40 per set

COCKTAIL LOUNGES
Bemelmans Bar

This upscale piano bar in The Carlyle hotel is named for Ludwig Bemelmans, children's book author of *Madeline* fame, who created the murals that adorn the hotel's walls. In exchange for his witty depictions of upper-crust New York life, the artist received free rooms. Even by the standards of the best cocktail bars, prices are high here, with drinks stretching well past the $20 mark, on top of the cover charged when music of the jazz standard piano variety begins at 9pm or 9:30pm nightly ($15/bar, $25/table

Sun.-Thurs., $15/bar, $35/table Fri.-Sat.). But the sumptuous atmosphere is alluring, evoking the upper-class New York of yesteryear.

MAP 7: 35 E. 76th St., 212/744-1600, www.rosewoodhotels.com/en/the-carlyle-new-york; noon-1am Tues.-Thurs., noon-1:30am Fri.-Sat., noon-12:30am Sun.-Mon.

CRAFT BEER
Bondurants

This modern pub is a rare find on the Upper East Side: a not-fancy spot that isn't a sports bar, with elevated grub and great beer at fair prices. Its 20-plus taps pour some of the city's best from the likes of Grimm and Other Half breweries, along with lesser-known offerings from the Hudson Valley and beyond. Snacks like tater tots and house-brined fried pickles are served in sharable portions and encourage lingering, as does the rustic-chic atmosphere of exposed brick and knotty wood. The modestly sized digs can get crowded, so try to nab a seat at the inviting U-shaped bar.

MAP 7: 303 E. 85th St., 929/279-1884, www.bondurantsnyc.com; 4pm-2am Mon.-Thurs., 3pm-4am Fri., 11am-4am Sat., 11am-2am Sun.

Dive 75

While not quite what its name implies, Dive 75 is a homey spot, complete with board games that draw a local crowd. With over 30 drafts, including prized microbrews like Grimm, it's also a prime place for beer drinkers to congregate. With four locations dotting the Upper West Side, the bar provides a good glimpse into the neighborhood's casually upscale residents. Dive 75 makes for a particularly good stop after a long trek through Central Park, which is just a block away.

MAP 7: 101 W. 75th St., 212/362-7518, http://divebarnyc.com; 5pm-4am Mon.-Wed., 4pm-4am Thurs., 2pm-4am Fri., noon-4am Sat.-Sun.

The Jeffrey

Situated on an oddly congested stretch near the entrance to the Queensboro Bridge, the Jeffrey is a respite of cool and understated beer culture. Tattered planks of knotty wood cover the bar and adjoining walls while couches in the backyard offer a casual place to unwind when the weather allows. The beer list is extensive, and the food is a notch above standard pub grub: Think breakfast quesadillas at brunch and locally made artisanal pretzels by Sigmund's anytime.

MAP 7: 311 E. 60th St., 212/355-2337, www.thejeffreynyc.com; 11am-2am daily

Harlem and Morningside Heights   Map 8

LIVE MUSIC
JAZZ
✪ Minton's Playhouse

It's hard to overstate Minton's importance in the history of jazz. The club, founded in 1938 by saxophonist Henry Minton, is credited as the birthplace of bebop, a style rooted in complex chord changes and intricately expansive improvisation—the backbone of contemporary jazz. A list of the musicians who have graced Minton's intimate stage reads like a who's who of the genre's greats: Miles Davis, Thelonious Monk, Charlie Parker, Bill Evans, Art Blakey, Billie Holiday, Ella Fitzgerald, Louis Armstrong, Sarah Vaughan, and so many more. Today the sleek lounge is a perfect place to linger over an epic meal of steaks, crab cakes, and empanadas, and the rousing, brassy sound of the J. C. Hopkins Biggish Band. Seating is available at the bar as well. Reservations can be made online but the spacious digs can usually accommodate walk-ins.

MAP 8: 206 W. 118th St., 212/243-2222, http://mintonsharlem.com; 6pm-midnight daily; $10-20 per set plus a two-drink minimum

Ginny's Supper Club

Gospel brunches abound in the area, but Ginny's Sunday brunch is the most lavishly decadent. Its all-you-can-eat buffet ($45 per person) is a great way to sample upstairs restaurant Red Rooster's menu, including mac-and-collard greens, chicken and waffles, and some of chef Marcus Samuelsson's Swedish-inspired specialties. Local gospel choirs raise the roof as diners devour heaping platefuls of food in plush booths. For dinner, an à la carte menu is served while musicians like Johnny O'Neal, one-time member of Art Blakey and the Jazz Messengers, hold court on stage. Dinner sets are typically 7pm and 9pm Thursday-Saturday. Reservations are recommended.

MAP 8: 310 Lenox Ave., 212/421-3821, www.ginnyssupperclub.com; 7pm-1am Thurs., 6pm-3am Fri.-Sat., 10am-2pm Sun.; $15-20 per set

COCKTAIL LOUNGES
67 Orange Street

The name of this upscale bar isn't a minimalist reference to its location, but the last address of one of the first black-owned bars in New York, Almack's, which was located in the crime-ridden Five Points neighborhood. Local art adorns the walls, and bottles perch on wooden shelves above the bar. The cocktail menu is divided by spirits, and the whiskey offerings are particularly strong. The best is Manhattan After Dark, which infuses the classic cocktail with the ginger liquor Domaine de Canton and a heavy dose of cigar smoke.

MAP 8: 2082 Frederick Douglass Blvd., 212/662-2030, www.67orangestreet.com; 5pm-midnight Mon.-Tues., 5pm-2am Wed.-Thurs., 5pm-4am Fri., 6pm-4am Sat., 6pm-midnight Sun.

CRAFT BEER
Bier International

Opened in 2010 as Harlem's first beer garden, this watering hole remains a popular hangout for those craving liters of German beer and local brews alike. As with most beer gardens in the city, the atmosphere is boisterous and prices tend to be a bit higher than at neighboring bars. A giant projection screen makes this a good spot to watch soccer matches, though, and a full menu with classic fare like bratwurst and pretzels provides sustenance. Brunch is actually a good deal and includes a beer. Seating is at long tables inside and doubles when the weather warms up with sizeable sidewalk dining at smaller café tables.

MAP 8: 2099 Frederick Douglass Blvd., 212/280-0944, www.bierinternational. com; 4pm-1am Mon.-Thurs., 4pm-2am Fri., noon-2am Sat., noon-1am Sun.

Harlem Hops

Owned by a trio of black entrepreneurs and Harlem residents, Harlem Hops is the first serious craft beer bar to open in the neighborhood. Sixteen taps—featuring beers mostly brewed within a 70-mile (113-km) radius—sit below an illuminated "Harlem" sign. Hearty grub, including thick bratwursts on pretzel rolls, is available to sate cravings, and a small backyard features tables fashioned out of beer barrels.

MAP 8: 2268 Adam Clayton Powell Jr. Blvd., 646/998-3444, https://harlemhops. com; 4pm-midnight Sun.-Thurs., 4pm-2am Fri.-Sat.

CRAFT BEER
The Brazen Head

Located on a stretch of Atlantic Avenue that has been massively transformed in recent years and is now overrun with shiny condos, the Brazen Head provides a bridge to the neighborhood's not-so-distant past and draws a mostly local crowd. Neither a dive nor an upscale watering hole, the bar frequently has complimentary tastings, hosts tap takeovers, and uses its backyard in warmer months to host an extensive cask beer festival and screen films like *The Last Waltz*.
MAP 9: 228 Atlantic Ave., 718/488-0430, http://brazenheadbrooklyn.com; noon-4am Tues.-Sat., noon-2am Sun.-Mon.

Circa Brewing

One of the newest additions to the craft beer scene is also one of the best. Located in the midst of the bustle of the Fulton Mall pedestrian street and a short walk from the Alamo Drafthouse, Circa sits in a cavernous space with plentiful seating for groups. Beer offerings are impressive and range from complex, floral IPAs to robust stouts with notes of chocolate and banana. A food menu hits several locavore comfort notes with Brussels sprouts and burgers as well as adds a bit of ingenuity with items like a shawarma pizza that comes with a lemon yogurt dipping sauce. Monday is trivia night, hosted by an affable Brit

Circa Brewing

who displays questions on a large TV screen and gives clues through songs.

MAP 9: 141 Lawrence St., 718/858-0055, http://circabrewing.co; 11am-midnight Sun.-Thurs., 11am-2am Fri.-Sat.

COCKTAIL LOUNGES

Long Island Bar

Closed in 2007 after serving Brooklynites since 1951, the Long Island Bar and its iconic neon sign have been revived by new owners. Inside, the atmosphere is a meld of retro warmth and smart modern style. Patrons sit in booths and sip classic cocktails like gimlets and boulevardiers as well as more inventive concoctions like a white negroni made with prosecco. The dinner menu puts a refined touch on the familiar with dishes like dry-aged meatloaf.

MAP 9: 110 Atlantic Ave., 718/625-8908, http://thelongislandbar.com; 5:30pm-midnight Sun.-Thurs., 5:30pm-2am Fri.-Sat.

BARS AND PUBS

Brooklyn Inn

There's old-school Brooklyn and then there's the Brooklyn Inn, one of the borough's historic watering holes. Open since 1885, it feels like the bar equivalent of a well-worn pair of sturdy boots. There's enough wood in the space to repopulate a barren forest; it's all carved impeccably, and scratches on the surfaces simply add more character to the place. Sidle up to the cash bar and order a mixed drink or local draft, which you can savor over a game of billiards in the back.

MAP 9: 148 Hoyt St., 718/522-2525; 4pm-4am Mon.-Thurs., 3pm-4am Fri., 2pm-4am Sat.-Sun.

Robert Bar

Pulling on a door with an outstretched fist for a knob reveals Robert Bar, a mellow, impossibly cool room where you'll wish everyone knew your name. The main space here features an intimate bar lit in soft tones at which to quaff retro-named drinks like Ricky Don't Lose That Number (Ford's gin, lime mint) and Another One Bites the Dust (mezcal, jalapeno syrup, pineapple), while a few tables are tucked into a cocooned corner. There's always a reliably tasty local microbrew on tap from brewers like Other Half, whose taproom is located just a bit south in the neighborhood of Carroll Gardens. Happy hour (5pm-8pm Mon.-Fri.) knocks a couple bucks off drinks.

MAP 9: 104 Bond St., 347/853-8687, www.robertbarbrooklyn.com; 5pm-2am Mon.-Thurs., 5pm-4am Fri.-Sat., 5pm-1am Sun.

Williamsburg, Greenpoint, and Bushwick

Map 10

NIGHTLIFE

LIVE MUSIC
ROCK
Baby's All Right

One of the area's best stages sits in the shadow of the Williamsburg Bridge, inside the Korean restaurant that bears its name. The intimate backroom stage of Baby's All Right is a place for new acts to be discovered and veterans to try new things. Singer-songwriter Phoebe Bridgers played a moving set shortly after Tom Petty's death, paying tribute to the fallen troubadour with a chilling cover of "It'll All Work Out." Other nights you can see comedians like David Cross try new material or side projects from bands like Ween and Thievery Corporation.

MAP 10: 146 Broadway, 718/599-5800, www.babysallright.com; 6pm-2am Mon.-Fri., 11am-4am Sat.-Sun.; free-$20

Knitting Factory

After spending decades in a funky building in Soho, this legendary club for experimental music of all genres moved to Williamsburg. In renovated digs, it's nearby like-minded venues like Baby's All Right. From bluegrass collectives to veteran local psych-pop acts, the programming is eclectic.

MAP 10: 361 Metropolitan Ave., 347/529-6696, http://bk.knittingfactory. com; box office opens 30 min. before doors on show nights; free-$35

Music Hall of Williamsburg

Formerly a club named Northsix that presented local indie favorites like Rainer Maria, the Music Hall of Williamsburg continues this legacy with a roster of buzzy new bands and also legendary acts like the Pixies. The acoustics are among the best for rock venues in the city, whether you're listening to former Hold Steady frontman and Greenpoint resident Craig Finn or electro crooner Perfume Genius. Shows are mostly standing room only and the hall holds 550 people. Check out the balcony level if the main floor becomes uncomfortably crowded.

MAP 10: 66 N. 6th St., 718/486-5400, www.musichallofwilliamsburg.com; door time varies by show; $15-55

AMERICANA
Skinny Dennis

Located down the block from Nitehawk Cinema, Skinny Dennis feels like it was ripped off the strip of clubs on Broadway in Nashville. The honky-tonk saloon features exposed wooden rafters and a portrait of Willie Nelson hanging above the bar. Rousing sets of foot-stomping Americana fill the cozy space nearly every night, and there's no cover on weekdays. The only thing that gives this place away as a Brooklyn bar is the abundance of craft beer available on tap (and massive weekend crowds). Prices are very good for the neighborhood.

MAP 10: 152 Metropolitan Ave., 212/555-1212, www.skinnydennisbar.com; noon-4am daily; free-$5

CRAFT BEER
✪ Beer Street

One of the smallest bars in the city is also one of the best. With room for a couple handfuls of people, this place feels like a secret you stumble into on a densely developed stretch of Graham Avenue. A wood mantelpiece is the focus of attention and contains a chalkboard listing the day's draft offerings. Proper glassware is used for each style of beer, and the bartenders are knowledgeable about what they pour. Prices run a bit high, but there are no lightweight offerings. You might pick from an intensely hoppy IPA or special collaboration sour. Bottles such as Grimm's Double Negative imperial stout are also available, as are growlers to go.

MAP 10: 413 Graham Ave., 347/294-0495, www.beerstreetny.com; 5pm-1am Mon.-Thurs., 5pm-2am Fri., 2pm-2am Sat.-Sun.

Braven Brewing Company

Braven has exploded recently, which is a good thing for hops lovers as well as fans of milder beers. Its pilsner, an often unsung beer, has received praise for its balanced flavor. Located in an industrial stretch of Bushwick, the taproom features limited-release offerings and bites to eat at its 60-seat restaurant on the premises.

MAP 10: 52 Harrison Pl., 929/295-6673, www.bravenbrewing.com; 5pm-midnight Wed.-Fri., noon-midnight Sat.-Sun.

The Diamond

The Diamond feels like home—that is, if your home has a shuffleboard table, a well-stocked and inviting semicircular bar, and amiable regulars who don't need to be reminded to adhere to the venue's no-shouting policy. In addition to great craft brews it has a decent wine selection, including two rosés in the summer months. Food is sparse but includes cheese from Murray's and a Thai chicken pot pie from a favorite

local purveyor. The Diamond also hosts the occasional comedy show.

MAP 10: 43 Franklin St., 718/383-5030, www.thediamondbrooklyn.com; 5pm-1am Mon.-Thurs., 5pm-2:30am Fri., 2pm-2:30am Sat., 2pm-1am Sun.

Greenpoint Beer and Ale

An expansive wood-bedecked room with concrete floors and a wood-burning stove make this a nice spot to while away the hours around a large central bar. From this perch, drinkers can glimpse the active brewery at work in the background while perusing a list of beers steeped in German, British, and Belgian traditions, infused with a dose of creativity, like a kolsch that blends Galaxy hops with notes of citrus. Names like "Was it Something I Said?" and "Flannel Shirt IPA" are fun to order, and prices are reasonable for the area.

MAP 10: 7 N. 15th St., 718/389-2940, www.greenpointbeer.com; 5pm-midnight Mon.-Thurs., 2pm-2am Fri., noon-2am Sat., noon-midnight Sun.

Grimm Artisanal Ales

One of the best breweries in the city now has its very own taproom in a bright, stylish space. Married couple Lauren and Joe Grimm began brewing out of their Brooklyn apartments more than a decade ago when they started dating. They don't have a flagship beer; rather the brewery's distinguishing feature is its experimentation. Each Saturday one of the 10-plus taps is devoted to a brand-new beer, and a quarter of this gleaming space is dedicated to making sours.

MAP 10: 990 Metropolitan Ave., no phone, http://grimmales.com; 5pm-midnight Thurs.-Fri., noon-midnight Sat., noon-10pm Sun., 5pm-10pm Mon.

Keg & Lantern Brewing Company

Keg & Lantern is a sports bar that brews its own beer, or a brewery that's really into sports—during big games it can get raucous inside. Beers are inventive and well executed, like a dry-hopped kettle sour or barrel-aged tripel on cask. The food menu leans toward comfort with bar food staples like mac and cheese gussied up with pulled pork and a Reuben with corned beef braised in the brewery's golden ale.

MAP 10: 97 Nassau St., 718/389-5050, www.kegandlanternbrooklyn.com; 11am-4am daily

Kings County Brewers Collective

Kings County Brewers Collective's offerings have quickly become an indispensable staple at many of the city's best craft beer bars, blending explosive flavors with smooth drinkability. Frequent collaborations with other breweries have yielded enviable results, including a delectably nuanced IPA made with Syracuse brewery Now & Later. Board games are on hand in the brewery's taproom and, while food isn't served, takeout is available from many nearby places, including Asian-inspired burger joint Strange Flavor, located next door at The Johnsons.

MAP 10: 381 Troutman St., 929/234-6557, www.kcbcbeer.com; 5pm-11pm Mon.-Thurs., 5pm-midnight Fri., noon-midnight Sat., noon-9pm Sun.

Left Hand Path

A craft beer bar with a cocktail soul, or possibly the other way around, Left Hand Path oozes retro cool but doesn't feel too scene-y. Table seating is located in the back, but the leather-covered barstools are a good idea for quick service. Eight drafts are culled mainly from local spots, with a couple of West Coast imports. The cocktail list includes classics like whiskey sours alongside more inspired concoctions made with Campari and absinthe.

MAP 10: 89 Wyckoff Ave., www.lefthandpathbk.com; 5pm-4am Mon.-Thurs., 4pm-4am Fri., 2pm-4am Sat.-Sun.

Spuyten Duyvil

Hidden behind a nondescript metal gate, Spuyten Duyvil was a pioneer in the Williamsburg craft beer scene. It has just half a dozen drafts but they're well curated and hew toward European-influenced offerings. An additional line serves up a rotating cask beer. The jukebox offerings range from Chet Baker to Radiohead, and the backyard is open year-round, making this a good place to hang out before a concert at the neighborhood's many venues.

MAP 10: 359 Metropolitan Ave., 718/963-4140, www.spuytenduyvilnyc.com; 5pm-2am Mon.-Thurs., 2pm-3am Fri., noon-3am Sat., noon-2am Sun.

Tørst

This sleek spot looks more like it should be an upscale wine bar, with its marble counters and small pours. But it's a beer bar and, though pricey to be sure, its owner's pedigree—Jeppe Jarnit-Bjergsø, founder of Denmark's Evil Twin Brewing—is impeccable. There's always a well-chosen selection of over 20 drafts, often including some rare ciders. A small but mouth-watering food menu features items like sourdough bread with yogurt butter and a dry-aged burger with caramelized onion aioli.

MAP 10: 615 Manhattan Ave., 718/389-6034, www.torstnyc.com; noon-midnight Sun.-Thurs., noon-2am Fri.-Sat.

CRAFT BEER OFF-THE-BEATEN-PATH

While craft beer might not be the first thing one thinks of when it comes to New York, the city has erupted with many first-class breweries in recent years. Some standouts have formal listings in these pages, but there are many more warranting attention. Because of space demands, these breweries are typically located far from where many tourists tread—but beer lovers are intrepid.

- In Brooklyn's residential Carroll Gardens neighborhood is **Other Half Brewing Company** (195 Centre St., 917/765-6107, info@otherhalfbrewing.com, http://otherhalfbrewing.com; noon-10pm Mon.-Wed., noon-midnight Thurs.-Fri., 10am-midnight Sat., 11am-10pm Sun.), located in a funky-cool warehouse and a must-stop for hopheads. Almost all of its 20 taps are IPAs and some—like a double dry-hopped version with broccoli—can only be found at the brewery. The Smith-9th Street F/G subway stop is just around the corner.

- For crisp European-style beers, it's hard to do better than **Folksbier Brauerei** (101 Luquer St., no phone, http://folksbier.com; 4pm-11pm Thurs.-Fri., 2pm-11pm Sat., 2pm-10pm Sun.), also located in Carroll Gardens and less than a 10-minute walk northwest of Other Half. The Old Bavarian Lager is quite sessionable while the bière de garde Selvina brewed with rosehips is one to savor. The nearest subway is the F/G at Carroll Street.

- Bordering Bushwick in Ridgewood, Queens, **Queens Brewery** (1539 Covert St., no phone, www.queensbrewery.com; 4pm-midnight Mon.-Fri., noon-midnight Sat.-Sun.) serves up delightfully hoppy concoctions—even its lager is dry-hopped. It also serves its own coffee and cold-brew cocktails. Games like a giant Jenga and cornhole make it easy to hang around, as do karaoke (9pm-midnight Tues.) and live music on the weekends. You can also sate your hunger here with the brewery's rotating menu of hot dogs and sausages. Queens Brewery is right next to the Halsey Street L train subway station, but if the L is down, take the M line to the next-closest station at Myrtle-Wyckoff Avenues.

- Also in Ridgewood, Queens, the mom-and-pop **Bridge and Tunnel Brewery** (15-35 Decatur St., 347/392-8593, rich@bridgeandtunnelbrewery.com, www.bridgeandtunnelbrewery.com; 5pm-10pm Fri., 1pm-9pm Sat.-Sun.), just down the block and around the corner from Queens Brewery (its closest subway stations are also Halsey Street and Myrtle-Wyckoff Aves.), serves up some of the city's most potently tasty dark beers, like the Slaughter House Stampede Black Rye IPA.

- **SingleCut Beersmiths** (19-33 37th St., 718/606-0788, http://singlecut.com; 4pm-midnight Thurs.-Fri., 11am-midnight Sat., 11am-9pm Sun.) is located in the northern reaches of the Astoria neighborhood of Queens, nearly 1 mile (1.6 km) from the N/W Astoria-Ditmars Boulevard stop. The trek is rewarded with hoppy concoctions like the double IPA Softly Spoken Magic Spells.

- If you're going to Citi Field in Flushing, Queens, for a Mets game, head out early or stay out late to hit up **Mikkeller Brewing NYC** (123-01 Roosevelt Ave., 718/766-2717, http://mikkellernyc.com; 4pm-10pm Wed.-Thurs., noon-midnight Fri.-Sat., noon-10pm Sun.). This outpost of the famed Danish brewery has 60 taps and several inventive sours made with unusual ingredients like the delicious shrub sea buckhorn. On game days/nights, it's open 2-3 hours before and 2 hours after events, in addition it its normal operating hours. The nearest subway is the 7 at Mets-Willets Point.

- Located in an industrial pocket of the south Bronx but a short walk from the 6 train Cypress Avenue stop, **Bronx Brewery** (856 E. 136th St., 718/402-1000, http://thebronxbrewery.com; 3pm-7pm Mon.-Wed., 3pm-8pm Thurs., 3pm-10pm Fri., noon-10pm Sat., noon-7pm Sun., reduced hours in winter, call ahead) is surprisingly accessible. Its pale ale is widely available around town, but you can get a variety of IPAs at the taproom along with a potent coffee stout and sour Berliner Weisse. In the warmer months, the backyard hosts a variety of events on the weekends, many with local DJs and dancing. Be sure to call ahead to confirm hours before venturing here because hours shorten in the colder months.

Tørst

The Well

The Well is possibly the largest bar in the city, closer in size to an airplane hangar than a watering hole. It has as many as 60 beers on tap, and the selection consistently includes obscure brews along with the usual local suspects from the likes of Brooklyn's Other Half, as well as craft ciders. A near-suburban-size back patio complete with cornhole makes this a great place for summer drinking.

MAP 10: 272 Meserole St., 347/338-3612, www.thewellbrooklyn.com; 4pm-1am Mon.-Thurs., 4pm-3am Fri., noon-3am Sat., noon-1am Sun.

COCKTAIL LOUNGES
✪ Noorman's Kil

Why not pair booze and grilled cheese? That's the guiding principle behind this elegant and woodsy Williamsburg bar serving a massive whiskey menu—over 400 bottles are neatly displayed on its knotty shelves. Bartenders are super friendly and happy to help you wade through the choices, among which is the rarely found Ardbeg Corryvreckan.

An accompanying menu of grilled cheese sandwiches combines ingredients like cheddar with hot honey and bacon, and brie with local mushrooms. The bar also has an excellent craft beer list.

MAP 10: 609 Grand St., 347/384-2526, http://noormanskil.com; 5pm-4am Mon.-Fri., noon-4am Sat., 2pm-4am Sun.

The Commodore

There are many places to savor a decent Manhattan in the city but, if you want to pair it with freshly made fried chicken, you've come to the right place. The Commodore evokes both Southern hospitality and Williamsburg cool in a retro diner shell. Locals put up with long waits to satisfy their cravings. Order at the counter (there's no wait service) and come before 9pm on weekends to avoid a maddening, raucous crowd.

MAP 10: 366 Metropolitan Ave., 718/218-7632; 4pm-4am Mon.-Fri., 11am-4am Sat.-Sun.

The Johnsons

The owners of quintessential Lower East Side dive bar Welcome to the Johnsons have gone slightly upscale with this Bushwick spot. It includes an enclosed front patio with fun seating and excellent burgers and green bean tempura care of Asian-inspired Strange Flavor, an awesome pop-up burger shack that shares space with the property. Inside, the atmosphere is sleeker than at its Manhattan sister spot, though $2 cans of Lionshead keep up the dive-y vibe. A gently priced cocktail menu benefits from an extended happy hour that runs until 9pm daily.

MAP 10: 369 Troutman St., 718/417-7100; 2pm-4am daily

ARTS AND CULTURE

New York City is the cultural capital of the United States, home to a dizzying array of world-class museums, performing arts venues, theaters, art galleries,

and independent cinemas—no other city in the country can lay claim to this level of artistry.

Many of the most renowned museums can be found on the Upper East Side's famous Museum Mile, but the city is also riddled with idiosyncratic gems, like the Museum of Sex, Mmuseumm—a miniature museum housed in a freight elevator down an alleyway—and the Rubin Museum of Art, focusing on the arts and culture of the Himalayas.

Chelsea has the densest concentration of art galleries, which are fun on most Thursdays, when they pop a few bottles of wine to celebrate the unveiling of new shows.

Most theatergoers flock to Broadway, but some of the best shows can be seen off the Great White Way. Meanwhile, multifaceted performing arts venues like Lincoln Center and the Brooklyn Academy of Music bring the best of the international arts scene to the city on numerous fronts.

Hamilton at the Richard Rodgers Theatre

The city is also a cinephile's paradise, with movie houses showcasing avant-garde cinema, retrospectives, and new independents, often with fun twists, particularly in downtown Manhattan and Brooklyn.

On any given day of the week, the city's arts and culture options overwhelm—the only way to stay sane is to pick your poison.

HIGHLIGHTS

✪ **BEST HIDDEN GEM:** Tucked away in an alley and housed in a freight elevator, **Mmuseumm** is one of the tiniest and most idiosyncratic museums in the world (page 216).

✪ **BEST THEATER FOR CHALLENGING, INTIMATE SHOWS:** You'll consistently find some of the most exciting theater in the city at tiny **Soho Rep** (page 218).

✪ **BEST THROWBACK MOVIE THEATER:** At the **Film Forum,** people still stand on line under a neon marquee to catch movies both classic and modern (page 219).

✪ **BEST GALLERY TO SEE LARGE-SCALE WORKS BY CONTEMPORARY ART GIANTS:** The signature gallery of an art dealer king, the **Gagosian** has the space for dramatic masterpieces (page 225).

✪ **BEST UNDER-THE-RADAR GALLERY:** Discover your next favorite artist at the pristine **Petzel Gallery** (page 225).

✪ **BEST UNDISCOVERED MUSEUM:** Don't overlook the **Rubin Museum of Art**'s impressive collection of Himalayan art and fun Friday night programs (page 228).

✪ **BEST PLACE TO SEE NEW AMERICAN PLAYS:** **Playwrights Horizons** has two state-of-the-art stages dedicated solely to new works (page 231).

✪ **BEST BANG FOR YOUR THEATER BUCK:** **Signature Theatre Company** offers the most affordable first-rate productions in the city (page 231).

✪ **BEST PLACE TO SOAK UP MYRIAD CULTURE:** Whatever your high art tastes, **Lincoln Center** delivers (page 244).

✪ **BEST PLACE FOR LARGE-SCALE EXPERIMENTAL THEATER:** **St. Ann's Warehouse** consistently delivers cutting-edge work with high production values (page 248).

✪ **BEST PLACE TO EXPERIENCE WORLD CULTURE IN BROOKLYN:** The **Brooklyn Academy of Music (BAM)** is a first-class performing arts center presenting the best theater, dance, and musical companies from around the world (page 249).

✪ **BEST CINEMA FOR FOOD-THEMED EVENTS:** Seeing a movie at **Nitehawk Cinema** is both a cinematic and culinary delight at events like its popular Film Feasts (page 252).

Lower Manhattan

Map 1

MUSEUMS

Fraunces Tavern Museum

Named for tavern owner Samuel Fraunces, who opened the Queen's Head Tavern on this site in 1762, this museum provides insight into the American Revolutionary era as well as the historic watering hole's role in the war, when it was a hotbed of social and political activity. Highlights include being able to stand in the room where then General George Washington bid farewell to his troops. The founding of the New York Chamber of Commerce also happened here, probably after several pints. A fully functioning on-site pub (212/968-1776; 11am-2am daily) allows you to join in the tradition and have a beer and bite.

MAP 1: 54 Pearl St., 212/425-1778, www. frauncestavernmuseum.org; noon-5pm Mon.-Fri., 11am-5pm Sat.-Sun.; $7 adults, $4 seniors, students, and children 5 and over, free for children under 5 and active military

Museum of Jewish Heritage

Self-described as "a living memorial to the Holocaust," this museum focuses not only on documenting and preserving the atrocities of the past but examining their reverberations in modern life. A permanent installation, *Garden of Stones*, features trees growing out of stones to conjure a sense of endurance and survival against the odds. A recent exhibit, *Eyewitness*, consisted of 31 portraits of Holocaust survivors living in New York. Admission

Fraunces Tavern Museum, where George Washington bade farewell to his officers after the end of the American Revolution

is free Wednesdays and Thursdays 4pm-8pm.

MAP 1: 36 Battery Pl., 646/437-4202, http://mjhnyc.org; 10am-6pm Sun.-Tues., 10am-8pm Wed.-Thurs., 10am-5pm Fri.; $12 adults, $10 seniors, $7 students

National Museum of the American Indian

Formerly the U.S. Customs House and designed by Woolworth Building architect Cass Gilbert, this stately building is now home to a museum preserving Native American cultural artifacts. It features both permanent exhibits—for instance, displays of the original garments and utensils of the Lenape people—as well as temporary exhibits, such as a recent offering focused on modern native peoples' fashion across the country and in Canada. Each gallery leads into the giant rotunda, which provides ample seating for the weary to rest. Look up and you might spot a portrait of Christopher Columbus—illustrating the country's morally complicated past.

MAP 1: 1 Bowling Green, 212/514-3700, http://nmai.si.edu; 10am-5pm Fri.-Wed., 10am-8pm Thurs.; free

9/11 Tribute Museum

Located just a few blocks south of the National September 11 Memorial & Museum, the 9/11 Tribute Museum is run by 9/11 families and provides unique insight not only into what it was like to be in the World Trade Center on that day but how the day has altered and shaped lives in the following decades. A section of the exhibit space is devoted to nonprofit organizations started by victims' families and survivors, detailing magnanimous acts in the wake of the attacks. For an extra fee, visitors can take a walking tour through the neighborhood with a survivor, offering a first-person perspective that museum exhibits can't capture.

MAP 1: 92 Greenwich St., 866/737-1184, http://911tributemuseum.org; 10am-6pm Mon.-Sat., 10am-5pm Sun.; $15 adults, $10 seniors, students, and military, $5 children 8-12

9/11 Tribute Museum

Skyscraper Museum

The small museum occupies a single floor in a modern high-rise building. Text-heavy exhibits illuminate the history of the towering buildings that line the streets of Manhattan, the first of which were created in the late 19th century. The invention of the elevator, unsurprisingly, played an important role. One of the most illuminating displays is a series of photos detailing the building up of what was formerly a cluster of piers north of The Battery using landfill. Another highlight is the original building plan and model of the World Trade Center from the 1960s.

MAP 1: 39 Battery Pl., 212/968-1961, www. skyscraper.org; noon-6pm Wed.-Sun.; $5 adults, $2.50 seniors and students

THEATER
3LD Art and Technology Center

The 3-Legged Dog, a production company and theater group, hosts shows in this intimate space using immersive video projections to create vivid backdrops for new plays that challenge traditional dramatic narrative structure. One viscerally charged production, *Tyson vs. Ali*, brought to life an imagined fight between the two famous boxers by surrounding a boxing ring with screens of various sizes projecting archival interviews with both men while actors sparred in the ring.

MAP 1: 80 Greenwich St., 212/645-0374, www.3ldnyc.org; $25-50

Soho and Tribeca   Map 2

MUSEUMS
✪ Mmuseumm
Housed in a freight elevator in an uncharacteristically quiet alleyway, this quirky museum is as tiny as it is carefully curated. While it's only open on weekends, you can see the whole exhibit at any time through a peephole—the exhibits are collections of small objects neatly organized on shelves that can be viewed via the small opening. A recent show, *Sarah Berman's Closet*, which transferred to The Metropolitan Museum of Art, featured the carefully folded all-white wardrobe of cofounder Alex Kalman's grandmother. (Fun fact: Alex Kalman's mother is the artist Maira Kalman.) Kalman cofounded the space with indie filmmakers Josh and Benny Safdie. A second freight elevator a few doors down houses a second and even smaller exhibit: Mmuseumm 2. Exhibits rotate and only a handful of people can fit "inside" either space at any given time.

MAP 2: 4 Cortlandt Alley, 888/763-8839, www.mmuseumm.com; noon-6pm Sat.-Sun.; $5 suggested donation

Leslie-Lohman Museum of Gay and Lesbian Art
Established as a nonprofit foundation to support gay and lesbian artists by Charles Leslie and Fritz Lohman in 1987, this small museum, which feels more like a casual-chic gallery, exhibits artists across the LGBTQ spectrum. Its permanent collection houses over 24,000 works, only a small fraction of which can be displayed at any one time in the museum's two intimate exhibition spaces. Well-curated shows illustrate the breadth of diversity in the queer community. A recent exhibit from the collection featured a drawing by sexually provocative artist Touko Laaksonen (aka Tom of Finland), a triptych of a lesbian African couple in loving embrace by Zanele Muholi, and a large-scale nude oil painting of

Mmuseumm

a trans woman by young Californian artist Janet Bruesselbach.

MAP 2: 26 Wooster St., 212/431-2609, www.leslielohman.org; noon-6pm Wed. and Fri.-Sun., noon-8pm Thurs.; $8 suggested donation

Leslie-Lohman Museum of Gay and Lesbian Art

New York City Fire Museum

This hidden gem of a museum is located in a firehouse built in 1904 for horse-drawn fire "engines"—picture ornate carriages decked out with bells and lights and large wheels for traction. A couple of these antiques are on display in the front room to the left of the main entrance. More modern items are on display as well, including a life-saving rope that was used to rescue victims from a burning apartment building on the Upper East Side in 2016. The museum has its own 9/11 exhibit, decidedly less flashy than the National September 11 Memorial & Museum; one highlight is a section of a pew from St. Paul's Chapel, which provided around-the-clock support for emergency workers, including firefighters.

MAP 2: 278 Spring St., 212/691-1303, www.nycfiremuseum.org; 10am-5pm Tues.-Sat., 10am-4pm Sun.; $8 adults, $5 seniors, students, and children

GALLERIES
Artists Space

Artists Space was founded in 1972 by an arts administrator and a critic—becoming a leading light in downtown's then-nascent arts scene—to support emerging artists, many of whom have gone on to mega careers, including the likes of Jeff Koons, Cindy Sherman, Laurie Anderson, John Baldessari, and Jenny Holzer. The nonprofit gallery moved in 2017 from its Soho home to a new space in Tribeca, but its mission remains the same. A recent show, *Ugo Rondinone: I (heart emoji) John Giorno*, took an exhibition from Palais de Tokyo in Paris and retooled it to focus on the native New Yorker artist/poet/activist's relationship with the city. Another recent highlight was an extensive retrospective of influential queer filmmaker and photographer Jack Smith that focused on a period in the 1970s and early 1980s.

MAP 2: 55 Walker St., 212/226-3970, www.artistsspace.org; noon-6pm Wed.-Sun.; free

Drawing Center

Somewhere between a gallery and a museum, the Drawing Center focuses on the eponymous skill as a driving force of creativity. Founded in 1977 by curator Martha Beck, it has the distinction of being the only one of its kind in the country. Exhibits range from the timeless to the topical. A couple of recent highlights include Judith Bernstein's *Cabinet of Horrors*, featuring charcoal and acrylic etchings that depict the Trump administration, and Jackie Ferrera's *Lines*, which rendered film titles in Morse code.

MAP 2: 35 Wooster St., 212/219-2166, www.drawingcenter.org; noon-6pm Wed.-Sun.; $5 adults, $3 seniors and students, free for children under 12

Kate Werble Gallery

With cement floors and exposed pipes, the atmosphere of this gallery echoes Soho's industrial past. Kate Werble hosts shows that cover a wide breadth of the art world, from Gareth Long's colorful sculptures to Melanie Schiff's ominous and electric photographs. Other recent highlights include the provocative *Sexting* show, which examined coupling in its various forms. MAP 2: 83 Vandam St., 212/352-9700, www.katewerblegallery.com; 11am-6pm Tues.-Sat.; free

Morrison Hotel Gallery

Taking its name from the Doors' classic album, this gallery features rotating photography exhibits of famous musicians, both in performance as well as in more contemplative poses. The narrow 2nd-floor gallery on Prince Street has a warm vibe. Its exposed brick is an attractive backdrop to, for instance, vivid portraits of Jimi Hendrix snapped by Karl Farris, creator of the iconic, psychedelic *Are You Experienced* album cover. The gallery also represents Henry Diltz, who was the official photographer at Woodstock. MAP 2: 116 Prince St., 2nd fl., 212/941-8770, www.morrisonhotelgallery. com; 11am-7pm Mon.-Sat., noon-6pm Sun.; free

The New York Earth Room

If you need a quick break from the bustle of urbanity, Walter De Maria's ongoing, aptly named gallery exhibit provides minimalist refuge, as it has since it was first unveiled in 1977. Made of earth, peat, and bark spread 22 inches thick across 3,600 square feet (334 sq m), the piece is both epic in its expanse and spare in its aspect. It was commissioned by the Dia Art Foundation, which maintains long-term exhibitions across the world, including Robert Smithson's *Spiral Jetty*. MAP 2: 141 Wooster St., 212/989-5566, http://diaart.org; noon-3pm and 3:30pm-6pm Wed.-Sun.; free

THEATER
✪ Soho Rep

Soho Rep shows make for thrilling evenings out, prizing ingenuity over big budgets and often completely transforming its tiny black-box theater for each production. Its season typically consists of only two or three plays, but there are rarely any duds. A recent highlight was Annie Baker's modern adaptation of Chekhov's *Uncle Vanya*, performed in a wood-covered cabin. Another was Branden Jacobs-Jenkins' penetrating examination of race as helmed by artistic director Sarah Benson, *An Octoroon,* in which the fourth wall comes crashing down, both figuratively and literally. The theater aims to give voice to underrepresented people through new works that gleefully play with the bounds of reality. Ticket prices are about half the cost of a normal Broadway show, and copies of the scripts are available for purchase in nicely bound editions in the lobby, making for special souvenirs. MAP 2: 46 Walker St., 212/941-8632, http://sohorep.org; $35-65

The Flea Theater

Founded by a trio of downtown artists in 1996, The Flea has a reputation for putting on challenging shows. The Off-Off-Broadway theater was the de facto home of the late playwright A. R. Gurney, who shined an incisive light on WASP culture, often with a humorous touch, and also acts as an incubator for new talent via an apprentice resident company, The

Bats. While The Flea may be best known for its Ground Zero-themed play, *The Guys*, it's at its best when producing provocative works by downtown master playwrights like Thomas Bradshaw. The company opened a gleaming new space in 2017 but has kept ticket prices on a sliding scale starting at just $15. Instead of being told to turn off your cell phone prior to a performance, you're (jokingly) directed to answer it and tell the caller you're at The Flea.

MAP 2: 20 Thomas St., 212/352-3101, http://theflea.org; $15-75 sliding scale

HERE

This space with two stages has become a mainstay of the Off-Off-Broadway community since it was founded in 1993. Diverse programming includes a mix of dance, theater, puppetry, and performance art by downtown legends like Taylor Mac and Basil Twist. The former's 2009 epic five-hour song cycle *The Lily's Revenge* was a precursor to the artist's groundbreaking 24-hour performance *A 24-Decade History of Popular Music*, while the latter developed his puppetry spectacular *Symphonie Fantastique* at HERE. A café in the lobby is an ideal place for a pre- or postshow drink and discussion.

MAP 2: 145 6th Ave., 212/647-0202, http://here.org; prices vary

CINEMA
✪ Film Forum

Stepping into the lobby of the only autonomous nonprofit movie theater in the city is like traveling through a time portal into the 1970s. You'll feel at home launching into a philosophical discussion while waiting in line for an old-school tub of popcorn. Screens are small but the programming is impressive, with a mix of first-run ultra-independent films and obscure classics. Recent highlights include a retrospective of master documentarian Frederick Wiseman and the U.S. premiere of a lost film by Italian neo-realism legend Vittorio De Sica, as well as acclaimed modern films like *Toni Erdmann, I Am Not Your Negro,* and *Amour.*

MAP 2: 209 W. Houston St., 212/727-8110, http://filmforum.org; $8-14

RADIO
The Greene Space

There really isn't another place in the city quite like The Greene Space, a pristine, light-filled room that acts as a broadcasting center for local public radio stations WNYC and WQXR as well as hosts uniquely cool events. When beloved radio program *This American Life* ventured into television, the space held an audiovisual smackdown event, pitting the show against similarly revered *Radiolab* inside a boxing ring to conceptually hash out which was better: TV or radio. Other highlights have included a birthday party concert for the *Soundcheck* music talk show host John Schaefer and the launch party for Jessica Williams's and Phoebe Robinson's personally reflective podcast *2 Dope Queens.*

MAP 2: 44 Charlton St., 646/829-4000, www.thegreenespace.org; prices vary

East Village and Lower East Side

Map 3

MUSEUMS

Merchant's House Museum

This preserved Greek Revival row house, once the home of successful merchant Seabury Tredwell, offers a glimpse of 18th-century New York life. Visitors enter at the parlor level and purchase tickets at the end of the entrance hallway. This floor contains two grand living spaces with soaring ceilings, but your self-guided tour will begin in the basement, which houses a more modestly sized family room and a faithfully re-created kitchen where servants prepared meals. It's impossible not to think about the class divisions. Lift the bucket of coal in the corner of the room to get a sense of the grueling physical labor demanded of the young Irish girls who worked for the Tredwells. Conclude the tour in their starkly furnished bedroom on the tiny top floor.

MAP 3: 29 E. 4th St., 212/777-1089, http://merchantshouse.org; noon-8pm Thurs., noon-5pm Fri.-Mon.; $15 adults, $10 seniors and students, free for children under 12

Museum at Eldridge Street

Housed in the spectacularly restored 1887 Eldridge Street synagogue, this museum captures the spiritual life of the neighborhood's many Jewish residents. There's an exhibit in the basement about the immigrants who made up the congregation and the architectural features of the building itself. But the main thrill comes from sitting in a temple pew and taking in the vibrant colors created by the dramatic chandeliers and large stained glass windows, which contrast with the intricate, dark woodwork. A standout is the circular stained glass window created by artist Kiki Smith and architect Deborah Gans.

MAP 3: 12 Eldridge St., 212/219-0302, www.eldridgestreet.org; 10am-5pm Sun.-Thurs., 10am-3pm Fri.; $14 adults, $10 seniors and students, $8 children 5-17, free for children under 5

New Museum

The New Museum, as its name suggests, focuses on contemporary art. Founded in the late 1970s by Marcia Tucker, the first female curator at the Whitney, the museum exhibited works by now-giants like Jeff Koons. Since constructing a gleaming new building on the Bowery in the aughts, complete with a theater and three floors of galleries, the non-collecting institution has become a premier exhibition space for working artists around the world, making this a good place to get a sense of the current international scene. Unlike other museums in the city, it often shows works by younger generations. One recent highlight showcased Australian painter Helen Johnson, who abstractly explores the ramifications of colonialism in vividly constructed large-scale works. Thursday evenings 7pm-9pm are pay-what-you-wish.

MAP 3: 235 Bowery, 212/219-1222, http://www.newmuseum.org; 11am-6pm Tues.-Wed. and Fri.-Sun., 11am-9pm Thurs.; $18 adults, $15 seniors, $12 students, free for children 18 and under

GALLERIES
Bullet Space

Of all the galleries on the Lower East Side, Bullet Space has the most dynamic history. This former tenement building is now owned by a group of artists who began squatting here in 1985 when many derelict buildings lay abandoned. The ground-floor gallery's name comes from a brand of heroin that was once sold on the block, and today it hosts shows and performances, such as poetry and play readings by the longtime residents who live in tiny apartments above. During two days in October, as part of Open House New York, they welcome visitors into their dwellings to talk about the changes in the neighborhood and the art they create.

MAP 3: 292 E. 3rd St., 917/841-5921, http://
bulletspace.org; box office 1pm-6pm
Sat.-Sun. or by appointment or chance; free

Perrotin

French owner Emmanuel Perrotin's namesake art gallery is one of the most pristine on the Lower East Side, with a focus on young contemporary artists. Housed in a former fabric factory—original signage from the early 20th century has been tweaked to cheekily advertise the art—the space is 25,000 square feet (2,323 sq m), roomy enough to host large-scale exhibitions.

MAP 3: 130 Orchard St., 212/812-2902,
www.perrotin.com; 10am-6pm Wed.-Sun.;
free

Sperone Westwater

Located in a stunning space a block north of the New Museum, this gallery was one of the first to exhibit acclaimed multimedia artist Bruce Nauman when it opened in Soho in 1975. The gallery also hosted abstract painter Susan Rothenberg's first show as well as artists like Julian Schnabel. An oversized elevator that doubles as an exhibition space and connects the building's five floors seamlessly is the signature design element of the gallery's current space, which it has occupied since 2010. Recent highlights include the whimsical and oversized canine Polaroids of William Wegman along with a new video installation by Nauman.

MAP 3: 257 Bowery, 212/999-7337,
www.speronewestwater.com; 10am-6pm
Tues.-Sat.; free

THEATER
Abrons Arts Center

A program of the not-for-profit social service agency Henry Street Settlement, Abrons Arts Center is one of the premier exhibitors of interdisciplinary theatrical performances that fall outside the mainstream. Its consistently adventurous works contrast with a classic auditorium atmosphere that feels like it was ripped from a well-heeled small town. Recent highlights include the Civilians theater company's porn industry musical *Pretty Filthy* and the Transport Group's gleefully subversive revival of *Once Upon a Mattress* starring Jackie Hoffman.

MAP 3: 466 Grand St., 212/598-0400,
www.abronsartscenter.org; prices vary

La Mama Experimental Theatre Club

It's hard to overstate the role La Mama has played in nurturing the talent of generations of renowned theater artists. Founded in 1961 by Ellen Stewart, the theater was the first home of playwrights Sam Shepard and Lanford Wilson and directors Robert Wilson and Mike Figgis. Far from a relic, the theater continues to produce over 80 works a year across three stages, and it also has an art gallery. Offerings can be hit or miss, but that's part of the thrill of a place that's never been satisfied with the status quo.

MAP 3: 66 and 74A E. 4th St., 212/352-3101, http://lamama.org; box office opens one hour before showtime; $10-25

New York Theatre Workshop

Best known for developing Jonathan Larson's megahit *Rent*, New York Theatre Workshop (NYTW) has consistently put on thought-provoking original plays and musicals since opening in 1979. NYTW has a long-running relationship with playwright Caryl Churchill and has produced some of her most eerie and challenging works, including the vividly drawn dystopia *Far Away* starring Frances McDormand. Other highlights over the decades at this 199-seat theater are Tony Kushner's sprawling epic about a woman who disappears in Afghanistan, *Homebody/Kabul*; Enda Walsh's adaptation of indie musical film hit *Once*; and Rick Elice's Peter Pan origin story. The latter two shows went on to successful Broadway runs.

MAP 3: 79 E. 4th St., 212/780-9037, www.nytw.org; box office noon-6pm Mon., noon-7pm Tues.-Wed., noon-8pm Thurs.-Sat., noon-7pm Sun., noon-6pm when not in performance; $29-69

Performance Space New York

Performance Space New York, formerly named P.S. 122 after the building's original purpose as a public school, is a downtown theatrical institution that's nurtured the talents of a wide range of artists, from Whoopi Goldberg to Reggie Watts. Spalding Gray performed his last monologue here, and Mindy Kaling launched her career writing and starring in the offbeat celebrity fantasia *Matt & Ben*.

The theater has also hosted renowned theater group Elevator Repair Service, playwright Young Jean Lee, playwright-director Richard Maxwell, and countless others. After a six-year renovation, it opened a gleaming new two-theater space in 2018.

MAP 3: 150 1st Ave., 212/477-5829, http://performancespacenewyork.org; prices vary

The Public Theater

Housed in an old Romanesque library, The Public Theater provides a home for plays and musicals that challenge convention, along with more classical offerings. Its track record of hits stretches from *Hair* to *Hamilton*. Expansive digs include five stages in addition to the sleek cabaret space, Joe's Pub. In the summer, The Public Theater's free, star-studded Shakespeare productions, held in Central Park, draw massive and diverse crowds. January is devoted to Under the Radar, a festival capturing cutting-edge offerings from established and up-and-coming artists alike. *The Late Late Show* bandleader Reggie Watts developed his unique blend of self-generated music and storytelling with several performances at the festival, and countless actors—from Meryl Streep to Oscar Isaac—have honed their craft at the Public.

MAP 3: 425 Lafayette Ave., 212/539-8500, www.publictheater.org; prices vary

Theater for the New City

Not to be confused with Brooklyn's Theater for a New Audience, Theater for the New City is an enduring reminder of the scrappy origins of Off-Broadway theater. Housed in a former school and minimally renovated since its founding by Crystal Field in 1970, this no-frills space offers emerging artists a chance to perform in professional productions. Producing 30-40 new American plays each year, it's one of the most prolific theaters in the country. Alumni of the Resident Theater Program include Sam Shepard, Moises Kaufman, Richard Foreman, and Charles Busch, as well as Hollywood stars Tim Robbins and Adrien Brody.

MAP 3: 155 1st Ave., 212/254-1109, www. theaterforthenewcity.net; $10-20

PERFORMING ARTS
Nuyorican Poets Cafe

Frustrated at the lack of opportunities for writers of color, poet Miguel Algarin founded the Nuyorican Poets Café—which began as an intimate salon for a growing circle of friends—in 1973 in his East Village apartment. Founding member and fellow Nuyorican (a term for New Yorkers of Puerto Rican descent) Miguel Pinero found success on Broadway with his play *Short Eyes*, and the group purchased a former tenement building in 1981, establishing a place in the downtown arts scene. They were pioneers of slam poetry and have helped nurture the talent of a wide range of artists, including slam poet and musician Saul Williams and playwright Sarah Jones, along with an older generation of artists like Amiri Baraka and Ntozake

Nuyorican Poets Cafe

Shange. Poetry slams are still a regular fixture, as is an open mic series on Monday nights. Other offerings include searing one-person shows such as Helena D. Lewis's *Call Me Crazy: Diary of a Mad Social Worker*, a first-person account of a descent into insanity.

MAP 3: 236 E. 3rd St., 212/780-9386, www. nuyorican.org; $10-15

CINEMA
Anthology Film Archives

A shrine to both the preservation and exhibition of avant-garde film, Anthology Film Archives opened in 1970 with the goal of showing the 330 films its five founders deemed essential. While they've expanded programming far beyond that goal, those original films still screen regularly as part of its Essential Cinema program ($9 general admission) and range from well-known classics like Orson Welles's *Citizen Kane* to lesser-known gems like Erich von Stroheim's intense silent film *Greed*. There are also premieres of new films. The archives' atmosphere falls somewhere between the sterility of a government building and the functionality of a school auditorium and has remained largely unchanged since its start.

MAP 3: 32 2nd Ave., 212/505-5181, http:// anthologyfilmarchives.org; $11 adults, $9 seniors and students, $7 children 12 and under

Metrograph

Metrograph is quite possibly the most aesthetically pleasing movie theater in the city, if not the country. The box office, concession stand, and other areas are labeled with the kind of nostalgic font you'd find in a Wes Anderson film. A bar to the left can make you a cocktail to enjoy on one of the small vintage couches. Snacks at the minimalist concession stand are stacked in neat rows on illuminated white shelves, while a restaurant upstairs serves dishes like steak tartare, burrata, and sea bass. Movies range from first-run indies to classic and cult films.

MAP 3: 7 Ludlow St., 212/660-0312, http://metrograph.com; 11am-midnight Sun.-Wed., 11am-2am Thurs.-Sat.; $15 adults, $12 seniors and children under 12

The Village and the Meatpacking District
Map 4

THEATER

Cherry Lane Theatre

Located on an idyllic dead-end street, this theater has produced world premieres of Edward Albee's *The Zoo Story* and Samuel Beckett's *Krapp's Last Tape,* among many others. Theater companies around the city rent out space here, so programming varies. Recent highlights include *The Daily Show* correspondent Hasan Minhaj's one-man-show, *Homecoming King,* and Nick Kroll and John Mulaney's *Oh, Hello,* which went on to become a sold-out Broadway hit.

MAP 4: 38 Commerce St., 212/989-2020, www.cherrylanetheatre.org; prices vary

Labyrinth Theater Company

The groundbreaking Labyrinth Theater was founded in 1992 with the mission of telling more diverse stories. It launched the careers of actor David Zayas and playwright Stephen Adly Guirgis, among others, and was the theatrical home of the late Philip Seymour Hoffman. Can't-miss productions over the years have included Guirgus's *Jesus Hopped the A Train* and *Our Lady of 121st Street,* and an evening of Eric Bogosian performing highlights from his penetrating one-man-shows.

MAP 4: 155 Bank St., 212/513-1080, www.labtheater.org; prices vary

Lucille Lortel Theatre

Named for actress-producer Lucille Lortel, who owned and ran it until her death in 1999, this theater hosts the Playwrights Walk of Fame on its front sidewalk—see stars for renowned playwrights including Edward Albee, Tennessee Williams, and Lanford Wilson. The 299-seat theater is also home to non-profit companies like Red Bull Theater, which imbues classic and forgotten plays with razor-sharp modern verve.

MAP 4: 121 Christopher St., 212/924-2817, www.lortel.org; prices vary

Rattlestick Playwrights Theater

As its name implies, this theater focuses on developing writers, and guarantees them a second production regardless of how the first one does. This unique credo has helped develop the talents of Adam Rapp, Annie Baker, Lucy Thurber, and Craig Wright, among others. The intimate 2nd-floor walkup, 99-seat theater recalls the neighborhood's scrappy bohemian past. Be warned the only bathroom is backstage and thus inaccessible during performances.

MAP 4: 224 Waverly Pl., 212/627-2556, www.rattlestick.org; prices vary

PERFORMING ARTS
Skirball Center for the Performing Arts

This 850-seat theater is located on New York University's campus, but its cutting-edge programming competes with the city's top venues. Recent highlights include James Sewell's ballet of Frederick Wiseman's searing documentary classic *Titicut Follies* and a concert by virtuoso jazz pianist Vijay Iyer, who transforms songs like MIA's "Galang" into a syncopated bebop frenzy.

MAP 4: 566 LaGuardia Pl., 212/992-8484, http://nyuskirball.org; prices vary

CINEMA
IFC Center

Formerly The Waverly, this art house theater features a combination of limited-release indie, documentary, and foreign films, as well as special events like the DOC NYC Festival. It also has midnight screenings (Fri.-Sat.) of cult classics like the original *Mad Max*, and evening conversations with directors like Ana Lily Amirpour (*A Girl Walks Home Alone at Night*).

MAP 4: 323 6th Ave., 212/924-7771, www.ifccenter.com; $10-15

Chelsea and Union Square

Map 5

GALLERIES
✪ Gagosian

With 16 locations across the world—including two a few blocks apart in Chelsea and three on the Upper East Side—Larry Gagosian's galleries are among the crown jewels of the contemporary art world, both for their big-name draws like Richard Serra, Diane Arbus, Chris Burden, and Jeff Koons and for their pristine, ridiculously spacious rooms. Gagosian clears a billion dollars in sales annually, and his sprawling spaces—this particular location in Chelsea clocks in at over 20,000 square feet (1,858 sq m)—are great for large-scale pieces such as Chris Burden's *Three Ghost Ships*, a trio of sailboats tilted to display their bare interiors.

MAP 5: 555 W. 24th St., 212/741-1717 and 212/741-1111, www.gagosian.com; 10am-6pm Tues.-Sat., free

✪ Petzel Gallery

Friedrich Petzel's namesake gallery shines a light on the best contemporary international artists, many of whom aren't household names but should be. This gleaming gallery is one of the largest in the area, encompassing 10,000 square feet (929 sq m) on one floor and making museum-sized exhibitions possible. Cuban artist and MacArthur Fellowship recipient Jorge Pardo recently received the full-gallery takeover treatment for his first show of giddily beautiful light/painting hybrids—giant portraits on wood blocks using strategically placed LED lights to make them pop. A second smaller gallery is located in a town house on the Upper East Side.

MAP 5: 456 W. 18th St., 212/680-9467, www.petzel.com; 10am-6pm Tues.-Sat., free

DIY CHELSEA GALLERY-HOPPING

For the uninitiated, art galleries in New York City can feel intimidating at first—but be assured that you are welcome. They're open to the public and free to enter, and unlike at some of the city's top boutiques, browsing without the intention to buy is the norm and not at all discouraged. The number of galleries in the city is ever fluctuating but has been counted as high as 1,500, and Chelsea has the densest concentration. Finding your personal favorite is part of the fun.

Most galleries in the neighborhood lie between 10th and 11th Avenues from about West 18th to West 27th Street, so weaving up and down these streets is a great way to spend a day. Most galleries are open 10am-6pm Tuesday-Saturday. If you need a break from gallery-hopping, you can pop up into the nearby High Line, which has easy access points in the neighborhood at 18th, 20th, 23rd, and 26th Streets, just off 10th Avenue.

Alternatively, opt for a night hop: Thursday evenings around 6pm or 7pm, galleries host opening parties for new exhibits, often popping bottles of wine to celebrate. The "Goings On About Town" section of the *New Yorker* is a great resource to find out about current gallery shows.

Bryce Wolkowitz Gallery

This tiny gallery features a few small rooms that lend a nice intimacy to the displayed works. Exhibits cover a range of media, from paintings to sculptures and installations. A recent standout, Stephen Wilkes's *Day to Night*, featured photos of cities from New York to Paris captured over a 24-hour span, with each distilling the shifting light of the day into a single scene through a blend of effects.

MAP 5: 505 W. 24th St., 212/243-8830, http://brycewolkowitz.com/h; 10am-6pm Tues.-Sat., free

David Zwirner

To many, David Zwirner represents the future of the art world; he combines massive financial success with a high level of artistic curation. His namesake galleries (two in Chelsea, one on the Upper East Side, and one each in London and Hong Kong) bring in 500 million a year and large crowds to boot. A rare show by Japanese artist Yayoi Kusama in 2017 drew crowds that stretched far around the gallery's wide block as people waited hours to glimpse her visceral and magical *Infinity Mirror Rooms*, displaying what appear to be endless reflective orbs.

Other highlights include new monolithic sculptures by legend Richard Serra. As impressive as his current Chelsea galleries are, Zwirner is working on opening a new Renzo Piano-designed gallery in the neighborhood in 2020.

MAP 5: 525 W. 19th St., 212/727-2070, www.davidzwirner.com; 10am-6pm Tues.-Sat., free

Friedman Benda

This eye-catching gallery features a large storefront window to tease its latest exhibition; you can quickly get a feel for whether you want to pop in for further exploration. Works are displayed in a series of smallish rooms and are often contemporary sculptures and other pieces that play with dimensionality. Misha Kahn's recent *Midden Heap* utilized the space well, with richly colored and decorated sculptures evoking a surreal realm between anthropomorphic objects and undiscovered life forms. Don't miss the basement gallery, which usually features a completely different exhibition.

MAP 5: 515 W. 26th St., 212/239-8700, www.friedmanbenda.com; 10am-6pm Tues.-Sat., free

Mary Boone Gallery

One of the major players in the 1980s art scene, Mary Boone represented Julian Schnabel and Jean-Michel Basquiat, among others. Fun fact: Parker Posey played her in Schnabel's *Basquiat* biopic. Her gallery (a second location is in Midtown) continues to present cutting-edge shows. Recent highlights include Peter Saul's *Fake News* paintings, incorporating art history stars and President Trump in surreal acrylic scenes featuring disembodied orange heads and colorful creatures like pilgrim ducks.

MAP 5: 541 W. 24th St., 212/752-2929, http://maryboonegallery.com; 10am-6pm Tues.-Sat., free

Pace Gallery

Considered one of the world's leading galleries, Pace represents over 70 top artists from David Hockney to James Turrell. It was founded in Boston in 1960 and relocated to New York in 1963. Past exhibitions have featured artists like Claes Oldenburg and Julian Schnabel. More recent shows include a retrospective of Richard Avedon's vivid portraits, ironically titled *Nothing Personal*, after a 1964 show he did with James Baldwin. The gallery also frequently exhibits the playfully shaped canvases of Elizabeth Murray, most recently exhibiting her paintings from the 1980s. Pace has nine galleries total around the world in cities from London to Beijing; its New York spaces include two in Chelsea and one on East 57th Street. A new flagship gallery down the block is slated for completion in fall 2019.

MAP 5: 510 W. 25th St., 212/255-4044, www.pacegallery.com; 10am-6pm Tues.-Sat., free

Paula Cooper Gallery

Sam Durant's glowing lightbox, *End White Supremacy*—installed here in the run-up to the 2008 election, taken down upon President Barack Obama's election, and now back on display indefinitely following the 2016 election of President Donald Trump—hangs above the entrance to Paula Cooper's namesake gallery, beckoning progressives into the space. You enter through a small door on the left side of the building into a small bookshop. Continue through the narrow passageway to access the more expansive gallery spaces. Recent highlights have included Cecily Brown's large-scale paintings that blur the line between abstract and figurative. Most of the gallery's shows (including at its second space on 26th St.) focus on minimalist and conceptual works.

MAP 5: 534 W. 21st St., 212/255-1105, www.paulacoopergallery.com; 10am-6pm Tues.-Sat., free

Paula Cooper Gallery

Robert Miller Gallery

Established in 1977 as a platform for underrepresented voices, this gallery has gone on to exhibit some of the biggest names in the business, from Andy Warhol to Ai Weiwei. A recent highlight featured over 30 gorgeously elusive abstracts by Lee Krasner; once known only as Jackson Pollock's wife, Krasner's five-decade-long career has solidified her place as a major artist of the modern art era.

MAP 5: 524 W. 26th St., 212/366-4774, www.robertmillergallery.com; 10am-6pm Tues.-Sat., free

Tanya Bonakdar Gallery

This duplex gallery exhibits roughly a dozen shows a year by major contemporary artists working in a range of media, like light installation artist Olafur Eliasson, perhaps best known for *The New York City Waterfalls* public art project featuring human-made waterfalls on the city's waterfront in 2008. Recent highlights include Phil Collins's (not the musician) futuristic film *Delete Beach*, which uses the anime genre to explore the ramifications of climate change.

MAP 5: 521 W. 21st St. #1, 212/414-4144, www.tanyabonakdargallery.com; 10am-6pm Tues.-Sat., free

MUSEUMS

✪ Rubin Museum of Art

This museum opened in 2004 to exhibit the intricately rich art of the Himalayas and surrounding regions, but it still feels like a secret. A striking central, circular staircase connects seven floors. The 2nd and 3rd floors display large tapestries and ancient artifacts from the permanent collection, like stone and bronze sculptures from 14th- and 15th-century Tibet, while the remaining floors house new exhibits. Examples of recent temporary shows include photographs Henri Cartier-Bresson took

of Gandhi just before his assassination and a sound exhibit utilizing the structure of a meditative drone to explore sonic textures and the ways they affect awareness and consciousness. On the ground floor, a café serves Himalayan food and drink, and doubles as a lounge—complete with a DJ—on Fridays when the Rubin keeps later hours and offers free admission (6pm-10pm). On these so-called K2 Friday Nights, you can hop on a 45-minute guided tour (7pm, free), watch a classic movie (9:30pm, $14) with a cocktail in hand, and, on select Fridays, see shows by live singer-songwriters (7pm, $25-35).

MAP 5: 150 W. 17th St., 212/620-5000, http://rubinmuseum.org; 11am-5pm Mon. and Thurs., 11am-9pm Wed., 11am-10pm Fri., 11am-6pm Sat.-Sun.; $15 adults, $10 seniors and students, free for children 12 and under

Museum at the Fashion Institute of Technology

Housed in the Fashion Institute of Technology (FIT)—the MIT of the fashion world—the college's free museum puts clothing in the context of history. Its three galleries feature items from its permanent collection—which rotate every six months—along with special exhibits and works by students and faculty. Exhibits often look like a runway show frozen in time, as faceless mannequins don all manner of clothing. A recent winter exhibit examined clothes made for survival and traced the origins of the parka to the "heroic era of polar navigation" from 1890 to 1922, while another examined how the cut of female garments influences the gaze of spectators.

MAP 5: 227 W. 27th St., 212/217-4558, www.fitnyc.edu/museum; noon-8pm Mon.-Fri., 10am-5pm Sat.; free

Museum of Sex

"Where titillation and history meet," could be the tagline for this sleek, sexy museum dedicated to opening uncensored discussions around sexuality. The adults-only museum has exhibited the celebrity sex tapes of Tommy Lee and Pamela Anderson along with the recent thought-provoking exhibit *NSFW: Female Gaze,* which called on over two dozen artists to create works evoking female sexuality. The museum doesn't shy away from videos and art depicting hardcore sex, but the curators aren't afraid to break out of that mold as well. One ongoing exhibit, *The Sex Lives of Animals,* features life-sized animals in the heat of carnal embrace but takes an anthropological approach to sexuality. Exhibitions tend to linger for long periods and draw from a considerable collection of over 20,000 pieces of art and historical sexual objects. Vibrators and other sex toys are available for purchase in the gift shop for those feeling inspired.

MAP 5: 233 5th Ave., 212/689-6337, www.museumofsex.com; 10am-9pm Mon.-Thurs., 10am-11pm Fri.-Sat., 11am-9pm Sun.; $17.50 Mon.-Fri. before 1pm, $19.50 Mon.-Fri. after 1pm, $20.50 all other times

THEATER

Atlantic Theater Company

Cofounded by playwright David Mamet and actor William H. Macy in 1985, the Atlantic Theater Company produces modern American and British dramas and musicals. Duncan Sheik's award-winning musical *Spring Awakening* premiered here, as did the political thriller *Farragut North* written by *House of Cards* creator Beau Willimon. Housed in an old Gothic Revival church, the theater features a soaring ceiling and exposed brick that gives the intimate 199-seat space

scene from the NYC Pride March outside the Museum of Sex

an inherently dramatic feel. Recent highlights include Simon Stephens's *On the Shore of the Wide World,* a sharp update on the sprawling mid-century family drama, and Martin McDonagh's *Hangmen,* which marks a welcome return to the theater for the witty provocateur who's lately been turning his talents to film.

MAP 5: 336 W. 20th St., 212/691-5919, http://atlantictheater.org; $70

The Cell

Housed in a brownstone with a wall of floor-to-ceiling windows, The Cell is one of the more unusual spaces in which to see a performance. Folding chairs are reconfigured based on the needs of productions. Classics like Moliére's savage social satires play particularly well here—the space oozes grandiosity—but lately the theater has been hosting a series of modern classic chamber concerts. Whatever the program, low ticket prices make taking a chance on an event more feasible.

MAP 5: 338 W. 23rd St., 646/861-2253, www.thecelltheatre.org; usually $15

Sleep No More at the McKittrick Hotel

Part site-specific installation and part Shakespearean fever dream, Punchdrunk theater company's immersive riff on *Macbeth* is as stylized as it is elusive. Your experience is what you make of it. This is no seated affair; instead you're free to wander the performance space (wear comfortable shoes!)—a five-story hotel completed in 1939—as you like, and for the full experience, you must engage. Many of the rooms are empty, and while examining their contents with a detective's eye can be fun, the real thrills come from hunting down the live scenes staged throughout the building.

Nothing separates the actors from the audience—except for the mask you'll be given and asked to don for the night. If a bloodied Lady Macbeth runs down the hall, chase her. If you hear the persistent thump of a house beat, follow its vibrations. The choose-your-own-adventure aspect of the production is so high that fans return multiple times to uncover new threads.

MAP 5: 530 W. 27th St., 212/904-1883, http://mckittrickhotel.com/sleep-no-more; arrivals scheduled 6pm-midnight; $100-300

PERFORMING ARTS
The Kitchen

This multidisciplinary performance space is one of the oldest in the city and has been dedicated to the experimental realm of a range of media since 1971. Originally located in Soho, the nonprofit helped launch the careers of many major artists, including Cindy Sherman, Robert Mapplethorpe, and Laurie Anderson. In the last decade, Arcade Fire violinist Sarah Neufeld has tested out new work here, and renowned downtown playwright-director Richard Maxwell has staged numerous challenging shows. Its small gallery has exhibited the early works of Sherman and Mapplethorpe and, more recently, those of mixed media artist Chitra Ganesh, who explores the relationship between gender and power in printmaking, sculpture, and video.

MAP 5: 512 W. 19th St., 212/255-5793, http://thekitchen.org; gallery 11am-6pm Tues.-Sat., performance times vary; gallery free, performances $15-25

New York Live Arts

Theater and dance gracefully collide at New York Live Arts, an unassuming and intimate performance space that hosts some of the country's most cutting-edge performance artists and dance companies. The immeasurably talented genderqueer punktress Taylor Mac did an early performance of a couple of decades from his epic *A 24-Decade History of Popular Music* here in 2016, and Anne Bogart's SITI Company—one of the premier dance-theater hybrids—performed its tour de force bio piece, *bobrauschenbergamerica*.

MAP 5: 219 W. 19th St., 212/691-6500, http://newyorklivearts.org; $10-25

DANCE
The Joyce Theater
Think of The Joyce as the Off-Broadway of the dance world: When you want a more intimate or experimental performance than the New York City Ballet or American Ballet Theater, this 472-seat theater satisfies, and there's hardly a seat without good sightlines. The lineup at any given time of year is packed with a who's who of the dance world, from Trisha Brown and Twyla Tharp to MOMIX and PHILANDANCO! Usually in residence for a week, each company's name appears on the old marquee preserved from the theater's former life as a 1940s movie palace.

MAP 5: 175 8th Ave., 212/691-9740, www.joyce.org; $26-81

Midtown, Hell's Kitchen, and Times Square   Map 6

THEATER
✪ Playwrights Horizons
Playwrights Horizons is a downtown theater that happens to be uptown, consistently producing new, boundary-pushing American plays. It produced the world premiere of Annie Baker's *The Flick*, which went on to win the Pulitzer Prize in 2014, as well as Doug Wright's absorbing gender-obscuring one-person show *I Am My Own Wife*, and the now-classic musicals *Sunday in the Park with George* and *Falsettos*. Artistic Director Tim Sanford has put together exceptionally exciting seasons recently with David Hyde Pierce delivering a shattering performance in Adam Bock's *A Life* and Robert O'Hara directing his wildly dystopic fantasia *Mankind*. The space includes the Mainstage Theater, which has some of the plushest leather seats in the city, and the intimate Peter Jay Sharp Theater.

MAP 6: 416 W. 42nd St., 212/564-1235, www.playwrightshorizons.org; box office noon-8pm daily; $39-99

✪ Signature Theatre Company
Founded in 1991 by James Houghton with the simple but ambitious goal of dedicating each of its seasons to one playwright, Signature Theatre Company quickly gained a reputation among theater lovers. Early seasons were devoted to heavy hitters like Edward Albee, Arthur Miller, and John Guare and featured revivals of classics alongside new plays written specifically for their season. The theater's mission has expanded since moving into its modern three-theater space, which also has a bookshop and café that often features live music. It

now produces some of the hottest new playwrights, such as Annie Baker and Branden Jacobs-Jenkins. Ticket prices for all regular runs are $35, a rarity for such an established theater. Performances often sell out, so it's best to buy at the beginning of previews or before.

The New Group (www.thenew group.org; $30-125), a critically acclaimed theater company, also performs out of the Signature Theatre space and often puts on some of the most exciting shows of the season. Some of the many highlights have included a feminist update of the musical *Sweet Charity* with Tony winner Sutton Foster, and Jesse Eisenberg's savage satire of privilege, *The Spoils*. Regular ticket prices are quite a bit more than the Signature's shows, but there are $30 rush tickets available one hour before curtain at the theater.

MAP 6: 480 W. 42nd St., 212/967-1913, www.signaturetheatre.org; box office 11am-6pm Tues.-Sun.; $35

Aladdin at the New Amsterdam Theatre

Based on the popular 1990s Disney film, this stage musical helmed by Casey Nicholaw, two-time Tony Award nominee for *The Drowsy Chaperone*, is just as satisfying for adults as it is for kids. A scat-singing Genie grants its eponymous hero wishes in show-stopping fashion. Chad Beguelin's script is filled with sharp dialogue that effortlessly connects songs like "One Jump Ahead," "Friend Like Me," and "A Whole New World." The show also features songs written by Alan Menken, Howard Ashman, and Tim Rice that were cut from the movie. Moments like the magic carpet ride retain their wonder; amid a wash of

stars so vivid, it's like being transported high above the world.

MAP 6: 214 W. 42nd St., 866/870-2717, www.aladdinthemusical.com; box office 9am-8pm Mon.-Fri., 10am-8pm Sat., 10am-6:30pm Sun.; $30-157

Ars Nova

Somewhere between a cabaret and an Off-Broadway theater, Ars Nova proves that great things happen in small spaces. A bar is situated near the entrance and seating is available at tables or auditorium-style. More than other Off-Broadway theaters, Ars Nova nurtures playwrights from their earliest beginnings: Lin-Manuel Miranda staged his first show, *Freestyle Love Supreme,* on this intimate stage. Ars Nova moved its mainstage shows (bigger Off-Broadway shows) to the larger Greenwich House Theater (27 Barrow St.) in the Village in 2019, allowing them to focus even more on emerging artists at this Midtown space, where ticket prices are more affordable.

MAP 6: 511 W. 54th St., 212/489-9800, http://arsnovanyc.com; box office opens 30 min. prior to performance; $15-65

The Book of Mormon at the Eugene O'Neill Theatre

Matt Stone and Trey Parker have long included theatrical flourishes in their work, most notably in the uproarious *South Park* movie musical, so it shouldn't be a surprise they've crafted a show that's as well made as it is outrageously obscene. Following a pair of young missionaries sent to Uganda, the musical takes on religious dogma as the Book of Mormon fails to provide answers for the protagonists' increasingly expanding world. One of its best songs, "Turn it Off," savagely rips into homophobia to an impossibly catchy melody; it's the kind of big Broadway score you'll be humming for weeks. Because the show has been on the boards for years it can often be found at TKTS discount booths for half price; otherwise, $32 lottery seats and $27 standing room tickets are available at each performance.

MAP 6: 230 W. 49th St., 877/250-2929, http://bookofmormonbroadway.com; box office 10am-8pm Mon.-Sat., noon-7pm Sun.; $27-169

Dear Evan Hansen at the Music Box Theatre

"When you're falling in a forest and there's nobody around, do you ever really crash or even make a sound?" The title character, a high school outcast suffering from social anxiety, wonders this aloud early on in this dark but uplifting musical. Evan's also quite a vivid liar and invents a friendship with a dead classmate in an effort to gain friends and the affection of the boy's sister. At its heart, *Dear Evan Hansen* is about the struggle to step into your true self, but Steven Levenson's sophisticated script takes us down a morally ambiguous path that resists easy solutions in favor of raw moments rarely found in mainstream musicals. *La La Land*-famous songwriting duo Justin Paul and Benj Pasek's soaring piano- and guitar-driven songs are charged with so much emotion they threaten to blow the roof off the Music Box Theatre, one of Broadway's most intimate spaces. Tickets are nearly as hard to come by as they are for *Hamilton*, but a lottery (www. dearevanhansenlottery.com) offers $42 tickets for each performance. Log onto the site through Facebook, Twitter, or Instagram to enter any time before 9am (matinee) or 2pm (evening) on the day of performance to enter. Winners are notified five minutes after closing and have two hours to purchase tickets.

MAP 6: 239 W. 45th St., 212/239-6200, http://dearevanhansen.com; box office 10am-8pm Mon.-Sat., noon-6pm Sun.; $42-499

Feinstein's/54 Below

Known as "Broadway's living room," this plush, inviting space beneath former club Studio 54 makes a good stop for fans looking to see their favorite performers in a more intimate light. Everyone from Chita Rivera to Melissa Errico has graced this stage with original cabaret performances. The space also hosts special one-night-only concert performances of short-lived but beloved shows like the porn industry musical *Pretty Filthy* by the late composer of *Bloody Bloody Andrew Jackson*, Michael Friedman.

MAP 6: 254 W. 54th St. St., 646/476-3551, http://54below.com; box office 5:15pm-midnight daily; $5-105

Hamilton at the Richard Rodgers Theatre

Lin-Manuel Miranda's hip-hop epic, drawn from Ron Chernow's biographical tome, lives up to all the hype. The songs, which merge soaring Broadway-inflected melodic hooks with meticulously constructed rap flows, are instantly memorable while serving to organically ratchet up the drama of the Founding Father's friendship and rivalry with politician Aaron Burr. Burr has generally been relegated by history to the role of villain but receives more complex treatment here. Miranda has a knack for conveying multitudes in simple lines. "Who lives, who dies, who tells your story" is a central theme here, as is Hamilton's

THE CENTER OF THE THEATRICAL UNIVERSE

There's nothing quite like watching live theater, and New York hosts the most diverse offerings in the world. On any given night you can pick from hundreds of shows. From black-box theaters where all the seats are within spitting distance of the actors to Broadway palaces where film stars and veteran theater actors alike bring to life the biggest shows on the planet, there is something for every taste and budget. Good sources for current listings include www.theatermania.com and *Time Out New York*.

Shows in New York are classified as either on Broadway, Off-Broadway, or Off-Off-Broadway, technical designations that have to do with contracts between the theater and performers, but which usually break down by the number of seats in a theater and geographical location. Still, productions within each classification tend to share some similarities that are useful to know.

BROADWAY

When people think of New York theater, they think of Broadway. While the length of the avenue stretches from south to north through the entire island of Manhattan, where the street converges with Times Square and the Theater District is its claim to fame. Broadway's theaters—comprising 41 venues surrounding Times Square and the Lincoln Center's Vivian Beaumont Theater—took in $1.45 billion in revenue in the 2016-2017 season, and audience attendance surpassed that of all 10 of the city's professional sports teams combined. Budgets for Broadway shows are lavish, with celebrity casting and high production values that are the theatrical equivalent of Hollywood blockbusters; applause for the theatrical sets alone is common. The number of seats in Broadway houses is 500 and up, with some theaters holding a seating capacity of nearly 2,000. Tickets commonly run up to $200, and can escalate dramatically for the biggest hits. While Broadway shows often comprise crowd-pleasing musicals and well-known revivals, recent years have seen an expansion to encompass shows by some of the most exciting American playwrights, as well as trends toward darker and sometimes subversive musicals, including *Dear Evan Hansen* (page 233), which tackles issues of depression and suicide, and, of course, *Hamilton* (page 233), which earns its hype by telling the history of the Founding Father through hip-hop.

OFF-BROADWAY

While there's still plenty of commercial fare on offer, you'll find many of Manhattan's best theaters and companies Off-Broadway. In these spaces—which hold 99-499 seats—it's hard to find a bad seat in the house, and the small scale allows for an intimacy between actors and audiences. Ticket prices are cheaper than on Broadway, though they can still top $100 for popular shows, particularly musicals. Here are some places to dip your toes into Off-Broadway:

determination to not throw away his "shot." Buy tickets up to a year in advance when new blocks are released, or try your luck with the $10 ticket lottery: Enter online (www.luckyseat.com/hamilton-ny) by 9am the day before your desired performance.

MAP 6: 226 W. 46th St., 212/221-1211, http://hamiltonmusical.com; box office 10am-8pm Mon.-Sat., noon-6pm Sun.; $10-749

Manhattan Theatre Club

Manhattan Theatre Club has been producing new plays and timely revivals since 1970. Beginning as an Off-Off-Broadway company, MTC has become a major force in the New York scene, with two Off-Broadway theaters and this one on Broadway, under the guidance of long-standing artistic director Lynne Meadow. She's directed some of its most popular

- **Soho Rep:** One of the smallest Off-Broadway theaters is also the best, consistently producing the most daring new playwrights in top-notch productions (page 218).

- **Playwrights Horizons:** Regularly producing boundary-pushing new plays, this theater has arguably made a greater contribution to modern American theater than any other in the country (page 231).

- **Signature Theatre Company:** Looking both to the past and the future, this company's gleaming three-stage space usually has something great to see, for only $35 (page 231).

Off-Broadway is also where you'll typically find immersive shows like *Sleep No More* (page 230) a choose-your-own adventure that takes place across five floors of a converted hotel. Immersive theater bulldozes the fourth wall that comfortably separates the audience from actors and often requires guests to actively participate by walking through various spaces and sometimes interacting with performers. Comfortable shoes are always a good idea, as is coming with an open mind and a fearless spirit.

OFF-OFF-BROADWAY

Off-Off Broadway theaters operate on the smallest budgets but can produce some of the most challenging theater in the city. More than a hundred such theaters are scattered across New York City, typically small black-box spaces that hold fewer than 99 people (and some with capacity for only a couple dozen people). Seating is often on metal folding chairs and production values are minimal. While these can be really hit-or-miss affairs and often feature a production in its initial stage of gestation, some real gems can be found, especially for fans of experimental theater. Ticket prices tend to be under $20. Here are some good places to start sampling Off-Off-Broadway:

- **The Flea Theater:** With a gleaming three-theater space, The Flea is the nicest Off-Off-Broadway theater, known for producing many plays by a younger generation of outspoken playwrights and offering tickets on a sliding scale (page 218).

- **HERE:** Diverse programming is afoot at HERE's cozy space, incorporating shows by seminal downtown theater artists as well as a mix of theater, dance, puppetry, and performance art (page 219).

- **Performance Space New York:** This legendary downtown space sparked the careers of a wide range of performers from Whoopi Goldberg to Mindy Kaling and continues to produce challenging new works (page 222).

productions, from Charles Busch's wild comedy *The Tale of the Allergist's Wife* to David Lindsay-Abaire's heart-wrenching *Rabbit Hole* starring Cynthia Nixon.

MAP 6: 261 W. 47th St., 212/239-6200, www.manhattantheatreclub.com; box office usually noon-6pm Mon.-Sat., with later and Sun. hours during performances; $38-199

New Victory Theater

Children's theater can get a bad rap, with too many shows that feel like dumbed-down productions of well-worn classics. The New Victory offers an alternative, with smartly conceived shows that respect the intelligence of kids of all ages. Offerings are rated for appropriate groups (6-plus, 10-plus, and so on) to give parents a guide. One of the most notable productions in recent years was the lauded Fiasco Theater company's production of Shakespeare's deliriously overstuffed *Cymbeline*. Running times tend to be distilled to a kid-friendly 60 minutes.

MAP 6: 209 W. 42nd St., 646/223-3000, www.newvictory.org; box office 11am-5pm Sun.-Mon., noon-7pm Tues.-Sat.; $16-38

Roundabout Theatre Company

With two Off-Broadway stages (at the Harold and Miriam Steinberg Center for Theatre) and two Broadway theaters (American Airlines Theatre, Studio 54), the Roundabout Theatre Company is one of the most prolific in the city, with wide-ranging offerings. It was one of the first to produce playwright Steven Levenson, of *Dear Evan Hansen* fame, as part of its Underground series that highlights emerging artists. It's also known for lavish set pieces that merit their own plaudits. Tickets at its Black Box Theatre are just $25 and offer one of the best opportunities to see professional theater at an affordable price.

MAP 6: Black Box Theatre at the Harold and Miriam Steinberg Center for Theatre, 111 W. 46th St., 212/719-1300, www.roundabouttheatre.org; box office noon-8pm Tues.-Sat., noon-6pm Sun.-Mon.; $25-154

Second Stage Theater

A bright orange wall welcomes visitors into the 2nd-floor lobby of this dynamic theater housed in a former bank. The box office sits in the former vault, its impressively impenetrable door on display. Theatrical offerings usually walk the line between accessible and daring. Some of the company's biggest hits include the sleek retelling of Ovid's *Metamorphoses* around a swimming pool and a pair of coming-of-age musicals, *The 25th Annual Putnam County Spelling Bee* and *Dear Evan Hansen*. Second Stage also frequently produces plays by two of the modern era's most interesting playwrights, Tracy Letts and Bruce Norris, and recently acquired the Helen Hayes Theatre on Broadway to allow larger audiences to see its work.

MAP 6: 305 W. 43rd St., 212/246-4422, http://2st.com; box office noon-6pm daily; $79-169

MUSEUMS
Gulliver's Gate

What if the world could be contained in a building? That's the concept behind Gulliver's Gate, a museum full of meticulously constructed miniature models ranging from the island of Manhattan to major monuments like Machu Picchu, the Eiffel Tower, and the Brandenburg Gate. The overall wow factor of this ambitious work-in-progress—new models are continuously being added—is high. Visitors receive a key upon entrance that can be inserted at various stations to animate an action in the miniature models—for instance, to prompt skiers to glide down slopes in Sochi. In-house craftspeople can be seen at work and also answer questions.

MAP 6: 216 W. 44th St., 212/235-2016, http://gulliversgate.com; 10am-8pm daily; $36 adults, $27 seniors and children 12 and under, free for active military in uniform

Intrepid Sea, Air & Space Museum

Before it was decommissioned in 1974, the *Intrepid* aircraft carrier saw intense battle in World War II—surviving five kamikaze attacks and a torpedo strike—the Cold War, and Vietnam. It now sits on the Hudson River west of Times Square as a National Historic Landmark. Its flight

STRATEGIES FOR SAVING ON THEATER TICKETS

Theater in New York can be expensive, there's no doubt. But many discounts are readily available.

TKTS
At any given time on Broadway there are a few shows—at the moment, *Hamilton* and *Dear Evan Hansen*—that are nearly impossible to get tickets for unless you luck into last-minute steals via lottery tickets (or purchase them full-price a year in advance). But there are also always plenty of other theatrical options. The most famous discount purveyor is the Times Square TKTS booth (Broadway and W. 47th St.; 3pm-8pm Mon. and Fri., 2pm-8pm Tues., 10am-2pm and 3pm-8pm Wed.-Thurs., 10am-2pm and 3pm-8pm Sat., 11am-7pm Sun.) run by the Theatre Development Fund. It offers same-day Broadway and Off-Broadway tickets for up to 50 percent off. It has a play-only line, which cuts down significantly on wait time if that's what you're after, and often features high-profile revivals along with new plays. Visit the TDF website (www.tdf.org/nyc/81/TKTS-Live) to check out current offerings; real-time listings are shown for each TKTS location. Plays are noted with the letter "P." If you're just interested in the shows themselves and don't need the Times Square TKTS line-waiting experience, head to any of the TDF's three other locations for shorter queues: South Street Seaport (190 Front St.; 11am-6pm Mon.-Sat., 11am-4pm Sun.), Downtown Brooklyn (1 Metrotech Center; 11am-6pm Tues.-Sat.), and Lincoln Center (61 W. 62nd St., noon-7pm Mon.-Sat., noon-5pm Sun.). The first two sell same-day tickets for evening performances and next-day tickets for matinees, while the latter sells day-of tickets for both evenings and matinees as well as next-day matinees. Similar discounts can also be found on websites like Theatermania (www.theatermania.com) and apps like TodayTix (www.todaytix.com). The latter offers rush tickets for many shows. For cheap Off-Off-Broadway tickets, you can join TDF for free (https://www.tdf.org/nyc/27/Off-Off-Broadway-Theatre-Dance-Music) to access $9 tickets.

PREVIEWS AND SPECIALS
A good rule of thumb for Broadway and Off-Broadway shows is to go during previews—before a show officially opens—for the best deals. New York Theatre Workshop sells preview tickets for as little as $25 while the Atlantic Theater Company also offers $25 tickets for preview performances.

Soho Rep sells tickets for select Sunday performances for just 99 cents (purchase in person on the day of), while The Public Theater gives away free tickets for the first preview of each performance and makes $20 rush tickets available for subsequent shows (via a lottery on TodayTix).

UNDER 30 AND 35 CLUBS
For those under 30 or 35, even more deals are available, with many theaters—mainly Off-Broadway—offering discounts to make shows more accessible and enticing to younger people. For example, Roundabout Theatre Company, Lincoln Center Theater, Second Stage Theater, and Manhattan Theatre Club all offer programs through their websites that allow you to purchase tickets in advance for $20-30. Some require enrolling in a free membership. As part of these programs, some theaters also throw an open-bar party for each show's run, free with a ticket purchase and making for an even more affordable evening out.

deck hosts a range of planes from an Avenger torpedo bomber to the A-12 *Blackbird*, a Cold War spy plane. Also on display is a prototype that paved the way for the space shuttle program. After checking out the aircraft, head below to the hangar deck to explore this massive floor divided between temporary exhibits as well as permanent exhibits on the ship's technology and fallen crewmembers. Overnight stays with educational activities are available for the price of a hotel room ($130).

MAP 6: Pier 86, at W. 46th and 12th Ave., 212/245-0072, www.intrepidmuseum.org; 10am-5pm daily; $33 adults, $31 seniors, $24 children 5-12

Intrepid Sea, Air & Space Museum

Japan Society

Founded in 1907 by prominent New Yorkers in an effort to enhance relations between the United States and Japan, this nonprofit has evolved into a premier exhibition space for Japanese culture. From exhibits on Japanese arts past and present to screenings of classic films like Akira Kurosawa's *Yojimbo* and Kenji Mizoguchi's *Ugetsu*, to talks on Japanese whiskey and *matcha* green tea, to theatrical performances like *Mugen Noh Othello*—a Noh interpretation of Shakespeare's classic—the Japan Society provides an impressive platform for the country's rich culture.

MAP 6: 333 E. 47th St., 212/832-1155, www.japansociety.org; noon-7pm Tues.-Thurs., noon-9pm Fri., 11am-5pm Sat.-Sun.; gallery admission $12 adults, $10 seniors and students, free for children 15 and under

The Morgan Library & Museum

Named after its original purpose as J. P. Morgan's private library—lined with triple tiers of Circassian walnut bookshelves capped by ornate murals that decorate its dome ceiling—this wonderfully intimate museum preserves the grandiose Italian Renaissance landmark. It programs engrossing exhibits often featuring rare manuscripts, letters, and other documents of Western civilization. Among the prized collection is an original Gutenberg Bible, letters of George Washington and Abraham Lincoln, and journals of Henry David Thoreau. Temporary exhibit highlights have included Tennessee Williams's letters and early drafts of plays, and a series of black-and-white portraits by brilliant downtown photographer Peter Hujar. Admission is free on Fridays 7pm-9pm.

MAP 6: 225 Madison Ave., 212/685-0008, www.themorgan.org; 10:30am-5pm Tues.-Thurs., 10:30am-9pm Fri., 10am-6pm Sat., 11am-6pm Sun.; $20 adults, $13 seniors and students, free for children 12 and under

The Morgan Library & Museum

Paley Center

For those who've ever wished that the culture of TV and radio could be celebrated communally, like that of theater, the Paley Center, formerly the Museum of Television and Radio, provides a space for precisely this purpose, with screenings and events held throughout the week. Visitors can also pick selections from the center's extensive archive of over 160,000 programs and advertisements to watch on individual screens. In the evenings, the center hosts panel discussions with the casts of TV shows like HBO's *Divorce* along with preview screenings of new films like Dan Klores's *Basketball: A Love Story.*

MAP 6: 25 W. 52nd St., 212/621-6600, http://media.paleycenter.org; noon-6pm Fri.-Sun. and Wed., noon-8pm Thurs.; suggested contribution $10 adults, $8 seniors and students, $5 children 13 and under

Scandinavia House

Home to all things Nordic, the Scandinavia House offers a variety of entry points to appreciate the region's culture. It has a gallery space with rotating exhibits—such as rare black-and-white photographs of famed Norwegian painter Edvard Munch—and also hosts concerts highlighting, for instance, folk songs from the Faroe Islands, and screenings of movies by the likes of Ingmar Bergman. In-house restaurant Smorgas Chef serves authentic fare, including Swedish meatballs and herring, with ingredients sourced from its farm upstate. Two-course dinner and a movie or concert pairings ($33, $41) are available 5pm-9pm nightly.

MAP 6: 58 Park Ave., 212/779-3587, www.scandinaviahouse.org; 11am-10pm Mon.-Sat., 11am-5pm Sun.; gallery admission free; film screenings $12; concerts $15-25

GALLERIES
Hirschl and Adler

Founded in 1952, Hirschl and Adler moved to this location in the art deco Fuller Building in 2018, and the gallery remains the epitome of well-appointed, old-school luxury. Walking through shows here can feel like perusing the prize pieces in a socialite's apartment, with spacious rooms housing stately pieces of art that would be at home in a penthouse on nearby Park Avenue. The gallery celebrated its move with a show examining the ways in which fashion both displays and obscures who we are.

MAP 6: 41 E. 57th St., 9th fl., 212/535-8810, www.hirschlandadler.com; 9:30am-5pm Mon., 9:30am-5:15pm Tues.-Fri., 9:30am-4:45pm Sat., free

Sean Kelly

Founded in 1991 in Soho, this gallery now sits opposite a gas station on a stretch of 10th Avenue north of Chelsea's cluster of galleries. Don't let its location fool you, though: plenty of interesting shows come here. British-born owner Sean Kelly focuses on contemporary pieces with an intellectual and conceptual bent. A recent exhibit of performance artist Marina Abramović's early work examined how the artist came to use her body as a canvas and engage her masochism to push the physical and emotional limits of her art.

MAP 6: 475 10th Ave., 212/239-1181, www.skny.com; 11am-6pm Tues.-Fri., 10am-6pm Sat., free

CONCERT VENUES

Carnegie Hall

Opened in 1891, there are few concert halls in the world that carry the same gravitas as Carnegie Hall. From Pyotr Ilyich Tchaikovsky's inaugural concert to seminal shows by Judy Garland, Duke Ellington, Bob Dylan, and the Beatles, it has remained the gold standard for artists across all genres of music. Today, famed orchestras like Staatskapelle Berlin grace the main stage, along with popular acts like Andrew Bird. Acoustics here are sublime and, holding just over 2,800 people, this National Historic Landmark is undeniably grand, with its Italian Renaissance architecture, intricate moldings, white arches, and seats the color of an exclusive red carpet.

Carnegie Hall opened Zankel Hall in 2003, a gorgeous basement space that's a smaller, edgier expression of the legendary venue, seating around 600 in an intimate but lofty subterranean room covered in sleekly polished wood, designed both for style and acoustics. Zankel's lineup ranges from chamber concerts with renowned musicians like violinist Joshua Bell and the genre-expanding Kronos Quartet to the equally adventurous bluegrass virtuoso mandolinist Chris Thile, who currently hosts *Live From Here.*

Carnegie Hall tours lasting 1-1.25 hours are given on select days at 11:30am and 12:30pm October-June. Tickets ($17 adults, $12 seniors, students, and children 12 and under) can be purchased on the website.

MAP 6: 881 7th Ave., 212/247-7800, www. carnegiehall.org; box office 11am-6pm Mon.-Sat., noon-6pm Sun.; $18-260

Madison Square Garden

It's not much to look at from the outside, but the Garden's place in history is undeniable. It was the venue for

Carnegie Hall

the "Fight of the Century" between Muhammad Ali and Joe Frazier and Marilyn Monroe's famous birthday serenade to JFK. Everyone from Simon & Garfunkel and Led Zeppelin to Lady Gaga and LCD Soundsystem have played here. With a maximum capacity of just over 20,000, if you're seeing a big event in the city—whether Beyoncé or Billy Joel, the New York Knicks or New York Rangers—it's likely to be here. A second theater space holds 5,600 and has hosted a range of events from big holiday theatrical shows like *A Christmas Carol* to comedians with large fan bases like Bill Maher. Celebrated, shuttered Carnegie Deli lives on at a pair of concession stands, serving the same corned beef and pastrami that made the deli famous (though in 12-ounce portions instead of the massive 1-pound sandwiches for which it was known).

MAP 6: 4 Pennsylvania Plaza, 212/465-6741, www.msg.com; prices vary

Terminal 5

Terminal 5 was once the site of Club Exit, where star DJs of yesteryear like Paul Oakenfold would spin late into the night. Now it's concert venue programming acts from They Might Be Giants to Run the Jewels. Acoustics in the three-tiered space, which holds 3,000 and is standing room only, have been compared to an airplane hangar, and indeed there are many places where sound might be muted and uneven; heading toward the center of the 1st floor is your best bet. A bar toward the back of the main floor is elevated for good sightlines, although there tends to be a lot of chatter here. Two balconies provide great birds-eye views if you arrive early enough to snag a space by the railing.

MAP 6: 610 W. 56th St., 212/582-6600, www.terminal5nyc.com; tickets for sale at PlayStation Theater box office (1515 Broadway) noon-6pm Mon.-Fri.; $25-250

Town Hall

Built in 1921 by the League for Political Education—instrumental in the passage of women's suffrage—as a place to exchange and be enriched by ideas, this 1,500-seat auditorium's architecture was intended to reflect democratic principles, hence no box seats or obstructed sightlines. Watching a concert at Town Hall—by the likes of, for example, Band of Horses, Regina Spektor, or Amanda Palmer and Neil Gaiman—is an intimate experience where you never feel too far away from the stage. The Moth has also held many storytelling events here in recent years. Free guided tours are given on select mornings at 10:30am and can be reserved in advance online.

MAP 6: 123 W. 43rd St., 212/997-1003, http://thetownhall.org; box office noon-6pm Mon.-Sat.; prices vary

Upper West Side and Upper East Side

Map 7

MUSEUMS

Asia Society and Museum

Founded by John D. Rockefeller III in 1956, the Asia Society aims to educate people about the continent's myriad cultures through exhibitions, talks, and arts events. It hosts the Asian American International Film Festival in the summer, as well as other screenings and topical talks throughout the year that wrestle with pressing issues like nuclear negotiations with North Korea and the state of Myanmar's developing democracy. Its museum holdings include traditional objects spanning Asian cultures, but it focuses on contemporary Asian and Asian American art acquisitions—the first U.S. museum to so focus its collection. Admission is free on Fridays 6pm-9pm.

MAP 7: 725 Park Ave., 212/288-6400, http://asiasociety.org; 11am-6pm Tues.-Sun.; $12 adults, $10 seniors, $7 students, free for children under 16

Cooper Hewitt

Founded in 1896, the Cooper Hewitt was the first Smithsonian museum to open outside of Washington DC and remains the only museum in the country dedicated to modern and contemporary design. In 1970, the museum moved to its current home, formerly Andrew Carnegie's mansion, which features intricate detailing in the lobby and a wondrously manicured garden that houses exhibits and an outdoor café. Saturday nights 6pm-9pm are pay-what-you-wish.

MAP 7: 2 E. 91st St., 212/849-8400, www.cooperhewitt.org; 10am-6pm Sun.-Fri., 10am-9pm Sat.; $18 adults, $12 seniors, $9 students, free for children 18 and under

The Frick Collection

Browse in a museum set in a stately mansion at The Frick. Chandeliers hang above wood-paneled walls and paintings by old masters—Rembrandt and Vermeer, to name two—line the galleries. The collection was established by the museum's namesake founder, Henry Clay Frick, an industrialist from Pittsburgh, in his former home. Despite the upper-class atmosphere, admission is pay-what-you-wish on Wednesdays (2pm-6pm) and free the first Friday evening (6pm-9pm) of every month except in September and January.

MAP 7: 1 E. 70th St., 212/288-0700, www.frick.org; 10am-6pm Tues.-Sat., 11am-5pm Sun.; $22 adults, $17 seniors, $12 students, children under 10 not admitted

The Jewish Museum

Founded in 1904, New York's Jewish Museum is one of the oldest such museums in the world. Rather than focus on history, it emphasizes the creative works and culture of Jewish people. Its *Scenes from the Collection* is an ongoing exhibit that showcases some of the museum's 30,000 artworks and artifacts—which span 4,000 years—on a rotating basis, with some scenes changing annually and one changing every six months. It also features compelling temporary exhibits, such as a retrospective of controversial cartoonist Art Spiegelman, of *Maus* fame, and early drawings of Amedeo Modigliani that shined a light on the famed artist's Italian Sephardic Jewish heritage.

The cultural experience extends to the museum's café, which is an outpost of the legendary Lower East Side appetizing store Russ & Daughters (note: admission isn't necessary to access it). Herring as fine as sashimi and pastrami-crusted salmon are a couple musts if you need a food break while here. Saturdays at the museum are free admission days, and Thursdays 5pm-8pm are pay-what-you-wish.

MAP 7: 1109 5th Ave., 212/423-3200, http://thejewishmuseum.org; 11am-5:45pm Fri.-Tues., 11am-8pm Thurs.; $18 adults, $12 seniors, $8 students, free for children under 18

The Met Breuer

Formerly the home of the Whitney Museum of American Art, The Met Breuer features temporary exhibits that draw in large part from The Met's collection of modern and contemporary art, such as a 2018 show, *Obsession*, which contrasted nude paintings by Gustav Klimt, Egon Schiele, and Pablo Picasso. Designed by Bauhaus architect Marcel Breuer, the building's five floors feel sleek yet intimate. Ticket lines are typically much shorter than at The Met, so buy your admission here—it's valid for three consecutive days and includes entrance to The Metropolitan Museum of Art as well as the Cloisters—and then you can breeze right into the former on nearby 5th Avenue.

MAP 7: 945 Madison Ave., 212/731-1675, www.metmuseum.org/visit/met-breuer; 10am-5:30pm Tues.-Thurs. and Sun., 10am-9pm Fri.-Sat.; $25 adults, $17 seniors, $12 students, free for children under 12

Museum of the City of New York

Historian Henry Collins Brown founded the Museum of the City of New York in 1923. Exhibitions detail New York's multiculturalism, along with the city's strong history as an epicenter of protest. Special exhibitions focus on New Yorkers' contributions to the city, as in a recent show of early photographs taken by legendary Bronx-born filmmaker Stanley Kubrick when he was working for *Look* magazine in his early twenties.

MAP 7: 1220 5th Ave., 212/534-1672, www.mcny.org; 10am-6pm daily; $18 adults, $12 seniors, free for children under 20

Neue Galerie

Housed in a beautiful beaux arts building that feels simultaneously grand and intimate, the Neue Galerie is devoted to German and Austrian art. The 2nd floor features a permanent collection, including a handful of paintings by Gustav Klimt, while the 3rd floor hosts special exhibitions such as a recent one examining art made under Hitler's rule, an illuminating window into the insularity of genocidal dictatorship. Café Sabarsky on the 1st floor transports visitors to Vienna with superb renditions of classic dishes like Wiener schnitzel and apple strudel, along with Austrian sodas. Note that because of the museum's relatively small size admission lines often stretch around the corner; this can be avoided by purchasing timed-entry premium admission online (a 50 percent upcharge). Admission is free 6pm-9pm the first Friday of the month.

MAP 7: 1048 5th Ave., 212/628-6200, www.neuegalerie.org; 11am-6pm Thurs.-Mon.; $20 adults, $15 seniors, $10 students

New-York Historical Society

The New-York Historical Society focuses on the history of the city and the people who have influenced it. Artifacts in the permanent collection include the cot George Washington slept on while leading troops at Valley Forge and a controller handle from the maiden voyage of the first subway car in 1904. Recent temporary exhibit highlights have included drawings from beloved modern children's book author Mo Willems's series *Knuffle Bunny* and Norman Rockwell's paintings of Franklin D. Roosevelt's Four Freedoms. A film showing in the museum's auditorium on the 1st floor is narrated by actor Liev Schreiber and tells the city's history through video projections that run on a continuous loop. Admission is pay-what-you-wish on Fridays 6pm-8pm.

MAP 7: 170 Central Park West, 212/873-3400, www.nyhistory.org; 10am-6pm Tues.-Thurs. and Sat., 10am-8pm Fri., 11am-5pm Sun.; $21 adults, $16 seniors, educators, and active military, $13 students, $6 children 5-13, free for children under 5

Nicholas Roerich Museum

This small museum, housed in a town house on the northwest edge of the Upper West Side, is devoted to exhibiting the works of prolific and multifaceted Russian-born painter Nicholas Roerich. (Among his accomplishments was a treaty, bearing his name, that he helped draft prioritizing the cultural preservation of artistic, educational, and scientific institutions in times of war as well as peace, which served as an important blueprint for creating international protections in the aftermath of World War II.) The museum's permanent collection consists of over 200 paintings, and many more drawings depicting natural landscapes, many with a spiritual bent. From October to May on Sunday evenings (5pm), the museum offers free classical concerts, recitals, and the occasional poetry reading.

MAP 7: 319 W. 107th St., 212/864-7752, www.roerich.org; noon-4pm Tues.-Fri., 2pm-5pm Sat.-Sun.; free

GALLERIES

Acquavella Galleries

Opened in 1921 and named for founder Nicholas Acquavella, who traded in paintings from the Italian Renaissance and introduced museums to these works, this gallery has in the decades since expanded its scope, with shows of modern masters from Monet to Picasso along with contemporary artists like British painter Lucian Freud and pop artist James Rosenquist. Recent shows include the most comprehensive exhibit in the United States of Spanish mixed-media artist and semi-abstract painter Joaquín Torres García.

MAP 7: 18 E. 79th St., 212/734-6300, www.acquavellagalleries.com; 10am-5pm Mon.-Sat.; free

PERFORMING ARTS

✪ Lincoln Center

Lincoln Center is the city's, and perhaps the country's, most comprehensive arts complex, hosting a range of renowned performing arts organizations. The New York City Ballet puts on both the classic works of Jerome Robbins and new works by principal dancer and choreographer Justin Peck, and the American Ballet Theatre performs here as well. The New York Philharmonic and Metropolitan Opera rank among the world's best. The latter stages extravagant operas for the city's old-school high society while also making $25 rush tickets available for each performance. Lincoln Center Theater, with its three stages, puts on lush musical revivals along with some of the best new American plays. The Film Society of Lincoln Center hosts year-round retrospectives of important world filmmakers as well as first-run indie features, organizes the city's most prestigious film festival, and publishes cinephile magazine *Film Comment*. The Chamber Music Society performs in the pristinely renovated Alice Tully Hall, oftentimes with young guest ensembles that represent the best of the next generation of classical music.

During the summer, the free festival Out of Doors takes over the center's Damrosch Park, with diverse events like family-friendly dance lessons from the Mark Morris Dance Group and performances by Sun Ra Arkestra, Dance Theatre of Harlem, and Carly Rae Jepsen. The Lincoln Center fountain, in the center of the main plaza, is quite scenic at night.

MAP 7: 10 Lincoln Center Plaza, 212/875-5456, www.lincolncenter.org; prices vary

French Institute Alliance Française

Besides offering French classes, this esteemed institution brings the best of French culture to New York audiences, from concerts and readings to wine tastings. The latter are as fun as they are informative, focusing on a particular region like the Loire or Rhone. Over the course of half a dozen pours, experts of the region and renowned critics like Eric Asimov of the *New York Times* explain what they love about the wines. Tickets are around $100. The institute is also home to the Crossing the Line Festival (Sept.-Oct.), which presents discipline-crossing works by French

Lincoln Center

and other international artists in one of the most important events of the year for the avant-garde community. The institute also offers a range of French language classes for students of all ages.

MAP 7: 22 E. 60th St., 212/355-6100, www.fiaf.org; 8:30am-8pm Mon.-Thurs., 8:30am-6pm Fri., 9am-5pm Sat.; prices vary

92nd Street Y

The 92nd Street Y was founded as a nonprofit epicenter of Jewish culture. It also hosts world-class talks with movie stars and world leaders alike. Since its founding in 1939 its Poetry Center has programmed readings from luminaries like Norman Mailer, W. H. Auden, Margaret Atwood, Susan Sontag, Tennessee Williams, and Sir Tom Stoppard. Recent events have included a reading by writer and commentator Roxane Gay and a concert by the inventive chamber music ensemble the Kronos Quartet. Devoted regulars are as old-school Upper East Side as they come.

MAP 7: 1395 Lexington Ave., 212/415-5500, www.92y.org; 5:30am-10:30pm Mon.-Thurs., 5:30am-9pm Fri., 7:30am-8pm Sat.-Sun.; $10-75

Park Avenue Armory

There are few more dramatically beautiful performing arts spaces in New York than the Park Avenue Armory. Originally the headquarters of the upper-class 7th New York Militia, an infantry regiment in the Union Army during the Civil War, this cavernously elegant Gothic Revival building now hosts art shows, exhibitions, concerts, and theatrical productions alike. The main space is 55,000 square feet (5,110 sq m) and has a barrel-vaulted roof that's 80 feet (24 m) high, making it one of the largest rooms in the city and an ideal home for avant-garde spectacles like Robert Wilson's *The Life and Death of Marina Abramović* and Eugene O'Neill's *The Hairy Ape* with Bobby Cannavale.

MAP 7: 643 Park Ave., 212/616-3930, www.armoryonpark.org; prices vary

Symphony Space

The 932-seat Symphony Space hosts creative programs across a number of fields, including talks with a diverse range of musicians and writers including Nick Cave and *Freakonomics* authors Steven Levitt and Steven J. Dubner. It also produces and hosts a popular reading series, *Selected Shorts*, that's broadcast across the country. Each show, organized around a theme, features readings by famous actors. Another series, Thalia Book Club, hosts authors of new books for lively discussions, while Secret Science Club engages astrophysicists and the like in heady conversation (followed by cocktails).

MAP 7: 2537 Broadway, 212/864-5400, www.symphonyspace.org; free-$85

CONCERT VENUES
Beacon Theatre

The Allman Brothers had a standing residency here for decades, and Jerry Seinfeld played a concert a month for a year. With a capacity just under 3,000, this historic theater, which first opened in 1929, feels intimate yet grand, with gold-colored statues flanking the stage. It's a great venue to see performers who usually grace much larger stages. For concerts, though, it's best to avoid sitting on the extreme sides of the orchestra because the sound can get muddy.

MAP 7: 2124 Broadway, 212/465-6500, www.msg.com/beacon-theatre; prices vary

Harlem and Morningside Heights   Map 8

GALLERIES
Long Gallery Harlem
It would be easy to miss this tiny gallery and its narrow storefront on a rapidly gentrifying stretch of 7th Avenue, but that would be a shame. Not only does it regularly put on shows as visually arresting as they are thought-provoking, the featured artists grapple with issues relevant to the surrounding community. One recent highlight, Delano Dunn's *No One Can Be This Tomorrow*, turned archival images of pivotal moments of struggle throughout black history into mixed-media collages awash in vibrant color. The gallery keeps regular weekend hours during exhibits, but otherwise is open by appointment; call ahead or check the website.
MAP 8: 2073 Adam Clayton Powell Jr. Blvd., 646/559-8368, www.long.gallery; noon-6pm Sat.-Sun. during exhibitions; free

Downtown Brooklyn, Dumbo, and Fort Greene   Map 9

MUSEUMS
Brooklyn Historical Society
Designed by architect George Post, whose many buildings include the New York Stock Exchange, the Brooklyn Historical Society's massive Queen Anne-style building with a terra-cotta facade stands out even in an area featuring some of the city's most stunningly beautiful streets, with big trees overhanging immaculately preserved brownstones. Its exhibits chart the borough's shifting history, as in a recent photography show on the borough's shuttered mom-and-pop shops. Talks are frequently held on the main floor and recent highlights include a reunion with original cast members of *Angels in America*—much of which is set in Brooklyn—to coincide with the Broadway revival of the play. A 2nd-floor library is also open to the public and dotted with dramatic wood columns and houses a treasure trove of materials, including an expansive collection pertaining to Brooklyn's history and culture. Author Jennifer Egan worked on her novel *Manhattan Beach* at a table in this room. The society also has an annex location at 55 Water Street next to Brooklyn Bridge Park.
MAP 9: 128 Pierrepont St., 718/222-4111, www.brooklynhistory.org; noon-5pm Wed.-Sun.; suggested admission $10 adults, $6 seniors and teachers, free for students and children under 12

New York Transit Museum
Housed in a decommissioned subway station in Downtown Brooklyn, the New York Transit Museum contains exhibits on fare collection and

vintage "no spitting" signs along with a bevy of old train cars. On Sundays from Thanksgiving to Christmas Eve, the museum breaks out a few of these pristinely kept relics and runs them on regular track lines throughout the city. Riding the whole route is a great way to spend a couple of hours, soak up the atmosphere, and savor the surprised expressions of riders as they board. The transit museum also has an annex in Grand Central Station.

MAP 9: Boerum Pl. and Schermerhorn St., 718/694-1600, http://www. nytransitmuseum.org; 10am-4pm Tues.-Fri., 11am-5pm Sat.-Sun.; $10 adults, $5 children 2-17 and seniors

GALLERIES
Janet Borden

Janet Borden is lauded for shining a light on contemporary artists with wild visions, as in a recent show by New York photographer David Brandon Geeting that featured vibrant and whimsical landscapes and still lifes. If you're lucky, you'll be greeted by Wilma, the gallery's unofficial poodle.

MAP 9: 91 Water St., 212/431-0166, http:// janetbordeninc.com; 11am-5pm Tues.-Sat.; free

Janet Borden

Klompching

Focusing on contemporary photography by up-and-coming artists as well as more established figures, Klompching's recent highlights include an emerging talent exhibition featuring dozens of unframed photographs pasted on the gallery's walls culled from submissions from over 160 countries. The gallery's FRESH Annual Summer Show is another opportunity for emerging photographers to win a space on the wall.

MAP 9: 89 Water St., 212/796-2070, www. klompching.com; 11am-6pm Wed.-Sat.; free

Smack Mellon

A small staircase at Smack Mellon's entrance leads to a lofty room supported by massive wooden columns. The gallery's space—formerly a warehouse—lends itself to large-scale works, such as a recent show featuring a botanically hued stained glass series by artist Summer Wheat. A second room usually features a few smaller canvases. Smack Mellon also hosts public talks with artists to further explore themes of their work.

MAP 9: 92 Plymouth St., 718/834-8761, http://smackmellon.org; noon-6pm Wed.-Sun.; free

THEATER
✪ St. Ann's Warehouse

For over three decades, this theatrical institution has brought cutting-edge and compelling productions to a hip, mostly local audience. When he was alive, Lou Reed could often be found in the front row. Shows have included productions by legendary downtown companies like the Wooster Group and Mabou Mines, including the latter's Ibsen reimagining, *Dollhouse*, which cast Nora as a towering woman amid a cast of male dwarfs. Other

highlights have included Taylor Mac's epic 24-hour song cycle *A 24-Decade History of Popular Music* and Duncan MacMillan's searing portrait of addiction, *People, Places & Things*. The institution also frequently produces shows by acclaimed playwright Enda Walsh and monologist Daniel Kitson. In 2015, St. Ann's moved into this cavernous theater, which can be configured in a variety of ways. Ticket prices are generally a bit lower than comparable theaters, and the TodayTix app offer same-day rush tickets for $20.
MAP 9: 45 Water St., 718/254-8779, http://stannswarehouse.org; box office 1pm-6:30pm Tues.-Sat.; from $35

Theatre for a New Audience

For years, Theatre for a New Audience operated out of rented spaces, staging stirring adaptations of Shakespeare and other classic works by actors and directors like Mark Rylance and Julie Taymor. The latter recently staged a visually stunning production of *A Midsummer Night's Dream* in the theater's equally captivating new home, located steps from BAM. Giant floor-to-ceiling windows give the lobby and café a dramatic feel that continues as theatergoers ascend to the three-tiered 299-seat theater designed to replicate an Elizabethan courtyard and inspired by London's National Theatre.
MAP 9: 262 Ashland Pl., 866/811-4111, www.tfana.org; box office 1pm-6pm Tues.-Sat.; $20-125

PERFORMING ARTS

✪ Brooklyn Academy of Music (BAM)

You can travel the world to find the best dance, theater, opera, and live music—or you can just go to BAM, America's oldest performing arts center, established in 1861. Its Next Wave Festival each fall invites companies

St. Ann's Warehouse

like Ivo Van Hove's Toneelgroep Amsterdam and the Schaubühne theater in Berlin to present radically deconstructed (and then furiously reconstructed) takes on classic and modern plays. Charlie Chaplin's grandson James Thiérrée is another regular and a physical wunderkind in his own right. His existential circuses are always season highlights, as are rare concerts by musicians like John Cale and Neutral Milk Hotel's Jeff Mangum. Some, like the Magnetic Field's Stephin Merritt and Sufjan Stevens, have staged elaborate shows that blur the boundaries between rock concert and play. Legendary dance companies, including Pina Bauch's and Trisha Brown's, have a big presence here as well. BAM also has three movie theaters.

MAP 9: 30 Lafayette Ave., 718/636-4100, www.bam.org; box office noon-6pm Mon.-Sat. (hours vary during summer); $20-150

CINEMA
Alamo Drafthouse

This outpost of the popular Austin-based movie theater chain is given a distinctly Brooklyn vibe with special shows like Fort Greene resident and former *Daily Show* correspondent Wyatt Cenac's "Shouting at the Screen," offering live commentary over classic blaxploitation films. In addition to an extensive menu of food and drinks that can be ordered in-seat, there's a dimly lit bar, House of Wax, which displays wax figures that might fit in comfortably with the Coney Island freakshow. Screenings tend to sell out, so buy tickets in advance, particularly for special events. If you can, opt for front-row seats—they recline.

MAP 9: 445 Albee Sq. W., 4th fl., 718/513-2547, http://drafthouse.com/nyc; box office opens 45 min. before first screening; from $12

Williamsburg, Greenpoint, and Bushwick   Map 10

MUSEUMS
The City Reliquary

A colorful awning beckons visitors into this bodega-sized museum. Past a turnstile, two cluttered rooms display a treasure trove of relics from the city's past. The permanent collection far exceeds the space, so items are rotated out often. But a sample exhibit might include old seltzer bottles, a collection of Jackie Robinson memorabilia, or mementos from the World's Fair. A back room houses temporary exhibits like *Empire Skate,* which explores the origins of roller disco.

MAP 10: 370 Metropolitan Ave., 718/782-4842, www.cityreliquary.org; noon-6pm Thurs.-Sun.; $7 adults, $5 students, teachers, and seniors, free for children 12 and under

Museum of Food and Drink

Located right off McCarren Park in perhaps the most developed stretch of Williamsburg, the Museum of Food and Drink aims to put beloved cuisines in the context of history. A recent exhibit, *Chow,* for example, traced 170 years of Chinese immigration and struggles for acceptance, with menus beginning from 1910 documenting how dishes were assimilated into American culture. The museum itself is small and in its incubation stage, but the curators strive for a full sensory experience. Tickets include fun food extras (e.g., unlimited fortune cookies at *Chow*) and a small tasting, with an option to upgrade to a full meal.

MAP 10: 62 Bayard St., 718/387-2845, www.mofad.org; noon-6pm Fri.-Sun.; $14-25

GALLERIES
The Bushwick Collective

The Bushwick Collective spans many blocks around the area near the Jefferson Street L train stop and features elaborate street art and graffiti. It began in 2011, born out of the desire of Bushwick native Joe Ficalora to shine the glow of creativity on a bleak and once crime-ridden landscape. His mother died that year and two decades earlier his father was murdered on the street. The project now features the work of legendary street artists Blek Le Rat, Case Ma'Claim, and Pixel Pancho. Wandering around these blocks is a great way to get a sense of the neighborhood's artistic pulse. The most concentrated block is on Troutman Street between Wyckoff and St. Nicholas Avenues. For a guided exploration, you can join a pay-what-you-wish tour (http://freetoursbyfoot. com/bushwick-graffiti-bushwick-collective) of this veritable open-air gallery. Tours are 1-2 times daily Friday-Monday.

Map 10: www.thebushwickcollective.com; 24 hours daily; free

56 Bogart Street

56 Bogart Street is an artists' loft building that contains about a dozen galleries open to the public. The art is often hit or miss, but the experience of walking on creaky paint-splattered floors, sometimes past artists at work, is a treat from the typical gallery experience. Gallery hours vary, but most are open Saturdays and Sundays 1pm-6pm.

MAP 10: 56 Bogart St., 718/599-0800, ext. 12, www.56bogartstreet.com; hours vary by gallery; free

THEATER
Bushwick Starr

Up a flight of rickety stairs and around a meandering corner is some of the most daring theater in New York. Productions like *Miles for Mary* and *Porto* captured the absurdity of formalities in public schools and dating in rapidly gentrifying Brooklyn, respectively, and both transferred to successful Off-Broadway runs. But it's always cooler to see a show at its source. The theater has a bar just past the makeshift box office where you can have a drink before nabbing seats, which are general admission. While the programming can be hit or miss, watching a show here feels thrilling, like the early days of the Soho Rep: experimental, fearless, and spanning a wide range of genres and forms.

MAP 10: 207 Starr St., 917/623-9669, www. thebushwickstarr.org; $25

CONCERT VENUES
Brooklyn Steel

Music clubs abound in Williamsburg, but larger concert venues are almost nonexistent. Brooklyn Steel, opened in 2017 and named after its former function as a steel manufacturing plant, is a cavernous addition to the neighborhood. With a capacity of 1,800, it draws big-name acts like LCD Soundsystem, the Mountain Goats, and the Arctic Monkeys and

Nitehawk Cinema

frequently sells out shows. The venue is a giant open space with general admission standing room, so crowds can become unwieldy. Hang by the sound booth for a chiller experience.

MAP 10: 319 Frost St., 888/929-7849, www.bowerypresents.com; door time varies by show; $15-75

National Sawdust

Gleaming from a previously industrial corner on Wythe Avenue, down the block from the Music Hall of Williamsburg, National Sawdust is a rare place: a sleek venue for experimental classical works with a buttoned-down but hip vibe. Its artistic advisory board includes a diverse array of musical talent from the experimental classical world (Laurie Anderson, Terry Riley, Philip Glass) and indie rock sphere (Bryce Dessner, James Murphy, Suzanne Vega). Stripped-down operas, rare solo recitals, and film screenings with live scores are just some of the types of events you can experience here via awesome Devialet Phantom speakers.

MAP 10: 80 N. 6th St., 646/779-8455, www.nationalsawdust.org; 10am-1am Mon.-Fri., noon-11pm Sat.-Sun.; free-$40

CINEMA
✪ Nitehawk Cinema

Q and A sessions with filmmakers are just the tip of the programming iceberg at this intimate movie triplex, which serves food and drink in its theaters. A very popular series of weekend morning cartoons from the 1940s to the 2000s is a brunch alternative, accompanied by alcoholic beverages like a Cinnamon Toast Crunch-infused rum and unlimited cereal. Midnight screenings of cult classics like David Lynch's *Blue Velvet* are also mainstays as are Film Feasts, five-course dinners paired with films like *Boogie Nights* and *Indiana Jones and the Temple of Doom*. The largest theater here seats 92 people and the smallest a third of that, making advance ticket purchase wise.

A ground-level bar with postshow specials encourages lingering, and there's also an extensive in-theater menu with savory bites like crispy tater tots with queso. Doors open 30 minutes prior to showtime and people line up well before for popular screenings; seating is first come, first served. Specialty drinks and food are created for most first-run films and can be ordered from your seat; for example at Wes Anderson's *Isle of Dogs*, you could pair the screening with a hibachi chili hot dog with wasabi mayo. **MAP 10:** 136 Metropolitan Ave., 718/782-8370, http://nitehawkcinema.com; $12 adults, $9 children and seniors, prices vary for special events

Festivals and Events

WINTER

Christmas in Rockefeller Center

Rockefeller Center hosts a giant Christmas tree each year, and its 50,000 string lights are lit for the first time each November with a grand ceremony. It's the official beginning of New York's holiday season, televised for all the country to see. The center's seasonal ice-skating rink, situated just below, is a popular place to take in the view. The tree remains lit and on display through early January. **Midtown:** Rockefeller Center, 45 Rockefeller Plaza, 212/332-6868, www.rockefellercenter.com; late Nov.-early Jan.; free

Christmas in Rockefeller Center

New Year's Eve in Times Square

An estimated million people converge on Times Square each New Year's Eve. Pop stars perform live in the lead-up to midnight, when the shiny Waterford crystal ball drops to mark the start of the New Year. Revelers wait upward of 12 hours to score a good viewing spot, and no alcohol is allowed, so it's as much an endurance test as a celebration.

Times Square: www.timessquarenyc.org; Dec. 31-Jan. 1; free

Winter Jazz Fest

For a jam-packed weekend in January, Winter Jazz Fest offers fans the chance to gorge on performances by veteran players like Dave Holland along with some of the most exciting musicians currently transforming the genre, like powerhouse saxophonist Donny McCaslin. In addition to the two-day marathon, there are special ticketed concerts.

The Village and East Village: various venues, http://www.winterjazzfest.com; early Jan.; marathon pass $50-95

Under the Radar Festival

For roughly two weeks in January, The Public Theater presents some of the newest and most exciting theater from around the world in this lauded festival. It's a great way to see top-notch plays and one-person shows at a fraction of the price The Public usually charges.

Various locations: various venues and The Public Theater, 425 Lafayette Ave., 212/539-8500, www.publictheater.org/Under-the-Radar; early-mid Jan.; most shows $25

Lunar New Year Parade

Every year Chinatown throws its festive, colorful Lunar New Year Parade, with a range of food offerings and performances. The parade begins at Mott and Canal Streets and ends on Eldridge and Forsyth Streets next to Sara D. Roosevelt Park.

Lower East Side: Chinatown, http://betterchinatown.com; 1pm late Feb.; free

New York City Beer Week

The NYC Brewers Guild, made up of about three dozen local brewers, organizes this yearly celebration to highlight their craft. This includes 10 days full of beer dinners, special tours, and one-off concoctions. In addition to ticketed events, many bars serve these specialty brews during the festivities.

Various locations: www.nycbrewed.com, late Feb.-early Mar.; prices vary

The Armory Show

The Armory Show takes over Piers 92 and 94 in Hell's Kitchen every March, and it's a great way to get a large overview of the New York as well as international art scene. Since its founding in 1994, hundreds of galleries from dozens of countries have exhibited compelling shows, including a survey of video artist Nam Jun Paik featuring previously unseen drawings and a talk with provocative photographer JR.

Midtown: Piers 92 and 94, 212/645-6440, www.thearmoryshow.com; early Mar.; $47-80

St. Patrick's Day Parade

New York's St. Patrick's Day Parade, which stretches from 44th to 79th Streets on 5th Avenue, features bagpipes and marching bands celebrating the luck of the Irish. Spectators are plentiful and the area surrounding the parade route is a giant party, with green beer flowing from every sports bar. Free tickets can be requested by mail for grandstand seating.

Midtown and Upper East Side: 718/231-4400, www.nycstpatricksparade.org/parade; 11am-5pm mid-Mar.; free

SPRING
PEN World Voices Festival

The PEN World Voices Festival organizes dozens of talks around downtown Manhattan and Brooklyn with best-selling writers and a focus on human rights. Highlights have included readings by Salman Rushdie and a panel on resistance in Ukraine after Russia's annexation of Crimea. The events support the organization's advocacy on behalf of imprisoned writers.

Various locations: 212/334-1660, https://pen.org/world-voices-festival; mid-Apr.; prices vary

Tribeca Film Festival

The Tribeca Film Festival premieres nearly 100 new indie films each April with talkbacks, longer conversational events, and virtual reality projects that push the boundaries of audience engagement. The fest was cocreated by Robert De Niro and Jane Rosenthal to draw business to the area after 9/11, and continues to bring crowds for its smart programming.

Tribeca and Chelsea: various venues, 212/941-2400, www.tribecafilm.com/festival; mid-late Apr.; prices vary

Rooftop Films

Starting in late spring and continuing through summer, Rooftop Films shows indie film premieres of movies like *The Miseducation of Cameron Post*, along with programs of short films, on rooftops around the city, as well as at sites like Brooklyn's Green-Wood Cemetery, with preshow concerts and postshow open-bar receptions. Times and locations vary.

Various locations: www.rooftopfilms.com; showtimes vary May-Sept.; free-$15

Governors Ball Music Festival

This three-day music festival in June takes place in the expansive fields of Randall's Island. People like Jack White and Eminem headline four stages of generally well-curated acts. It's no Coachella, but it's the closest thing New York has to it.

Greater New York City: Randall's Island Park, 20 Randall's Island, www.governorsballmusicfestival.com; early June; $115-2,190

Puerto Rican Day Parade

A series of community arts and culture events culminate in the Puerto Rican Day Parade—New York City's largest parade, drawing nearly three million people each year. It celebrates Puerto Rican heritage, including those who've made an indelible mark on greater American culture, such as *Hamilton* composer Lin-Manuel Miranda and New York Yankee great Jorge Posada. The parade begins on 42nd Street and 5th Avenue and stretches north to 79th Street.

Midtown and Upper East Side: 917/685-1607, www.nprdpinc.org; second Sun. in June; free

Puerto Rican Day Parade

SUMMER

Jazz Age Lawn Party

You don't need a time machine to partake in this Prohibition-era-inspired daytime jazz party—just your finest flapper threads and a desire to dance like it's 1929. A brassy orchestra led by local favorite Michael Arenella draws thousands, so be sure to buy tickets in advance.

Lower Manhattan: Colonel's Row on Governor's Island, http://jazzagelawnparty. com; one weekend in June and one weekend in Aug.; $35-300

Shakespeare in the Park

The Public Theater puts on two productions each summer, often starring high-profile actors, in Central Park's open-air Delacorte Theater. Past highlights include Meryl Streep in Bertolt Brecht's *Mother Courage and Her Children* and Amy Adams in Stephen Sondheim's *Into the Woods*. Tickets for the free shows go quickly, so you'll need to be dedicated.

Upper West Side and Upper East Side: Central Park, Delacorte Theater, www.publictheater.org; June-Sept. 8pm; free

Coney Island Mermaid Parade

Watch alongside thousands of spectators or join in and express your inner mermaid at this DIY parade where judgement is shed and flippers are donned to celebrate the magical sea creature in all of us. A community celebration, the parade features handmade costumes, floats, and antique cars, and toasts the arts, summer solstice, and seaside rituals. It heads east from West 21st Street and Surf Avenue, turns south on West 10th Street, and heads back west on the boardwalk, ending at Steeplechase Plaza.

Greater New York City: Coney Island, www.coneyisland.com; 1pm mid-June; $15-30 registration, free for spectators

NYC Pride March

Summer gets into gear with the NYC Pride March, an inclusive celebration of all queer communities. Allies are welcome. It starts at 16th Street and 7th Avenue and heads south before circling back up to 29th Street and 5th Avenue. In addition to the march, there's a monthlong series of events, from a family movie night to rooftop parties and a conference on human rights.

The Village and Chelsea: http://2019-worldpride-stonewall50.nycpride.org; last Sun. in June; free

BRIC Celebrate Brooklyn! Festival

For decades, Celebrate Brooklyn has programmed a free lineup of artists each summer that would normally sell out large venues with pricey tickets. Performances take place in Prospect Park's open-air bandshell. Recent highlights have included shows by rapper Common, folk singer Aimee Mann, and alt-pop group the Breeders. Arrive when doors open for the best seats.

Greater New York City: Prospect Park Bandshell, Brooklyn, 718/683-5600, www. bricartsmedia.org; June-Aug.; free

Bryant Park Movie Nights

Nestled on the lush lawn of Bryant Park amid the glow of Midtown skyscrapers, this film festival is insanely popular, often showing contemporary classics like *When Harry Met Sally . . .* and *The Breakfast Club*. To get a spot, it's essential to arrive by 5pm when the lawn opens. Movies don't start until sundown but there are food vendors to keep you fed.

Midtown: Bryant Park, http://bryantpark.org/programs sunset; Mon. June-Aug.; free

SummerStage

Central Park's free outdoor concert series programs live acts from around the world, from the likes of seminal local underground '70s punk band Television to beloved Beninese Grammy Award-winning singer Angélique Kidjo. Shows are occasionally held at various other parks around the city.

Upper East Side: Rumsey Playfield, Central Park, 212/360-2777, http://cityparksfoundation.org/summerstage; June-Sept.; free

Forest Hills Stadium Summer Concerts

Built on farmland in 1923, this stadium was the original home of the U.S. Open. During the 1960s, the Beatles, Rolling Stones, Jimi Hendrix, and Frank Sinatra all played shows in this expansive open-air venue. The historic space lay dormant for some years but was brought back to life and now features a stellar lineup of legends past and present each summer, from Bob Dylan and Paul Simon to the National and Arctic Monkeys. The venue seats 14,000 on bleacher seats and on the floor, which alternates between standing room and rows of folding chairs. For an additional $65 you can get bottomless wine at the City Winery's outpost along with tasty caprese sandwiches to keep you going all night. The E train and Long Island Railroad stop nearby, making the trip from Midtown easy.

Greater New York City: 1 Tennis Pl., Forest Hills, Queens, http://foresthillsstadium.com; June-Sept.; prices vary

Macy's 4th of July Fireworks Show

The largest July 4th show in the country takes place in New York, lighting up the city's famous skyline.

Various locations: www.macys.com/social/fireworks; July 4; free

Nathan's Famous International Hot Dog Eating Contest

What's more festive than hot dogs on the Fourth of July? All the hot dogs. Each year the world's top competitive eaters vie to take home the Nathan's Mustard Belt, while tens of thousands of spectators look on. Participants, vetted through an advance prequalifying round, down as many dogs and buns as they can in 10 minutes. The current record is nearly 75.

Greater New York City: Coney Island, corner of Surf and Stillwell Aves., Brooklyn, 718/333-2202, http://nathansfamous.com; 10am-2pm July 4; free

Broadway in Bryant Park

On select Thursdays in the summer, the Broadway in Bryant Park series brings casts from Broadway shows to perform their biggest hits in hour-long concerts. The midday performances provide a nice lunch break for the area's many office workers as well as lucky tourists.

Midtown: Bryant Park; 12:30pm select Thurs. July-Aug.; free

Movies with a View

Since 2000, over half a million people have flocked to outdoor screenings in Brooklyn Bridge Park—both for the dramatic bridge and Manhattan skyline views from the waterfront as well as the films, curated in part by BAM. From classics like *Casablanca* to the Madonna-starring *Desperately*

FREE FUN IN THE SUMMERTIME

Bryant Park Movie Nights

New York doesn't let the often-stifling heat and humidity of its summers stop it from cultural engagement—the city embraces it, programming amazing outdoor arts and entertainment during this season, gloriously free of charge. Rules of thumb: Go early because it can get crowded, and bring a picnic and a book, friends, or family to enjoy the wait until showtime.

FREE LIVE MUSIC

- **BRIC Celebrate Brooklyn! Festival** at Prospect Park programs artists who would usually sell out paid shows.

- **SummerStage** brings local and international talent to an outdoor stage in Central Park.

FREE MOVIES

- **Bryant Park Movie Nights,** a wildly popular series, shows contemporary classics against the Midtown skyline.

- **Movies With a View** screens classics and crowd-pleasers on the Brooklyn waterfront with the impressive backdrop of the Manhattan skyline and Brooklyn Bridge.

- **SummerScreen** shows cult favorites at Williamsburg's McCarren Park.

FREE THEATER

- **Shakespeare in the Park,** by The Public Theater, brings two productions to Central Park's Delacorte Theater each summer, often starring celebrities.

- **Broadway in Bryant Park** offers lunchtime accompaniment in Midtown, with Broadway casts performing their biggest hits in an hour-long concert.

Seeking Susan, offerings tend to be crowd-pleasers.

Downtown Brooklyn, Dumbo, and Fort Greene: Harbor View Lawn, Brooklyn Bridge Park, www. brooklynbridgepark.org; 8pm Thurs. July-Aug.; free

SummerScreen

Crowds gather each summer for six screenings of modern cult favorites like *Office Space* and *Donnie Darko* on a concrete expanse in the southwest corner of Williamsburg's McCarren Park. Programmed by Northside Media, this series draws large local crowds. Chairs and dogs are both welcome, and the space begins filling up when the "doors" open at 6pm. Preshow concerts start at 7pm and past acts have included Sean Lennon and indie singer-songwriter Ducktails.

Williamsburg: McCarren Park, www. summerscreen.org; 8pm Wed. July-Aug.; free

Socrates Sculpture Park Outdoor Cinema

Curated mostly by the Film Forum, with a few organized by Rooftop Films, this outdoor series at the Socrates Sculpture Park is geared toward foreign cinema aficionados, with offerings like recent Turkish feline indie *Kedi* and beloved French musical *The Young Girls of Rochefort*. Preshow music or dance performances (starting at 7pm) from the film's country of origin set the worldly mood, as do the food offerings. Arrive early to snag a spot close to the screen, which is set up against the backdrop of the East River.

Greater New York City: Socrates Sculpture Park, 32-01 Vernon Blvd., Long Island City, Queens, http://socratessculpturepark.org/programs/films; sunset Wed. July-Aug.; free

U.S. Open

The summer ends with the U.S. Open, one of tennis's biggest events. Two weeks of nail-biting matches are played in Arthur Ashe and Louis Armstrong Stadiums. While matches can be expensive, qualifying rounds are free to watch and offer opportunities to see the next generation of rising stars up close while traipsing through the impeccably manicured grounds.

Greater New York City: USTA Billie Jean King National Tennis Center, Flushing Meadows-Corona Park, Queens, 718/760-6363, www.usopen.org; late-Aug.-early-Sept.; prices vary

Feast of San Gennaro

The 11-day Feast of San Gennaro is when Little Italy's place as the first Italian American community comes into focus through colorful religious-tinged parades, live music, and a cannoli-eating contest.

Soho: Mulberry St. between Canal St. and Houston St. and Grand St. and Hester St. between Mott St. and Baxter St., Little Italy, 212/768-9320, www.sangennaro.org; mid-Sept.; free

FALL
New York Film Festival

Over the course of a couple of weeks, the prestigious Film Society of Lincoln Center's New York Film Festival showcases some of the most exciting recent works of film art from around the world, often with Q&A sessions following the screenings. The highest-profile screenings take place inside the pristinely renovated Alice Tully Hall.

Upper West Side: Lincoln Center, 212/875-5610, www.filmlinc.org; late-Sept.-mid-Oct.; prices vary

New Yorker Festival

Organized by the *New Yorker* magazine, this festival hosts talks, specialty tours, and other events with high-profile artists and culture makers. Events almost always sell out, and with good reason, with inventive programming including experiences like being led in a meditation by performance artist Marina Abramović and participating in a protest sing-along with former Rage Against the Machine guitarist Tom Morello.

Various locations: http://festival. newyorker.com; early Oct.; prices vary

New York City Wine & Food Festival

This festival is a highlight for foodies. Events are on the extravagant side, including dinners with celebrity chefs and rooftop parties like Rachael Ray's Burger Bash. "Cheap eats" include events under $100. Net proceeds go to charities to end childhood hunger.

Various locations: 800/764-8773, http:// nycwff.org; mid-Oct.; prices vary

FringeNYC

For almost every summer since 1997, FringeNYC, formerly the New York International Fringe Festival, has taken over dozens of theaters to put on a couple hundred shows that vary in subject as much as they do in quality. With a chaotic mix of amateur and professional shows, the fest forces theatergoers to play an artistic game of Russian roulette. Both thrilling and terrifying, it's a magnified version of the feeling you get whenever the lights go down in a theater and you wonder: Where is this going to take me?

Various locations: http://fringenyc.org; Oct.; $22 adults, $16 seniors

White Light Festival

Of all of Lincoln Center's festivals, the White Light Festival is the most enigmatic. Its name comes from Arvo Pärt's description of his music as "white light," containing all the colors but needing the listener to act as the prism that makes them appear. An example of the festival's programming sensibility: a screening of Carl Theodor Dreyer's meditative masterpiece *The Passion of Joan of Arc*, set to an original score by Portishead's Adrian Utley.

Upper West Side: Lincoln Center, 212/875-5456, www.lincolncenter.org/ white-light-festival; mid-Oct.-mid-Nov.; prices vary

Village Halloween Parade

On Halloween, 50,000 participants don their most elaborate or outrageous costumes and march down 6th Avenue from Canal Street to 16th Street. Massive crowds come to watch, and the enthusiasm is palpable. The event is televised on local news station NY1.

Tribeca, The Village, and Chelsea: http://halloween-nyc.com; Oct. 31; free

New York City Marathon

With a route tracing through all five boroughs, the New York City Marathon is a great opportunity for runners to see this city from a different perspective. The city's largest race also provides ample opportunity for spectators and supporters to glimpse this feat of endurance. It starts on Staten Island and ends in Central Park.

Various locations: 855/569-6977, www. tcsnycmarathon.org; first Sun. in Nov.; $255-358 registration, free for spectators

Macy's Thanksgiving Day Parade

The Macy's Thanksgiving Day Parade kicks off the end-of-year holidays. It dates back to 1924 and features massive and increasingly elaborate helium-filled balloons and culminates with an appearance from Santa Claus. The parade starts at Central Park West and 77th Street and ends at 6th Avenue and 34th Street. For a different view, head over to the American Museum of Natural History the night before when the giant characters are inflated, and the public is free to watch.

Midtown and Upper West Side: www.macys.com/social/parade; late Nov.; free

RECREATION

New York is perhaps the most urban of all cities, defined by its skyscrapers and sidewalks. And walking to get from place to place is such a way of life here that most people don't make any distinction between city living and outdoor activity.

Hudson River Greenway

This is the most densely populated city in the country, but 8 out of 10 New Yorkers live within a 10-minute walk of a large park, and share about 3 acres (1 ha) per 1,000 people. So there are plenty of places to stretch out, unwind, and occasionally even break a sweat here. Central Park is the most obvious green refuge, offering walking, running, biking, and boating opportunities. Besides this most high-profile of green spaces, Manhattan and Brooklyn have in recent years seen spectacular renovations that have transformed former wastelands into recreation spaces, such as the piers of Hudson River Park and docks of Brooklyn Bridge Park. The artful landscaping of each takes advantage of the boroughs' prime waterfront.

More and more in recent years, biking is gaining traction as a commuting option or recreational delight, even in this car-trafficked metropolis.

And come winter, there's nothing more idyllic or classic than taking to one of the city's ice-skating rinks for a spell.

New York also offers a wealth of spectator sports. With professional baseball, basketball, football, and hockey teams, there is always a game on, no matter the season.

HIGHLIGHTS

⭐ **BEST FREE SIGHTSEEING:** Glimpse the Statue of Liberty, Ellis Island, and the Manhattan skyline from aboard the free **Staten Island Ferry,** and maybe enjoy a beer while you're at it to boot (page 265).

⭐ **BEST BIKEWAY:** Stretching the entire western edge of Manhattan, the **Hudson River Greenway** offers a scenic stretch from downtown to uptown (page 265).

⭐ **BEST PARK FOR PEOPLE-WATCHING:** Master chess players, street musicians, and NYU students all congregate at **Washington Square Park** (page 267).

⭐ **BEST MANHATTAN SKYLINE VIEWS:** With its elevated perspective above the waterfront, the **Brooklyn Heights Promenade** offers sweeping panoramas of the city's skyscrapers (page 275).

⭐ **BEST HIKING WITHIN CITY LIMITS:** Walk the trails in **Inwood Hill Park** to experience Manhattan's only remaining forest. It's as close as you can get to seeing what New York looked like half a millennium ago (page 281).

Staten Island Ferry

Lower Manhattan

Map 1

PARKS

The Battery

Formerly named Battery Park, The Battery encompasses 25 acres (10 ha) at the southern tip of Manhattan, a refuge in the middle of the densely concentrated Financial District. In addition to providing ample picnicking areas under large shade trees and hosting free summertime concerts by bands like the New Pornographers, it has a number of historical attractions. Inside the park is Castle Clinton National Monument (www.nps.gov/cacl, 7:45am-5pm, free), built as a fort to defend against British invasion in 1812; it also served as the country's first immigration center prior to Ellis Island. Free 20-minute tours are given by park rangers daily at 10am, 12pm, 2pm, and 4pm. Ellis Island and Statue of Liberty ferries also depart from the park; you can buy tickets at Castle Clinton. A range of other monuments are also in the park, including the New York Korean War Veterans Memorial and Battery Cannon, the latter of which dates back to the Revolutionary War. Make sure to visit the nautically themed Seaglass Carousel (10am-10pm daily Apr.-Dec., hours vary Jan.-Mar., $5) if you have children in tow; in place of standard horses there are seashells that are lit up after sundown.

MAP 1: State St. and Battery Pl., 212/344-3491, www.thebattery.org; 24 hours daily; free

Bowling Green

A lot of history has gone down at New York City's oldest park, unassumingly tiny as it is—its triangular shape barely covers a city block. Today consisting mainly of an elegant fountain and several benches, it was originally council ground for Native American tribes as well as where soldiers and sailors knocked down a statue of King George III during the Revolutionary War. Arturo Di Moca's *Charging Bull* statue is also here, installed in an act of guerilla art to represent American resilience after the stock market crash of 1987—though in popular conception it has since become a symbol of Wall Street aggression and greed. It's said to be good luck to rub the bull's horn. The now equally iconic *Fearless Girl* statue served as a corrective to male aggression when installed in 2017 until she was moved to the New York Stock Exchange in 2018. *Charging Bull* might join her soon if Mayor Bill de Blasio gets his way.

MAP 1: Broadway and Whitehall St., 212/408-0100, www.nycgovparks.org; 9am-5pm daily; free

The Battery

Zuccotti Park

Zuccotti Park is where the 2011 Occupy Wall Street protests against economic inequality were birthed. Today this plaza has reverted back to its function as a place for Financial District workers to bask in open air during lunch breaks.

MAP 1: between Trinity Pl., Broadway, Liberty St., and Cedar St.; 24 hours daily; free

BOATING

✪ Staten Island Ferry

This free commuter ferry has been transporting people to and from the city's most remote borough since before any bridges were built. It remains the only way to access Staten Island without a car and features amenities like free Wi-Fi (both on the vessel and in Manhattan's Whitehall Terminal and Staten Island's St. George Terminal) and beer for sale on board. The trip takes about 25 minutes and passes the Statue of Liberty and Ellis Island, so it's a lovely sightseeing option for those who just want a close glimpse of the landmarks, as well as nice views of the Manhattan skyline. Ferries depart every 15-30 minutes. Avoid peak commuting hours (5pm-6:45pm leaving from Whitehall, 7am-8:45am leaving from St. George) for a pleasant ride, and note that you'll need to disembark when you reach Staten Island and then line up to reboard if you're not planning to stay here.

MAP 1: Whitehall Terminal, 4 Whitehall St., Manhattan, www.siferry.com; 24 hours daily; free

Manhattan By Sail

For a more intimate experience on the water, it's hard to beat a ride on one of this small company's two sailboats: a schooner built in 1929 that holds 48 passengers and a tall ship that holds around 130. Options range from a standard day cruise that pulls up near the Statue of Liberty to excursions including craft beer- or wine-tasting, brunch, and even burlesque show cruises. Most weekdays there's a 12:30pm departure that sails up close past the Statue of Liberty, but check the website for schedules. Rides last 1-2 hours and there are typically 9-10 sailings each day with different themes. Private charters are also available.

MAP 1: The Battery, Slip 2 and North Cove Marina at Brookfield Pl., 212/619-6900, www.manhattanbysail.com; $25-95

BIKING

✪ Hudson River Greenway

Biking around the city can be quite treacherous (note the white-painted two-wheelers known as "ghost bikes" mounted at intersections where cyclists have been killed), but this 11-mile (17.7-km) path along Manhattan's west side is completely car-free. Stretching the entire length of the island from Battery Park to the Cloisters, this route is popular with cyclists as well as runners and walkers. Chelsea Piers and the General Grant National Memorial are accessible from this path, as is a lighthouse that sits underneath the George Washington Bridge. There are several Citi Bike kiosks located along the way where you can grab a bike, including one at Little West Street and 1st Place right at the start of the greenway next to Battery Park. The stretch from Lower Manhattan north through Greenwich Village is quite nice.

MAP 1: southern trailhead Battery Pl.; 24 hours daily; free

BIKE SHARING

Citi Bike (www.citibikenyc.com) is New York's popular bike share program, with 12,000 bicycles available at 750 stations throughout Manhattan and Brooklyn as well as Queens. Bikes rides or passes can be purchased through its app. Single rides are $3 for up to 30 minutes, or you can buy a day pass for $12, which is good for unlimited 30-minute rides in a 24-hour period. For rides over 30 minutes, an additional $4 charge is assessed per 15 minutes. On the app and website you can also find real-time info on how many bikes and dock spaces are available at each station. Helmets aren't included or available with rentals.

Soho and Tribeca   Map 2

PARKS
Hudson River Park

Comprising 550 acres (223 ha) along Manhattan's west side, between Battery Place in Lower Manhattan and 59th Street in Midtown, Hudson River Park is one of the most significant green additions to the city. It has transformed formerly abandoned piers along this stretch into scenic destinations for locals and tourists alike. Hudson River Park encompasses the southern part of the Hudson River Greenway that begins at Battery Place, and the path serves as a link people can walk or bike between the park's piers. The stretch from Tribeca's **Pier 25**—the southernmost and longest pier in the park, which boasts seasonal oyster bar Grand Banks, as well as a mini golf course—to **Chelsea Piers** is particularly scenic and popular among families, dog walkers, and couples out for a romantic stroll. **Christopher Street Pier (Pier 45)** in Greenwich Village features great views of One World Trade Center. **Pier 84** in Midtown has a generous lawn for picnics as well as kayak rentals ($7 for 30 min.). Free kayak rentals are available at **Pier 26** and **Pier 96** in the warmer months.

MAP 2: Battery Pl. to W. 59th St., 347/756-3813, https://hudsonriverpark.org; 6am-1am daily; free

East Village and Lower East Side   Map 3

PARKS
Tompkins Square Park

Once a den for heroin addicts, this park is now a popular slice of greenery in the East Village. Its central location makes it a cool spot to enjoy food from nearby hole-in-the-wall eateries like Superiority Burger and Crif Dogs, and the park also hosts arts events like the drag festival Wigstock, the Howl! Festival honoring beat poet Allen Ginsberg, and the Charlie Parker Jazz Festival, which puts on free concerts at the end of August. Tompkins

Square Park is also the ending point for Unsilent Night, Phil Kline's annual modern take on winter holiday caroling.

MAP 3: between Ave. A and Ave. B, E. 7th St. and E. 10th St., 718/813-8971, www.nycgovparks.org/parks/tompkins-square-park; 6am-midnight daily; free

The Village and the Meatpacking District

Map 4

PARKS

✪ Washington Square Park

This urban park has served many purposes since the dedication of Stanford White's famous arch, modeled on the Arc de Triomphe, in 1895. It's been a cemetery, parade ground, gathering spot for artists and performers, and playground for kids and dogs alike. While the park is now surrounded by New York University buildings, it never feels like you're in an insular quad. As the neighborhood has become increasingly upscale, this remains a place where students, finance workers, artists, and everyone in between can come together on a nice day. One constant in recent decades has been the master chess hustlers who play intense matches around the clock in the park's southwest corner; challenge them at your own peril. A particularly good place for people-watching is near the central fountain.

Washington Square Park

MAP 4: between MacDougal St. and University Pl., W. 4th St. and Waverly Pl., http://washingtonsquareparkconservancy.org; 24 hours daily; free

Christopher Street Pier (Pier 45)

This pier is one of the longest in the city at 850 feet (269 m), stretching out into the Hudson River and away from the bustle of the West Side Highway. Part of Hudson River Park, its stretches of green lawn provide space for all comers, from sunbathers and picnickers to practicing yogis and martial artists. The pier has also long been a gathering spot for the LGBTQ community. The boardwalk is great for an extended stroll, and the pier's location provides expansive views of Lower Manhattan and One World Trade Center in particular. The developing skyline of Jersey City is in full view and, if you get hungry, Wafels and Dinges serves inventively topped Belgian waffles at Belgo Landing, a café at the foot of the pier, on weekends during the warmer months.

MAP 4: Christopher St. and West St., 212/627-2020, www.hudsonriverpark.org; 6am-1am daily; free

Jefferson Market Garden

Occupying land that once housed a women's prison, this public green space has become a refuge for neighborhood locals as well as visitors. A koi pond and rose garden surround a variety of trees from crabapple to weeping birch. The garden hosts a variety of events both public and private. Fans of *Sex and the City* will recognize it as the spot where Miranda and Steve get married.

MAP 4: 70 A Greenwich Ave., 212/777-7662, www.jeffersonmarketgarden.org; 10am-5pm Tues.-Sun. Apr.-Oct.; free

Chelsea and Union Square   Map 5

PARKS

Gramercy Park

You can't actually go inside the gated Gramercy Park in this gilded old-money neighborhood—unless you have a coveted key, which is given only to occupants of the buildings that line each side of the quaint green space, including members of The Players private social club, founded by Shakespearean actor Edwin Booth (you might glimpse a statue of him as Hamlet in the center of the park). But the appeal of this privileged park for the public is simply strolling its leafy perimeter. Gothic architecture abounds, as does a rare tranquility in an otherwise bustling neighborhood.

MAP 5: between E. 20th St. and E. 21st St., Gramercy Park W. and Gramercy Park E.; not open to the public

Madison Square Park

A green spot amid the skyscrapers, this park is popular during the warmer months with office workers on lunch break and sunbathers, with its many benches and spacious-for-the-city lawns. There are also often art installations here; one recent highlight was Erwin Redl's *Whiteout*, which suspended hundreds of LED orbs among

Gramercy Park

the barren trees during winter. The park is also home to the original Shake Shack.

MAP 5: between 23rd St. and 26th St., 5th Ave. and Madison Ave., 212/520-7600, www.madisonsquarepark.org; 6am-midnight daily; free

RECREATION CENTERS

Chelsea Piers

This sports complex, housed in a series of renovated piers and part of Hudson River Park, is as expansive as it is state-of-the-art, playing host to an array of athletic pursuits from barre to boxing. The four-story driving range is a particular draw for golfers, combining a commanding view of the Hudson River with a 200-yard fairway and balls that tee themselves up using an automated system. An ice-skating rink hosts ice hockey leagues and figure skating championships, but welcomes novices ($12 entry, $6 skate rental) to bumble around the massive space, which also has views of the Hudson River; it's particularly invigorating to go in extreme weather. The fitness center is one of the city's top gyms, featuring a climbing wall, spa, and sundeck along with an array of exercise equipment. Day passes are available, and a multisport passport includes access to the fitness center, golf club, and more. But just wandering near the marina is a fun activity in and of itself.

MAP 5: 62 Chelsea Piers, 212/336-6666, www.chelseapiers.com; 5:30am-11pm Mon.-Thurs., 5:30am-10pm Fri., 8am-9pm Sat.-Sun.; prices vary

Midtown, Hell's Kitchen, and Times Square

Map 6

PARKS

Bryant Park

This park sits next to the main branch of the New York Public Library and is a popular spot for lunching office workers, with its numerous bistro tables and open lawn space, and it also hosts beloved events. In the summer, people stake out spots hours before sundown for free screenings amid the Midtown skyscrapers during Bryant Park Movie Nights, and on select Thursdays at 12:30pm the free Broadway in Bryant Park series brings casts from Broadway shows to perform their biggest hits in hour-long concerts. In winter, the pop-up Winter Village at Bryant Park hosts an ice-skating rink as well as an open-air holiday market. And year-round there's free Wi-Fi and food kiosks, including a Wafels & Dinges stand near the 42nd Street and 6th Avenue entrance that serves up elaborately topped Belgian concoctions; try the "Elvis" with bacon, peanut butter, and banana for an unconventionally sweet lunch. The park also has a couple of sit-down bar-restaurants, though you'll pay outsized prices for the privilege of the scenic setting.

MAP 6: between W. 40th St. and W. 42nd St., 5th Ave. and 6th Ave., 212/768-4242, http://bryantpark.org; 7am-10pm daily; free

ICE-SKATING

The Rink at Rockefeller Center

Skating beneath Rockefeller's towering Christmas tree is the draw of this seasonal rink. It's the smallest and priciest place to ice-skate in the city, but this doesn't stop the crowds. Avoid weekends during the prime December season to increase your chances of gliding straight onto the ice. With a $60 VIP Igloo pass, which includes skate rental, visitors can bypass lines and receive complimentary hot beverages and cookies.

MAP 6: 600 5th Ave., 212/332-7654, http://therinkatrockcenter.com; 8:30am-midnight Oct.-Apr.; $25-32 adults, $15 seniors and children 10 and under, $12 skate rental

Winter Village at Bryant Park

Winter Village at Bryant Park

For those wanting to skate amid the Midtown skyline and avoid the high prices of Rockefeller Center, Bryant Park provides a nice alternative. Admission is free, which means the lines can be long, particularly on the weekends. Organized activities, where experts provide impromptu lessons in the brisk winter atmosphere—like frozen-finger juggling—add extra entertainment. An outpost of popular local chain Joe Coffee is located in the park and convenient for warming up.

MAP 6: between W. 40th St. and W. 42nd St., 5th Ave. and 6th Ave., 212/768-4242, http://bryantpark.org; 8am-10pm daily Oct.-Mar. weather permitting; free admission, $20 skate rental

SPECTATOR SPORTS
BASKETBALL
New York Knicks

Despite not having won a championship since 1973 (or perhaps because of it), the Knicks have retained a loyal fan base that packs Madison Square Garden for each of its home games. Founded in 1946, the team holds the distinction of being one of the original NBA franchises, and its arena is the second oldest in the league. As at most arenas security lines can be quite long, so plan to arrive early. You can grab a quick meal at the on-site Carnegie Deli stand. Stubhub (www.stubhub.com) is a good place to find last-minute tickets to games.

MAP 6: Madison Square Garden, 4 Pennsylvania Plaza, 212/465-6741, www. nba.com/knicks; box office 10am-6pm Mon.-Sat.; from $62

HOCKEY
New York Rangers

The New York Rangers share Madison Square Garden with the Knicks, and the arena is the oldest in the National Hockey League. The team has won four Stanley Cup championships (though three were before 1940). Celebrations spilled outside the arena when they won in 1994, and fans are primed for another Cup. Cheap tickets are impossible to come by due to the limited number of home games. Your best bet for finding tickets is on StubHub, or aim for a preseason game if you happen to be here in September. You can

save a little cash by having a beer at the Pennsy food hall (located next to the main entrance) before a game; it always features a selection of crafts on draft for less than a Bud at the arena.

MAP 6: Madison Square Garden, 4 Pennsylvania Plaza, 212/465-6741, www. nhl.com/rangers; box office, 10am-6pm Mon.-Sat.; $89-1,853

TOURS
NBC Studios Tours

TV fans can take The Tour at NBC Studios (212/664-3700, www. thetouratnbcstudios.com; $33 adults, $29 seniors and students) for a behind-the-scenes look at the television production process, which includes visits to at least two working studios—the selection depends on production schedules but might include *Saturday Night Live*, *The Tonight Show Starring Jimmy Fallon*, or *Late Night with Seth Meyers*, among others. You'll be guided by an NBC page (think Kenneth on *30 Rock*). The tour lasts just over an hour, and booking in advance is recommended. It leaves every 20 minutes 8:20am-2:20pm Monday-Thursday, 8:20am-5pm Friday, and 8:20am-6pm on select Saturdays and Sundays.

Free tickets to attend NBC Studios show tapings (212/664-3056, www. nbc.com/tickets; free) can be reserved online. Tickets are released about a month in advance, and popular shows like *Late Night with Seth Meyers* sell out very quickly. *Saturday Night Live* tickets are by lottery only. The lottery is held during the month of August for the following season. To enter send an email (snltickets@nbcuni.com) explaining why you want to attend.

MAP 6: NBC Studios, 30 Rockefeller Plaza; 212/664-3700, 212/664-3056, www.nbc. com; The Tour at NBC Studios $29-33, NBC Studios show tapings free

Upper West Side and Upper East Side

Map 7

PARKS

Carl Schurz Park

This small green respite encompasses almost 15 acres (6 ha) and also serves as the backyard for the mayor's residence, Gracie Mansion. It was created in 1910 and named after German-born Secretary of the Interior Carl Schurz, who resided in the city for the last quarter century of his life. A wide promenade on the East River overlooking Roosevelt Island makes for a good stroll, and multiple dog runs make this a popular place for local canines.

MAP 7: between E. 84 St. and E. 90th St., East End Ave. and the East River, 212/459-4455, www.carlschurzparknyc.org; 6am-midnight daily; free

Riverside Park

Overlooking the Hudson River and stretching 4 narrow miles (6.4 km) from the Upper West Side north into Morningside Heights and Harlem, this park designed by Frederick Law Olmsted—creator of Central Park—is a favorite of locals. Some of these locals live on houseboats near the 79th Street Boat Basin marina, which features a casual café; the views outshine the menu of American fare here, so perhaps simply pause for a look or a drink. With the exception of Grant's Tomb, the park isn't filled with attractions but operates more like a large public backyard.

Riverside Park

MAP 7: between W. 59th St. and W. 155th St., Riverside Dr. and the Hudson River, 212/870-3070, http://riversideparknyc.org; 24 hours daily; free

BOATING
The Loeb Boathouse

Skip the pedicabs offering rides through Central Park and opt instead to tool around the lovely Lake in a rowboat. Holding up to four, the rowboat rentals ($15 per hour, $4 each additional 15 min., cash only) provide a great opportunity to navigate the lake's nooks and crannies, and under a scenic bridge or two while spotting birds or some of the two dozen species of butterfly that call the area home. The skyline is also visible through the trees. Gondola tours ($45 per half hour for up to six people) are also available.

MAP 7: E. 72 St. and Park Drive N., 212/517-2233, www. thecentralparkboathouse.com; 10am-dusk daily Apr.-Nov. weather permitting; rowboat rental $15 per hour, gondola tour $45

BIKING
Central Park Bike Rentals and Tours

Well-paved roads—now closed to cars—trace scenic and popular routes through Central Park. You can choose from three loops ranging 1.7-6.1 miles (2.7-9.8 km) via these roads. West Drive begins at 7th Avenue and Central Park South and weaves all the way to the north end of the park where it runs into East Drive at roughly 7th Avenue and Central Park North. East Drive curves south around the Harlem Meer and runs all the way down to 59th Street and 5th Avenue. A third road, Center Drive, begins at 6th Avenue and Central Park South and connects to both the West and East Drives. Beware of pedestrians. You can find bike rentals ($15-30 for 1-5 hours, $40 full day) to take a ride on your own, or hop on a bike tour ($50-75 adults, $35-50 children) lasting one or two hours that will point out the park's many attractions.

MAP 7: 208 W. 80th St., 917/993-3141, www.centralpark.com; 8am-8pm daily Apr.-Aug., 9am-6pm Mon.-Fri. and 8am-8pm Sat.-Sun. Sept.-Mar.; bike rental $15-40, bike tour $35-75

ICE-SKATING
Wollman Rink

Outside of Rockefeller Center and Bryant Park, this is Manhattan's most accessible ice-skating rink and much larger than the other two at 33,000 square feet (3,066 sq m). Originally opened in 1950, the ice-skating venue is now owned by the Trump family and, like everything else they own, has their surname emblazoned on the perimeter walls. Fees are relatively reasonable, the lines shorter than at Rockefeller, and the setting in southern Central Park scenic and iconic. Wollman Rink's little sister, Lasker Rink (110 Lenox Ave., www.laskerrink.com; 9:30am-4pm Mon.-Tues. and Thurs., 9:30am-2:30pm Wed., 9:30am-4:50pm and 6pm-11pm Fri., 1pm-11pm Sat., 12:30pm-4:30pm Sun. late Oct.-Apr.; $8.50 adults, $4.50 children, $2.25 seniors, $7.50 skate rental), also Trump-owned, is located at the northern edge of Central Park and features a slightly more local crowd and cheaper prices.

MAP 7: 830 5th Ave., 212/439-6900, www. wollmanskatingrink.com; 10am-2:30pm Mon.-Tues., 10am-10pm Wed.-Thurs., 10am-11pm Fri.-Sat., 10am-9pm Sun. late Oct.-Apr.; $12-19 adults, $5-9 seniors, $6 children under 12, $5 spectators, $9 skate rental

TOURS

Central Park Horse Carriage Tours

Before there were cars, New Yorkers traveled by horse carriage. This mode of transport is now strictly a tourist amusement, and controversial because of the strain it puts on the horses. If you do choose to take a ride, you'll find the carriages on the park side of Central Park South between 5th and 6th Avenues. Reservations aren't necessary, though they can be made online. Rides are 30 minutes ($110) or 45 minutes ($145) for up to four adults, two adults and three children under 12, or one adult and four children under 12. Seating is on two benches that face each other and the ride goes through the park, past popular sites like Bethesda Fountain. A few other things to note: There are no rides when the temperature is above 89 degrees Fahrenheit or below 19 degrees Fahrenheit, and during the holiday season (Dec. 10-Jan. 5) all rides are 45 minutes and $235.

MAP 7: W. 59th St. and 5th Ave., www. centralpark.com/tours/horse-carriage-rides; tours depart 10am-11:30pm Mon.-Fri., 9am-11:30pm Sat.-Sun.; $110-235

Central Park horse carriage tours

5th and Park Walking Tour

Museum Mile contains the largest cluster of world-class museums in the city, and the area also hosts a lot of city history that doesn't necessarily announce itself, particularly on the Upper East Side in the area known as Carnegie Hill—named for Andrew Carnegie's mansion, which now houses the Cooper Hewitt museum. Local resident and film critic Cole Smithey guides small-group walking tours that weave together sights with movie trivia, as numerous famous films have also been shot in the area (including *Marathon Man* and *Rosemary's Baby*). The 95-minute tour also passes by the homes of famous recluse J. D. Salinger and surrealist filmmaker Luis Buñuel, among many others. It meets at the Guggenheim, heads up to the Central Park Reservoir, and concludes in front of The Met.

MAP 7: meeting point Guggenheim Museum, 212/369-3937, www.colesmithey. com/tour; noon Sun.-Fri.; $35 adults, free for children under 2

Harlem and Morningside Heights Map 8

PARKS

Crack is Wack Playground

During the height of the urban crack epidemic in the mid-80s, artist Keith Haring decided to take a whimsical yet powerful antidrug stance to an afflicted area in far east Harlem, painting a massive double-sided mural on the wall of a handball court on the East River. While it was unauthorized at the time, the park has since been renamed after the work, which remains Haring's most prominently enduring piece in the city. A snake is seen chasing down a group of people—all marked with an "X"—on one side of the wall, while the other displays a skeleton and tangle of bodies in an arrestingly bright red.

MAP 8: E.127th between 2nd Ave. and Harlem River Dr., 212/639-9675, www.nycgovparks.org; 24 hours daily; free

Morningside Park

This skinny stretch of green separates Morningside Heights from Harlem and is primarily used by neighborhood locals and students from nearby Columbia University. Original designs by Central Park landscape architects Frederick Law Olmsted and Calvert Vaux were reworked by architect Jacob Wrey Mould until his death, at which point Olmsted and Vaux took over the project again. Morningside Park is located in one of the city's hilliest areas, so you can gain a bit of elevation here; the park is named for its sunrise views, which are impressive from its western ridge. Another defining feature is its pond and waterfall near the southern end, and there are also several playgrounds.

MAP 8: between W. 110th St. and W. 123rd St., Morningside Dr. and Manhattan Ave./Morningside Ave., www.nycgovparks.org; 6am-1am daily; free

Downtown Brooklyn, Dumbo, and Fort Greene Map 9

PARKS

✪ Brooklyn Heights Promenade

Long before Brooklyn Bridge Park, the Brooklyn Heights Promenade was the choice spot for waterfront greenery. While it's no longer a neighborhood secret, it remains a treasure. Sporting dramatic views of the East River, Brooklyn Bridge, and Lower Manhattan skyline as well as benches on which to sit and take it all in, the promenade is ideally perched above the piers. This gives it a secluded feeling despite the stroller crowds that often flood through on weekends. The backs of brownstones line the path. The promenade has been featured in multiple movies, including *Prizzi's*

Brooklyn Heights Promenade

Honor and *Moonstruck*. The walkway is about a third of a mile long (just over half a kilometer) and elevated four stories aboveground.

Enjoy this beloved stretch now while you can: The city has plans to repair the Brooklyn-Queens Expressway (BQE) upon which the Brooklyn Heights Promenade sits, possibly forcing its closure for up to six years. Plans are still being discussed, and a decision isn't expected to be reached until 2020 at the earliest.

MAP 9: northern entrance Orange St. and Columbia Heights, southern entrance Remsen St. and Montague Terrace, 718/722-3214, www.nycgovparks.org; 7am-1am daily; free

Brooklyn Bridge Park

Once a series of derelict docks, this meticulously planned waterfront park is now one of the city's most well-maintained green spaces. It spans 85 acres (34 ha) from the Manhattan Bridge and south down to Pier 6 and offers beautiful views of the Manhattan skyline and Brooklyn Bridge. Wander paths through clusters of plantings that muffle the noise of the nearby BQE, or stretch out on the expanse of lawn called **Empire Fulton Ferry Park,** popular for picnicking and serious lounging on weekends. Nearby is **Jane's Carousel**

Fort Greene Park

(www.janescarousel.com; 11am-7pm Wed.-Mon. mid-May-mid-Sept., 11am-6pm Thurs.-Sun. mid-Sept.-mid-May; $2), created in 1922 and glass-encased for year-round rides with great views. A spot underneath the roar of the Manhattan Bridge sports an outdoor climbing wall and a patch of rocky beach, aptly named Pebble Beach. Bocce courts and Ping-Pong tables on Pier 2 and free kayak rentals on Pier 4 are just some of the other available amusements. MAP 9: 334 Furman St., 718/222-9939, www.brooklynbridgepark.org; 6am-1am daily (select piers close earlier); free

Fort Greene Park
Elevated above its namesake brownstone-lined neighborhood, Fort Greene Park is a great place to stretch out and read on a warm afternoon or eat takeout from a restaurant on DeKalb or Myrtle Avenue, which form its southern and northern borders, respectively. The site of a former Revolutionary War fort, the land was designated a public park in 1845 with the help of Walt Whitman—then an editor for a local daily newspaper in Brooklyn that championed the project. In 1867, landscape architects Frederick Law Olmsted and Calvert Vaux, the designers of Central Park, helmed a redesign. They also designed the Prison Ship Martyrs' Monument, a towering granite pillar in the center of the park that pays tribute to the thousands of American prisoners of war who died in British captivity during the war. MAP 9: Myrtle Ave., DeKalb Ave., Washington Park, and St. Edward's St., 212/639-9675, www.nycgovparks.org; 5am-1am daily; free

SPECTATOR SPORTS
BASKETBALL
Brooklyn Nets
"We go hard" is the rallying cry for this NBA team, which moved from New Jersey to Brooklyn to play in the shiny new Barclays Center. While the team often ranks a few notches below the Knicks, it's still possible to see a thrilling contest aided by the center's state-of-the-art sound system—which sets each game to a hip-hop soundtrack. The acoustics were designed by the company responsible for the Sydney Opera House and the Pompidou Center in Paris, and the center regularly draws a diverse array of musical acts from Billy Joel to JAY-Z. The Nets game experience is also enhanced by a Brooklyn-focused food court offering options from local eateries, including "Brooklyn Bangers" from The Vanderbilt and cheesecake from Junior's Restaurant and Bakery. Local dance troupes perform tightly choreographed routines in between quarters. MAP 9: 620 Atlantic Ave., 917/618-6100, www.nba.com/nets; box office noon-6pm Mon.-Fri., noon-4pm Sat. (varies on game days and for concerts), prices vary

A DAY AT THE BEACH

Rockaway Beach

No one comes to New York for its beaches, but if you have a day to spare, an excursion to one of the city's sandy stretches offers a nice change of scenery, a festive atmosphere, and a chance to hang out among a diverse range of locals.

ROCKAWAY BEACH

Featured in the Ramones song that bears its name and located on the far southeastern edge of Queens, **Rockaway Beach** (Beach 9th St. to Beach 149th St., 718/313-4000, www.nycgovparks.org; 7am-midnight daily; free) is the city's premier beach community, with sandy stretches and a boardwalk. On weekends it fills with sunbathers and swimmers, from Puerto Rican families to fashionistas who couldn't make it farther east to the Hamptons. The prime gathering areas—paralleling the subway stops at Beach 90th, Beach 98th, Beach 105th, and Beach 116th Streets—can get packed, but as the street numbers go up, the crowds thin. Rockaway Beach also offers the only legal surfing stretches within city limits, with beaches located between Beach 68 and 71 Streets, 87 and 91 Streets, and 110 and 111 Streets designated for surfers. A number of shops on Rockaway Beach Boulevard and in designated surf areas offer board rentals ($10-40 per day). While some are open just during the summer, others remain open year-round; some of the best waves arrive late September to early November.

Don't bother packing a picnic for a day here because there are great eats along the beach's boardwalk and nearby streets, such as **Rockaway Beach Surf Club** (302 Beach 87th St., www.rockawaybeachsurfclub.com; 11am-11pm daily spring-summer; $) and

Caracas Arepa Bar (106-01 Shore Front Pkwy., www.caracasarepabar.com; noon-8pm Mon.-Thurs. and 11am-9:30pm Fri.-Sun. summer; $) near Beach 105th Street.

To get here, take the A subway to Beach 90th, Beach 98th, Beach 105th, or Beach 116th Streets. NYC Ferry (www.ferry.nyc) also runs a Rockaway route from Wall Street/Pier 11 in Lower Manhattan. The ride takes about an hour, costs the standard $2.75 fare, and lands at Beach 108th Street and Beach Channel Drive. Free shuttle buses can transport riders between the beach areas.

THE PEOPLE'S BEACH AT JACOB RIIS PARK

Farther southwest along the same stretch as Rockaway Beach is The People's Beach at Jacob Riis Park (157 Rockaway Beach Blvd., http://nyharborparks.org; 7am-midnight daily, lifeguard on duty 10am-6pm Memorial Day-Labor Day; free) a chiller, LGBTQ-friendly beach where women often go topless. Go a touch farther southwest and you'll find a tranquil section near the former military base Fort Tilden (Breezy Point, http://nyharborparks.org; 7am-midnight daily, lifeguard on duty 10am-6pm Memorial Day-Labor Day; free). A nature preserve is also here, with trails that weave from the beach to several batteries that provide dramatic views of the Rockaways. MoMA also puts on installations by notable artists like Yayoi Kusama in the abandoned buildings here in the summer.

Casual eats abound at the Riis Park Beach Bazaar (16702 Rockaway Beach Blvd., http://riisparkbeachbazaar.com), a 1930s art deco beachside bathhouse recently converted into a food hall. Here you'll find two outposts of the city's best ice cream, Ample Hills Creamery (Bay 9 and Bathhouse; noon-8pm daily summer; $), as well as the Rockaway Clam Bar (Bay 9, http://rockawayclambar.com; 11am-9pm daily summer), which does a lobster boil ($30) with live music on Friday nights in the summer. Hours vary by vendor, and most are only open in the summer, but The Meat Up Grill (Bay 9 and Bathhouse, 708/632-8871, www.themeatupgrill.com; hours vary seasonally; $) is open year-round and has indoor seating.

To get here, take the Rockaway route on the NYC Ferry (www.ferry.nyc) from Wall Street/Pier 11 in Lower Manhattan. The ride takes about an hour, costs the standard $2.75 fare, and lands at Beach 108th Street and Beach Channel Drive. A free shuttle bus from the ferry dock can transfer you, or you could walk the approximately 2.5 miles (4 km) to reach Jacob Riis Park.

BRIGHTON BEACH

East of Coney Island on Brooklyn's south waterfront is Brighton Beach (Ocean Pkwy. to Corbin Pl., 718/946-1350, www.nycgovparks.org; 5am-1am daily, lifeguard on duty 10am-6pm Memorial Day-Labor Day; free), popular for swimming and sunbathing. The surrounding neighborhood is nicknamed "Little Odessa" for its many Russian-speaking immigrants and Russian culture. Boardwalk restaurants serve heaping portions of comfort food from the old country in an Eastern European nightclub atmosphere—and with plenty of vodka. You'll find authentic eats slightly farther inland. Varenichnaya (3086 Brighton 2nd St., 718/332-9797; 10am-9pm daily; $), is named after the sublime Russian dumpling, which is the thing to get here. The dumplings are served in heaping portions with a dollop of sour cream. For a beach picnic, head to Brighton Bazaar (1007 Brighton Beach Ave., 718/769-1700; 8am-10pm daily), a Russian supermarket with an extensive buffet of dishes like thick pieces of chicken kotleti (cutlets) and fresh blintzes.

To get here, take the Q or B subway to the Brighton Beach station and walk south two blocks to hit the boardwalk and beach.

Williamsburg, Greenpoint, and Bushwick
Map 10

PARKS

East River State Park

Formerly a shipping dock during the 19th century and then abandoned for decades, East River State Park is now a well-manicured waterfront park that offers great views of the Williamsburg Bridge and Manhattan skyline. It's also home of the seasonal and ever-popular Smorgasburg (11am-6pm Sat. Apr.-Oct.), the world's largest open-air food market. The park is also a favorite spot for locals to bask in the sun or have an impromptu picnic with friends. The NYC Ferry conveniently stops here, making a 20-minute ride from Manhattan's East 34th Street dock.

MAP 10: 90 Kent Ave., 718/782-2731; 9am-9pm daily; free

McCarren Park

It says something about the neighborhood's population that there was a public outcry when it was announced that the outdoor pool at McCarren Park—which had long been drained and recently repurposed as a summer concert venue drawing bands like the Black Keys and Bloc Party—was going to be revitalized and reopened for swimming. The pool is now open (11am-3pm and 4pm-7pm daily Memorial Day-weekend after Labor Day; free), concerts are still held in the park (Brian Wilson played *Pet Sounds* one recent summer), and hipster locals continue to sunbathe, walk their dogs, and hang out at this gathering spot, located in Williamsburg at its border with Greenpoint.

MAP 10: 776 Lorimer St., 212/639-9675, www.nycgovparks.org; 6am-1am daily; free

BOWLING

Brooklyn Bowl

Because the city is so starved for space, bowling is quite pricey. At least at Brooklyn Bowl, you can also eat the Blue Ribbon restaurant empire's awesome fried chicken—among other offerings—and imbibe a beer, wine, or cocktail while trying to score a strike. The lanes also make prime viewing spots during the venue's many live shows that cover a diverse range of genres. Jam band Joe Russo's Almost Dead has played to many packed crowds as has Interpol frontman Paul Banks and the Roots' Questlove, who seems to show up just about everywhere.

MAP 10: 61 Wythe Ave., 718/963-3369, www.brooklynbowl.com/brooklyn; 6pm-close Mon.-Fri., noon-close Sat.-Sun.; concert cover free-$75, bowling $25 per lane per 30 min.

HIKING

✪ Inwood Hill Park

New York City is not exactly a hiking destination, and the city itself is fairly flat—but the terrain gets hillier at the northern tip of Manhattan. Inwood Hill Park encompasses Manhattan's only forest, and its nearly 200 acres (81 ha) hosts several trails (white, orange, blue) measuring 1.2, 1.3, and 1.7 miles (1.9, 2.1, and 2.7 km), respectively. All three provide elevated views of the Hudson and Harlem Rivers. The park offers the best example of what New York looked like half a millennium ago. Trails wind past woodland plants, glacial potholes, and caves the Lenape people used for shelter, as well as skirt the island's last remaining salt marsh, home to great blue herons and other waterfowl.

The blue trail passes Shorakapok Rock, which is marked by a plaque as the place where Dutch trader Peter Minuit purchased Manhattan from the Lenape (although the sale has also been linked to other sites in Manhattan).

To get here, take the A subway to the Dyckman Street station. Walk two blocks northwest on Dyckman Street and turn right on Payson Avenue, where you can access the park.

MAP 11: between Dyckman Ave., Payson Ave./Seaman Ave., Hudson River, and Harlem River, Manhattan, 212/639-9675, www.nycgovparks.org/parks/inwood-hill-park; 6am-1am daily; free

BOATING

Lefrak Center at Lakeside Prospect Park

From the center of the lake in Prospect Park, only trees are visible. Paddle out in a rental paddleboat or kayak, and pretend you've transported back in time to the city's bucolic past. Inside the lake, the tiny and aptly named Duck Island is a good place to spot waterfowl. Weekday afternoons are the best times to enjoy the stillness of the water, while weekends are popular with families, who rent multiple boats for some marine hangout time.

MAP 11: 171 East Dr., Brooklyn, 718/462-0010, http://lakesidebrooklyn.com; 11am-sunset daily late Mar.-late June and early Sept.-late Sept., 9am-sunset daily late June-early Sept., 11am-sunset Fri.-Sun. Oct.; paddleboat rental $26-36 per hour, kayak rental $16-25 per hour or $30-38 half day, $40-45 full day

SPECTATOR SPORTS

BASEBALL

New York Mets

The New York Mets have seen their share of struggles since their triumphant 1986 World Series win. This endears them to some fans and exasperates others such as Jon Stewart, who launched into more than a few rants about it during his tenure as host of *The Daily Show*. Politically incorrect commentator and comedian Bill Maher is a minority shareholder and longtime fan. Even when the team is losing, it's possible to have a good time at the tricked-out Citi Field stadium in Queens, with its open-air center field food court that includes offerings from Momofuku's Fuku and Milk Bar, Shake Shack, and others. Mikkeller opened a brewery inside the stadium featuring 60 drafts and a killer food menu of its own—and you don't even need a ticket to the game to visit. Citi

FIELD TRIP FOR FOOTBALL FANS

The New York Giants and New York Jets may be rivals, but it doesn't stop them from playing out of the same stadium in New Jersey. Bruce Springsteen played a set of concerts to close out the old Giants Stadium before it was torn down and replaced with the $1.6 billion MetLife Stadium (MetLife Stadium Dr., East Rutherford, NJ, 212/559-1515, www.metlifestadium.com). It was the most expensive stadium ever built when it opened in 2010 and is the second largest in the NFL. The parking lots open five hours prior to games and events for tailgating. If eating here, check out Fat Rooster for its hot chicken sandwich, the Grater Mac Shop for a variety of mac 'n' cheese options, and Global Pies for empanadas, including a s'mores version.

To get there, hop on a train via NJ Transit (www.njtransit.com) from Midtown Manhattan's Penn Station (7th Ave. and W. 32nd St.). Transfer at Secaucus Junction to its Meadowlands line, which stops right in front of the stadium. Services are every 10-30 minutes in the 3.5 hours leading up to the event, once an hour during, and 10-30 minutes for the two hours following. A round-trip ticket is $11 and the journey takes about half an hour. Coach USA (800/877-1888, ext. 3, www.coachusa.com) also runs buses from Midtown Manhattan's Port Authority (625 8th Ave.) to the stadium via its route 351 Meadowlands Express for $7 one-way. It takes about 20 minutes, and frequency of bus departures is based on the event.

Field typically opens 1.5 hours before the first pitch, or 2 hours prior Monday-Friday so fans can watch batting practice.

To get here, take the 7 subway to the Mets-Willets Point station, which is across the street from the stadium.

MAP 11: Citi Field, 123-01 Roosevelt Ave., Queens, 718/507-8499, www.mlb.com/mets/ballpark; prices vary

New York Yankees

Love them or hate them, the New York Yankees have won far more World Series championships than any other team—27 and counting. Open since 2009, the current Yankee Stadium in the Bronx is across the street from the site of the original, which is now a public park. You're more relegated to your seating section in this incarnation, as wandering around is discouraged. That said, the sightlines in the upper deck grandstand feel closer to the action and the railing is clear glass for improved viewing. Food options are much more standard than at rival Citi Field, but you're here to watch the game, right? The venue typically opens 1.5 hours before the first pitch, or 3 hours prior on Friday nights and for all Saturday games to allow fans to watch batting practice.

To get here, take the B, D, or 4 subway to the 161st Street-Yankee Stadium station, which is just across the street from the ballpark.

MAP 11: Yankee Stadium, 1 E. 161st St., Bronx, 718/293-4300, www.mlb.com/yankees/ballpark; prices vary

SHOPS

Whether you're searching for used books for a dollar or haute couture that costs a month's rent, New York City offers retail therapy for every budget—even some of the city's most elegant corners have scrappy backstories. One symbol of New York luxury, Barneys New York, got its start reselling showroom samples and overstock at a discount.

The most iconic of upscale shopping, with haute couture flagships as well as the city's most lavish department stores can be found on 5th Avenue, as well as Madison Avenue. Many of these stores can feel like museums, with lines forming outside during the busiest times. Soho and the Meatpacking District are also high-end shopping areas. While there's some overlap with the glitzy stores uptown, these neighborhoods boast more independent boutiques, as downtown neighborhoods generally do.

For all things indie, head to Brooklyn. Williamsburg has numerous notable shops. Regular markets, like the Brooklyn Flea, also operate on this side of the river for those seeking vintage goods and handmade items by local designers.

Abode

SHOPPING DISTRICTS

Soho

Cobblestone streets that once housed lofts for struggling artists are now full of gleaming boutiques. Stores on Broadway lean toward mainstream chains while the more charming side streets are home to smaller upscale boutiques. As an entry point, you might start exploring Soho's shops by looping east and

HIGHLIGHTS

✪ **BEST CHOCOLATE STORE THAT DOUBLES AS A MUSEUM:**
Jacques Torres Chocolate offers sweets with a side of history (page
289).

✪ **BEST GALLERY-LIKE SHOP: Ingo Maurer**'s unique lighting creations delightfully blur the line between decor and art (page 290).

✪ **BEST PLACE TO SHOP IN A NEIGHBORHOOD LANDMARK:**
Housed in the hallowed former digs of CBGB, this **John Varvatos**
store has preserved some of the original graffiti and artifacts of the
legendary punk club (page 290).

✪ **BEST BOOKSTORE:** Spend hours browsing for books to fit any
budget at **The Strand** (page 291).

✪ **BEST SHOP TO GET A GLIMPSE OF THE MEATPACKING
DISTRICT'S PAST LIFE:** Popular women's clothing store **Madewell**
sits in the former space of a famed late-night restaurant from the
neighborhood's slaughterhouse days (page 293).

✪ **BEST BROWSING:** Beautiful design meets fun and function at the
MoMA Design Store (page 299).

✪ **BEST PLACE TO SPOT THE LATEST FASHION TRENDS:**
Fivestory is like Barneys distilled into a brownstone and curated by a
savvy thirtysomething (page 300).

✪ **BEST PLACE TO EMBRACE CLASSIC NEW YORK STYLE:** Head
to **Barneys New York** to find a classic city department store that's
made a graceful leap into the 21st century (page 300).

✪ **BEST THRIFT STORE:** Secondhand threads by designers are available for a song at **Beacon's Closet** (page 304).

✪ **BEST RECORD STORE THAT'S ALSO AN AWESOME MUSIC
CLUB: Rough Trade** sells rare vinyl and also happens to have one of
the best live music stages in the city (page 304).

The Strand

Meatpacking District

back west down the parallel streets of Prince and Spring Streets, or north and south via the parallel Wooster and Greene Streets, and so on, and then just let yourself wander from there.

MAP 2: W. Houston St. to Canal St. and 6th Ave. to Crosby St.

Meatpacking District

The former grit of this once industrial neighborhood has now nearly vanished. Cavernous warehouse spaces today house high-end designers, and the atmosphere feels more South Beach than Soho—a bit brash and flashy. Some major shopping thoroughfares in the neighborhood are 14th Street and Washington Street, but shops are scattered in the surrounding side streets as well.

MAP 4: W. 14th St. to Gansevoort St. and 10th Ave. to Hudson St.

5th Avenue

High-end New York department stores like Bergdorf Goodman and Saks Fifth Avenue call 5th Avenue home, and the grandest international brands, such as Tiffany & Co., keep their flagship stores here as well, along with more accessible ones like Uniqlo and Topshop.

MAP 6: 5th Ave. from 42nd St. to 59th St.

Williamsburg

Bedford Avenue is the main thoroughfare of the hipster Brooklyn of which you've heard. Crowds stream down the narrow sidewalks to shop at indie boutiques for clothing, books, bags, and more. Stores are dotted along the side streets as well.

MAP 10: Bedford Ave. between Broadway and McCarren Park

BEST SOUVENIRS

Chelsea Market

GOURMET GOODIES

Unfortunately, New York bagels and pizza are hard to take home with you. But you can still bring back some foodie goodness by way of packaged treats, like chocolates or a spicy hot chocolate mix from **Jacques Torres Chocolate** (page 289) or any number of items from **Chelsea Market** (page 92).

BOOKS AND MUSIC

New York is full of bibliophiles and audiophiles, and stores here cater to them. Take advantage and hunt down that rare book or signed edition at **The Strand** (page 291) or vinyl album at **Rough Trade** (page 304) or **Jazz Record Center** (page 295).

LOCAL GOODS

Bypass standard souvenirs for something unique, and support local artists and designers at the same time. You'll find an assortment of distinctive and handcrafted items at the city's artisan markets, like **Artists and Fleas** and **The Market NYC,** which have multiple outposts (page 303).

THEATER MEMORABILIA

While most theaters sell consumer-baiting merchandise that's uninspired at best, keep your eyes peeled for special finds that will remind you of that great show. **Soho Rep** (page 218), for instance, has nicely bound scripts made for each production. Or if you see *Sleep No More* (page 230), your souvenir is already included in the ticket price— you'll get to take the mask you're required to wear during the show home with you.

MUSEUM STORE SOUVENIRS

Museum stores may be a generic go-to for gifts in many cities, but New York has the **MoMA Design Store** (page 299), a phenomenally fun store to browse with beautifully designed accessories, housewares, and more.

NYC TCHOTCHKES

If you just can't leave the city without a classic I Heart NYC T-shirt, New York's City's official store, **CityStore** (page 287), has you covered. You'll also find more unusual souvenirs to remember your time in the city; if you've become fond of the enviable mass transit system while here, for instance, you can toast your memories with a shot glass imprinted with the colorful subway map.

Lower Manhattan Map 1

DEPARTMENT STORES
Century 21

For fashionistas who don't want to pay retail, this discount department store offers an array of clothing, shoes, and accessories from designers like Giorgio Armani and Jimmy Choo. It's common to see prices slashed 50-70 percent. This six-level flagship store is Century 21 at its swankiest and largest.

MAP 1: 22 Cortlandt St., 212/227-9092, www.c21stores.com; 7:45am-9pm Mon.-Wed., 7:45am-9:30pm Thurs.-Fri., 10am-9pm Sat., 11am-8pm Sun.

GIFTS AND HOME
CityStore

The official store of the City of New York offers visitors a chance to take home a piece of the city, literally. You can buy real city signs, nonoperational taxicab medallions, and merchandise licensed by the NYPD, FDNY, NYC Parks, NYC Subway, and NYC Taxi. You can also get your classic I Heart NYC T-shirts here.

MAP 1: 1 Centre St., 212/386-0007, http://a856-citystore.nyc.gov; 9am-5pm Mon.-Fri.

Soho and Tribeca Map 2

CLOTHING AND ACCESSORIES
Agent Provocateur

With its purple neon sign above the small entrance, this luxury lingerie boutique indicates there's an art to undressing. Corsets, thongs, and aptly named playsuits (tassels included) walk a fine line between artful elegance and primal sexuality, while accessories like a crystal-tipped riding crop take a more aggressive stance. Prices are prohibitive (few items are under three figures), so you might view a visit here as akin to going to a gallery in Chelsea.

MAP 2: 133 Mercer St., 212/343-7370, www.agentprovocateur.com; 11am-7pm Mon.-Sat., noon-7pm Sun.

INA

Melding the best attributes of a cozy boutique and a bohemian thrift store, this midrange consignment shop features twin stores for men and women and a well-curated selection of designer threads from Ben Sherman to Burberry. While it would be easy to spend a lot here, a rotating sale section in the back makes it equally easy to land a bargain without sorting through the endless bounty.

MAP 2: 19 and 21 Prince St., 212/334-9048, www.inanyc.com; noon-8pm Mon.-Sat., noon-7pm Sun.

Opening Ceremony

Opening Ceremony offers an impressively diverse glimpse of global couture via its own fashion line as well as precise curation of designers from across the world. A sample of these offerings include a casual unisex suit handmade in Portugal by Bonne Suits, a virgin wool crewneck sweater by French designer Ami, and colorful plaid pants by local designer Miaou. The retailer's name references the Olympics, and in the vein of that international event's traveling style, Opening Ceremony showcases items from a different country each year. The New York store is the brand's original location.

MAP 2: 35 Howard St., 212/219-2688, www.openingceremony.com; 11am-8pm Mon.-Sat., noon-7pm Sun.

UNTUCKit

As its name implies, this store is the answer to every man's dream of not having to tuck in his shirt for work. The fitted tops convey cool yet put-together and come in a variety of colors and patterns. Simple checkered designs are particularly versatile. A wrinkle-free line gives added convenience. While UNTUCKit now has many shops across the country, this Soho location was its original brick-and-mortar store.

MAP 2: 129 Prince St., 888/992-3102, www.untuckit.com; 11am-7pm Mon.-Thurs., 10am-7pm Fri.-Sat., 11am-6pm Sun.

UNTUCKit

Warby Parker

The brick-and-mortar flagship of the popular online eyewear retailer lets you try on way more than the five frames you're limited to via the website. Eyeglasses and sunglasses are displayed on tall, sleek, white bookshelves that line the perimeter of the store, creating a distinctly stylish and literary vibe. For each pair purchased, this socially conscious company donates a pair to someone in need.

MAP 2: 121 Greene St., 646/568-4720, www.warbyparker.com; 11am-8pm daily

VINTAGE

A Second Chance

A Second Chance

Owned and run by two generations of a New York family, this classy consignment shop features vintage Chanel jewelry, Hermès bags, and deep discounts on threads by high-end designers like Balenciaga and Prada. Think of it as Bergdorf Goodman's second-hand shop. Its colorful pink awning stands out on a tree-lined street.

MAP 2: 155 Prince St., 212/673-6155, www. asecondchanceresale.com; 11am-7pm Mon.-Fri., 11am-6pm Sat., noon-5pm Sun.

What Goes Around Comes Around

Founded in 1993 by partners Seth Weisser and Gerard Maione, this flagship store has attracted a celebrity clientele from Jennifer Aniston to Miley Cyrus for its unparalleled selection of rare vintage items ranging from Levi's jeans and band T-shirts to a 1932 Hermés bag named after Grace Kelly and priced at nearly six figures. It's like a museum where everything is for sale and the people-watching is prime.

MAP 2: 351 W. Broadway, 212/343-1225, www.whatgoesaroundnyc.com; 11am-8pm Mon.-Sat., noon-7pm Sun.

DEPARTMENT STORES
Pearl River Mart

Revered shopping institution Pearl River Mart was opened by a group of Chinese immigrants in 1971—before the United States had normalized relations with China—and represents the kind of ballsy ingenuity that makes this city great. From clothes to dinnerware to lights and other home furnishings, the department store remains a one-stop-shop for Eastern designs at prices that often rival Ikea.

MAP 2: 395 Broadway, 212/431-4770, www.pearlriver.com; 10am-7:20pm daily

BOOKS
Housing Works Bookstore

The soaring ceilings and well-worn wood floors of this used bookstore perfectly capture the bohemian ghost of Soho's artsy, literary past. All inventory is donated, so browsing here is sort of like looking through a well-read New Yorker's apartment, and all proceeds go to help end homelessness and AIDS. Lingering is encouraged, and there's a café serving Intelligentsia coffee and pastries from local bakeries. On select nights, the bookstore hosts events ranging from The Moth's storytelling slams to book readings to concerts by musicians like Glen Hansard of *Once* fame.

MAP 2: 126 Crosby St., 212/334-3324, www.housingworks.org; 9am-9pm Mon.-Fri., 10am-5pm Sat.-Sun.

McNally Jackson

This local indie bookstore is a pristine shrine to good books. An entire bookcase near the front is devoted to individual staff picks, and a café serves Stumptown coffee and a dizzying array of organic teas and snacks from nearby restaurant Balthazar, among other renowned eateries. Readings take place almost nightly and regular book clubs convene here, further encouraging a sense of community at this cozy literary refuge.

MAP 2: 52 Prince St., 212/274-1160, www. mcnallyjackson.com; 10am-10pm Mon.-Sat., 10am-9pm Sun.

GOURMET GOODIES
✪ Jacques Torres Chocolate

The city has no shortage of great chocolate, but French-born chocolatier Jacques Torres's concoctions are among the best. He served as executive pastry chef for over a decade at famed fine-dining institution Le Cirque before opening his first chocolate store and factory in 2000. The hot chocolate is uniquely satisfying—for a spice kick, try the Wicked version—and a cheap alternative to truffles (though these are excellent as well). This Soho location also houses a museum ($15 adults, $12 seniors, $10 youth) for those wanting to delve deeper into the history and production process behind this timeless sweet.

MAP 2: 350 Hudson St., 212/414-2462, www.mrchocolate.com; 8:30am-7pm Mon.-Fri., 9am-7pm Sat., 10:30am-5pm Sun.

Chamber Street Wines

Known for an exceptionally knowledgeable staff who can guide you to the perfect bottle at almost any price point, this shop offers that rare blend of value and refinement. It offers everything from a red zinfandel blend for around $15 to a 1989 bordeaux for $100, with a large selection of organic and biodynamic wines to boot. Several tastings are held each week to deepen your knowledge on a variety of regions; check the website for the current schedule.

MAP 2: 148 Chambers St. A, 212/227-1434, www.chambersstwines.com; 10am-9pm Mon.-Sat., noon-7pm Sun.

GIFTS AND HOME
✪ Ingo Maurer

This lighting store feels like an art gallery, each piece carefully crafted by its namesake owner. Pieces range in price from three figures to amounts adequate to purchase a nice car, and walk the fine line between style and function. Maurer transforms utilitarian objects into stunning statements of expression, with a knack for teasing magic out of the mundane. One of his simplest creations is a single bare bulb flanked by angel wings—which might sound silly until you see it glow in person.

MAP 2: 89 Grand St., 212/965-8817, www.ingo-maurer.com/en; 11am-7pm Tues.-Sat., noon-6pm Sun.

ARTS AND CRAFTS
Purl

If you've run out of yarn while knitting a scarf or just want to stock up for future projects, this unassuming storefront packs an astonishing variety of options inside its tiny footprint. From Romanian wool to baby alpaca, natural fibers abound in an array of colors. The owners are fanatic hobbyists themselves and happy to answer questions, make recommendations, and generally geek out. For more formal instruction, they offer a variety of classes on how to make various wardrobe items.

MAP 2: 459 Broome St., 212/420-8796, www.purlsoho.com; noon-7pm Mon.-Fri., noon-6pm Sat.-Sun.

East Village and Lower East Side Map 3

CLOTHING AND ACCESSORIES
✪ John Varvatos

Rumor has it John Varvatos decided to open this store when he heard a bank was going to raze it to open a new branch. It's the hallowed ground of legendary punk club CBGB, opened in 1976 and host to numerous bands before they became legends—including the Ramones, Talking Heads, Blondie, and Patti Smith, who played the club's last show in 2006. Varvatos has done a pretty admirable job of preserving the space (sections of the original flyer-filled walls and the stage remain) though it is a bit jarring to see designer men's threads in a place that previously only knew ripped jeans and T-shirts. But at least Varvatos is more punk than his haute couture contemporaries; he can say Iggy Pop has worn his suits.

MAP 3: 315 Bowery, 212/358-0315, www.johnvarvatos.com; noon-8pm Mon.-Fri., 11am-8pm Sat., noon-6pm Sun.

Yumi Kim

This flagship store of designer Kim Phan features bold floral prints inspired by the traditional Vietnamese dresses her mother wore. From flowing tops to off-the-shoulder rompers and maxi dresses, she combines downtown sophistication with laid-back West Coast brightness. Most dresses hover around $200, though sales can reduce the price dramatically.

MAP 3: 105 Stanton St. #1, 212/420-5919, http://yumikim.com; noon-7pm daily

VINTAGE

Edith Machinist

Fans of this vintage accessory and clothing store rave about the array of shoes displayed in neat pairs along the shop floor's perimeter. From 1960s studded alligator loafers to suede platform heels, the selection is eclectically curated, with items from the 1940s-1980s in pristine condition for their age; note that the footwear tends to run smaller than the printed sizes. The store also sells colorful scarfs by designers like Givenchy and other eye-catching accessories like Christian Dior belts and clutches. The entrance, a few steps below street level, tucks away the store's presence.

MAP 3: 104 Rivington St., 212/979-9992, www.edithmachinist.com; noon-6pm Sun.-Mon. and Fri., noon-7pm Tues.-Thurs. and Sat.

Tokio 7

This consignment shop takes its name from the owner's home city of Tokyo and features a range of vintage and offbeat items from iconic high-end brands like Chanel and Christian Louboutin, along with local neighborhood designers. While it can be a pricey affair, some items can be had for a steal. Comparison shopping by searching on eBay is a good way to get a sense of a find's value.

MAP 3: 83 E. 7th St., 212/353-8443, http://tokio7.net; noon-8pm daily

BOOKS
❂ The Strand

Named for a street in London where authors like Charles Dickens and William Makepeace Thackeray used to gather, The Strand is a New York institution containing 18 miles (29 km) worth of used and new books on its soaring shelves. The original store opened in 1927 around the corner in the midst of a cluster of dozens of bookstores known as Book Row. Today it's the only one remaining and has been at its current location since 1957. It's the kind of place where floorboards creak and the clerks are as well-read as the customers; don't be afraid to ask for a recommendation as you browse the massive collection. Great finds can be had at any price point, from the dollar book bins outside to the Rare Book Room holding first-edition collectibles selling for thousands. The room also hosts a variety of author readings and signings by the likes of people such as Patti Smith, Salman Rushdie, acclaimed sociologist Eric Klinenberg, and playwright Sarah Ruhl, among others. Admission ranges from free to about $15.

MAP 3: 828 Broadway, 212/473-1452, www.strandbooks.com; 9:30am-10:30pm Mon.-Sat., 11am-10:30pm Sun.

The Strand

Forbidden Planet

Containing one of the largest inventories of comics, graphic novels, toys, and all things sci-fi, Forbidden Planet has been selling to collectors of all stripes since 1981. Wide aisles and a knowledgeable staff make shopping here a pleasant experience, and a visit here nicely complements a stop at The Strand next door. Forbidden Planet periodically hosts special events where you can win prizes like a clothbound set of George R. R. Martin's *A Song of Ice and Fire.*

MAP 3: 832 Broadway, 212/473-1576, www.fpnyc.com; 9am-10pm Mon.-Tues., 8am-midnight Wed., 9am-midnight Thurs.-Sat., 10am-10pm Sun.

BATH AND BEAUTY
Kiehl's

This flagship store opened in 1851 as an apothecary. It now offers a host of skin and body care products for women as well as men; Andy Warhol was a fan of the Blue Astringent Herbal Lotion. Popular offerings range from an avocado eye treatment to a rare earth cleansing mask. The store itself retains its old-school signage and facade, but the interior is decidedly modern, with polished floors and gleaming displays.

MAP 3: 109 3rd Ave., 212/677-3171, http://stores.kiehls.com; 10am-9pm Mon.-Sat., 11am-7pm Sun.

CLOTHING AND ACCESSORIES

✪ Madewell

Popular casual-chic clothing designer Madewell caters to young women who want to look effortlessly put-together. Sure, it's a chain, but this Meatpacking store is housed in the former space of legendary gender-bending restaurant Florent, which was a fixture for those in the know during the years when slaughterhouses populated the neighborhood. Madewell has kept the original storefront intact (it reads "R & L Restaurant," which is the diner that occupied the space before Florent), allowing shoppers to glimpse a piece of the city's lore while buying a new pair of skinny jeans. Unfortunately, the inside just looks like another Madewell. **MAP 4:** 69 Gansevoort St., 646/486-7073, www.madewell.com; 10am-7pm Mon.-Thurs., 10am-8pm Fri.-Sat., 11am-6pm Sun.

Aedes De Venustas

This perfumery sells luxury fragrances organized in categories of unisex, masculine, and feminine; it has something for you no matter where you fall on the gender spectrum. The centerpiece of the red-walled store is a gleaming chandelier that would be at home in a French palace.

Madewell

MAP 4: 7 Greenwich Ave., 212/206-8674, www.aedes.com; noon-8pm Mon.-Sat., 1pm-7pm Sun.

Flight 001

If your luggage broke mid-journey and you need another bag to haul back all your souvenirs, or just a colorful eye mask for the ride home, this cute shop with high-end travel gear and accessories has you covered. Shaped like the inside of a mod airplane with shelves placed inside its curved walls, Flight 001 provides a fun environment in which to browse.

MAP 4: 96 Greenwich Ave., 212/989-0001, www.flight001.com; 11am-7pm Mon.-Sat., noon-6pm Sun.

Ports 1961

An outpost of Italian fashion designer Tia Cibani, this clothing boutique for men and women also features a gallery and design studio, but shoppers' eyes will immediately be drawn to a huge glass cube in the center with a skylight above. Cibani's designs are a haute couture interpretation of nature and favor boldness over practicality.

MAP 4: 3 9th Ave., 917/475-1022, www.ports1961.com; 11am-7pm Wed.-Mon.

Stephen F

The flagship store of this men's designer concentrates on well-tailored clothes made from high-quality materials. The sleek designs have attracted famous patrons like *Hamilton* star Daveed Diggs and model Alex Lundqvist, who shop in the store's private VIP room in the basement. Above ground, items are sparsely hung and dramatically displayed on elevated mannequins that line a whole wall.

MAP 4: 829 Washington St., 212/633-9100, www.stephen-f.com; 11am-7pm Mon.-Thurs. and Sat., 11am-8pm Fri., noon-6pm Sun.

VINTAGE
Hamlet's Vintage

Hamlet's Vintage holds a vast collection of clothing and accessories, including hats and bags, from the 1940s to the 1980s. With an emphasis on casual attire for men and women, the shop's rotating inventory is organized into basic categories, like "Shirts"—otherwise it's up to you to find that gem.

MAP 4: 146 W. 4th St., 212/228-1561, www.hamletsvintage.com; noon-8pm daily

BOOKS
Idlewild Books

There aren't many places where you can buy an obscure Italo Calvino novel and learn another language, but Idlewild is just that place. The bookstore offers classes in French, Spanish, Italian, and German, along with a trove of international literature. The well-traveled staff creates recommendation lists with the wanderlust-driven in mind. For a blustery autumn, they'll recommend a graphic novel by Iranian-born Parisian Marjane Satrapi or an autobiographical exploration of the season by Norwegian author Karl Ove Knausgaard.

MAP 4: 170 7th Ave. S., 212/414-8888, www.idlewildbooks.com; noon-8pm Mon.-Thurs., noon-6pm Fri.-Sun.

Three Lives & Company

Dubbed one of the greatest bookstores on earth by Pulitzer Prize-winning author Michael Cunningham, this beloved shop has been hawking a curated selection of new releases and classics since 1968. The well-read staff are happy to make recommendations as well as place special orders. The store also hosts the occasional reading.

MAP 4: 154 W. 10th St., 212/741-2069, www.threelives.com; noon-8pm Mon.-Tues., 11am-8:30pm Wed.-Sat., noon-7pm Sun.

GOURMET GOODIES
Murray's Cheese Shop

A mecca for dairy lovers, Murray's flagship was founded in 1940 and features a dizzying array of delectable mold, from brie to blue and stinky to smoky. It also sells a wide range of finely cured meats and specialty items such as olives and dried fruits to make DIY cheese-plating or picnicking easy; Washington Square Park is a five-minute walk east. For those wanting to consume immediately, the sit-down Murray's Cheese Bar (264 Bleecker St., 646/476-8882, www. murrayscheesebar.com; 4pm-10pm

Mon.-Tues., 4pm-midnight Wed.-Thurs., noon-midnight Fri., 11am-midnight Sat., 11am-10pm Sun.) is a couple of doors down.

MAP 4: 254 Bleecker St., 212/243-5001, www.murrayscheese.com; 8am-8pm Mon.-Sat., 9am-7pm Sun.

GIFTS AND HOME
Considerosity

The postage-sized Considerosity sells an array of handmade necklaces and earrings along with Unwined handcrafted candles made from reused wine bottles and other inventive small items. A whimsical card from the Rifle Paper Company reads "This is a Birthday Cardi" in a nod to the famous pop singer. Basically, this is the place to pick up a thoughtful gift that feels like you could have made it if you had the time (and were ridiculously skilled).

MAP 4: 191 W. 4th St., 646/397-4438; 11am-8pm Mon.-Sat., 11am-6pm Sun.

Chelsea and Union Square

Map 5

BOOKS AND MUSIC
Books of Wonder

Books of Wonder is a children's bookstore, but its meticulous level of curation will be just as appreciated by adults, with new releases, classic titles, and rare editions (a first edition of *Where the Wild Things Are* will set you back north of $20,000). Founded in 1980, it's the city's oldest children's bookstore, and beloved—it served as the model for Meg Ryan's shop in *You've Got Mail*. Books of Wonder hosts free story times (11am Sat.,

11:30am Sun.) and author-attended events including signings and readings. Another location is on the Upper West Side.

MAP 5: 18 W. 18th St., 212/989-3270, http://booksofwonder.com; 10am-7pm Mon.-Sat., 11am-6pm Sun.

Jazz Record Center

Its 8th-floor office building location, gray carpet, and metal shelves don't make the Jazz Record Center stand out—this is the kind of place you need to seek out, and when you do you're rewarded with a carefully curated collection of vinyl albums, CDs, books, T-shirts, and posters, as well as a crowd of like-minded people. The store specializes in rare and out-of-print items, and its website looks like it was made shortly after the its opening in 1983, so it's best to stop by to peruse the full inventory.

MAP 5: 236 W. 26th St. #804, 212/675-4480, www.jazzrecordcenter.com; 10am-6pm Mon.-Sat.

Rizzoli

Lit by elaborate chandeliers, Rizzoli was a Midtown respite for sophisticated book nerds for decades, established in 1964. Its current location is a bit south near Madison Square Park but no less grand. Trading the cozy environs of a six-story town house for a more modern, lofty space, with towering black marble columns and huge dark wood bookshelves, the store's name is still emblazoned out front in gold lettering—in the same font that marks the book shelf categories, from magazines to literature. This is a place to come to peruse pristine editions of the shop's namesake coffee table-worthy tomes on art, architecture, and fashion.

MAP 5: 1133 Broadway, 212/759-2424, www.rizzolibookstore.com; 10:30am-8pm Mon.-Fri., noon-8pm Sat., noon-7pm Sun.

GIFTS AND HOME
ABC Carpet & Home

A rich breadth of furniture, from streamlined Eames designs to industrial-chic melds of metal and wood, and a wide array of unique home goods from across the world are displayed across six massive floors. You could travel to India or Turkey for a fine rug—or just come here (check out the silk rug sample sale, which can cut prices by more than 50 percent). From an Italian floor lamp that emits an ethereal glow of the cosmos to an Indian steel bookshelf that's a feat of intricate geometry, just browsing here has its pleasures.

MAP 5: 888 Broadway, 212/473-3000, www.abchome.com; 10am-7pm Mon.-Wed. and Fri.-Sat., 10am-8pm Thurs., 11am-6:30pm Sun.

STORY

STORY

This unique boutique is a breath of fresh air, changing its inventory every 4-8 weeks and organizing it around fresh themes. Out of Office, for instance, conjured a beachy vacation vibe, featuring floaties, flip-flops, and taffy, while Remember When hearkened back to the 1990s and childhood, with slime, Keds, and composition books for sale, with some items displayed on classroom desks.

MAP 5: 144 10th Ave., 212/242-4853, http://thisisstory.com; 11am-8pm Mon.-Wed. and Fri.-Sat., 11am-9pm Thurs., 11am-7pm Sun.

Midtown, Hell's Kitchen, and Times Square

Map 6

CLOTHING AND ACCESSORIES

Tiffany & Co.

Immortalized by Audrey Hepburn in *Breakfast at Tiffany's*, the flagship of this famed jewelry store has been dealing diamonds to the city's elite since 1837. It has been housed in this limestone and granite art deco building since 1940. While Tiffany's sells some smaller items like charm bracelets in the under $250 category, it's not uncommon for necklaces and rings to cost more than the average house. Don't worry; you won't be alone if you go in just to browse.

MAP 6: 727 5th Ave., 212/755-8000, www.tiffany.com; 10am-7pm Mon.-Sat., noon-6pm Sun.

Tiffany & Co.

Topshop

This beloved British-based retailer focuses on bold fashions at reasonable prices. This location is its second largest in the country at 40,000 square feet (3,716 sq m) and features an extensive array of women's clothes and shoes, a section for men, as well as a whole floor devoted to boutique collaborations; the limited-edition offerings are restricted to five items per person. A shopping experience here is high energy, with Top 40 songs pumping through the sound system and neon lights illuminating clothing displays on all four floors.

MAP 6: 608 5th Ave., 212/757-8240, http://us.topshop.com; 10am-8pm Mon.-Wed., 10am-9pm Thurs.-Sat., 11am-8pm Sun.

Uniqlo

New York's flagship store of the Japanese clothing brand is the largest Uniqlo in the world. Among its usual offerings of men's, women's, and children's wear is a rotating line called SPRZ NY, which fuses fashion with art. From fleece pajamas adorned with Andy Warhol's Velvet Underground banana to winter hats stamped with Jean Michel-Basquiat's crown, there's an endless array of fun items that embody the brand's focus on creating an unbeatable combination of style, function, and value. Uniqlo's Ultra Light down jackets are a quintessential travel item, providing substantial outerwear that packs down to conveniently fit in your bag.

MAP 6: 666 5th Ave., 877/486-4756, www.uniqlo.com; 10am-9pm daily

DEPARTMENT STORES

Bergdorf Goodman

More fashion palace than department store—it's housed in an eight-floor art deco building on land that previously held a Vanderbilt mansion—Bergdorf

Goodman is in a shopping class of its own. With pristinely folded sweaters that cost a month's rent and dresses singularly displayed and lit like priceless pieces of art, it's a rarefied environment, to be sure, with clientele including New York socialites, Saudi princesses, and celebrities alike. The store's buyers regularly attend fashion shows all over the world and display new designs by haute couture royalty like Manolo Blahnik and Stella McCartney. A store restaurant serves standard New American-European high-end fare along with high tea and overlooks Central Park, as do the dressing rooms. For those wanting a glimpse of haute couture up close, there's no better place to browse.

Bergdorf Goodman

MAP 6: 754 5th Ave., 212/753-7300, www.bergdorfgoodman.com; 10am-8pm Mon.-Sat., 11am-7pm Sun.

Macy's

Macy's stores may be shuttering across the country, signaling the end of an era, but from its appearances in the classic film *Miracle on 34th Street* to David Sedaris's darkly hilarious "Santaland Diaries" essay about his experience working as an elf here during the Christmas season, this flagship location is embedded in New York's, as well as the country's, culture. Covering a whopping one million square feet (92,903 sq m) across 11 floors, this location opened in 1902, and wooden escalators installed in 1920 and 1930 remain functional to this day. Men's fashion can be found on the quirkily situated floor 1½, set away from the bustle of the rest of the store with its own escalator. This Macy's also has the largest shoe selection of any store in the world. During the end-of-year holidays, Macy's sponsors the city's Thanksgiving Day Parade, and

Santaland takes over the 8th floor, depicting Santa's fabled North Pole home base with colorful and detailed diorama scenes. And while all of New York's big department stores now host elaborate window displays during the season, Macy's was the first, beginning in 1899.

MAP 6: 151 W. 34th St., 212/695-4400, www.macys.com; 10am-10pm Mon.-Sat., 10am-9pm Sun.

Saks Fifth Avenue

Saks Fifth Avenue

Borne out of the luxe ambitions of two retail store operators, Horace Saks and Bernard Gimbel, Saks Fifth Avenue established this original flagship location in 1924. The 10-story department store stretches a full city block, and while its original signage in gold lettering remains above the store's 5th Avenue entrances, its interiors are now sleekly modern, covered in marble and host to elegantly arranged displays of high-end designer clothing and accessories. Saks is also famous for its holiday window displays, often creating vivid tableaus with themes rooted in pop culture. It celebrated, for instance, the 80th anniversary of Disney's *Snow White and the Seven Dwarfs* with displays incorporating meticulously detailed custom gowns for the titular princess, designed by Alberta Ferretti among others.

MAP 6: 611 5th Ave., 212/753-4000, www.saksfifthavenue.com; 10am-8:30pm Mon.-Sat., 11am-7pm Sun.

GIFTS AND HOME
✪ MoMA Design Store
If after a day of browsing galleries you're itching to bring a bit of artistic flair back home, head to the MoMA Design Store, just across the street from the museum and more than just another museum gift shop. Placing a premium on well-designed objects, the store's inventory ranges from children's toys to scarves to glassware and furniture. Some items can be overpriced, but a large part of the fun comes simply from examining the unconventional pieces you'll stumble upon, like a bowl that doubles as a sculpture, a clear glass pot that puts the water-boiling process on full display, and ThePresent Clock by Scott Thrift, awash in colors that wildly and seamlessly bleed into each other to capture a full year in a single rotation, beginning with the brilliant white light of winter solstice.

MAP 6: 44 W. 53rd St., 212/767-1050, http://store.moma.org; 10am-6:30pm Sun.-Thurs., 10am-9pm Fri.-Sat.

Muji
Walls of exposed brick and wood add warmth to this expansive Japanese catchall store, the brand's North American flagship. Muji, which roughly translates to "brand-less"— refreshingly, its wares are indeed unbranded—sells everything from flannel shirts to suitcases, not to mention stationery, housewares, and furniture, in a signature style that emphasizes simplicity. Prices range from cheap to reasonable, and the breadth of offerings can make you feel like you're walking through a sleeker Ikea.

MAP 6: 475 5th Ave., 212/447-1690, www.muji.com; 10am-9pm Mon.-Sat., 11am-8pm Sun.

Upper West Side and Upper East Side   Map 7

CLOTHING AND ACCESSORIES

✪ Fivestory

Located discreetly in a luxury town house, Fivestory is a boutique interpretation of the Barney's or Bergdorf shopping experience—though only for women. Prices are on the high end but sales can knock off 50 percent; though the deals are nice, they're not the main draw. Go for the curated experience and personalized styling advice on everything from wildly printed palazzo pants to a pink lizard clutch. Millennial founder Claire Distenfeld has a fondness for 1980s styles, so expect to see a lot of those mixed with items she's spotted around the world, from Paris to Morocco.

MAP 7: 18 E. 69th St., 212/288-1338, www.fivestoryny.com; 10am-6pm Mon.-Wed. and Fri., 10am-7pm Thurs., noon-6pm Sat.-Sun.

DEPARTMENT STORES

✪ Barneys New York

Barneys specializes in high-end men's and women's clothing and accessories and exudes classic city style: Its raincoat has long been a staple of well-heeled New Yorkers. This flagship department store sleekly stretches across nine floors and makes for an aesthetically pleasing shopping experience, with its muted cream colors, spacious layout, and digital directories. Staff are very attentive as well, especially if you dress the part and come in your dapper best. This store was also the site of a famous *Seinfeld* scene wherein Elaine is convinced Barneys mirrors make her look slimmer.

MAP 7: 660 Madison Ave., 212/826-8900, www.barneys.com; 10am-8pm Mon.-Tues. and Sat., 10am-9pm Wed.-Fri., 11am-7pm Sun.

Zitomer

This trilevel Upper East Side mainstay opened in 1950 as a pharmacy and has evolved into a full-fledged beauty shop geared toward women, with a select few skin care products for men. From natural bug repellents to high-end anti-humidity hair sprays and an array of makeup, sun hats, and lingerie, this family-owned store is a one-stop-shop for the well-polished.

MAP 7: 969 Madison Ave., 212/737-5560, www.zitomer.com; 9am-8pm Mon.-Fri., 9am-7pm Sat., 10am-6pm Sun.

BOOKS

Albertine

Housed in the former mansion of businessman and philanthropist Payne Whitney, and sharing space with the French embassy, this elegant bookshop features a range of French authors from Simone de Beauvoir to modern playwright Yasmina Reza, available in both English and French editions. The store's location on Museum Mile makes it a welcome place to take a break in between art gazing. Cozy up to one of its reading nooks. A ceiling painted like the night sky adds to the tranquility.

MAP 7: 972 5th Ave., 212/650-0070, www.albertine.com; 11am-7pm Mon.-Sat., 11am-6pm Sun.

Dylan's Candy Bar

some scenes with Julianne Moore and Millicent Simmonds here.

MAP 7: 2246 Broadway, 212/362-0706, http://westsiderbooks.com; 10am-9pm Mon.-Fri., 10am-10pm Sat., 11am-8pm Sun.

Westsider Rare and Used Books

This delightfully cluttered store, with bookshelves that stretch to the soaring ceilings, is a relic from when bookstores rather than department stores and chains lined Broadway. It's a better place to browse than to go looking for something specific, though the staff is knowledgeable. There's a dollar shelf of books piled high outside and many first editions inside. Todd Haynes's *Wonderstruck* shot

GOURMET GOODIES
Dylan's Candy Bar

The boutique chain of gourmet confections now has stores dotted around the country, but this three-floor original flagship still stands as its grandest incarnation. Think of it as an artful take on the classic candy shop, where the colorful lollipops—which come in flavors like rainbow sherbet—look like abstract paintings and come with a hidden message inside the stick. Other offerings include truffle peanut butter cups and artisanal gummies packaged both for everyday consumption and gifting.

MAP 7: 1011 3rd Ave., 646/735-0078, www.dylanscandybar.com; 10am-9pm Sun.-Thurs., 10am-11pm Fri.-Sat.

Harlem and Morningside Heights — Map 8

MARKETS
Malcolm Shabazz Harlem Market

This open-air market showcases vendors selling authentic African crafts and threads such as wax skirts and hand-carved figurines. Hair-braiding stalls are one of the more unique offerings. The worn banner that marks the entrance reads, "building a better community is our job," alluding to a time when the neighborhood was neglected by government officials. Bargaining with vendors is allowed though prices are generally reasonable.

The market's location just north of Central Park makes it an easy stop after meandering.

MAP 8: 52 W. 116th St., 212/987-8131; 10am-8pm daily

GOURMET GOODIES
Harlem Wine Gallery

Located just down the block from the Long Gallery Harlem and a short stroll up Adam Clayton Powell Jr. Boulevard from the north entrance of Central Park, this hip wine shop has a well-curated selection of fine varietals, with an emphasis on smaller vineyards. Staff picks are displayed via individual pedestals on a chalkboard wall, and the knowledgeable owners are happy to offer pairing suggestions.

MAP 8: 2067 Adam Clayton Powell Jr. Blvd., 646/912-9365, www. harlemwinegallery.com; 3pm-9pm Mon.-Tues., noon-9pm Wed.-Thurs. and Sun., noon-10pm Fri., 10am-10pm Sat.

Downtown Brooklyn, Dumbo, and Fort Greene Map 9

BOOKS
POWERHOUSE Arena

Situated in the shadow of the Manhattan Bridge, this store doesn't look like much upon first glance. Walk inside and its treasures begin to snap into focus. Near the entry, new releases are stacked in neat piles on a table, many signed by their Brooklyn-based authors. Local art for sale adorns the walls. Venture farther in and you'll find a series of church pews, used for the store's frequent readings.

MAP 9: 28 Adams St., 718/666-3049, www.powerhousebooks.com; 10am-7pm Mon.-Fri., 11am-7pm Sat.-Sun.

Williamsburg, Greenpoint, and Bushwick Map 10

CLOTHING AND ACCESSORIES
Better Than Jam

This tiny Bushwick storefront sells local handcrafted items, from pillows with quirky prints to rustic one-of-a-kind jewelry pieces, made at its onsite communal workshop. Browsing here is a great way to get a sense of the neighborhood talent. While there's a definite DIY vibe, prices aren't cheap. The store offers workshops so you can explore your own inner designer, and it also rents workspaces by the hour.

MAP 10: 20 Grattan St., 929/441-9596, http://betterthanjamnyc.com; 1pm-7pm Mon., Thurs., and Sun., 1pm-8pm Fri., noon-8pm Sat.

Brooklyn Industries

Before Brooklyn was a brand recognized around the world there was Brooklyn Industries, hawking borough-emblazoned T-shirts. Its first products were messenger bags fashioned out of recycled materials, so it's fitting that the stores now run on 100 percent wind power. The store has expanded to other locations since opening this first shop in Williamsburg in 2001 and now sells all sorts of threads and accessories for men and women looking to exude the neighborhood's muted cool.

MAP 10: 162 Bedford Ave., 718/486-6464, http://brooklynindustries.com; 11am-8pm Sun.-Thurs., 11am-9pm Fri.-Sat.

Hester Street Fair

New Yorkers hate malls, but they love a good market, which typically allows for the browsing of many vendors while snacking on something delicious. It is as much a social affair as it is a way to come away with a couple of unique souvenirs. While bargaining isn't always successful, it doesn't hurt to ask if sticker shock overwhelms.

- **Brooklyn Flea:** Brooklyn artisanal style comes to life with hundreds of vendors hawking vintage wares, handmade furniture, and collectible antiques spanning a range of budgets. The flea market (www.brooklynflea.com) holds court April-October 10am-5pm on Saturdays at cavernous renovated warehouse complex **Industry City** (241 37th St.) in the Sunset Park neighborhood and Sundays in Dumbo next to the **Manhattan Bridge archway** (80 Pearl St.).

- **Artists and Fleas:** With locations in **Williamsburg** (70 N. 7th St.; 10am-7pm Sat.-Sun.), **Chelsea Market** (88 10th Ave.; 10am-9pm Mon.-Sat., 10am-8pm Sun.), and **Soho** (568 Broadway; 11am-8pm Mon.-Sun.), Artists and Fleas (www.artistsandfleas.com) is situated near the city's epicenters of style. Think of it as a sanitized and pricier version of your neighborhood flea market with the possibility of celeb sightings. Local artists and photographers sell their prints alongside vendors of vintage threads, funky-chic jewelry, rare vinyl, and premium candles.

- **The Market NYC:** Market NYC (www.the marketynyc.com) has two locations—**The Market NYC Nolita** (290 Mulberry St.; noon-8pm Mon. and Wed.-Thurs., noon-9pm Fri., 11pm-9pm Sat., 11pm-7pm Sun.) and **Market34NYC** (130 W. 34th St.; 11am-9pm daily)—at which shoppers can talk with the emerging designers hosting the variety of stalls and maybe bargain down the already-discounted prices (note: this does not mean it's cheap). Items range from handmade soaps to jewelry to T-shirts and dresses.

- **Hester Street Fair:** This Lower East Side street fair (corner of Hester St. and Essex St., http://hesterstreetfair.com; 11am-6pm Sat., Apr.-Oct.) features homespun threads and jewelry along with food vendors who have turned their passion projects into careers, such as Melt Bakery and the Arancini Brothers; the latter now sells its inventively flavored rice balls at Madison Square Garden. Fairs are sometimes themed, such as an annual all-female vendors day. Special events are held on Sundays mid-late April.

Treehouse Brooklyn

Locally designed clothes and vintage items hang next to each other—sometimes from branches—at this woodsy-chic boutique. Located a few doors down from Beer Street, Treehouse is perfectly situated for buzzed browsing. From oversized dresses made of eco-friendly materials to a line of feather-based accessories by a local trapeze artist, the offerings walk a line between comfort-focused and eccentric. The store also sells its own in-house jewelry line that combines woven chains with shiny crystals.

MAP 10: 430 Graham Ave., 718/482-8733, www.treehousebrooklyn.com; 1pm-8pm Wed.-Sun.

VINTAGE
✪ Beacon's Closet

The original flagship location of this local favorite was just 900 square feet (84 sq m) when it opened in 1997 in Williamsburg on the cusp of the neighborhood's gentrification transformation. In 2014, it moved into this cavernous space—5,500 square feet (511 sq m)—just north in Greenpoint, allowing for even more perusing possibilities. Unlike other boutique vintage stores with these name brands, Beacon's Closet is surprisingly affordable; go ahead and hunt for that $15 Paul Smith shirt or vintage pair of Versace jeans.

MAP 10: 74 Guernsey St., 718/486-0816, http://beaconscloset.com; 11am-8pm daily

BOOKS AND MUSIC
✪ Rough Trade

Part record store and part performance venue, Rough Trade is a great place for music lovers. The front shop stocks rare vinyl-issued albums and often hosts record release parties, while a backroom performance

Beacon's Closet

space has great acoustics and regularly books top-notch indie acts like Father John Misty, Amanda Palmer, and the Bad Plus. For packed shows, try heading to the upstairs balcony for a better view.

MAP 10: 64 N. 9th St., 718/388-4111, www. roughtrade.com/us; 11am-11pm Mon.-Sat., 11am-9pm Sun.

Book Thug Nation

Secondhand literary fiction, film, and philosophy books line the shelves of this homespun spot created by a group of vendors who used to sell their volumes on the street. The small storefront also houses collections of plays, erotica, sci-fi, and poetry. Emphasis is placed on accessibility for all, borne out in the gently priced books and occasional community events. They'll buy your books, too—though given the store's well-curated nature, they're picky.

MAP 10: 100 N. 3rd St., www. bookthugnation.com; noon-8pm daily

Desert Island

Graphic novels have brought a new respect to the artistry of comics, and there's no better place in the city to explore the medium than at Desert Island. Housed in a former Italian bakery whose signage has been humorously amended with the words "and comic booklets," this small shop contains a comprehensive collection, from old issues of *Mad* magazine to free copies of the shop's own comic anthology *Smoke Signals*. It's a fun place to spot new talent.

MAP 10: 540 Metropolitan Ave., 718/388-5087, http://desertislandcomics. tumblr.com; noon-7pm Tues.-Sun.

WORD

This beloved Greenpoint bookstore hosts a bevy of events, including author readings and Q and A sessions, book group discussions to dissect works like Joan Didion's *Slouching Towards Bethlehem*, and trivia nights where you can win money to buy all the staff picks, which consistently feature some of the best new literary fiction. Events take place in the cozy basement, considered the store's living room. The bookstore answers questions and takes orders through its Twitter account, which has almost 35,000 followers.

MAP 10: 126 Franklin St., 718/383-0096, www.wordbookstores.com; 10am-9pm daily

GIFTS AND HOME
Abode

Abode is packed with the cluttered intensity of a vintage thrift shop but filled with a curated selection of artful and upscale homewares. From a Danish-designed set of carving knives to naturally cooling ceramic ice buckets from Finland, this shop has tons of nifty items you probably never thought you needed. Browse the limited edition art prints and hand-blown glass birds that riff on classic preppy mallard carvings to your heart's content, if not necessarily your wallet's.

MAP 10: 42 West St., 718/388-5383, http:// abode-newyork.com; noon-7pm Mon. and Wed.-Sat., noon-6pm Sun.

WHERE TO STAY

From bare-bones rooms with shared baths to suites overlooking Central Park, accommodations in New York City are as diverse as the residents of this melting pot city. That said, rooms in New York are pricey even for basic digs. And save for the highest-end accommodations, room sizes are considerably smaller than is typical for U.S. cities; it's not uncommon for standard rooms to offer little more than a bed and a narrow perimeter to walk around it. But you're not here to sleep, right? The best thing about New York City is that no matter where you decide to lay your head for the night, you're almost always guaranteed to be within spitting or walking distance of some form of entertainment—or at least a subway station that will get you there.

WestHouse Hotel

Traditional chain hotels are found across Manhattan and Downtown Brooklyn but are most concentrated in Midtown and Lower Manhattan's Financial District. Smaller guesthouse accommodations with private and shared baths can be found in prime areas like Chelsea for a relative bargain, while more upscale guesthouses can be found in the Village. Boutique hotels also abound in downtown neighborhoods like Soho and the Lower East Side. Meanwhile, the Upper East Side has some of New York's most historic and elegant hotels—think The Plaza—which are among the priciest in the city. On the other side of the spectrum, new hostels in Bushwick offer bare-bones prices for artfully constructed communal housing, and Harlem has affordable historic brownstone and town house options.

HIGHLIGHTS

✪ **BEST HOTEL FOR WATERFRONT VIEWS:** For stellar views in a tranquil setting, the **Conrad Hotel** can't be beat (page 310).

✪ **BEST BUDGET HOTEL FOR ART LOVERS:** At the stylish hostel-alternative **Carlton Arms Hotel**, you can spend the night beneath a Banksy mural, among many other options (page 317).

✪ **BEST HISTORIC HOTEL:** Stay in storied style at **The Plaza**, the chateau-style landmark where the powerful and famous have cavorted and slept (page 317).

✪ **BEST BOUTIQUE HOTEL:** Find downtown chic and a convenient Midtown location at the **WestHouse Hotel** (page 318).

✪ **BEST HOTEL WITH A LITERARY LEGACY:** Dorothy Parker traded barbs in the famous roundtable at the **Algonquin Hotel**, where you can spend the night in art deco digs (page 319).

✪ **BEST HOTEL TO HANG WITH THE LOCALS:** With an excellent rooftop bar, restaurant, and intimate cabaret venue, **Yotel** draws locals and out-of-towners alike (page 320).

✪ **BEST HOTEL TO FEEL LIKE ONE OF NEW YORK'S ELITE:** The **Surrey** replicates the feel of some of the city's most exclusive apartment buildings (page 321).

✪ **BEST HOTEL IN HIPSTER CENTRAL:** A stylish hideaway in the middle of Williamsburg, the **Wythe Hotel** balances the intimacy of a boutique hotel with the service of a large one (page 325).

PRICE KEY

$	Less than $200 per night
$ $	$200-350 per night
$ $ $	More than $350 per night

Conrad Hotel

CHOOSING WHERE TO STAY

Lower Manhattan

Once deserted after business hours, Lower Manhattan is an increasingly residential neighborhood and also home to some of the most extravagant hotels. These accommodations tend to offer more spacious digs as well as great views of the waterfront and the Statue of Liberty, and they charge for it. The area still has a somewhat staid corporate vibe—it is home, after all, to the Financial District—but some top-notch cocktail bars liven nighttime options, and you're conveniently close to the ferry dock for the Statue of Liberty and Ellis Island.

Soho and Tribeca

Cobblestone streets along with modern restaurants and cocktail bars appeal to locals and visitors alike. These downtown neighborhoods are moneyed but have a hip edge, and the hotels here reflect this sensibility, with lushly appointed but understated accommodations that tend toward the boutique.

East Village and Lower East Side

Hip restaurants, bars, theaters, and music clubs abound in the East Village and Lower East Side, sharing space with the tenement buildings resonant of the neighborhoods' immigrant, working-class past. The previous blight of certain areas, such as Alphabet City, has given way to gentrification, so while the neighborhoods retain their character, some parts have also been homogenized, with more banks and chains. Accommodations can be found across a wide range of budgets.

The Village and the Meatpacking District

A number of flashy hotels are in the Meatpacking District; smaller but no less pricey digs are in Greenwich Village. Meatpacking District hotels give you access to scene-y spots, while the Village boasts some of the prettiest blocks in the city, with leafy, cobblestoned streets. Both neighborhoods are desirable, and priced accordingly, although the Village offers more of a range.

Chelsea and Union Square

Chelsea is a nice alternative to Midtown—close enough to the action and almost as convenient, but far enough away to retain a sense of tranquility. It's a great place to stay if you want to be near galleries, the Theater District, and the Village, but without the madding crowds.

Midtown, Hell's Kitchen, and Times Square

Midtown offers the most convenience to major attractions, within walking distance of major sights like the Empire State Building, Rockefeller Center, and Times Square, and with easy access to subway lines that can take you anywhere else in the city. Options are available in a range of budgets here, and concentration is dense. The downside is the crowds and somewhat corporate workaday and touristy vibe. Hell's Kitchen on the west side feels more neighborhood-y but is still close to the action.

Upper West Side and Upper East Side

Museum fanatics and those who want to be near Central Park would do well to stay in either of these uptown

YOU WANT COMMANDING VIEWS:
Stay in **Lower Manhattan,** where many hotels have rooms overlooking the Hudson and East Rivers, along with the Statue of Liberty.

YOU WANT TO STAY IN THE CHICEST BOUTIQUE HOTELS:
Stay in **Soho,** where high-end properties cater to discerning guests.

YOU CRAVE CHARM ALONG WITH ACCESS:
Stay in **The Village,** particularly the West Village, where you'll be surrounded by quaint restaurants and bars on tree-lined streets.

YOU WANT TO PARTY:
Stay in the **Meatpacking District** if you're interested in the scene-y, clubby nightlife, or opt for **Williamsburg** or the **East Village and Lower East Side** for indie bars and live music.

YOU ONLY HAVE ONE WEEKEND:
Stay in **Midtown** or **Chelsea,** where the city's major amusements will be at your fingertips.

YOU LIKE TO GO FOR A MORNING WALK OR RUN:
Stay on the **Upper West Side** or **Upper East Side** and enjoy proximity to Central Park and its many paths, as well as a popular running route around its reservoir.

YOU'RE TRAVELING ON A BUDGET:
Stay in **Harlem** or **Bushwick,** which are farther out from the city center but give you more bang for your buck.

neighborhoods. More reasonably priced accommodations are on the Upper West Side, while the Upper East Side boasts some of the best five-star hotels in the city. Both areas are otherwise largely residential and leafy for those who want more of an escape from the throngs.

Harlem and Morningside Heights

Harlem is a good choice for reasonably priced accommodations, although transportation isn't quite as convenient. The A train is your best bet for getting to and from the neighborhood.

Downtown Brooklyn, Dumbo, and Fort Greene

Newly minted hotels in these Brooklyn neighborhoods put you within easy striking distance of some of the borough's attractions as well as downtown Manhattan.

Williamsburg, Greenpoint, and Bushwick

If you want to be in the midst of hipster culture, these neighborhoods are where it's at. The most luxurious hotels are in Williamsburg, offering sweeping river and skyline views along with a plethora of bars and restaurants within a short stroll. Bushwick is for the slightly more adventurous traveler looking for cool spots at more affordable price points and a rawer arts scene, and who doesn't mind a little more walking or longer train ride.

ALTERNATIVE LODGING OPTIONS

Many Airbnb (www.airbnb.com) listings are available throughout New York's many neighborhoods, with prices varying wildly from cheap to extravagant. Note that Airbnb has been particularly controversial here as the company's services impact the city's housing supply and contribute to price inflation in a city already known for high rents. While numerous regulations are in place to try to curb this, there isn't a way to check or guarantee that your Airbnb rental is technically legal.

All of the major chains have hotels near the airports, but staying in these locations isn't recommended as they're inconveniently located to the city; even with a car, commutes to Midtown can take more than an hour.

Lower Manhattan   Map 1

✪ Conrad Hotel $$$

Spacious modern digs with waterfront views are the draw of this outpost of the high-end brand of Hilton Hotels. You'll feel the elegance immediately upon entering the cavernous lobby, with its soaring ceilings and a larger-than-life Sol LeWitt abstract painting. Each of the 463 suites average over 430 square feet (40 sq m), unusually spacious for Manhattan lodging. Another bonus is the moderately priced Salvatore Barber Salon located in the hotel's atrium. A stellar restaurant and a rooftop bar complete the offerings.

MAP 1: 102 North End Ave., 212/945-0100, www.conradnewyork.com

The Beekman $$$

While the hotel itself has only been open since 2016, the site of The Beekman has a rich history. It hosted the New York premiere of *Hamlet* in 1761 and became a library frequented by Henry David Thoreau, Mark Twain, and Edgar Allan Poe in the 1800s. Rooms at the five-star property are eclectic, with custom-made beds featuring leather headboards and Carrara marble bathrooms with sliding barn doors. The Eat and Drink package offers a $50 credit per day that can be used at Tom Colicchio's Temple Court and Keith McNally's Augustine, both of which are located on the property.

MAP 1: 123 Nassau St., 212/233-2300, www.thebeekman.com

Andaz Wall Street $$

This four-star offshoot of the Hyatt brand features free Wi-Fi as well as complimentary snacks and nonalcoholic drinks in each of its 253 loft-style rooms. An outdoor plaza transforms into a beer garden serving local craft brews in the warmer months and also hosts a local farmers market. You can enjoy a complimentary wine hour served nightly year-round in the lobby.

MAP 1: 75 Wall St., 212/590-1234, http://wallstreet.andaz.hyatt.com

Gild Hall $$

This boutique hotel is designer Jim Walrod's stylish interpretation of a country lodge. With walls of rich knotty wood, elegantly appointed sofas, and a chandelier made of antlers in the lobby, plus claw-foot tubs in select rooms, Gild Hall stands out among the business hotels in the area. If you want to stay in the Financial District but feel like you're in Soho, this is the place.

MAP 1: 15 Gold St., 212/232-7700, www.thompsonhotels.com

Conrad Hotel

Soho and Tribeca   Map 2

SOHO
Crosby Street Hotel $$$

Light and airy elegance abound at
this 86-room boutique hotel, where
each room is individually styled by
owner Kit Kemp. Accommodations
range from standard rooms to two-
bedroom suites and all feature dramatic floor-to-ceiling windows and
generous-for-the-city proportions;
the smallest room is 340 square feet
(32 sq m). A screening room in the
basement regularly hosts film industry events, so don't be surprised to see
actors, writers, and directors passing
through the well-appointed hall-
ways. Every Sunday, the hotel hosts
dinner-and-a-movie events that are
open to the public, screening films
like *Wonder Woman* and featuring
a three-course feast from the on-site
restaurant, which has a lovely garden
terrace.

MAP 2: 79 Crosby St., 212/226-6400,
www.firmdalehotels.com

The James $$$

Tiny but stylish is the theme at this
well-situated boutique hotel. A standard room holds little more than a bed,
but it's quite a plush one and framed
by walls of floor-to-ceiling windows.

The James

The rooftop pool is likewise compact, a place to quietly soak while wearing sunglasses rather than swim laps. By late afternoon, the pool closes to make way for the hotel's trendy cocktail bar, Jimmy, which takes over the outdoor space. Drinks here veer toward the sweet and simple, and DJs typically bring a complex array of rhythmic mixes. Complimentary snacks can be found in a lounge near check-in, and the David Burke Kitchen is on-site. You have a lot to occupy you here, but venturing out is easy with multiple train lines a few blocks away at Canal Street. MAP 2: 27 Grand St., 212/465-2000, www.jameshotels.com

The Mercer Hotel $$$

This five-star hotel sits on a bustling corner in the heart of Soho, steps from the subway and surrounded by world-class restaurants, including Jean-Georges' Mercer Kitchen, located on the premises. Housed in a landmark Romanesque brick building and providing 24-hour room service, this boutique hotel of course comes with a high price tag. The 75 rooms at this sister property to Hollywood's Chateau Marmont start at over $500 a night for a cozy room and go up to nearly a grand for a lofted room. Suite prices are available on request. MAP 2: 147 Mercer St., 212/966-6060, www.mercerhotel.com

Soho Grand $$$

This iconic hotel wears the carefully chosen clothes of a boutique hotel but is much larger in size, with 365 rooms all decorated with stylized restraint and echoes of the neighborhood's industrial past. Unlike other dens of sophistication, it happily welcomes pets for no extra charge; notify the hotel in advance and staff will trick your room out with organic treats, bedding for your furry friend, water bowls, and doggy bags (the hotel also has its own dog park). Alternatively, those wanting a temporary pet for their trip can request a goldfish in their room, on the house. MAP 2: 310 W. Broadway, 212/965-3000, www.sohogrand.com

TRIBECA
The Greenwich Hotel $$$

Occupying a wrought-iron building on a charming cobblestone stretch of Greenwich Street, this hotel is the brainchild of legendary actor Robert De Niro. It exudes the same rough-hewed old-world charm as the excellent Italian restaurant Locanda Verde, also housed in the building. Each of the hotel's 88 rooms is uniquely designed and features silk rugs from Tibet, Moroccan tiles, or Italian Carrara marble, as well as Duxiana mattresses. An array of gadgets—including laptops—are available to guests for use at no charge, whether you're staying in a standard courtyard room or the 2,800-square-foot penthouse for $15,000 a night. MAP 2: 377 Greenwich St., 212/941-8900, www.thegreenwichhotel.com

Duane Street Hotel $$

Minutes from the World Trade Center, Chinatown, Hudson River Park, and multiple train lines, this boutique hotel appeals to a wide swath of travelers. With just 43 rooms, it can provide personal touches like a lending library of classic books, complimentary iPads, and bicycles to explore the city. The 11-foot ceilings give the rooms the airy feel of the loft residences that abound in the neighborhood. Fine Italian linens by Bellino, toiletries by L'Occitane, and Egyptian cotton bathrobes by Scandia complete the picture MAP 2: 130 Duane St., 212/964-4600, www.duanestreethotel.com

East Village and Lower East Side   Map 3

EAST VILLAGE

The Bowery Hotel $$$

A wood-paneled lobby with well-appointed furniture and tropical plants welcomes guests to the stylishly quirky Bowery Hotel. It blends a modern sensibility—amenities include 400-thread-count sheets and free bike and laptop rentals—with Old New York elegance and is popular with musicians and filmmakers; don't be surprised to see someone like Nick Cave relaxing in a club chair near reception.

MAP 3: 335 Bowery, 212/505-9100, http://theboweryhotel.com

LOWER EAST SIDE

Hotel on Rivington $$

Soak in an oversized tub while peering out through floor-to-ceiling windows at the Williamsburg Bridge and East River in select rooms at this luxe spot. The clientele are often refined, hip, and eager to be in the heart of the LES. The J, M, Z, and F subway lines down the block make getting around easy, an endless array of restaurants are nearby, and one of the city's best dive bars—Welcome to the Johnsons—is across the street.

MAP 3: 107 Rivington St., 212/475-2600, www.hotelonrivington.com

The Ludlow Hotel $$

With Marshall amps mounted to the ceiling in its lofty atrium and some rooms featuring record players and Ramones records, The Ludlow exudes a punk-chic vibe. The 175-room hotel is one of the newest lodging additions to the neighborhood and at a price point lower than the similarly stylish Bowery Hotel. Oak-paneled walls, antique chandeliers, and skyline views through large casement windows create a dramatic backdrop for your home base. Located across the street from Katz's Deli, around the corner from the Mercury Lounge, and just a three-minute walk to the F subway line, the location is prime for soaking up LES culture.

MAP 3: 180 Ludlow St., 212/432-1818, http://ludlowhotel.com

SIXTY LES Hotel $$

A sleek black-and-white color scheme drives the design of the minimalist SIXTY LES Hotel, which delivers a four-star experience at three-star prices. With the F line down the block, the hotel is ideally situated to make uptown sightseeing trips easy while keeping a downtown base. Dirt Candy, the New Museum, and Doughnut Plant are nearby, as is the Metrograph, New York Theatre Workshop, and countless other nightlife options. Rainfall showers and plush robes are a few of the standard in-room amenities.

MAP 3: 190 Allen St., 877/460-8888, www.sixtyhotels.com/lower-east-side

The Village and the Meatpacking District

Map 4

GREENWICH VILLAGE

Walker Hotel $$$

This property's Georgian facade makes for a distinctive entrance, standing in contrast to the prewar buildings it abuts. This 113-room, four-star hotel is located on a quiet, leafy side street but is just a stroll from Village hot spots. Each of the rooms is named for a street in the neighborhood and decorated with retro flair to emphasize the area's history.

MAP 4: 52 W. 13th St., 212/375-1300, www.walkerhotel.com

The Marlton Hotel

The Marlton Hotel $$

A former single-room-occupancy hotel turned NYU dorm was again transformed in 2013 into this boutique hotel, quickly shedding its utilitarian skin. Although rooms are tiny, with room for little more than the comfy beds, the common lounge areas are spacious and inviting, with dim lighting, a nearly year-round fireplace, and a skylighted restaurant that serves a complimentary continental breakfast. It's also located just a couple of blocks from Washington Square Park. Creative types looking for inspiration can take note that Jack Kerouac wrote his 1958 interracial romance novella *The Subterraneans* while staying in the hotel's SRO incarnation.

MAP 4: 5 W. 8th St., 212/321-0100, http:// marltonhotel.com

The Jane Hotel $

Once a sailors' home and more recently a rent-by-the-hour motel, the Jane is now a gussied-up 200-room design hotel, located in the charming West Village, the western end of Greenwich Village. Its motto, though, is to house guests with "more dash than cash," and to that end it offers cheap prices on single and bunk bed cabins with shared baths. For theater lovers, the original production of *Hedwig and the Angry Inch* was performed in the hotel's now lavishly appointed ballroom. Perks include free Wi-Fi and bikes, the latter of which you can ride along the Hudson River just across the street.

MAP 4: 113 Jane St, 212/924-6700, www. thejanenyc.com

MEATPACKING DISTRICT

Hotel Gansevoort $$$

This trendy hotel has 186 guest rooms with 400-thread-count Egyptian cotton linens. It has a pool table in the lobby and a year-round rooftop bar featuring both indoor and outdoor spaces that, on a warm night, feels like a portal to Miami with its clean white lines and house music pulsing throughout. Hotel guests have exclusive access to the rooftop pool, even at night, an unusual amenity for the city.

MAP 4: 18 9th Ave., 212/206-6700, www.gansevoorthotelgroup.com

The Standard $$$

Located in the Meatpacking District right on The High Line, this luxury hotel is ideal for people who have cash to burn and want to be in the middle of everything. The Standard features a beer garden, rooftop bar Le Bain, an art gallery, a seasonal ice-skating rink, and a penthouse club (Top of the Standard) that hosts exclusive celeb-saturated events like the Met Gala's after-party. The 338 rooms are pretty nice, too, with floor-to-ceiling windows and a retro-chic style.

MAP 4: 848 Washington St., 212/645-4646, www.standardhotels.com/newyork

Chelsea and Union Square

Map 5

Ace Hotel $$

With plaid comforters and boxy wooden bed frames, the hip Ace Hotel has dorm room chic down. Just north of Madison Square Park, it has everything from rooms with bunk beds and a mini-fridge for late-night food binges to loft suites. The hotel lobby is always bustling and a favorite of locals and guests alike for its comfy couches, while the basement features an event space often rented out for film press junkets—so you might see big-name actors and directors floating through.

MAP 5: 20 W. 29th St., 212/679-2222, www.acehotel.com/newyork

Chelsea Pines Inn $$

Contained in an 1850s five-story walk-up row house, this tiny gay-owned and -operated inn is decorated with old Hollywood film posters. Common space is minimal but there's a small lounge/kitchen where a continental breakfast is set out each morning and which can be enjoyed in the lush private garden. The inn sits on the south border of Chelsea, putting it steps away from the Whitney Museum, The High Line, and trains that will take you uptown or out to Brooklyn in less than 20 minutes.

MAP 5: 317 W. 14th St., 888/546-2700, http://www.chelseapinesinn.com

The GEM Hotel $$

This three-star boutique hotel punches above its class. It has a charming, well-appointed lobby decked out with stylish furniture and a tiny six-stool bar, and rooms are equally cozy: They barely fit a full- or queen-size bed but incorporate fresh, modern decor and nice perks like down pillows and free Wi-Fi. The hotel's location on a pleasant tree-lined street off 8th Avenue in Chelsea puts it within walking distance of many restaurants and bars in the surrounding blocks.

MAP 5: 300 W. 22nd St., 212/675-1911, www.thegemhotel.com

I REMEMBER YOU WELL: THE LEGENDARY CHELSEA HOTEL

By the time novelist/poet-turned-troubadour Leonard Cohen sang "Chelsea Hotel No. 2" about his hookup with Janis Joplin in one of its rooms, the Hotel Chelsea (more often known by its inverse, the Chelsea Hotel) already had a rich history colored by some of the country's most important artists. Built as cooperative apartment housing in the 1880s by Philip Hubert at 222 West 23rd Street and conceived as something of a utopic community, it originally housed people from various socioeconomic realms, from blue-collar workers to artists to wealthy families. It went bankrupt in 1905, when it took a turn as a luxury hotel. From then until World War II, it attracted an upscale clientele, including Mark Twain.

Postwar, the hotel fell into decline, but began earning its true fame. During the 1950s, painter Jackson Pollock, theater critic Kenneth Tynan, and poet Dylan Thomas all called it home for a time. Thomas died here in 1953. Arthur Miller lived here after his split with Marilyn Monroe, and Bob Dylan wrote songs in room 211, just two floors down from Cohen and Joplin's tryst. William Burroughs spent time writing in the hotel, as did Arthur C. Clarke, who dreamed up *2001: A Space Odyssey* while here. Beat generation titan Jack Kerouac spent a night of passion with erudite wit Gore Vidal, and punk rock star Sid Vicious was accused of killing his girlfriend Nancy Spungen at the hotel. The density of artists was not a coincidence; longtime innkeeper Stanley Bard let many whose work he admired stay for free in exchange for paintings and other works, turning the hotel into a de facto artist colony. In 2011, Bard was outvoted by his co-owners and the hotel was sold to real estate magnate Joseph Chetrit for $80 million. An upscale boutique hotel is in the works by developers SIR, who bought the space in 2016. Opening is slated for 2019 with amenities including a greenhouse and a rooftop gym and spa. Fifty apartments of long-time residents will be preserved under the New York City Rent Stabilization Act, and art will continue to decorate the walls.

Gramercy Park Hotel $$

Stay here if you want access to the city's only private park. Other perks include a rooftop deck and an exclusive bar featuring custom furniture designed by Julian Schnabel and occasional intimate performances by national acts like the Head and the Heart. Walls are lined with a rotating selection of art from masters like Andy Warhol and Jean-Michel Basquiat and rooms are appointed in vibrant colors, grafting a modern sensibility onto the hotel's throwback elegance. While rooms here are by no means cheap, they are considerably less than many other luxe options.

MAP 5: 2 Lexington Ave., 212/920-3300, www.gramercyparkhotel.com

The NoMad Hotel $$

This modern hotel, named for the neighborhood in which it sits, features king-size beds in sleek rooms and a casual eatery created by Eleven Madison Park's Daniel Humm that's known for its lavish burger. Most of the 168 rooms have claw-foot bathtubs and all have handmade vintage Heriz rugs from Iran. Free Wi-Fi, 24-hour room service, and loaner laptops and iPads round out the amenities.

MAP 5: 1170 Broadway, 212/796-1500, www.thenomadhotel.com

W New York - Union Square $$

Housed in a landmark 1911 beaux arts building, this W has more history than most of the chain's locations. High ceilings and archways in the lobby welcome guests, as does a dramatic winding staircase. Many rooms on the upper floors feature expansive city views. It's directly across from Union Square and its hub of subway lines, which makes it an exceptionally convenient location as well as puts you at the crossroads of various neighborhoods and proximate to numerous restaurants, bars, and theaters.

MAP 5: 201 Park Ave S., 212/253-9119, www.wnewyorkunionsquare.com

✪ Carlton Arms Hotel $

A single room with a shared bathroom can be had for as little as $60 during the winter at this quirky, stylish hostel-alternative, while a room with private bath during prime season goes for about double that. Besides a prime location that combines convenience and tranquility, just north of Gramercy Park, the main draw to this hotel is the unique artwork adorning its guest-room walls. From oversized portraits to lush landscapes, most of the art has been done by up-and-comers who painted the rooms in exchange for a free stay. Room 5B features colorful murals of cartoonish animals by none other than famed street artist Banksy—he painted them in 1999 when he was just another struggling artist.

MAP 5: 160 E. 25th St., 212/679-0680, http://carltonarms.com

Midtown, Hell's Kitchen, and Times Square   Map 6

✪ The Plaza $$$

Easily the city's most recognizable hotel and a National Historic Landmark, The Plaza was designed in the style of a chateau and stands out even among the elegant buildings of adjacent Central Park and 5th Avenue. Inspired by Louis XV French decor and now managed by Fairmont Hotels, it retains its allure. When it opened in 1907 it was just $2.50 a night. Adjusted for inflation, that would be roughly $60 now, about a tenth of the cost of a standard room today. The Beatles stayed here during their first visit to the United States in 1964, and Truman Capote hosted his famous Black and White Ball here in 1966 to promote the release of *In Cold Blood*.

Standard rooms come with a king-size bed and a bathroom decked out with 24-karat-gold fixtures that might make you feel like the kid in *Home Alone 2* playing adult. Family-size rooms sleep six on two queen beds and a pullout sofa and feature a marble wet bar.

The Plaza's dining room, the Palm Court, remains a quintessential place for afternoon tea, with its vaulted dome ceiling and tropical plant greenery. For an added kick, order an Orson Welles Negroni or Gatsby Mint Julep. A food hall in the basement offers excellent sandwiches from No. 7 Sub, as well as uniquely thin pizza—meant to be eaten rolled up—from Pizza Rollio. These are nice

The Plaza

WestHouse Hotel

amenities for guests as well as good options for those who just want a taste of The Plaza's glamour without shelling out for a room.

MAP 6: 768 5th Ave., 212/759-3000, www.fairmont.com/the-plaza-new-york

○ WestHouse Hotel $$$

WestHouse is located steps from storied institutions such as Carnegie Hall and MoMA, and just north of Times Square. While the city pulsates just outside the hotel's doors, its gleaming wood-paneled lobby and lounge offer tranquility; the latter is a perfect spot to sip a rare whiskey or just unwind. Breakfast, served from the perch of the 23rd-floor terrace, is included in your stay, as are a selection of alcoholic drinks and bites from 5pm to 8pm daily. Room have a luxuriously plush feel with oversized padded headboards and supple leather chairs.

MAP 6: 201 W. 55th St., 800/355-9378, www.westhousehotelnewyork.com

The Chatwal $$$

Although just feet from Times Square, soundproofing keeps the noise down in The Chatwal's art deco rooms, which feature oversized rainfall showers, Jacuzzi tubs, and bidets. Many also feature balconies or terraces on which to enjoy a predinner cocktail, while the in-house restaurant is Jeffrey Zakarian's Lambs Club. Open to the public, the restaurant features an 18th-century French fireplace popular for private parties for the city's literary and artistic elite. Also on-site is a spa with a dimly lit pool designed for unwinding.

MAP 6: 130 W. 44th St., 212/764-6200, www.thechatwalny.com

Four Seasons New York $$$

I. M. Pei designed this 52-story art deco icon rife with Old New York elegance, featuring high ceilings and French limestone columns. Standard rooms offer shoeshine services, unlimited health club access, and complimentary rides in a Rolls-Royce within a 12-block radius. The hotel's prime location on the border of Midtown and the Upper East Side makes sightseeing from here easy, and the luxurious rooms—with handmade king-size beds, custom oak desks, and oversized bathrooms covered in rare Italian marble—make coming back home after a day out a treat in itself. Sweeping views from Central Park to the Hudson River are a bonus.

MAP 6: 57 E. 57th St., 212/758-5700, www.fourseasons.com/newyork

Kimpton Ink48 Hotel $$$

With their free evening cocktail hour and reliably plush beds, Kimpton Hotels are always a good choice. Several locations are in the city but this Hell's Kitchen outpost sports a massive roof deck with commanding views of the Hudson River to the west and the gleaming Midtown skyline to the east. It also features a locavore restaurant perfect for times when leaving the building for dinner after a long day of sightseeing is too much to bear. Rooms are bright and airy, with cozy beds, walk-in showers, and soaking tubs. Many also have sweeping skyline or river views.

MAP 6: 653 11th Ave., 877/843-8869, http://www.ink48.com

The London $$$

Modern swank dominates the spacious digs at this all-suite hotel. The lobby features towering ceilings, a strikingly patterned floor, and large abstract paintings at which to gaze while awaiting check-in. Rooms are a minimum of 500 square feet (46 sq m) and many sport views of nearby Central Park and the Hudson River. A gym and free Wi-Fi are added bonuses along with dual showerhead stalls. A hotel bar serves food all day, including an express lunch of plates like fish-and-chips and steak frites.

MAP 6: 151 W. 54th St., 212/307-5000, www.thelondonnyc.com

✪ Algonquin Hotel $$

Opened in 1902, the Algonquin has a rich literary history. Designated a Literary Landmark, the hotel was host to the legendary Algonquin Round Table, composed of creatives including writers and actors, who met daily at Algonquin's restaurant between 1919 and 1929 for quick-witted repartee over lunch. Members included Dorothy Parker as well as Harold Ross, who founded the *New Yorker* in 1925 after winning a lucrative game of poker against fellow members. The hotel's restaurant operates to this day serving standard American fare at inflated prices. The Algonquin's 181 rooms underwent a sleek renovation in 2012 while maintaining their art deco allure. In addition to well-appointed furniture, each room comes with the latest issue of the *New Yorker* and a privacy door sign that reads, "Quiet Please. Writing the Great American Novel."

MAP 6: 59 W. 44th St., 212/840-6800, www.algonquinhotel.com

Viceroy Central Park $$

Located a couple of blocks south of Central Park and down the block from Carnegie Hall, Viceroy offers a great location for those who want the city's top institutions at their fingertips while maintaining a sense of tranquility. The hotel's smartly appointed rooms can be had for a relative bargain, particularly in the winter months, despite an annoying $29 amenity fee per night per room (which includes bottled water, high-speed

Algonquin Hotel

Internet access, and gym use) and $10 room service/mini-bar credit. On-site restaurant **Kingside** serves a wide-ranging menu from sushi to steak and is operated by the Gerber Group, which owns the famed Campbell bar in Grand Central.

MAP 6: 120 W. 57th St., 212/830-8000, www.viceroyhotelsandresorts.com/en/newyork

Warwick New York $$

If you'd like MoMA in your backyard and Central Park just a few blocks away, the Warwick will be your perfect home away from home. Built by William Randolph Hearst in 1926 for his mistress, Marion Davies, the hotel has updated interiors but retains its historic charm. It has spacious standard rooms as well as one-bedroom suites, the latter of which feel more like prewar apartments than hotel rooms, with terraces overlooking the Midtown skyline. The lobby also has a by-gone-days elegance, with chandeliers

illuminating elevators marked with the phrase "this car up." Fittingly, Internet access isn't free here, but daily newspapers are.

MAP 6: 65 W. 54th St., 212/247-2700, http://warwickhotels.com/new-york

✪ Yotel $

Tiny rooms at (relatively) tiny prices should be the motto at this Hell's Kitchen spot. Depending on the season, you can snag a room for as little as $75 a night. While it'll feature little more than a place to sleep, these micro-dwellings are well appointed with comfy beds, floor-to-ceiling windows, and rain showers (located just steps from the bed). The 4th floor is a giant social space that's also popular with New Yorkers. It features a massive rooftop terrace with Midtown skyline views and is home to an excellent Israeli restaurant, the **Green Fig**. Movies are screened there in the summer. A cabaret space in Yotel, the **Green Room 42**, also serves the restaurant's food and hosts occasionally intimate shows by Broadway performers like Alice Ripley.

MAP 6: 570 10th Ave., 646/449-7700, www.yotel.com

citizenM $

A Netherlands-based chain aiming to provide "affordable luxury," citizenM is a beacon of hip in the Times Square area with its eye-catching combination of steel, glass, and concrete. The lobby feels like a stylish apartment, with towering bookshelves and comfy couches in place of bellhops. Self-check-in and checkout are designed for expediency while rooms—though small—feature neat amenities like iPad-controlled blackout blinds and king-size beds.

MAP 6: 218 W. 50th St., 212/461-3638, www.citizenm.com

Hotel Edison $

For bargain accommodations in Times Square, wedged between Broadway theaters and nearby several subway lines, it's hard to beat the Edison. This massive art deco hotel features renovated digs with amenities that punch above their price class, like C. O. Bigelow bath products, free walking tours, and complimentary light bites, wine, and live jazz in the lobby (5pm-6pm Tues.-Wed. and Fri.). Rooms are simple and modern, featuring USB charging ports, free daily bottled water, and either two queen beds or one king.

MAP 6: 228 W. 47th St., 800/637-7070, www.edisonhotelnyc.com

Upper West Side and Upper East Side   Map 7

UPPER EAST SIDE

✪ The Surrey $$$

Walking into this boutique hotel feels a lot like entering one of the storied apartment buildings on nearby Park Avenue. The intimate lobby—it's not designed to hold many because it's intended for the privileged few—conveys its exclusivity. An art gallery containing works by William Kentridge and Jenny Holzer is tucked behind reception for hotel guests and locals in the know. The hotel has a measured elegance, with simple, often muted color schemes, stylish furniture that's never flashy, and service that's attentive but not hovering. Acclaimed chef Daniel Boulud's Café Boulud and adjoining Bar Pleiades are located here. Despite a cozy feeling in the public areas, including the guests-only roof deck, rooms are quite large and feature luxe Duxiana beds.

MAP 7: 20 E. 76th St., 212/288-3700, www.thesurrey.com

The Carlyle $$$

Built in 1930, The Carlyle is the most iconic hotel on the Upper East Side, a mix of residences and hotel rooms. During her life, actor and singer Elaine Stritch lived here, and President John F. Kennedy also owned an apartment here in which rumor has it his affair with Marilyn Monroe took place; she would allegedly sneak in through the hotel's secret tunnels, designed to maximize guest privacy. The 190 guest rooms are done up in classic style by designers like Dorothy Draper and Thierry Despont, and some rooms boast great views of Central Park. The on-site Café Carlyle is an exclusive cabaret that features a weekly big band jazz show by Woody Allen, and countless others have graced the stage as well; with hefty prices, it's mainly a nightlife den for the wealthiest New Yorkers.

MAP 7: 35 E. 76th St., 212/744-1600, www.rosewoodhotels.com/en/the-carlyle-new-york

The Mark Hotel $$$

This five-star Renaissance Revival hotel offers a remarkable number of luxury amenities to those staying in its 156 rooms and suites. It hosts a restaurant run by master chef Jean-Georges Vongerichten, a hair salon by celebrity stylist Frederic Fekkai, and personal shoppers from Bergdorf Goodman, and it makes available a fleet of monogrammed custom-built Republic bicycles and Jean-Georges-created picnic baskets for enjoyment at nearby Central Park. The Mark also offers to set up a tent for children staying in suites for a rarefied "fort" experience, and Maclaren strollers are available to help cart little ones around. Sweet treats by French bakery Ladurée are left bedside on your first night, while pups enjoy dog beds and custom place mats.

MAP 7: 25 E. 77th St., 212/744-4300, www.themarkhotel.com

The Pierre $$$

Built in the 1920s, The Pierre is a fixture of elegance on 5th Avenue, and a designated historic landmark. Its location near Central Park means some of its 189 rooms boast spectacular views of it. In addition to complimentary shoeshine and dog amenities for pups under 15 pounds, the hotel will cart you around the neighborhood in a Jaguar, gratis. Despite an extensive $100 million renovation in 2007, it's retained many of its neo-Renaissance flourishes, including the famous rotunda with a preserved mural by Edward Melcarth depicting a bucolic landscape with prominent New Yorkers such as Jacqueline Onassis and mythical figures alike. Guest rooms have a more modern look and start at a spacious 300 square feet (28 sq m).

MAP 7: 2 E. 61st St., 212/838-8000, www.thepierreny.com

UPPER WEST SIDE

Mandarin Oriental New York $$$

Mandarin Oriental's lavish New York hotel sits atop the Time Warner Center mall on Columbus Circle. Its 244 guest rooms and suites look out onto the Hudson River, Central Park, and/or the city skyline, and feature floor-to-ceiling windows to maximize views. Dame Helen Mirren and architect I. M. Pei are among the hotel's many fans. The restaurant, lounge, and cocktail bar are decorated with the kind of bold fancy that's central to the hotel's brand, with shimmering chandeliers and lushly appointed spaces that fuse Western and Eastern opulence. Private yoga sessions and a naturally lit lap pool are probably the hotel's subtlest touches.

MAP 7: 80 Columbus Cir., 212/805-8800, www.mandarinoriental.com/new-york

The Empire Hotel $$

Located across the street from Lincoln Center, The Empire Hotel was once home to famed composer Aaron Copland. It has a seasonal rooftop pool deck for guests. A separate rooftop restaurant-lounge is open to the public and a popular spot for parties thrown by Comedy Central and the like. The hotel's iconic red neon sign has been lighting up the Upper West Side for decades, and you can get up close to it from the roof deck. Rooms are smallish but come equipped with nice amenities like rain showers and cotton bathrobes. Wi-Fi is, unfortunately, not free outside of the lobby and mezzanine, but there is a 24-hour complimentary fitness center.

MAP 7: 44 W. 63rd St., 212/265-7400, http://empirehotelnyc.com

Hotel Beacon $$

This 1928 beaux arts hotel is named not for the theater next door, but an airway beacon built on its roof. It's conveniently located: Central and Riverside Parks, as well as the 2/3 subway line, are just a stone's throw away. The stylish hotel bar offers a couple of happy hours (10pm-close Sun.-Thurs. and 3pm-6pm daily) while the diner

Viand Cafe next door is good for quick and casual bites. The 270-plus guest rooms come with a kitchenette, perfect for reheating leftovers or preparing a simple meal bought at Fairway Market across the street.

MAP 7: 2130 Broadway, 212/787-1100, www.beaconhotel.com

Hostelling International New York $

New York City's only outpost of the HI hostel chain offers its usual clean dorm-style lodging as well as an expansive backyard and free/cheap walking tours of Central Park, the Brooklyn Bridge, and other landmark attractions. Wi-Fi is complimentary, and some rooms include breakfast and slippers for the bathroom. It also hosts a bevy of free events, like a comedy night and afternoon tea and cookies, to encourage mingling with fellow guests.

MAP 7: 891 Amsterdam Ave., 212/932-2300, www.hiusa.org

Harlem and Morningside Heights   Map 8

HARLEM

Aloft Harlem $$

Aloft Harlem is much like the Starwood brand's other hotels, offering dorm-room chic. But a pool table in the lounge encourages lingering and draws a youthful crowd, as does the 24/7 grab-and-go food options. King-size beds provide comfort while the hotel's location near the express A train puts Midtown a mere 20 minutes away. Charles' Country Pan Fried Chicken and Red Rooster are

both a short walk away, and the Apollo Theater is even closer.

MAP 8: 2296 Frederick Douglass Blvd., 212/749-4000, www.aloftharlem.com

The Harlem Flophouse $

This historic Victorian town house was built in 1890 as a private residence before being converted to low rent-lodging in 1917. The term "flophouse" came about during the Harlem Renaissance when artists were looking for cheap shelter. Though it was renovated in

2000 with refinished wood floors and period furniture in double-bedded rooms bearing the names of famous local musicians like Thelonious Monk and Duke Ellington, prices remain quite reasonable. Be warned of some no-frills aspects: no air-conditioning or housekeeping service, and no check-in after 11pm. Book early because the five rooms sell out quickly.

MAP 8: 242 W. 123rd St., 646/632-1960, http://harlemflophouse.com

Harlem Grand $

Harlem Grand's rooms feature en suite baths, some with claw-foot tubs, and a ramshackle arrangement of cozy furniture. The accommodation also has some lavish furnishings and a piano room. It sits on the edge of Harlem just down the block from Morningside Park. The A train is nearby, making travel to Midtown, Chelsea, the Village, and Lower Manhattan cheap and easy.

MAP 8: 343 W. 122nd St., 646/807-9789

The Melva Inn $

Located in a turn-of-the-century brownstone, Melva offers a similar experience as The Harlem Flophouse; one notable difference is that it has air-conditioning. (New York summer nights can be unbearably sticky: Playwright Arthur Miller wrote an essay for the *New Yorker* of the trying experience titled "Before Air-Conditioning.") Sexy Taco/Dirty Cash and Amy Ruth's are just a couple blocks away, and Central Park is about a 10-minute walk south on Lenox Avenue, making this a convenient place to call home. The five newly renovated guest rooms are named after famous Harlem residents like Langston Hughes and Maya Angelou and retain historic details like fireplaces and exposed brick.

MAP 8: 68 W. 120th St., 646/650-5240 (email themelvainn@gmail.com prior to calling), http://themelvainn.com

Downtown Brooklyn, Dumbo, and Fort Greene   Map 9

Hotel Indigo Brooklyn $

Located in Downtown Brooklyn alongside both towering modern structures as well as old row houses, Hotel Indigo is just a couple stops from Manhattan on subway lines that are steps away. The style is on the bland side of nice, but the prices are quite good, pets are allowed, and there's a roof deck along with free Wi-Fi. Artwork from the Brooklyn Arts Council helps to create a cultured neighborhood vibe and brownstone

Brooklyn is within easy walking distance.

MAP 9: 229 Duffield St., 718/254-7800, www.ihg.com/hotelindigo

NU Hotel $

Equal parts chic and cheap, NU Hotel features high-ceilinged rooms that lend a loftiness to the digs and provide ample space for murals in its Perspective rooms—select guest rooms with hand-painted murals by local artists featuring Brooklyn

NU Hotel

themes. There are also standard queen and king rooms, as well as a bunk bed suite that sleeps four with a bunk bed and a queen bed. Free Wi-Fi, a pets-welcome policy, loaner bikes, and complimentary continental breakfast round out the perks. The hotel's location on Smith Street puts you in the midst of dozens of bars and restaurants and within walking distance of BAM and Brooklyn Bridge Park.

MAP 9: 85 Smith St., 718/852-8585, www.nuhotelbrooklyn.com

The Tillary Hotel Brooklyn $

The Tillary offers some of the most stylish digs in its price class, combining mid-century modern furniture with carefully measured bursts of gold and dramatic light fixtures. While it's located in a bit of a dead zone that's currently awash in new condo development, Dumbo and Fort Greene are within walking distance, as are several train lines. Frette linens and soundproof windows add comfort to the rooms, and there's a beer garden on-site and free Wi-Fi throughout.

MAP 9: 85 Flatbush Ave Ext., 718/329-9537, www.thetillaryhotel.com

Williamsburg, Greenpoint, and Bushwick — Map 10

WILLIAMSBURG
The William Vale $$$

Even if it didn't have an artisanal doughnut shop on its premises (it's home to Du's Donuts and Coffee), this five-star hotel has a lot to offer: A pool with cabanas, commanding East River and Manhattan skyline views, and 181 rooms all featuring balconies and floor-to-ceiling windows. Also here is a burger joint that's run out of a vintage Airstream helmed by acclaimed Locanda Verde chef Andrew Carmellini, who also oversees other on-site dining options here. The hotel is located in Williamsburg, just south of Greenpoint, and down the block from McCarren Park.

MAP 10: 111 N. 12th St., 718/631-8400, www.thewilliamvale.com

✪ Wythe Hotel $$

Housed in a former factory building on a once industrial stretch of its namesake avenue, the 70-room Wythe Hotel was the first sleek accommodation to open in the area. Pieces by local artists like whimsical street art guru ESPO hang on the walls, and custom beds are made from wood reclaimed from the building's original ceiling. Radiant floor heating and

The William Vale

iPhone-controlled surround sound are among the amenities. With striking views over the East River and Manhattan skyline from the roof deck bar and select rooms, the hotel's a chic resting place both away from the city congestion and right in the heart of Williamsburg's lively nightlife. With hotel events, Brooklyn Bowl across the street, and countless venues within a short stroll, it's easy to have a memorable night out without straying too far. The in-house restaurant, Reynard, is run by Andrew Tarlow, a Brooklyn restaurant pioneer who has amassed a mini-empire in the neighborhood. MAP 10: 80 Wythe Ave., 718/460-8000, http://wythehotel.com

McCarren Hotel and Pool $$

Located just off McCarren Park, the rooftop pool of this hotel gets title billing here for a reason: It's huge (by New York City standards, anyway), not one of those decorative puddles

the fashionable sit around—although guests will feel pretty posh on the oversized daybeds with poolside service. Free Wi-Fi extends outdoors, making for a sweet summer workday. Rooms have an understated sleekness and feature oversized windows and rainfall showers. Deep discounts can be found outside of summer. MAP 10: 160 N. 12th St., 718/218-7500, www.mccarrenhotel.com

McCarren Hotel and Pool

Urban Cowboy B&B $$

As its name implies, the Urban Cowboy B&B brings rustic style to one of the trendiest areas in the city. Opened by a thirtysomething couple yearning to create a space of tranquil natural splendor away from the Midtown bustle, this eye-catching town house is adorned with beautiful woodwork and country features like wood-burning stoves and claw-foot tubs. Smaller rooms can be had for a bargain while a standalone cabin suite is perfect for those looking to splurge on added seclusion.

MAP 10: 111 Powers St.,
www.urbancowboy.com

GREENPOINT
Box House Hotel $$

This larger sister property of the Henry Norman Hotel is located in the northernmost reaches of Greenpoint, closer in fact via a walk over the Pulaski Bridge to Queens than the Greenpoint Avenue subway station. It offers many of the same amenities as the Henry Norman, including steam showers and saunas. One unique touch is that its complimentary shuttle service is via authentic 1970s taxicabs, giving guests a window into the city's past each time they set off to catch the subway or explore the neighborhood. Another bonus are the rooms themselves, most of which have terraces or balconies, in sweeping proportions that are hard to find in the city. A two-bedroom duplex loft sleeps six adults and features a full kitchen and a large curved living room flooded with light.

MAP 10: 77 Box St., 718/383-3800, www.theboxhousehotel.com

Henry Norman Hotel $$

While its location could be more convenient—the hotel is located deep in

Urban Cowboy B&B

Greenpoint a bit of a trek from the subway, though a courtesy car is available for trips within a 1 mile (1.6 km) radius—this is quite the place to retire to after a long day out and about. The 50-room boutique hotel is housed in a 19th-century warehouse, and rooms sport steam rooms and saunas, high ceilings, and walls adorned with local art. Some rooms feature terraces or private roof access.

MAP 10: 239 N. Henry St., 718/951-6000, www.henrynormanhotel.com

BUSHWICK

BKLYN House Hotel $$

For a solid design hotel in Bushwick near transportation, BKLYN House Hotel is a good bet. Its 113 rooms feature pillowtop queen beds, some with two in a room—great for groups. A continental breakfast adds to the value, as does its location a couple blocks from the M train, which can take you to the heart of the Village in about 25 minutes. It's also a short walk to cool bars and restaurants like the Brooklyn Cider House.

MAP 10: 9 Beaver St., 718/388-4433, www.bklynhousehotel.com

NY Moore Hostel $

This renovated hostel is located near Roberta's and at the core of where Bushwick gentrification began. With a graffiti-covered courtyard and spacious rooms with high ceilings, these digs provide a communal living experience (private rooms are available for about triple the price) ideal for solo budget travelers who'd rather spend their money on experiences. Book early; there aren't many places like it in the neighborhood.

MAP 10: 179 Moore St., 347/227-8634, www.nymoorehotel.com

BACKGROUND

The Landscape

GEOGRAPHY

The United States is the third-largest country in the world, both in terms of land mass and population, and New York, located on the East Coast, is its most populous city with over 8.5 million people. It's also the most densely populated: Roughly 1.6 million New Yorkers live on the island of Manhattan, a long and thin landmass of less than 23 square miles (60 sq km). Four other boroughs compose New York City, which covers just over 300 square miles (777 sq km) in total. Staten Island lies to Manhattan's south. The Bronx is separated from Manhattan by the Harlem River and lies to its northeast, and is the only borough located on the North American mainland proper. Queens and Brooklyn lie east of Manhattan, separated from it by the East River, and are located on the western end of Long Island. Brooklyn is home to 2.6 million people

United Nations Headquarters

spread across 70 square miles (181 sq km); if it were a separate city it would be the fourth largest in the country, and the second most densely populated. New York's natural harbor is located where the Hudson River meets the Atlantic Ocean. The state of New Jersey lies west of Manhattan, across the Hudson River.

CLIMATE

The climate in New York is fairly moderate as far as coastal cities in the U.S. Northeast go. January is the coldest month with an average high of 39°F (4°C) and low of 27°F (-3°C). July and August are the warmest months, with average highs around 85°F (29°C) and lows of 69°F (21°C). However, the city's mass amounts of concrete retain heat, making nights almost as warm and humid as the days in summer; 85 percent humidity is not uncommon. It's an oven effect that gives New York its reputation for sweltering summers. Spring and fall are much more moderate in temperature, which makes them desirable times for travelers. Spring weather can be highly variable, but May's average highs and lows are 72°F (22°C) and 54°F (12°C), respectively. September's are 76°F (24°C) and 61°F (16°C). The city gets about 45 inches of rain per year, 28 of which are from snow.

ENVIRONMENTAL ISSUES

New York has generally been spared massive natural disasters due to its protected estuaries. This changed in 2012 with deadly Hurricane Sandy. The storm flooded Lower Manhattan and parts of Brooklyn and Queens and left millions without power. Major damage was done to the subway tunnels, which are still being repaired.

New York accounts for just 1 percent of the country's greenhouse gas emissions while housing 2.7 percent of its population. Still, air quality has been a concern. The city is in the process of transitioning to an all-electric bus fleet by 2040. It's also working on cleaning up the Gowanus Canal Superfund site. This has not slowed the gentrification of this hip slice of Brooklyn.

History

THE CITY'S FOUNDING

In 1613, the Dutch established a trading post on the island of Manhattan, then inhabited by the Lenape people. After years of mutually beneficial trades, members of the Lenape sold the land to the Dutch in 1626 in exchange for goods worth just 60 guilders (about $24). A series of laws enacted in the following years, including a ban on sexual relations between the Dutch and the Lenape people and attempts to tax the Lenape, lead to escalating tensions and violent conflicts. The National Museum of the American Indian in Lower Manhattan is a great resource for learning about this dark history.

The British gained control of the land in 1664. As one of Great Britain's original 13 colonies, New York initially enjoyed a high level of autonomy. The first pavement in the city was installed on Wall Street in 1693. This marked the transformation of the area from quiet residential stretch to commercial hub and allowed New York to compete with more populous cities such as Boston and Philadelphia. By the 1750s, the colonies began increasingly working together, and this created a sense of American identity and a growing furor over "taxation without representation."

REVOLUTIONARY WAR AND AMERICAN INDEPENDENCE

The British government, its coffers stretched thin from the French and Indian War (1754-1763), tried to raise money through taxes on the colonies on everything from sugar to paper. Because the colonies had no representatives of their own in Parliament, these taxes were viewed as unjust. A tea tax was the breaking point, igniting boycotts of all British goods; the protests began in Boston and reached New York, which had its own rebellious tea party in 1774 following the more famous Boston Tea Party the year prior, in which protestors dumped British shipments of tea into the harbor in protest. This also prompted New York to send delegates to the First Continental Congress in Philadelphia, during which the colonies organized their opposition to the Intolerable Acts, a punitive step taken by the British to strip Massachusetts of its powers of self-government. The Revolutionary War broke out the following year in 1775, and the United States issued its Declaration of Independence on July 4, 1776, at the Second Continental Congress.

A third of all the war's battles took place in New York, including the first major battle following the country's Declaration of Independence, the Battle of Long Island, the site of which is now Brooklyn's Green-Wood Cemetery. The 1783 Treaty of Paris officially ended the war, and New York City served as the nation's capital from 1785 to 1790. George Washington was inaugurated as the first president of the United States in 1789 at Lower Manhattan's Federal Hall.

SLAVERY AND THE CIVIL WAR

Slavery was legal in all 13 colonies at the time of independence. By the 1830s, the abolitionist movement was gaining steam and the moral acceptance of slavery in the North began to erode. In 1838, William H. Seward was elected governor of New York and used his office to strengthen rights for the city's black residents. That same year, Frederick Douglass escaped from slavery and became a free man in New York, founding an abolitionist newspaper that Seward financially supported. After losing the 1860 Republican presidential primary to Abraham Lincoln, Seward became Lincoln's secretary of state. Just a month after President Lincoln was inaugurated in 1861, seven Southern states seceded from the Union and soon after formed the Confederate States of America, to be joined by four more states in the following months.

New York City served as a major source of supplies and troops for the Union Army during the Civil War, although the local business community was divided as many benefited from the slave trade themselves and cheap exports produced in Southern states. The country as a whole was still young, and notions of what democracy would look like and whether it could sustain as a governing force were an open question. On Rikers Island, now a prison, white and black soldiers trained in a Union military camp.

In 1863, a draft riot broke out in Lower Manhattan over the Civil War's conscription inequities—the wealthy could be excused from service by paying a fee—and quickly morphed into a race riot as working-class Irish American resentment over job competition with African Americans rose to the surface. The riots lasted for days and more than a hundred New Yorkers were killed in what remains the deadliest riot in U.S. history.

Battles between the Union and Confederate armies also claimed immense casualties—as many as 750,000 by the end of the war, which culminated in a Union victory in 1865.

NEW YORK CITY EXPANDS

Ellis Island opened in 1892 and became the country's primary immigration checkpoint. By the time it closed in 1954, more than 12 million people had passed through the gateway. Many Ellis Island immigrants would make New York City their home.

In 1898, New York City expanded from Manhattan to include the Bronx, Brooklyn, Queens, and Staten Island. The creation of the first subway line in 1904, which ran from City Hall to 145th Street in 26 minutes and cost just five cents, was the beginning of the most comprehensive underground transportation system in the world, helping spur growth and commerce in the city.

By the time World War II (1939-1945) broke out, New York was the largest city in the world, with more than seven million residents in its boroughs and several million more in its suburbs. It played a large part in the war effort, contributing 900,000 service members and hosting the country's shipbuilding hub at the Brooklyn Navy Yard. By the end of the war, given the devastation in Europe, New York, physically untouched, emerged as the world's preeminent city.

SEPTEMBER 11, 2001

On the morning of September 11, 2001, Al-Qaeda terrorists hijacked four planes and crashed two into the twin towers of Lower Manhattan's World Trade Center. Both buildings collapsed, killing more than 2,600 people in the deadliest attack on U.S. soil since Pearl Harbor. President George W. Bush interpreted this as an act of war and invaded Afghanistan, where the Taliban provided safe haven for Al-Qaeda and its leader, Osama bin Laden. The Bush administration also used the attacks as a justification for the larger "War on Terror" and invasion of Iraq. September 11 also impacted domestic policies, especially privacy rights, and stricter security measures at airports as well as seaports and major arenas were put in place. While the city's psyche has proven defiantly resilient, many first responders continue to suffer from the toxic air they breathed in the aftermath.

CONTEMPORARY TIMES

While New York is a liberal melting pot, it's also home to the largest financial institutions in the world, not least of which is the New York Stock Exchange. "Greed is good," a motto coined by fictional character Gordon Gecko in Oliver Stone's *Wall Street,* has been a driving force for many bankers, businesspeople, and politicians from the era of Boss Tweed through the present. The financial crisis of 2007-2008 began here, following risky subprime mortgage lending by the big banks and lax oversight, becoming international in scope following the collapse of global bank Lehman Brothers, headquartered in New York. Taxpayer-funded bailouts ensued to avoid an even more catastrophic economic disaster, and the Great Recession began. While financial institutions have rebounded, many people are still feeling the effects of the greatest economic downturn since the 1929 stock market crash.

New York's Financial District was also the birthplace of the Occupy Wall Street movement in 2011. The first protest in Zuccotti Park was organized in response to Wall Street greed and a lack of government regulation of the financial industry. With the rallying cry, "we are the 99 percent," the movement's protests against financial and social inequality struck a chord, spreading across the country and the world. While the Zuccotti Park occupation lasted a little less than two months, its impact can be still be felt in the city and country today, with progressive U.S. politicians, such as 2016 presidential candidate Bernie Sanders, incorporating the movement's ethos into their platforms.

In recent years, as in many cities in the county, gentrification has impacted New York City. Shiny high-rise condos have been replacing smaller tenement buildings across all boroughs. This construction has resulted in formerly industrial neighborhoods being transformed into residential communities for young professionals. A New York City comptroller's office report from 2017 provides stark statistics that fall along racial lines: From 2007 to 2012 black-owned businesses in New York decreased from 8,067 to 5,532 as major black neighborhoods in Brooklyn gentrified. One of the most pronounced examples is Bushwick, where the white population increased from 3,207 in 2000 to 22,776 in 2015. The borough's most affluent neighborhoods, Brooklyn Heights and Fort Greene, have seen a white population increase of 70 percent during this period and decrease of 28 percent in their black population.

Local Culture

DIVERSITY

New York is an immigrant city. Its most iconic landmarks, including the Empire State Building and the Brooklyn Bridge, were built by Italian, German, and Irish immigrants. The city's most iconic foods also hail from immigrants: Italian Americans set up pizza shops beginning in 1905 with Gennaro Lombardi, and bagels arrived in the city along with Eastern European Jewish immigrants as early as the 1880s.

The city's incredible diversity is what makes New York so special. According to a 2018 study by the World Population Review, the city's racial composition is 44.6 percent white, 25.1 percent black, and 11.8 percent Asian. Hispanic people of any race account for 27.5 percent of the population.

But these numbers hardly do justice to the city's multicultural richness. Over 3 million New Yorkers are foreign-born, a quarter of whom arrived after 2000. The city has the largest Chinese population of any city outside of Asia, as well as the largest population of Dominicans and Puerto Ricans outside of the West Indies. There are over 2.4 million Hispanic people and

1.89 million black non-Hispanic people here, more than double that of any other city in the United States. There are 1.1 million Jewish people, the largest population outside of Israel. Half of all New Yorkers speak a language other than English in their daily lives, and over 200 languages are spoken in homes across the five boroughs. This is as apparent on a crowded subway car as it is waiting in line for takeout, and part of what makes the city so enthralling.

RELIGION

According to the Public Religion Research Institute's 2016 survey, 30 percent of New Yorkers identify as Catholic. Jewish people comprise the largest non-Christian religious group, representing about 7 percent of the city's population. Muslims are the next largest, with 3 percent of the population, followed by Hindus and Buddhists with 1 percent each. Meanwhile, 25 percent of New York City residents are unaffiliated. However, religious affiliations in New York City vary widely between the boroughs. For example, Manhattan is the least religious of the five with 38 percent of citizens identifying as unaffiliated; in Staten Island that number is 13 percent.

THEATER

Theater is alive and well in New York, from the shining lights of the Great White Way to the hundreds of Off- and Off-Off Broadway theaters. Because it's the epicenter of American theater, many of the industry's top players have made the city their home and often premiere their works here. The late Edward Albee and Arthur Miller were both longtime residents. Lin-Manuel Miranda grew up in Washington Heights (detailed in his musical *In the Heights*), and Kenneth Lonergan grew up on the Upper West Side, where he set his play *This is Our Youth*. Stephen Sondheim remains a fixture and can be seen at play premieres.

LITERATURE

New York has a rich literary history. The late Tom Wolfe, in his iconic white suit, is just one of the countless literary icons who've made their lives here. Norman Mailer and Truman Capote both lived in Brooklyn, and the borough continues to claim a treasure trove of contemporary talent, including Paul Auster, Nicole Krauss, Jonathan Franzen, and Jennifer Egan. Founded by Harold Ross in the 1920s, *The New Yorker* remains the preeminent literary magazine in the country. New Yorkers also love to read. Evidence of this can be found during any morning commute or by perusing the long waitlists for popular books at the public library. A good way to find free books is to stroll the brownstone streets in Brooklyn's Park Slope, where books are frequently discarded for the taking on stoops throughout the neighborhood. Many local authors participate in free readings and signings at the city's independent bookstores.

VISUAL ARTS

New York doesn't just have the largest concentration of the country's best museums, it's also been home to many of the artists whose works populate those museums. In the 1950s, the rivalry between Willem de Kooning and Jackson Pollock played out in the beach enclave of the Hamptons, just outside the city. Andy Warhol's Factory thrived in three separate

Manhattan locations from the 1960s to the 1980s and nurtured many artists, including Jean Michel Basquiat. Robert Mapplethorpe lived and worked in the East Village, and countless other artists built careers here, from Keith Haring to Jeff Koons. The list is as long as it is varied, and while cheap studio space is increasingly hard to find, artists continue to make New York their home and take inspiration from it. Many exhibit at gallery shows and are present for the openings.

MUSIC AND DANCE

Brooklyn alone gave birth to the Beastie Boys, Lou Reed, JAY-Z, Notorious B.I.G., George Gershwin, and Aaron Copland. It's impossible to trace the history of many genres of music, from classical to hip-hop, without running through New York. Woody Guthrie made some of the best music of his life while living in Brooklyn's Coney Island, while the Ramones spent their formative years in Forest Hills, Queens. From storied venues like Carnegie Hall and Lincoln Center to intimate jazz clubs like the Village Vanguard and legendary now-shuttered spaces like CBGB, New York has been a place for musical ground breaking.

While game-changing choreographers Martha Graham and Alvin Ailey weren't born here, they both developed their creative voices in New York, and in the process forever changed the world of modern dance. Today companies from across the world thrive at venues like The Joyce Theater in Chelsea and the Brooklyn Academy of Music in Fort Greene. Classical traditions are alive and well at the New York City Ballet, even as the company develops boundary-pushing new works by rising star Justin Peck.

FOOD

There are as many kinds of meals to be devoured in New York as there are different kinds of people. What's impressive about New York food is how it encompasses every cuisine and budget, from iconic and affordable comfort staples like bagels and pizza to extravagant dozen-course *omakase* and tasting menus by chefs lauded the world over. There are restaurants that require booking months in advance and cost more than a nice hotel room, and others you can wander into for an epic meal at 2am. Many Manhattan eateries are open until midnight or later, and there are also 24-hour delis and halal food carts for cheap, filling meals after a long night out. When all the better options are closed, $1 pizza joints can be a life-saving snack.

ESSENTIALS

Transportation

subway

GETTING THERE
BY AIR

New York City is primarily served by three airports, all of which are connected to various taxi and mass transit options for getting into the city. Lyft (www.lyft.com) and Uber (www.uber.com) also run services from all of the airports into the city. Major car rental companies have offices at each of the airports, although driving into the city is not recommended.

John F. Kennedy International Airport

John F. Kennedy International Airport (JFK, Jamaica, Queens 11430, 718/244-4444, www.jfkairport.com) is a major international gateway with nonstop flights from across the United States, Canada, Mexico, Europe, South America, Asia and the Pacific, and Africa. The airport is approximately 16 miles (26 km) southeast of Midtown Manhattan, and so large that it has its own zip code.

New York City's yellow taxis (www.nyc.gov) charge a flat rate of $56.50 4pm-8pm Monday-Friday, and $52 at all other times, not including tip, and can take anywhere from 30 to 90 minutes to get to Midtown Manhattan; an hour is about standard. The AirTrain (www.jfkairport.com/to-from-airport/air-train) costs $5 one-way and connects the airport terminals to subway lines (E, J/Z) and Long Island Rail Road trains at Jamaica station, as well as subways (A) at Howard Beach station. The trip takes about an hour to Midtown.

The Port Authority also operates the NYC Express Bus (718/777-5111, www.nycairporter.com; 11am-7pm daily), which takes travelers to Grand Central Terminal and near Times Square (42nd St. between 5th Ave. and 6th Ave.). It's $18 one-way and takes about an hour.

Newark Liberty International Airport

Newark Liberty International Airport (EWR, 3 Brewster Rd., Newark, NJ, 973/961-6000, www.newarkairport.com) is another major international gateway with nonstop flights from across the United States, Canada, Mexico, Europe, South America, Asia and the Pacific, and Africa.

The airport is approximately 15 miles (24 km) southwest of Midtown, a trip of about 45 minutes by car. There is no flat taxi rate from Newark airport; taxis will be metered plus add a surcharge of $17.50, which can add up to anywhere from $60 to $90 to Midtown, not including tip. The AirTrain (www.newarkairport.com/to-from-airport/air-train) costs $5.50 each way and takes riders from the airport terminals to Newark Liberty Airport Station, where you can board New Jersey (NJ) Transit and Amtrak to Penn Station in Midtown. The trip takes about 40 minutes. The Newark Airport Express (877/894-9155, http://newarkairportexpress.com; approx. 4:45am-1:45am Manhattan-EWR, 4am-1am EWR-Manhattan) bus runs every 20-30 minutes to Grand Central, Bryant Park, and the Port Authority terminal near Times Square and costs $17 one-way. The trip takes about 45-60 minutes.

LaGuardia Airport

LaGuardia Airport (LGA, Queens 11371, 347/468-3927, www.laguardiaairport.com) is both smaller and closer to the city—about 10 miles (16 km) northeast of Midtown—than JFK. It mostly runs domestic flights, but it does have select nonstops to Europe, Asia, and South America. It's currently in the middle of an $8 billion overhaul, projected to be completed by 2021, in the hopes of improving its ranking as one of the country's worst airports. It'll continue to operate during this period.

Taxis are metered from the airport, and a trip to Midtown can cost anywhere from $30 to $70 without tip and take 30-60 minutes. The Q-70 bus stops at all terminals as well as the Jackson Heights-Roosevelt Avenue subway station, where you can connect with E, F/M, R, and 7 trains. The trip typically takes about an hour, though allowing a lot of extra time is wise. It costs the standard $2.75 bus/subway fare. The NYC Express Bus (718/777-5111, www.nycairporter.com; 11am-7pm daily) brings travelers to Grand Central Terminal and Times Square and takes about 45-60 minutes depending on traffic. It's $16 one-way.

BY CAR

Major highways into Manhattan from the west include U.S. 9 via the George Washington Bridge ($15 toll incoming traffic), I-78 via the Holland Tunnel ($15 toll incoming traffic), and Route 495 via the Lincoln Tunnel ($15 toll incoming traffic).

If you're driving from the north, a popular alternative is entering Manhattan via Route 9A over the Henry Hudson Bridge ($6 toll each way). Another artery from the north is I-278, which becomes the Brooklyn-Queens Expressway; it's a popular way to get to these boroughs without going through Manhattan. On this highway, a toll is applicable when crossing over the Robert F. Kennedy Bridge ($8.50 toll each way).

All toll booths accept E-ZPass or cash, except for the Henry Hudson Bridge, which only accepts E-ZPass; if you don't have an account, you'll automatically be sent a bill for the toll based on your license plate. If you have a rental car, check with your agency to see how such tolls are processed.

BY TRAIN

National rail carrier Amtrak (800/872-7245, www.amtrak.com) runs trains to New York from cities small and large throughout the Northeast, though service can be spotty outside of main service routes like Washington DC (3.25 hours) and Boston (4.15 hours). Trains can be dated but offer plush seating, Wi-Fi, and power outlets in both economy and business class. Book early for the best fares.

Metro-North and Long Island Rail Road (http://www.mta.info/schedules) are commuter rails run by the Metropolitan Transit Authority (MTA) to Westchester County and the Hudson Valley in New York, as well as Connecticut and Long Island. Some destinations overlap with Amtrak, which is pricier. New Jersey (NJ) Transit (www.njtransit.com) is a commuter rail that connects the state with New York.

Grand Central Terminal (89 E. 42nd St.; 24 hours daily) is the major train hub for Metro-North and Amtrak. Penn Station (7th Ave. and W. 32nd St.; 24 hours daily), also in Midtown, is the other major train station in the city, and serves Amtrak, the Long Island Rail Road, and NJ Transit.

BY BUS

Port Authority Bus Terminal (625 8th Ave.; 24 hours daily), near Times Square, is New York's major long-distance bus hub. Greyhound (214/849-8966, www.greyhound.com) runs bus services to Port Authority from across Canada and the United States, including Atlantic City, Boston, Philadelphia, Washington DC, Albany, and Baltimore.

Other long-distance bus services include BoltBus (877/265-8287, www.boltbus.com), OurBus (844/800-6828, http://ourbus.com), and Megabus (877/462-6342, http://us.megabus.com). OurBus leaves mostly from Port Authority and serves college towns like Ithaca and Syracuse, while BoltBus and Megabus tend to leave from corners in far west Midtown, depending on the route. Popular routes include Washington DC, Boston, and Philadelphia.

GETTING AROUND
PUBLIC TRANSPORTATION

New York's public transportation is run by the Metropolitan Transit Authority (MTA, www.mta.info). Subways and buses in the city run 24 hours daily. Unlike in some cities, there are no zones here and you can ride to the farthest reaches of Manhattan, the Bronx, Brooklyn, and Queens on a single fare. Single rides for a local bus or subway ride are $2.75, and transfers between subway lines and local buses are free within two hours. Google Maps is pretty accurate for planning your route, and the MTA Weekender App notes delays and scheduled work in real time;

if you have access to a phone during your trip, this app is a must.

Subway

Walking is a wonderful way to get around New York City, but taking the subway is just as much a part of the city experience. Even with its many delays, the subway is the best motorized way to get around the city for speed and economy. New York's track system is the most extensive in the country, and you can often get within a few blocks of your destination with one transfer or less.

In order to use the subway, you'll need to first buy a MetroCard at one of the many kiosks located at every subway station. A regular Pay-Per-Ride card costs $1 and can be refilled. One ride costs $2.75, but you'll receive a 5 percent bonus if you put $5.50 or more on the card. To use the card, simply swipe once at the turnstile entrance. MetroCards can be used by up to four people at the same time. However, if you're planning on traveling a lot over a week or more, consider a 7-Day ($32) or 30-Day ($121) Unlimited Card (note that these can only be used by one person).

Screens on subway platforms provide real-time arrivals. Keep in mind that during summer, heat gets trapped underground and turns the subway into a sauna, so for the actively inclined walking is a better bet on hot days for short trips. Large maps are displayed at subway stations, as well as inside each subway car. Cars also have electronic strip maps that display the current and all future stops on the given line.

Bus

Buses aren't as efficient as subways and tend to be best for uptown crosstown travel. Like the subway, the bus costs $2.75 per ride. Local buses stop every 2-3 blocks, while Limited buses make fewer stops. For Limited buses, you'll find machines at each stop, and you'll typically need a MetroCard so you can get a receipt prior to boarding. For local buses, you can pay by MetroCard or exact change, no bills. If you pay in cash, ask your bus driver for a transfer and you'll receive a single-use MetroCard valid for two hours.

TAXI

Yellow taxis are the easiest way to get around in New York City, if not the most economical. The meter starts at $2.50 and adds $0.50 every 0.2 mile (0.3 km) or every minute in slow traffic (less than 12 mph/19 kph). A number of other surcharges will be added onto a taxi ride as well, including $0.50 for trips ending in New York City (or surrounding counties), $0.50 for trips between 8pm and 6am, and $1 for trips between 4pm and 8pm Monday-Friday, excluding holidays. A $0.30 improvement surcharge is also added. This doesn't include a tip (15-20 percent is customary). Payment by cash, credit card, or debit card is acceptable.

To hail a cab, walk out on any corner in Manhattan and stick out your hand. Cabs that are available will have their four-digit medallion illuminated on the car's roof, making them easy to spot. During rush hour or rain, it can be hard to find an available taxi, but often a cab is never more than a couple of minutes away.

UBER AND LYFT

Uber (www.uber.com) and Lyft (www.lyft.com) both operate in the city and are often cheaper than taxis. Lyft tends to be more cost-effective, with fewer price surges. The downside is that drivers often aren't always as familiar with the roads and might need some additional directions, which can be challenging if you don't know the way around yourself. It can also be time-consuming if your driver gets lost, which happens on a not-infrequent basis. For price, though, you can't beat the Lyft Line shareable option; it's often the same cost as the subway.

DRIVING

Driving in New York City is a stressful experience. Confusing one-way streets abound, traffic jams are unavoidable, parking is scarce and expensive (from about $20 an hour to $60 a day), frustrations run high, and you'll need to dodge numerous pedestrians and bicyclists. It's also an inefficient way to get around; you might notice that some fast-walking locals are making better time. So leave the car behind if at all possible and take advantage of the city's great walkability and public transit system.

But if you do require a car, you'll find ZipCars (www.zipcar.com) in almost every garage in Manhattan, though using them requires a membership with the car-sharing company. Major rental car companies like Budget (800/214-6094, www.budget. com), Avis (800/352-7900, www.avis. com), and Enterprise (855/266-9565, www.enterprise.com) serve all three of the major area airports and also have offices throughout the city.

FERRY

The NYC Ferry (www.ferry.nyc; $2.75 one-way) whisks riders from the east side of Manhattan—the most convenient docks are East 34th Street in Midtown and Wall Street/Pier 11 in Lower Manhattan—to popular areas in Brooklyn such as Dumbo, Williamsburg, and Greenpoint. In the summer ferries go to Governors Island, and there's also a direct trip to popular beach destination Rockaway Beach. Ferries have fully stocked bars inside and limited seating on top where you can take in the views. Tickets can be bought through the ferry app or at machines before boarding. MetroCards cannot yet be used to purchase fares. The ferry's combination of cheap, fast, and pleasant ensures large crowds, so allow extra time for waiting in line.

The Staten Island Ferry (4 Whitehall St., www.siferry.com; 24 hours daily; free) provides free shuttle service between Lower Manhattan and Staten Island. The trip takes about 25 minutes, and no tickets are required. For those taking the ferry as a scenic trip, note that you need to disembark when you reach Staten Island and then line up to reboard.

Travel Tips

WHAT TO PACK

Traveling light is always recommended, but particularly so in New York. Public transportation to airports requires a good bit of walking and sometimes stairs, making big suitcases cumbersome. Good walking shoes are a must since you'll likely end up doing more than you realize in this most walkable of cities; if they can double as dress shoes, even better. While there aren't many places that still have mandatory dress codes, New Yorkers are a fashionable crowd and wearing logo T-shirts, shorts, and sneakers is generally frowned upon at nice restaurants and cultural events.

ACCESS FOR TRAVELERS WITH DISABILITIES

All of New York's buses are wheelchair accessible, and some subway stops have elevator access. Most attractions and museums have ramps and elevators. Hotels likewise have ramps and elevators, although some have small bathrooms that could be challenging to navigate with a wheelchair. Note that accessibility exemptions are in place for some older historic buildings. The city's official tourism site (www.nycgo.com/plan-your-trip/basic-information/accessibility) is a good resource. For booking accessible tickets for arts and cultural events, you can contact individual venues directly for assistance. Sites like Yai Arts and Culture (https://yaiartsandculture.org) also arrange experiences for travelers with disabilities.

TRAVELING WITH CHILDREN

New York can be a challenging destination for families with very young children—navigating the city with a stroller can be trying, especially in heavily crowded areas like the Times Square and Midtown neighborhoods, and subway access is challenging since only some stations have elevators. Buses are a popular way for families to get around, though you'll need to budget for longer travel times. Those with slightly older children are likely to find the city fairly family friendly, with many museums and other venues offering free or discounted admission for children. Many restaurants, even some of the fine-dining ones, have kids' menus. And many of the city's big winter holiday draws are the stuff kids' dreams are made of, from the giant Thanksgiving Day Parade balloons to the elaborate department store window displays to the open-air ice-skating rinks.

WOMEN TRAVELING ALONE

Women traveling alone should feel comfortable and safe in New York City. However, commonsense precautions are always wise, for people of any gender. You may want to avoid taking the subway very late at night, and it's best to walk the better-lit main thoroughfares rather than side streets. Unfortunately, catcalling still occurs on occasion. If you feel uncomfortable don't hesitate to let others know; New Yorkers are ready to aid those in need.

SENIOR TRAVELERS

Many attractions and hotels offer discounts for seniors 65 and older, although this can vary so it never hurts to ask. While the city streets are fairly fast-paced, taxis are readily available when you need a break from walking.

GAY AND LESBIAN TRAVELERS

New York has a large and thriving gay, lesbian, bisexual, and transgender community woven into a multitude of neighborhoods across the city. The West Village and Chelsea are particular hubs. The LGBT Center (http://gaycenter.org) offers a wealth of information for travelers, but you can feel at ease that any hotel will welcome you with open arms.

INTERNATIONAL TRAVELERS

Although credit cards are widely accepted, having U.S. dollars on hand is particularly helpful because many venues in the city are cash-only, particularly smaller independent restaurants. Debit cards may not work depending on your bank. Major hotels have international electrical adaptors, but it's always a good idea to carry your own.

Health and Safety

HOSPITALS AND EMERGENCY SERVICES

In the United States, 911 is the number to call for assistance in an emergency.

There's no shortage of hospitals in New York City with 24-hour emergency rooms. Ambulance rides can be quite expensive, however, so if it's not a dire emergency consider taking a cab. The top three hospitals are New York-Presbyterian (525 E. 68th St., 212/746-5454, www.nyp.org), Mount Sinai Hospital (1 Gustave L. Levy Pl., 877/326-9053, www.mountsinai. org), and NYU Langone (550 1st Ave., 212/263-7300, https://nyulangone.org).

For less pressing issues, try an urgent care facility like City MD (www. citymd.com), which has well over a dozen locations throughout the city and provides real-time wait estimates for each location through its website.

PHARMACIES

Pharmacies are plentiful in the city; in some neighborhoods, you'll find one every few blocks. Duane Reade (www.walgreens.com/topic/duane-reade/duane-reade) and CVS (www. cvs.com) are the biggest ones. Check their websites for the branch nearest your location.

CRIME

Long gone are the days of *Taxi Driver*. New York is now the safest city in the country per capita. That doesn't mean you shouldn't be alert, but violent crime is exceedingly rare and theft is down as well. It would still be wise not to carry a wallet in your back pocket, and you should be aware of your surroundings when walking down a deserted street late at night; those unaware are the easiest targets. Walking with purpose is a good deterrent.

Information and Services

VISITORS CENTERS

NYC Official Information Centers (www.nycgo.com) offer visitors maps, guides, sightseeing brochures, and coupons for discounted attractions. There are locations in Herald Square (151 W. 34th St. between 7th Ave. and Broadway, 212/484-1222; 9am-7pm Mon.-Fri., 10am-7pm Sat., 11am-7pm Sun.), Times Square (44th and 45th St. between 7th Ave. and Broadway, 212/484-1222; 8am-7pm daily) and City Hall (southern tip of City Hall Park at Broadway and Park Row, 212/484-1222; 9am-6pm daily).

POST OFFICE

Dozens of U.S. Post Office (www. usps.com/welcome.htm) locations are throughout the city. You can buy stamps and even mail letters and packages without waiting in line at many of them. Check the website for specific branch details.

New York's main post office, the James A. Farley Post Office (421 8th Ave.), two blocks long and an architectural landmark built in 1912, is currently being converted into an extension of Penn Station, slated for completion in 2020—but you can still admire the old post office's facade.

RESOURCES

Suggested Reading

FICTION

Capote, Truman. *Breakfast at Tiffany's*. New York: Random House, 1958. A novella about the darkness of chasing glamour.

Cole, Teju. *Open City*. New York: Random House, 2011. This acclaimed slice-of-life novel follows an immigrant on the precipice of completing his studies in psychiatry as he forges connections with people across the city.

Lethem, Jonathan. *The Fortress of Solitude*. New York: Doubleday, 2003. A pre-gentrification coming-of-age tale in 1970s Brooklyn.

McCann, Colum. *Let the Great World Spin*. New York: Random House, 2009. Acclaimed novel about Philippe Petit's daring World Trade Center tightrope walk in the 1970s, and so much more.

Trillin, Calvin. *Tepper Isn't Going Out*. New York: Random House, 2002. This cutting satire focuses on a man who's let the quest for the perfect parking space take over his life.

CULTURE AND HISTORY

Koolhaas, Rem. *Delirious New York*. New York: The Monacelli Press, 1978. An architectural and cultural history of the city by innovative Dutch architect Rem Koolhaas.

Lopate, Phillip. *Waterfront: A Walk Around Manhattan*. New York: Crown, 2004. A native New Yorker delves into the history of the city through walks along its once-neglected shorelines.

Mitchell, Joseph. *Up in the Old Hotel*. New York: Pantheon, 1992. A collection of Joseph Mitchell's *New Yorker* essays from 1943 to 1964 vividly bring to life eccentrics on the fringes of society who would have otherwise been forgotten.

Murphy, James T., and Karla L. Murphy. *Storefront: The Disappearing Face of New York*. New York: Gingko Press, 2009. Documents the loss of mom-and-pop businesses throughout the city through eye-catching photographs.

MEMOIR

Gornick, Vivian. *The Odd Woman and the City*. New York: Farrar, Straus and Giroux, 2015. A memoir about engaging the city on foot and being open to spontaneous encounters.

Smith, Patti. *Just Kids*. New York: Ecco, 2010. Punk rock icon Patti Smith details her young romance with Robert Mapplethorpe and the city.

Whitehead, Colson. *The Colossus of New York*. New York: Doubleday, 2003. The lauded New York novelist's nonfiction love letter to making New York your home.

Internet Resources

GENERAL INFORMATION

NYCgo
www.nycgo.com
New York's official tourism website offers info on attractions, restaurants, and lodging, along with discounted promotional events.

ENTERTAINMENT

Flavorpill
www.flavorpill.com
This weekly newsletter gathers the coolest culture and nightlife listings.

The New Yorker
www.newyorker.com
The great literary magazine is also a font of information for cultural events around town. Nonsubscribers get 10 free articles a month.

Theatermania
www.theatermania.com
Find comprehensive theater listings and reviews along with discount offers.

Time Out New York
www.timeout.com/newyork
Reviews and listings of the best things to do in every category.

FOOD

Eater
http://ny.eater.com
One of the most comprehensive online publications for restaurant news and reviews.

NEWS

Gothamist
http://gothamist.com
From subway shutdowns to art installation pop-ups, Gothamist reports on the pulse of the city.

The New York Times
www.nytimes.com
The newspaper of record for the city (and possibly the world). Nonsubscribers get five free articles a month.

The Village Voice
www.villagevoice.com
The legendary underground weekly now lives solely online.

Index

Restaurants Index

Nightlife Index

Shops Index

Hotels Index

Photo Credits

All photos © Christopher Kompanek except page 4 © (top left) jerry coli | dreamstime. com; (top right) eileen tan | dreamstime.com; (left middle)francoisroux | dreamstime. com; (right middle)jerry coli | dreamstime.com; (bottom) vitalyedush | dreamstime.com; page 5 © demerzel21 | dreamstime.com; page 12 © (bottom) kmiragaya | dreamstime. com; page 13 © zhukovsky | dreamstime.com; page 14 © vvoevale | dreamstime.com; page 16 © (top) jjfarq | dreamstime.com; page 17 © ryan deberardinis | dreamstime. com; zhukovsky | dreamstime.com; page 18 © (bottom) ymgerman | dreamstime.com; page 20 © (bottom) erica schroeder | dreamstime.com; page 22 © (top) palinchak | dreamstime.com; page 31 © jovannig/123rf.com; helen louise haigh | dreamstime. com; jerry coli | dreamstime.com; courtesy of the dead rabbit; page 33 © courtesy of city winery; courtesy of jungsik; edichenphoto | dreamstime.com; page 35 © jennifer walz | dreamstime.com; mark soskolne | dreamstime.com; evan sung, courtesy of dirt candy; spirer/123rf.com; page 37 © (top) boggy | dreamstime.com; page 38 © (top) courtesy of the summit bar; page 39 © achilles | dreamstime.com; page 41 © ginamcleanphoto / shutterstock.com; courtesy of minetta tavern; page 44 © (bottom) littleny | dreamstime.com; page 45 © (top) jay beiler | dreamstime.com; page 47 © jake chessum; bigapplestock | dreamstime.com; danielle delre, courtesy of upland; page 50 © yooran park / 123rf.com; page 51 © (top) janifest | dreamstime.com; (top) peter aaron/esto; page 53 © yooran park / 123rf.com; daniel krieger, courtesy of le bernardin; david pereiras villagrá / 123rf.com; page 55 © julie feinstein | dreamstime.com; john anderson | dreamstime.com; meagan marchant / shutterstock; boggy | dreamstime.com; page 57 © deanpictures | dreamstime.com; bumbleedee | dreamstime.com; victorianl | dreamstime.com; tanyabird777 | dreamstime.com; page 59 © (top) jiawangkun | dreamstime.com; page 60 © (top) jesse seniunas / shutterstock; page 61 © (bottom) nuvisage | dreamstime.com; page 63 © jim lawrence | dreamstime.com; courtesy of bella gioia; teddy wolff, courtesy of st. ann's warehouse; ehblake | dreamstime.com; page 64 © (bottom) davidevison | dreamstime.com; page 66 © (top) image courtesy of smack mellon. photo by etienne frossard; page 67 © sampete | dreamstime.com; page 69 © zhukovsky | dreamstime.com; young kim, courtesy of brooklyn cider house; carly rabalais, courtesy of beacon's closet; courtesy of nitehawk cinema; page 71 © (top) littleny | dreamstime.com; page 72 © (bottom) jumiss | dreamstime.com; page 73 © (top) courtesy of tørst; page 74 © meinzahn | dreamstime.com; page 76 © (bottom) jerry coli | dreamstime.com; page 78 © (top) pumppump | dreamstime.com; page 79 © (bottom) ritu jethani | dreamstime.com; page 80 © edichenphoto | dreamstime.com; page 84 © ymgerman | dreamstime.com; page 86 © bigapplestock | dreamstime.com; page 88 © (bottom) tinamou | dreamstime.com; page 90 © (top) yooran park | dreamstime.com; page 92 © (bottom) saloni1986 | dreamstime.com; page 93 © yooran park | dreamstime. com; page 94 © (bottom) yooran park | dreamstime.com; page 96 © ivan cholakov | dreamstime.com; page 97 © yooran park | dreamstime.com; page 98 © ymgerman | dreamstime.com; page 100 © silvapinto | dreamstime.com; page 103 © (top) ymgerman | dreamstime.com; page 105 © (bottom) kmiragaya | dreamstime.com; page 109 © debra reschoff ahearn | dreamstime.com; page 114 © ritu jethani | dreamstime.com; page 115 © (bottom) dmitrii sakharov | dreamstime.com; page 118 © (top) byelikova | dreamstime. com; page 120 © priscille canivet, courtesy of the fiat café; page 124 © (bottom) noah fecks, courtesy of locanda verde; page 127 © courtesy of the odeon; page 129 © (bottom) courtesy of estela; page 137 © bradley skaggs, courtesy of veselk; page 155 © evan sung, courtesy of gabriel kreuther; page 156 © courtesy of 5 napkin burger; page 163 © courtesy of jacob's pickles; page 166 © courtesy of red rooster; page 167 © julian cragnaz, courtesy of the cecil steakhouse; page 168 © courtesy of hudson jane; page 169 © (top) courtesy of bella gioia; page 170 © courtesy of yaso tangbao; page 173

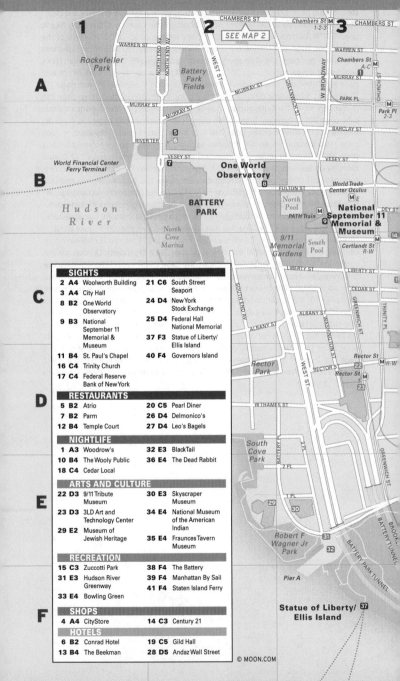

CHAMBERS ST

SEE MAP 2

Chambers St Ⓜ 1-2-3

CHAMBERS ST

1

2

3

Rockefeller Park

WARREN ST

Battery Park Fields

WARREN ST

Chambers St A-C Ⓜ

WEST ST

MURRAY ST

MURRAY ST

W BROADWAY

MURRAY ST

GREENWICH ST

PARK PL

CHURCH ST

Park Pl Ⓜ 2-3

A

MURRAY ST

MURRAY ST

RIVER TER

BARCLAY ST

5
6

VESEY ST

7

One World Observatory

VESEY ST

World Financial Center Ferry Terminal

8

World Trade Center Oculus

Ⓜ E

DEY ST

B

H u d s o n River

BATTERY PARK

FULTON ST

North Pool

PATH Train

National September 11 Memorial &

Ⓜ

14

North Cove Marina

9

South Pool

9/11 Memorial Gardens

Cortlandt St R-W

LIBERTY ST

LIBERTY ST

CEDAR ST

SOUTH END AV

GREENWICH ST

TRINITY PL

C

SIGHTS			
2 A4	Woolworth Building	**21** C6	South Street Seaport
3 A4	City Hall		
8 B2	One World Observatory	**24** D4	New York Stock Exchange
9 B3	National September 11 Memorial & Museum	**25** D4	Federal Hall National Memorial
		37 F3	Statue of Liberty/ Ellis Island
11 B4	St. Paul's Chapel	**40** F4	Governors Island
16 C4	Trinity Church		
17 C4	Federal Reserve Bank of New York		

ALBANY ST

WASHINGTON ST

ALBANY ST

Rector Park

Rector St Ⓜ R-W

RECTOR ST

Rector St **23** Ⓜ

D

RESTAURANTS			
5 B2	Atrio	**20** C5	Pearl Diner
7 B2	Parm	**26** D4	Delmonico's
12 B4	Temple Court	**27** D4	Leo's Bagels

WEST ST

W THAMES ST

1 PL

GREENWICH ST

NIGHTLIFE			
1 A3	Woodrow's	**32** E3	BlackTail
10 B4	The Wooly Public	**36** E4	The Dead Rabbit
18 C4	Cedar Local		

South Cove Park

2 PL

ARTS AND CULTURE			
22 D3	9/11 Tribute Museum	**30** E3	Skyscraper Museum
23 D3	3LD Art and Technology Center	**34** E4	National Museum of the American Indian
29 E2	Museum of Jewish Heritage	**35** E4	Fraunces Tavern Museum

E

1 PL

BROOK- BATTERY TUNNEL

BATTERY PARK TUNNEL

RECREATION			
15 C3	Zuccotti Park	**38** F4	The Battery
31 E3	Hudson River Greenway	**39** F4	Manhattan By Sail
33 E4	Bowling Green	**41** F4	Staten Island Ferry

29

30

Robert F Wagner Jr Park

31

32

Pier A

SHOPS			
4 A4	CityStore	**14** C3	Century 21

Statue of Liberty/ Ellis Island

37

F

HOTELS			
6 B2	Conrad Hotel	**19** C5	Gild Hall
13 B4	The Beekman	**28** D5	Andaz Wall Street

© MOON.COM

SEE MAP 3

4

5

6

To ④ CityStore

M Chambers St
J-Z
4-5-6 M Brooklyn Bridge-
City Hall

M City Hall
R-W

**City
③ Hall**

City Hall
Park

**Woolworth
Building
②**

⑩

SPRUCE ST

PARK ROW

BEEKMAN ST

BROOKLYN BRIDGE
BROOKLYN BRIDGE

⑫

⑬

NASSAU ST

**St. Paul's
⑪ Chapel**

ANN ST

FULTON ST

M A-C

PECK SLIP

Fulton
St M J-Z

Fulton
St M 2-3

M Fulton St
4-5

FULTON ST

JOHN ST

GOLD ST

CLIFF ST

PEARL ST

WATER ST

FRONT ST

BEEKMAN ST

**Federal Reserve
Bank of New York
⑰**

MAIDEN

LIBERTY ST

**FINANCIAL
DISTRICT**

NASSAU ST

⑲

PLATT ST

⑱

LA.

FLETCHER ST

⑳

JOHN ST

MAIDEN LA

**South Street
㉑ Seaport**

**Trinity
Church
⑥**

M Wall St
4-5

PINE ST

M Wall St
2-3

**㉕ Federal Hall
National Memorial**

**New York
㉔ Stock Exchange**

WALL ST

NEW STREET

M Broad St
J-Z

EXCHANGE PL

WALL ST

㉘

WATER ST

FRONT ST

FDR DRIVE

Pier 16

Pier 15

⑳ ⑳

㉖

BROAD ST

S. WILLIAM ST

BEAVER ST

㉗

OLD SLIP

OLD SLIP

**Pier 11
Ferry Terminal**

**Bowling
Green
㉝**

Bowling Green
4-5

㉞

STONE ST

BRIDGE ST

PEARL ST

STATE ST

㉟ ㊱

WATER ST

Vietnam
Veterans
Plaza

*East
River*

R-W
M Whitehall St

STATE ST

BROADWAY

FDR DRIVE

Lower Manhattan
Heli Port Pier

㊲

*The
Battery*

South Ferry
M 1

㊶

National Park
Service Pier

㊴

Governors
Island
㊵

Staten Island
Ferry Pier

0 — 200 yds
0 — 200 m
Distance Across Map: 1.35mi or 2.2km

478

Pier 45 Park
Pier 45

1
2
3

MORTON ST
GREENWICH ST
James J
Walker Park
DOWNING ST

Houston St M 1-2

WASHINGTON ST
LEROY ST
CLARKSON ST
VARICK ST

WEST ST
W HOUSTON ST
HUDSON ST

KING ST
18
19

A

CHARLTON ST

Hudson River
Park Ball
Fields

VANDAM ST
20
21

Pier 40

B
22

SPRING ST

DOMINICK ST

Canal
Park
32
BROOME ST

HOLLAND
TUNNEL
ENTRANCE
RAMPS

WATTS ST
CANAL ST
HUDSON ST

WEST ST
DESBROSSES ST
VESTRY ST

WASHINGTON ST
GREENWICH ST
LAIGHT ST

HUBERT ST

BEACH ST

Pier 26
50
52

Pier 25
49
48

HARRISON ST

Washington
Market Par

CHAMBERS ST

Rockefeller
Park

WARREN ST

NORTH END AV
NORTHFIELD

Battery
Park
Fields

WEST ST

© MOON.COM

SIGHTS
60 F5 African Burial Ground National Monument

RESTAURANTS
2 A4	Blue Ribbon Sushi	**31 B6**	Fiat Cafe
3 A4	Raoul's	**33 C4**	David Burke Kitchen
10 A5	The Mercer Kitchen		
13 A5	Lure Fishbar	**47 D6**	Forlini's
15 A6	Estela	**48 E2**	Grand Banks
24 B4	Aquagrill	**50 E3**	Locanda Verde
25 B4	Altesi Downtown	**52 E3**	Tribeca Grill
28 B5	Balthazar	**53 E3**	Sarabeth's
29 B6	Osteria Morini	**54 E4**	Jungsik
30 B6	Lombardi's Pizza	**56 E4**	The Odeon

NIGHTLIFE
5 A4	Pegu Club	**32 C3**	Ear Inn
12 A5	Fanelli Cafe	**42 C5**	The Ship
21 B3	City Winery	**55 E4**	The Bennett

ARTS AND CULTURE
1 A3	Film Forum	**23 B4**	HERE
6 A4	The New York Earth Room	**37 C4**	Drawing Center
8 A5	Morrison Hotel Gallery	**38 C4**	Leslie-Lohman Museum of Gay and Lesbian Art
19 B3	The Greene Space		
20 B3	Kate Werble Gallery	**43 D5**	Soho Rep
22 B3	New York City Fire Museum	**44 D5**	Artists Space
		46 D5	Mmuseumm
		58 E5	The Flea Theater

RECREATION
49 E2 Hudson River Park

SHOPS
4 A4	A Second Chance	**26 B5**	Agent Provocateur
7 A4	UNTUCKit	**36 C4**	What Goes Around Comes Around
9 A5	Warby Parker		
14 A5	Housing Works Bookstore	**39 C5**	Purl
		40 C5	Ingo Maurer
16 A6	McNally Jackson	**41 C5**	Opening Ceremony
17 A6	INA	**45 D5**	Pearl River Mart
18 B3	Jacques Torres Chocolate	**59 F4**	Chambers Street Wines

HOTELS
11 A5	The Mercer Hotel	**51 E3**	The Greenwich Hotel
27 B5	Crosby Street Hotel		
34 C4	The James	**57 E4**	Duane Street Hotel
35 C4	Soho Grand		

4 | **5** | **6**

SEE MAP 4

W. HOUSTON ST
W. HOUSTON ST

Broadway-Lafayette St
B-D-F-M

5

BOWERY

6

14

9
11
10 13

Prince St
N-Q-R-W

15

W HOUSTON ST
W HOUSTON ST

PRINCE ST

3
4 7

8
12

16

17

2

Spring St
A-C-E

26

Prince St
N-Q-R-W

24 25

SPRING ST

6TH AVENUE
THOMPSON ST
W BROADWAY
SULLIVAN ST
WOOSTER ST
GREENE ST
MERCER ST
BROADWAY
CROSBY ST
LAFAYETTE ST
MULBERRY ST
MOTT ST
ELIZABETH ST

47

Spring St
4-6

SOHO

23

5TH AVE

28

27

30
31

29

KENMARE ST

LITTLE
ITALY

BROOME ST

39

36

37

38 40

CENTRE ST

33

WATTS ST

GRAND ST

34

GRAND ST

35

CENTRE MARKET

42

SEE MAP 3

Canal St
1-2

Duarte
Square

Albert
Capsouto
Park

CANAL ST

HOWARD ST
41

HESTER ST

HESTER ST
MULBERRY ST
BAXTER ST
MOTT ST

Canal St-
Holland Tunnel
A-C-E

Tribeca
Park

6TH AVENUE
CHURCH ST

LISPENARD ST

R-W

Canal St
N-Q

4-6
Canal St

Canal
St
J-Z

CANAL ST

CHINATOWN

ERICSSON PL

43

WALKER ST

44 45

LAFAYETTE ST
CENTRE ST

47

N MOORE ST

WHITE ST

Franklin St
1-2

FRANKLIN ST

46

BAYARD ST

FRANKLIN ST

Collect
Pond
Park

Columbus
Park

54

TRIBECA

HUDSON ST
STAPLE ST

LEONARD ST

WORTH ST

WORTH ST

WAY ST

THOMAS ST
58

BROADWAY

56

55

57

DUANE ST

DUANE ST

PEARL ST

BOWERY

READE ST

African Burial Ground
National Monument

60

Chambers St
M J-Z

59

Chambers St
1-2-3

CHAMBERS ST

WARREN ST

City Hall
Park

SEE MAP 1

Chambers St
A-C

City Hall
R-W

0   200 yds
0   200 m
Distance Across Map: 1.35mi or 2.2km

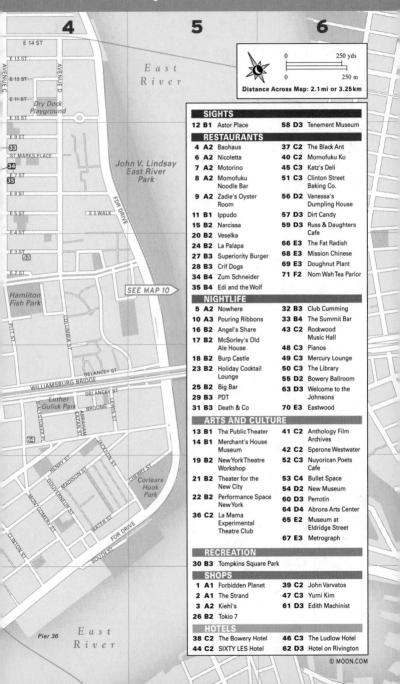

E 14 ST
E 13 ST
E 12 ST
E 11 ST
E 10 ST
E 9 ST
ST MARKS PLACE
E 7 ST
E 6 ST
E 5 ST · E 5 WALK
E 4 ST
E 3 ST
E 2 ST

AVENUE C
AVENUE D

East River

Dry Dock Playground

John V. Lindsay East River Park

FDR DRIVE

Hamilton Fish Park

PITT ST
COLUMBIA ST

SEE MAP 10

WILLIAMSBURG BRIDGE

DELANCEY ST
DELANCEY ST
BROOME ST

Luther Gulick Park

BIALYSTOKER PL
ABRAHAM E KAZAN ST
LEWIS ST
JACKSON ST

HENRY ST
MADISON ST
CHERRY ST

Corlears Hook Park

MONTGOMERY ST
GOUVERNEUR ST
CLINTON ST
WATER ST

FDR DRIVE

SOUTH ST

Pier 36

East River

Distance Across Map: 2.1mi or 3.25km

0   250 yds
0   250 m

SIGHTS

| 12 B1 | Astor Place | 58 D3 | Tenement Museum |

RESTAURANTS

4 A2	Baohaus	37 C2	The Black Ant
6 A2	Nicoletta	40 C2	Momofuku Ko
7 A2	Motorino	45 C3	Katz's Deli
8 A2	Momofuku Noodle Bar	51 C3	Clinton Street Baking Co.
9 A2	Zadie's Oyster Room	56 D2	Vanessa's Dumpling House
11 B1	Ippudo	57 D3	Dirt Candy
15 B2	Narcissa	59 D3	Russ & Daughters Cafe
20 B2	Veselka		
24 B2	La Palapa	66 E3	The Fat Radish
27 B3	Superiority Burger	68 E3	Mission Chinese
28 B3	Crif Dogs	69 E3	Doughnut Plant
34 B4	Zum Schneider	71 F2	Nom Wah Tea Parlor
35 B4	Edi and the Wolf		

NIGHTLIFE

5 A2	Nowhere	32 B3	Club Cumming
10 A3	Pouring Ribbons	33 B4	The Summit Bar
16 B2	Angel's Share	43 C2	Rockwood Music Hall
17 B2	McSorley's Old Ale House	48 C3	Pianos
18 B2	Burp Castle	49 C3	Mercury Lounge
23 B2	Holiday Cocktail Lounge	50 C3	The Library
25 B2	Big Bar	55 D2	Bowery Ballroom
29 B3	PDT	63 D3	Welcome to the Johnsons
31 B3	Death & Co	70 E3	Eastwood

ARTS AND CULTURE

13 B1	The Public Theater	41 C2	Anthology Film Archives
14 B1	Merchant's House Museum	42 C2	Sperone Westwater
19 B2	New York Theatre Workshop	52 C3	Nuyorican Poets Cafe
21 B2	Theater for the New City	53 C4	Bullet Space
22 B2	Performance Space New York	54 D2	New Museum
36 C2	La Mama Experimental Theatre Club	60 D3	Perrotin
		64 D4	Abrons Arts Center
		65 E2	Museum at Eldridge Street
		67 E3	Metrograph

RECREATION

| 30 B3 | Tompkins Square Park |

SHOPS

1 A1	Forbidden Planet	39 C2	John Varvatos
2 A1	The Strand	47 C3	Yumi Kim
3 A2	Kiehl's	61 D3	Edith Machinist
26 B2	Tokio 7		

HOTELS

| 38 C2 | The Bowery Hotel | 46 C3 | The Ludlow Hotel |
| 44 C2 | SIXTY LES Hotel | 62 D3 | Hotel on Rivington |

© MOON.COM

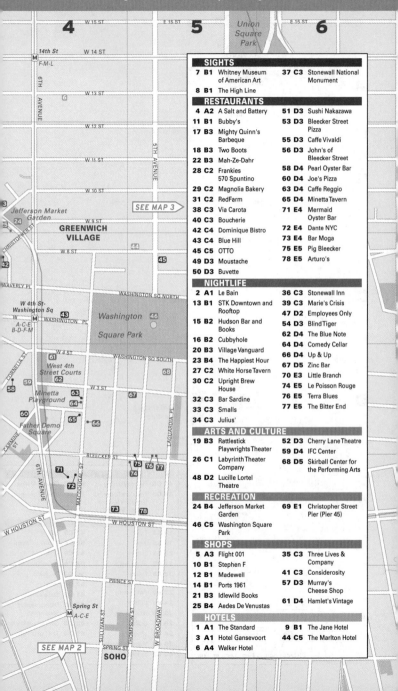

4 W 15 ST   **5** W 15 ST   Union Square Park   **6** E 15 ST

14th St M F-M-L   W 14 ST

6TH AVENUE   W 13 ST

6   W 12 ST

5TH AVENUE   W 11 ST

W 10 ST

SEE MAP 3

Jefferson Market Garden   W 9 ST   3   24

13   GREENWICH VILLAGE   44   W 8 ST

CHRISTOPHER ST   42   45

WAVERLY PL

WASHINGTON SQUARE NORTH

W 4th St-Washington Sq M A-C-E B-D-F-M   43   WASHINGTON PL   Washington Square Park   46

W 4 ST   WASHINGTON SQUARE SOUTH

West 4th Street Courts   61   62   W 3 ST   67   68

CORNELIA ST   58   59   Minetta Playground   63   64   66

60   65

Father Demo Square

CARMINE ST   BLEECKER ST   75 76 77   74

6TH AVENUE   71

72   73   78

W HOUSTON ST   W HOUSTON ST

PRINCE ST

Spring St M A-C-E

SEE MAP 2   SPRING ST   SOHO

MACDOUGAL ST   SULLIVAN ST   THOMPSON ST   W BROADWAY   LAGUARDIA PL   5TH AVENUE

SIGHTS
7	**B1**	Whitney Museum of American Art	**37 C3**	Stonewall National Monument
8	**B1**	The High Line		

RESTAURANTS
4	**A2**	A Salt and Battery	**51 D3**	Sushi Nakazawa
11	**B1**	Bubby's	**53 D3**	Bleecker Street Pizza
17	**B3**	Mighty Quinn's Barbeque	**55 D3**	Caffe Vivaldi
18	**B3**	Two Boots	**56 D3**	John's of Bleecker Street
22	**B3**	Mah-Ze-Dahr	**58 D4**	Pearl Oyster Bar
28	**C2**	Frankies 570 Spuntino	**60 D4**	Joe's Pizza
29	**C2**	Magnolia Bakery	**63 D4**	Caffe Reggio
31	**C2**	RedFarm	**65 D4**	Minetta Tavern
38	**C3**	Via Carota	**71 E4**	Mermaid Oyster Bar
40	**C3**	Boucherie	**72 E4**	Dante NYC
42	**C4**	Dominique Bistro	**73 E4**	Bar Moga
43	**C4**	Blue Hill	**75 E5**	Pig Bleecker
45	**C5**	OTTO	**78 E5**	Arturo's
49	**D3**	Moustache		
50	**D3**	Buvette		

NIGHTLIFE
2	**A1**	Le Bain	**36 C3**	Stonewall Inn
13	**B1**	STK Downtown and Rooftop	**39 C3**	Marie's Crisis
15	**B2**	Hudson Bar and Books	**47 D2**	Employees Only
16	**B2**	Cubbyhole	**54 D3**	Blind Tiger
20	**B3**	Village Vanguard	**62 D4**	The Blue Note
23	**B4**	The Happiest Hour	**64 D4**	Comedy Cellar
27	**C2**	White Horse Tavern	**66 D4**	Up & Up
30	**C2**	Upright Brew House	**67 D5**	Zinc Bar
32	**C3**	Bar Sardine	**70 E3**	Little Branch
33	**C3**	Smalls	**74 E5**	Le Poisson Rouge
34	**C3**	Julius'	**76 E5**	Terra Blues
			77 E5	The Bitter End

ARTS AND CULTURE
19	**B3**	Rattlestick Playwrights Theater	**52 D3**	Cherry Lane Theatre
26	**C1**	Labyrinth Theater Company	**59 D4**	IFC Center
48	**D2**	Lucille Lortel Theatre	**68 D5**	Skirball Center for the Performing Arts

RECREATION
24	**B4**	Jefferson Market Garden	**69 E1**	Christopher Street Pier (Pier 45)
46	**C5**	Washington Square Park		

SHOPS
5	**A3**	Flight 001	**35 C3**	Three Lives & Company
10	**B1**	Stephen F	**41 C3**	Consideravly
12	**B1**	Madewell	**57 D3**	Murray's Cheese Shop
14	**B1**	Ports 1961	**61 D4**	Hamlet's Vintage
21	**B3**	Idlewild Books		
25	**B4**	Aedes De Venustas		

HOTELS
1	**A1**	The Standard	**9 B1**	The Jane Hotel
3	**A1**	Hotel Gansevoort	**44 C5**	The Marlton Hotel
6	**A4**	Walker Hotel		

1

**HUDSON
YARDS**

Entrance

2

*Entrance
(elevator)*

United States
Postal Service

3

Madison Square
Garden

W 31 ST

A

W 30 ST

W 29 ST

Entrance   1

W 28 ST

*The
High
Line*

Chelsea Park

W 28 ST

3

W 27 ST

4

W 27 ST

7

8   *Entrance*

9

W 26 ST

13

B

10

W 25 ST

12

5 6

W 24 ST

11

W 24 ST

111TH AVENUE

Pier 64

*Entrance
(elevator)*

W 23 ST

23rd St

M

W 23 ST

35

A-C-E

36

34

10TH AVENUE

Pier 62

22

38

37

29 30

CHELSEA

W 21 ST

C

Entrance

W 20 ST

CHELSEA
PIERS

28

39

Pier 61

31

41

43

32

33

40

W 19 ST

42

59

60

11TH AVENUE

Pier 60

Entrance

55

W 18 ST

9TH AVENUE

61

8TH AVENUE

Pier 59

W 17 ST

D

56

**Chelsea
Market**

58

Pier 57

57

W 16 ST

*Entrance
(elevator)*

W 15 ST

62

14th St
A-C-E-L

63

64

M

*Entrance
(elevator)*

W 14 ST

*The
High
Line*

Hudson

River

Pier 54

Pier 53

Pier 52

E

10TH AVENUE

F

SIGHTS

46 C5	Flatiron Building		**58 D2**	Chelsea Market
49 C5	Theodore Roosevelt Birthplace National Historic Site		**72 D6**	Union Square

RESTAURANTS

12 B3	Txikito		**47 C5**	Cosme
19 B5	Junoon		**50 C6**	Gramercy Tavern
20 B5	Eataly		**51 C6**	Craft
21 B5	Shake Shack		**52 C6**	Union Square Cafe
22 B5	Eleven Madison Park		**56 D2**	Del Posto
23 B6	Park Avenue		**57 D2**	Toro
24 B6	Upland		**61 D3**	Stella's Pizza
25 B6	Blue Smoke		**62 D3**	Old Homestead Steakhouse
26 B6	Dhaba		**63 D3**	Gansevoort Market
34 C3	aRoqa		**65 D4**	The Donut Pub
36 C3	Murray's Bagels			
40 C3	Salinas			

0   200 yds

0   200 m

Distance Across Map: 1.9mi or 3km

© MOON.COM

SEE MAP 6

NOMAD

TENDERLOIN

FLATIRON DISTRICT

Madison Square Park

Madison Square

Flatiron Building

Theodore Roosevelt Birthplace National Historic Site

GRAMERCY

Gramercy Park

Union Square

Union Square Park

WEST ADDRESSING

EAST ADDRESSING

Union Square

SEE MAP 4

NIGHTLIFE

1	A2	Death Ave
3	B1	Porchlight
4	B1	The Eagle NYC
37	C3	Barracuda
42	C3	Cooper's Craft & Kitchen
43	C3	REBAR

ARTS AND CULTURE

5	B1	Gagosian
6	B1	Mary Boone Gallery
7	B2	Sleep No More at the McKittrick Hotel
8	B2	Friedman Benda
9	B2	Robert Miller Gallery
10	B2	Pace Gallery
11	B2	Bryce Wolkowitz Gallery
14	B4	Museum at the Fashion Institute of Technology
16	B5	Museum of Sex
29	C2	Paula Cooper Gallery
30	C2	Tanya Bonakdar Gallery
31	C2	David Zwirner
32	C2	The Kitchen

45	C5	Flatiron Lounge
59	D3	Bathtub Gin
60	D3	Gym Sportsbar
67	D4	Raines Law Room
69	D6	Old Town Bar
70	D6	Pete's Tavern
73	D6	Irving Plaza

ARTS AND CULTURE (continued)

35	C3	The Cell
39	C3	Atlantic Theater Company
41	C3	The Joyce Theater
44	C3	New York Live Arts
55	D2	Petzel Gallery
66	D4	Rubin Museum of Art

RECREATION

18	B5	Madison Square Park
28	C1	Chelsea Piers
54	C6	Gramercy Park

SHOPS

13	B3	Jazz Record Center
17	B5	Rizzoli
33	C2	STORY
48	C5	ABC Carpet & Home
68	D5	Books of Wonder

HOTELS

2	A5	Ace Hotel
15	B5	The NoMad Hotel
27	B6	Carlton Arms Hotel
38	C3	The GEM Hotel
53	C6	Gramercy Park Hotel
64	D3	Chelsea Pines Inn
71	D6	W New York – Union Square

Lexington Ave-
59th St
4-5-6
N-R-W

QUEENSBORO BRIDGE

E 60 ST
E 59 ST

5th Ave-59th St
N-R-W

E 58 ST

57th St
F

E 57 ST

E 56 ST

E 54 ST

Museum of Modern Art (MoMA)

Lexington Ave-
53rd St

5th Ave-53rd St

E 53 ST

E-M

E 52 ST

E-M

Radio City Music Hall

51st St
4-6

E 51 ST

St. Patrick's Cathedral

E 50 ST

Rockefeller Center

MIDTOWN

E 49 ST

TURTLE BAY

47th-50th Sts-
Rockefeller Ctr
B-D-F-M

E 48 ST

E 47 ST

E 46 ST

E 45 ST

Grand Central Terminal

E 43 ST

United Nations Headquarters

Chrysler Building

42nd St-
Bryant Pk
B-D-F-M

5th Ave-
Bryant Pk
7

Grand Central-
42nd St
S
4-5-6

E 42 ST

E 41 ST

E 40 ST

Bryant Park

New York Public Library Main Branch

MURRAY HILL

E 39 ST
E 38 ST

TUDOR CITY

QUEENS-
MIDTOWN
TUNNEL

E 37 ST

E 36 ST

St. Vartan
Park

Herald
Square
B-D-F-M
Herald Sq-
34th St
N-Q-R-W

Empire State Building

E 35 ST

TUNNEL
ENTRANCE
RAMPS

33rd St
4-6

E 34 ST

E 33 ST

E 32 ST

© MOON.COM

ARTS AND CULTURE

1 A1	Terminal 5	
2 A3	Carnegie Hall	
8 A4	Hirschl and Adler	
10 B2	Ars Nova	
13 B3	Feinstein's/54 Below	
16 B3	*The Book of Mormon* at the Eugene O'Neill Theatre	
23 B4	Paley Center	
35 C1	Intrepid Sea, Air & Space Museum	
40 C2	Signature Theatre Company	
41 C2	Playwrights Horizons	
50 C3	Second Stage Theater	
51 C3	Manhattan Theatre Club	

53 C3	*Hamilton* at the Richard Rodgers Theatre	
54 C3	*Dear Evan Hansen* at the Music Box Theatre	
55 C3	Gulliver's Gate	
56 C3	New Victory Theater	
57 C3	*Aladdin* at the New Amsterdam Theatre	
59 C3	Roundabout Theatre Company	
62 C3	Town Hall	
70 C6	Japan Society	
73 D2	Sean Kelly	
82 D4	The Morgan Library & Museum	
83 D3	Scandinavia House	
84 E3	Madison Square Garden	

RECREATION

26 B4	NBC Studios Tours	
27 B4	The Rink at Rockefeller Center	
77 D4	Bryant Park	

78 D4	Winter Village at Bryant Park	
85 E3	New York Knicks	
86 E3	New York Rangers	

SHOPS

7 A3	Bergdorf Goodman	
21 B4	MoMA Design Store	
24 B4	Uniqlo	
29 B4	Tiffany & Co.	

30 B4	Topshop	
31 B4	Saks Fifth Avenue	
80 D4	Muji	
87 E3	Macy's	

HOTELS

3 A3	Viceroy Central Park	
5 A4	WestHouse Hotel	
6 A4	The Plaza	
9 A4	Four Seasons New York	
14 B3	The London	
17 B3	citizenM	

20 B4	Warwick New York	
36 C1	Kimpton Ink48 Hotel	
52 C3	Hotel Edison	
61 C3	The Chatwal	
63 C4	Algonquin Hotel	
72 D2	Yotel	

MAP 7

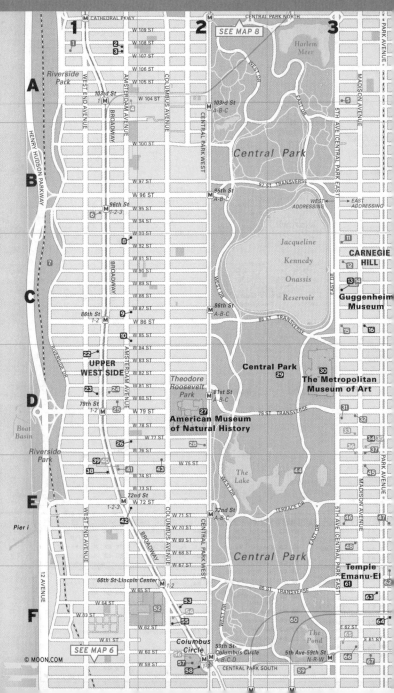

SIGHTS

13	C3	Guggenheim Museum
20	C5	Gracie Mansion
27	D2	American Museum of Natural History
29	D3	Central Park
30	D3	The Metropolitan Museum of Art
61	E3	Temple Emanu-El
69	F4	Roosevelt Island

RESTAURANTS

2	A1	Taqueria Y Fonda
3	A1	Thai Market
8	C1	Gennaro
9	C1	Barney Greengrass
10	C1	Jacob's Pickles
16	C3	Ristorante Morini
18	C4	Papaya King
22	D1	Maison Pickle
23	D1	Zabar's
26	D1	Levain Bakery
38	E1	Fairway Cafe
39	E1	Viand Cafe
42	E1	Gray's Papaya
49	E4	Candle Cafe
50	E4	JG Melon
51	E4	2nd Floor Bar and Essen
53	F2	Bar Boulud
55	F2	Rosa Mexicano
58	F2	Per Se
63	F3	Daniel
64	F3	Vaucluse

NIGHTLIFE

19	C4	Bondurants
34	D3	Bemelmans Bar
43	E2	Dive 75
57	F2	Dizzy's Club Coca-Cola
70	F4	The Jeffrey

ARTS AND CULTURE

1	A1	Nicholas Roerich Museum
5	A3	Museum of the City of New York
6	B1	Symphony Space
11	C3	The Jewish Museum
12	C3	Cooper Hewitt
15	C3	Neue Galerie
17	C4	92nd Street Y
28	D2	New-York Historical Society
32	D3	Acquavella Galleries
41	E1	Beacon Theatre
45	E3	The Met Breuer
46	E3	The Frick Collection
47	E3	Asia Society and Museum
52	F3	Lincoln Center
62	F3	Park Avenue Armory
67	F3	French Institute Alliance Française

RECREATION

7	C1	Riverside Park
14	C3	5th and Park Walking Tour
21	C5	Carl Schurz Park
25	D1	Central Park Bike Rentals and Tours
44	E3	The Loeb Boathouse
59	F3	Central Park Horse Carriage Rides
60	F3	Wollman Rink

SHOPS

24	D1	Westsider Rare and Used Books
31	D3	Albertine
37	D3	Zitomer
48	E3	Fivestory
66	F3	Barneys New York
68	F4	Dylan's Candy Bar

HOTELS

4	A1	Hostelling International New York
33	D3	The Mark Hotel
35	D3	The Carlyle
36	D3	The Surrey
40	E1	Hotel Beacon
54	F2	The Empire Hotel
56	F2	Mandarin Oriental New York
65	F3	The Pierre

0   0.25 mi

0   0.25 km

Distance Across Map: 3.3mi or 5.3km

SIGHTS

1	A2	Hamilton Grange National Memorial	
2	A3	Abyssinian Baptist Church	
6	C1	General Grant National Memorial	
9	C3	Apollo Theater	
15	C4	Langston Hughes House	
17	D1	Riverside Church	
18	D2	Columbia University	
28	E2	Cathedral of St. John the Divine	

RESTAURANTS

3	B3	Charles' Country Pan Fried Chicken	
5	C1	Dinosaur Bar-B-Que	
12	C3	Red Rooster	
14	C3	Sylvia's	
20	D3	The Cecil Steakhouse	
22	D3	Amy Ruth's	
24	D3	Sexy Taco/ Dirty Cash	
26	D5	Patsy's Pizzeria	
27	E2	Hungarian Pastry Shop	
32	E5	Blue Sky Deli (Hajji's)	

NIGHTLIFE

4	B3	Harlem Hops	
13	C3	Ginny's Supper Club	
21	D3	Minton's Playhouse	
30	E3	Bier International	
31	E3	67 Orange Street	

ARTS AND CULTURE

10	C3	Long Gallery Harlem	

RECREATION

16	C5	Crack is Wack Playground	
29	E2	Morningside Park	

SHOPS

11	C3	Harlem Wine Gallery	
23	D3	Malcolm Shabazz Harlem Market	

HOTELS

7	C3	Aloft Harlem	
8	C3	The Harlem Flophouse	
19	D2	Harlem Grand	
25	D3	The Melva Inn	

Map labels:

4 · 5

87

138th St-Grand Concourse 4-5

E 138 ST

BRONX

5 AVENUE

E 131 ST

E 130 ST

E 128 ST

MANHATTAN

HARLEM RIVER DR

E 128 ST

E 127 ST

E 126 ST

15

Langston Hughes House

125th St 4-5-6

E 125 ST

E 124 ST

E 123 ST

Marcus Garvey Park

E 122 ST

E 121 ST

E 120 ST

MADISON AVENUE

PARK AVENUE

LEXINGTON AVENUE

3RD AVENUE

2ND AVENUE

E 119 ST

E 118 ST

E 117 ST

26

1ST AVENUE

PLEASANT AV

E 116 ST

116th St 4-6

E 115 ST

EAST HARLEM

E 113 ST

E 112 ST

Thomas Jefferson Park

Randall's Island Park

W 111 ST

110th St 4-6

E 111 ST

E 110 ST

32

F.D.R. DRIVE

Harlem Meer

RANDALL'S-WARDS ISLANDS

WEST ADDRESSING

EAST ADDRESSING

E 105 ST

103rd St 4-6

E 104 ST

E 103 ST

SEE MAP 7

E 102 ST

E 101 ST

E 100 ST

5 AVENUE

Harlem River

MADISON AVE BRIDGE

PARK AV

RIDER AV

MORRIS AV

CANAL PL

3 AVE BRIDGE

0		0.25 mi
0		0.25 km

Distance Across Map: 3mi or 4.8km

MAP 9

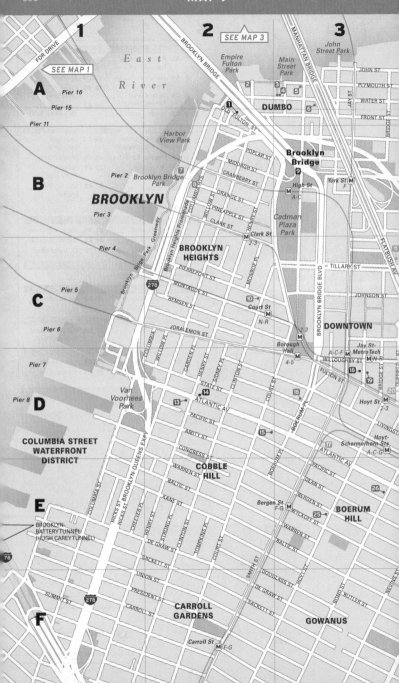

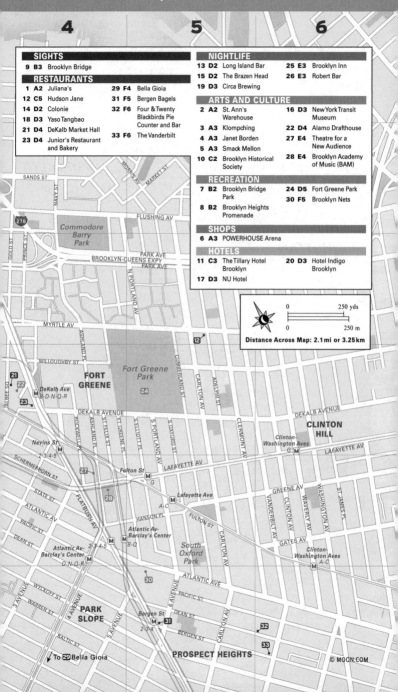

SIGHTS
9 B3 Brooklyn Bridge

RESTAURANTS
1 A2 Juliana's
12 C5 Hudson Jane
14 D2 Colonie
18 D3 Yaso Tangbao
21 D4 DeKalb Market Hall
23 D4 Junior's Restaurant and Bakery
29 F4 Bella Gioia
31 F5 Bergen Bagels
32 F6 Four & Twenty Blackbirds Pie Counter and Bar
33 F6 The Vanderbilt

NIGHTLIFE
13 D2 Long Island Bar
15 D2 The Brazen Head
19 D3 Circa Brewing
25 E3 Brooklyn Inn
26 E3 Robert Bar

ARTS AND CULTURE
2 A2 St. Ann's Warehouse
3 A3 Klompching
4 A3 Janet Borden
5 A3 Smack Mellon
10 C2 Brooklyn Historical Society
16 D3 New York Transit Museum
22 D4 Alamo Drafthouse
27 E4 Theatre for a New Audience
28 E4 Brooklyn Academy of Music (BAM)

RECREATION
7 B2 Brooklyn Bridge Park
8 B2 Brooklyn Heights Promenade
24 D5 Fort Greene Park
30 F5 Brooklyn Nets

SHOPS
6 A3 POWERHOUSE Arena

HOTELS
11 C3 The Tillary Hotel Brooklyn
17 D3 NU Hotel
20 D3 Hotel Indigo Brooklyn

Distance Across Map: 2.1mi or 3.25km

© MOON.COM

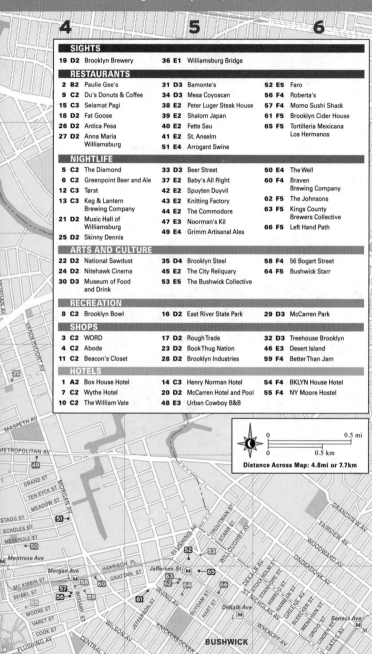

SIGHTS
19 D2 Brooklyn Brewery	36 E1 Williamsburg Bridge	

RESTAURANTS
2 B2 Paulie Gee's	31 D3 Bamonte's	52 E5 Faro
9 C2 Du's Donuts & Coffee	34 D3 Mesa Coyoacan	56 F4 Roberta's
15 C3 Selamat Pagi	38 E2 Peter Luger Steak House	57 F4 Momo Sushi Shack
18 D2 Fat Goose	39 E2 Shalom Japan	61 F5 Brooklyn Cider House
26 D2 Antica Pesa	40 E2 Fette Sau	65 F5 Tortilleria Mexicana
27 D2 Anna Maria Williamsburg	41 E2 St. Anselm	Los Hermanos
	51 E4 Arrogant Swine	

NIGHTLIFE
5 C2 The Diamond	33 D3 Beer Street	50 E4 The Well
6 C2 Greenpoint Beer and Ale	37 E2 Baby's All Right	60 F4 Braven Brewing Company
12 C3 Tørst	42 E2 Spuyten Duyvil	
13 C3 Keg & Lantern Brewing Company	43 E2 Knitting Factory	62 F5 The Johnsons
	44 E2 The Commodore	63 F5 Kings County Brewers Collective
21 D2 Music Hall of Williamsburg	47 E3 Noorman's Kil	
	49 E4 Grimm Artisanal Ales	66 F5 Left Hand Path
25 D2 Skinny Dennis		

ARTS AND CULTURE
22 D2 National Sawdust	35 D4 Brooklyn Steel	58 F4 56 Bogart Street
24 D2 Nitehawk Cinema	45 E2 The City Reliquary	64 F5 Bushwick Starr
30 D3 Museum of Food and Drink	53 E5 The Bushwick Collective	

RECREATION
8 C2 Brooklyn Bowl	16 D2 East River State Park	29 D3 McCarren Park

SHOPS
3 C2 WORD	17 D2 Rough Trade	32 D3 Treehouse Brooklyn
4 C2 Abode	23 D2 Book Thug Nation	46 E3 Desert Island
11 C2 Beacon's Closet	28 D2 Brooklyn Industries	59 F4 Better Than Jam

HOTELS
1 A2 Box House Hotel	14 C3 Henry Norman Hotel	54 F4 BKLYN House Hotel
7 C2 Wythe Hotel	20 D2 McCarren Hotel and Pool	55 F4 NY Moore Hostel
10 C2 The William Vale	48 E3 Urban Cowboy B&B	

0   0.5 mi

0   0.5 km

Distance Across Map: 4.8mi or 7.7km

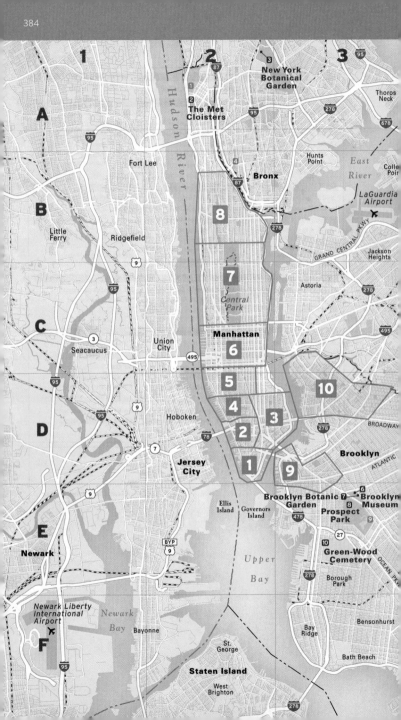

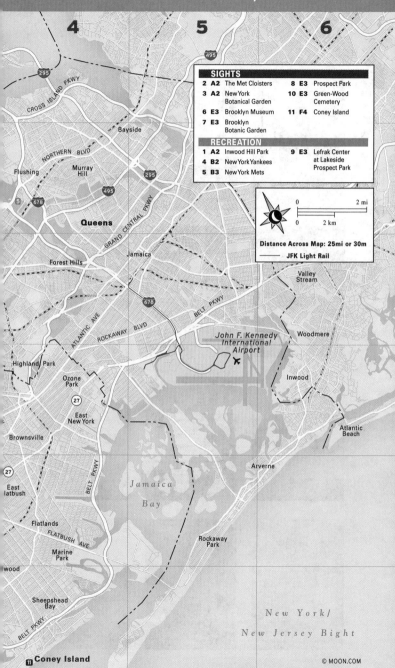

SIGHTS

2	A2	The Met Cloisters	8	E3	Prospect Park
3	A2	New York Botanical Garden	10	E3	Green-Wood Cemetery
6	E3	Brooklyn Museum	11	F4	Coney Island
7	E3	Brooklyn Botanic Garden			

RECREATION

1	A2	Inwood Hill Park	9	E3	Lefrak Center at Lakeside Prospect Park
4	B2	New York Yankees			
5	B3	New York Mets			

0   2 mi
0   2 km

Distance Across Map: 25mi or 30m
—— JFK Light Rail

© MOON.COM

MOON TRAVEL GUIDES TO EUROPE

GO BIG AND GO BEYOND!

These savvy city guides include strategies to help you see the top sights and find adventure beyond the tourist crowds.

OR TAKE THINGS ONE STEP AT A TIME

Gear up for a bucket list vacation

or plan your next beachy getaway!

More Guides for Urban Adventure

ASHEVILLE & THE GREAT SMOKY MOUNTAINS

BOSTON

BUENOS AIRES

CHICAGO

CHARLESTON

CLEVELAND

LOS ANGELES

MEXICO CITY

MONTRÉAL

NASHVILLE

NEW YORK CITY

PITTSBURGH

PORTLAND

QUÉBEC CITY

REYKJAVÍK

SAN DIEGO

SAVANNAH

SEATTLE

VANCOUVER

WASHINGTON DC